GERMAN PIETISM AND THE PROBLEM
OF CONVERSION

 PIETIST, MORAVIAN, AND ANABAPTIST STUDIES

EDITOR

Craig D. Atwood
Director of the Center for Moravian Studies, Moravian Seminary

Volumes in the Pietist, Moravian, and Anabaptist Studies Series take multidisciplinary approaches to the history and theology of these groups and their religious and cultural influence around the globe. The series seeks to enrich the dynamic international study of post-Reformation Protestantism through original works of scholarship.

ADVISORY BOARD

Bill Leonard, *Wake Forest University*
Katherine Faull, *Bucknell University*
A. G. Roeber, *Penn State University*
Jonathan Strom, *Emory University*
Hermann Wellenreuther, *Georg-August-Universität Göttingen*
Rachel Wheeler, *Indiana University–Purdue University Indianapolis*

JONATHAN STROM

GERMAN PIETISM AND THE PROBLEM OF CONVERSION

The Pennsylvania State University Press
University Park, Pennsylvania

Library of Congress Cataloging-in-Publication Data

Names: Strom, Jonathan, author.
Title: German pietism and the problem of conversion / Jonathan Strom.
Other titles: Pietist, Moravian, and Anabaptist studies.
Description: University Park, Pennsylvania : The Pennsylvania State
    University Press, [2018] | Series: Pietist, Moravian, and Anabaptist studies
    | Includes bibliographical references and index.
Summary: "Explores how conversion and religious experiences developed
    within German Pietism, arguing that the Pietist relationship with
    conversion was much more complex and problematic than it is often
    presented to be"—Provided by publisher.
Identifiers: LCCN 2017033582 | ISBN 9780271079349 (cloth : alk. paper)
Subjects: LCSH: Pietism—Germany—History. | Conversion—
    Christianity—History.
Classification: LCC BR1652.G3 S77 2018 | DDC 273/.7—dc23
LC record available at https://lccn.loc.gov/2017033582

Copyright © 2018 The Pennsylvania State University
All rights reserved
Printed in the United States of America
Published by The Pennsylvania State University Press,
University Park, PA 16802–1003

The Pennsylvania State University Press is a member of the Association of
American University Presses.

Material from chapter 6 appeared in an earlier form in "Pietism and
Conversion in Dargun," *Pietismus und Neuzeit* 39 (2013): 150-192. It is
used here by permission of Vandenhoek & Ruprecht.

It is the policy of The Pennsylvania State University Press to use acid-free
paper. Publications on uncoated stock satisfy the minimum requirements of
American National Standard for Information Sciences—Permanence of
Paper for Printed Library Material, ANSI Z39.48–1992.

CONTENTS

Preface vii
Abbreviations ix

   Introduction 1
1 August Hermann Francke's
   Conversion 15
2 Early Pietism and the Diverse
   Cultures of Conversion................. 28
3 Conversion in Light of Death:
   Von Schönberg and Henckel's
   Last Hours 50
4 The *Bußkampf* and Conflicting
   Views of Conversion After Francke 61
5 Pietist Periodicals and the
   Conversion Narrative 71
6 Conversion in Dargun 90
7 Execution Narratives 122
   Conclusion........................... 144

Notes 159
Bibliography 201
Index 221

PREFACE

This book began by accident. Working on another project, I wanted a few colorful examples to illustrate how early Pietists employed conversion narratives. Everyone seemed to acknowledge the paradigmatic nature of August Hermann Francke's autobiographical conversion narrative and how important it had been. With some strategic forays into the archives and Pietist publications, I planned to locate a number of vivid examples that were similar to Francke's and move on. My investigations found, however, far fewer descriptions of conversion experiences than I expected, and despite its supposedly model character, Francke's autobiography was not something Pietist contemporaries regularly cited. The accounts I found often did not fit the so-called *Bußkampf* model well, even those from Halle. There were other oddities. Many of the Pietist "patriarchs"—such as Joachim Justus Breithaupt, Joachim Lange, and Paul Anton—had written short autobiographies, but they did not mention a distinct conversion experience. Pietists, to be sure, wrote and talked a great deal about conversion as a goal. They printed grisly tales of conversion of convicted criminals, but, it seemed, they were remarkably circumspect about publishing the experiences of ordinary individuals. When they did appear, it was almost always after their death, and the authors clearly selected and shaped the narratives in quite deliberate ways. In many respects, conversion emerged as much a problem as it was a solution to the spiritual issues that Pietists raised. Questions about Pietist conversion and the standard narrative continued to nag at me, and what began as a background chapter turned into something more substantial.

Much of the work on this project was completed on sabbatical in Berlin in 2010–11, where professor Dorothea Wendebourg graciously welcomed me as a visiting scholar at the theology faculty of Humboldt University. I am grateful to my colleagues at Emory's Candler School of Theology and especially Dean Jan Love for affording me time away from teaching to devote to this project. I have benefited from the advice and counsel of many friends and colleagues as this project has emerged. Brooks Holifield has always been an engaging discussion partner on the issues I have encountered, and I am particularly grateful for his perceptive reading of the manuscript. Two anonymous reviewers carefully scrutinized the text and provided suggestions that strengthened the book throughout. Craig Atwood, the series editor, provided much needed encouragement and direction at critical junctures, and Kathryn Yahner has been wonderfully supportive in shepherding the project to fruition with Penn State University Press. Ulrike Guthrie was a delight to work with on editorial issues. Candler students Mary Button and Nicolette Paso Schoemake provided superb research assistance. Many others have been generous with their advice and suggestions, including Hartmut Lehmann, Wolfgang Breul, Markus Meier, Doug Shantz, Peter Yoder, Sabine Pettke, Ben Marschke, Hans Schneider, Johannes Wallmann, Klaus vom Orde, Manfred Jakubowski-Tiessen, and Kelly Whitmer. Their insights have improved the project in countless ways.

I am especially grateful for the assistance of archivists and librarians at the institutions where I have been privileged to conduct my research. Like almost all scholars of Pietism, I have come to appreciate the marvelously organized and supportive atmosphere of the library and archives of the Franckesche Stiftungen. Other archives and libraries were instrumental for this project as well, including the Forschungsbibliothek Gotha, Staatsbibliothek zu Berlin–Preußischer Kulturbesitz, Universitätsbibliothek Rostock, Universitätsarchiv Rostock, Landeshauptarchiv Schwerin, Landesarchiv Sachsen-Anhalt in Wernigerode, Universitäts- und Landesbibliothek Sachsen-Anhalt in Halle, and Landesarchiv Thüringen–Staatsarchiv Gotha. German archivists and librarians are remarkably generous to international scholars, for which I am deeply thankful. Here in Atlanta, the staff at Candler's Pitts Theology Library have given every assistance.

This is dedicated to my wife, Siri, and my daughter, Solveig, who over the years have tolerated more discussion of Pietism than is healthy for anyone. Their good humor and support made this book possible.

September 2017

ABBREVIATIONS

AFSt	Archiv der Franckeschen Stiftung, Halle
Altes und Neues	*Altes und Neues aus dem Reich Gottes und der übrigen guten und bösen Geister*, 1733–39
CSNM	*Closter-Bergische Sammlung nützlicher Materien zur Erbauung im wahren Christenthume*, 1745–61
FSAM	*Fortgesetzte Sammlung auserlesener Materien zum Bau des Reichs Gottes*, 1735–37
LASA Wernigerode	Landesarchiv Sachsen-Anhalt, Abteilung Magdeburg, Standort Wernigerode
LHA Schwerin	Landeshauptarchiv Schwerin
SAMR	*Sammlung auserlesener Materien zum Bau des Reichs Gottes*, 1731–34
StBPK	Staatsbibliothek zu Berlin–Preußischer Kulturbesitz, Berlin
VSAM	*Verbesserte Sammlung auserlesener Materien zum Bau des Reichs Gottes*, 1737–43

INTRODUCTION

Religious conversion goes to the heart of the Pietist movement and exemplifies the value it placed on lived experience in the Christian faith. Conversion aimed to distinguish the true Christian from the lukewarm believer, the ardent follower of Christ from the nominal adherent. Yet, almost from the start, conversion experiences and their accounts were fraught with difficulty for Pietists. Questions about their authenticity, orthodoxy, and stability proliferated, as did attempts to control and even constrain the process and narration of conversion. Conversion plays such a prominent role in the historical imagination surrounding Pietism that it is tempting to see such experiences as a neat resolution that both provided confirmation and assurance to those who doubted their salvation and allowed Pietists to separate neatly the unconverted from the converted. Yet in practice, conversion and conversion narratives proved deeply problematic in eighteenth-century Germany, not only for Pietist leaders but also for everyday Christians. This book is an account of that uneasy history.

Emerging in the second half of the seventeenth century, Pietism became the most important renewal movement within German Protestantism after the Reformation. Pietists sought to revitalize Christianity through renewed emphasis on the Christian life and innovative practices of devotion and community.[1] Most Pietists chose to remain inside the existing Protestant churches and reform them from within, though some left and formed new communities of faith. Even at the height of the movement in the eighteenth century, Pietism never encompassed a majority of Protestants in any German territory or region, but the movement did leave profound marks on modern Protestantism. It shaped how people read the Bible, interpreted religious experiences, and judged authentic Christianity. And central to much Pietist discourse on the Christian life was discussion of conversion and related terms of regeneration and rebirth.

We will deal predominantly with how Pietists described the experience of conversion. Accounts of conversion appeared quite late in German Protestantism, especially when compared with the English Puritan tradition. In part, this had doctrinal roots. Early German Protestantism, especially Lutheranism, understood conversion not as a discrete event in the believer's life, but as a lifelong process tied closely to repentance, a view that tended to preclude narrative description until Pietists reframed the understanding of regeneration, repentance, and conversion at the end of the seventeenth century.

The dramatic story of August Hermann Francke's conversion in 1687 dominates descriptions of Pietist conversion and often stands as the paradigmatic case. In the turning point of his autobiographical account, Francke described how, amid many tears and atheistic doubts, he fell to his knees in intense spiritual travail and suddenly found himself transformed: "My doubt vanished as quickly as one turns one's hand; I was assured in my heart of the grace of God in Christ Jesus and I knew God not only as God but as my Father. All sadness and unrest of my heart was taken away at once, and I was immediately overwhelmed as with a stream of joy so that with full joy I praised and gave honor to God who had shown me such great grace. I arose a completely different person from the one who had knelt down."[2] Yet, although no history of conversion narratives in Pietism can avoid dealing with Francke's narrative—one of the most compelling from the early Pietist movement—it is unlikely that Francke's experience was well known during his lifetime or indeed during much of the eighteenth century, and its current prominence in the historiography obscures other ways of describing conversion in Pietist periodicals and publications. These other narratives recounted experiences that occurred in places ranging from the gallows in Wernigerode to conventicles in Pomerania and had far greater currency in the eighteenth century than did Francke's narrative.

What do we mean by conversion in this early modern context? At its most basic, religious conversion refers to a profound turn or change in one's life, a reorientation with regard to the world as well as to the divine. Language of conversion has deep roots in Christian scriptures and tradition. In the modern study of religion, especially after William James, it has become one of the central terms for exploring fundamental changes in a person's affiliation and experience.[3] Yet the semantic field of conversion is extraordinarily broad, and historians employ the term to describe a wide swath of religious changes and transformations that often have little apparent affinity.

There are three overarching categories of conversion in early modern studies. First, conversion can refer to the change in religious identity from one tradition to another, as when a Jew is baptized and adopts Christianity, or when a Christian becomes Muslim.[4] In the Middle Ages, this form of conversion could be a mass phenomenon, as rulers and missionaries induced entire communities to adopt Christianity, sometimes with the threat of force.[5] By the early modern era, conversion in Europe had largely become synonymous with individual religious experiences, though the expansion of Western Christianity beyond Europe afforded new opportunities for group or mass conversion, at least in the Western imagination.

Second, the Reformation in the sixteenth century and the ensuing division of Western Christendom created a new mode for religious conversion—the cross-confessional conversion. Here an individual could reject a previous Christian identity and affiliate with a new confessional group, as when a Lutheran became Roman Catholic or a Catholic was rebaptized and joined an Anabaptist community. Turning from one Christian confessional community to another often entailed dramatic social or political consequences for prominent figures as well as ordinary laypeople.[6] Conversion in this sense almost never refers to changes among the major Protestant confessions, from Lutheran to Reformed, for instance, but rather signifies more fundamental changes in affiliations that contemporaries perceived as incompatible with one another.

Third, conversion can represent an inward change of heart or powerful transformation in a nominal Christian, whose faith subsequently becomes qualitatively different. This type of conversion shared elements of the medieval understanding of the *conversio in se*, which signaled profound growth in interiority and spirituality, but such conversions could also manifest themselves in marked changes in morality and comportment in the life of a Christian that echoed a *conversio vitae*. Protestants obviously lacked the opportunity to enter religious orders, a decision that often signaled a *conversio vitae* in the Middle Ages.[7] Puritan conversions, with their long-standing tradition of published narratives, are the best-known Protestant variety of this mode of conversion, and this is the form most often associated with Pietism. Yet German Pietists would have described all three modes as *Bekehrungen* (conversions).

Modern scholars of religion have created typologies that can help historians categorize conversion in the early modern world. Lewis Rambo, for instance, identifies five types of religious conversion: (1) *tradition transition*, the move from one worldview, ritual system, or symbolic universe to another; (2) *institutional transition*, movement from one community to another within a tradition; (3) *affiliation*, in which one who has minimal or no commitment becomes involved with a community of faith or institution; (4) *intensification*, in which one who has a previous affiliation undergoes a revitalized commitment within this faith; and finally (5) *apostasy or defection*, the rejection of one religious tradition without the acceptance of another.[8]

Without great difficulty, Rambo's typology can encompass the three aforementioned forms of conversion as tradition transition, institutional transition, and intensification. Given the compulsory nature of religious identity in the early modern period, the mode Rambo describes as affiliation would have little significance and could be incorporated as part of intensification. Historians rarely treat apostasy or defection as a form of conversion in the early modern period, but the rise of un-conversion narratives in the eighteenth century—such as the autobiography of Johann Christoph Edelmann, who described his rejection of Christianity in favor of reason as a form of conversion—suggests that Rambo's last type may also have historical utility.[9]

Rambo recognizes the limitations of his typology for the modern context, and the difficulties for the historian are even greater. Categorization of conversion can depend largely on one's point of view. Many Pietists would have rejected an interpretation of their personal conversion as merely a kind of intensification, instead seeing it as a fundamental move away from their former atheism and unbelief to true faith and complete rebirth, even though they remained in the same tradition and confession. Indeed, a trope in a number of Pietist conversion narratives was the rejection of a prior "atheism" in favor of true Christianity.[10] For many Pietists, conversion from utter unbelief would have represented a transition as significant as that of a Jew baptized into Christianity. Likewise, both Protestants and Catholics viewed the conversion to or from Catholicism not as a matter of selecting a new institutional expression for their faith, but rather as a statement about the nature of true Christianity and interior conviction.[11] For others in the early modern world, the gap between Protestant and Catholic ritual systems and their symbolic universes may have appeared as large as the gap many twenty-first-century observers perceive between distinct religions today. This does not invalidate the usefulness of a typology, but it does suggest that we should recognize their analytical limits and avoid reifying these as discrete types that have little to do with one another, at least in the eyes of historical subjects.

Studies of early modern conversion often focus on one type of conversion to the exclusion of others. Even in collections on conversion broadly conceived, individual contributions tend to treat one specific form of conversion.[12] In recent years, examinations of cross-confessional conversion in early modern Germany have been especially prominent. A major study by Duane Corpis, along with an extensive collection of essays edited by Ute

Lotz-Heumann and others, have given this aspect of conversion detailed attention in the historiography on early modern Germany, though both explicitly exclude from their analysis the intensification form of conversion typical of Pietism.[13] Jewish–Christian conversion in early modern Europe in both directions has received attention,[14] but conversion among Pietists much less so.

Dealing with a distinct variety of conversion has a methodological clarity that can yield strong conclusions, but the exclusion of the intensification mode of conversion typical of Pietism is striking.[15] In part, this reflects a linguistic division in contemporary German between *Konversion* and *Bekehrung* that does not exist in English. There has been a semantic shift in the term *Bekehrung* since the early modern period, and today it carries connotations in German that "conversion" does not in English. Scholars frequently employ the term *Konversion* for the alternation between Protestant and Catholic adherence—and now increasingly between Judaism and Christianity—whereas they tend to reserve *Bekehrung* for the inward form of Christian transformation and intensification of religious sensibility.[16] There are, of course, confessional connotations to these terms,[17] but *Konversion* appears in recent years to be gaining ground as the accepted term to cover all forms of conversion in a social-scientific context—apart from the Pietist variety. Historians of Christianity as well as Germanists continue to use *Bekehrung* to designate conversion within a Christian tradition, especially the tradition associated with Pietism, although some recent studies seem to use the two terms synonymously.[18] It is telling, perhaps, of the conceptual fuzziness in Germany that some Protestant German pastoral theologians today are hesitant to apply *Bekehrung* to the process of inner-Christian transformation, identifying it as "tainted, trying, [and] diseased," and preferring the ostensibly more neutral and less loaded term *Konversion*.[19]

Linguistic distinctions applied to related phenomena can serve to avoid facile identities, but at the same time they tend to import current conceptions of *Konversion* and *Bekehrung* back into historical material in which these contrasts were not drawn as clearly—and this can obscure connections among different forms of conversion by treating them in isolation. By emphasizing the external change in affiliation and identity, scholars especially marginalize what Karl Morrison describes as the "supernatural" aspect of religious conversion that nearly all medieval and early modern actors would have identified as the essential precondition of authentic conversion, and it particularly excludes attention to inner-Christian forms of conversion as intensification.[20] One might see the increasing use of *Konversion* as a bleeding over of British and American usage of "conversion" into German linguistic conventions, but there is an irony here: the theoretical literature on *Konversion* frequently cited by German scholars who exclude *Bekehrung* from their analysis is drawn largely from an Anglo-American scholarly tradition that stretches from William James to Lewis Rambo, for whom personal conversion within Christianity—that is, *Bekehrung*—is a central rather than marginal phenomenon.[21] The distinction between *Konversion* and *Bekehrung* may say more about the uneasiness of modern German scholars in dealing with the messy topic of religious experience than it does about seventeenth- or eighteenth-century understandings.

Even as we categorize conversion into distinct types—Protestant–Catholic, Jewish–Christian, intensification within Christianity—the language of conversion can have several different, sometimes diffuse senses for the historian that we can locate within three broad fields. When we speak or write about conversion, we can be referring to the experience of individuals, accounts or descriptions of that experience, or theological reflection on the meaning of the concept. Historians may examine all three uses of the term "conversion," but none is identical with the others. It is perhaps natural that for narrative purposes one might collapse the experience itself and the account of conversion, but there is inevitably an interpretive move between any experience and a verbal expression of it.[22] This is as true of a first-person autobiographical account as it is of a third-person narrative, though we might prize the apparent immediacy of autobiography and be more skeptical of later retellings by others.[23] Nonetheless, whether as simple oral testimonies or highly literate narrative texts, all conversion accounts represent interpretations of an original experience and contain the possibility of subtle shading, misdirection, and even outright falsification. The sources themselves do not allow us to penetrate to the experiences, though that fact does not deprive them of historical meaning.

We can, of course, engage accounts of conversion, and these remain a prime avenue for comprehending how their authors in the seventeenth and eighteenth centuries wanted their audiences to understand conversion experiences. One of the arguments of this book is that by examining a broad range of Pietist conversion narratives and accounts rather than a select few, we can arrive at a richer understanding of how Pietists sought to portray conversion in the eighteenth century. Acknowledging the interpretive distance between a recorded expression and the original experience does not mean we can negate such experiences altogether. Even as we recognize the limits of our historical evidence, the variety of historical evidence that points toward conversion experiences is substantial. Furthermore, there is little reason to doubt that most authors of conversion accounts *thought* they were providing accurate descriptions of experience, whether their own or that of others. Yet, even as we posit some relation between them, we should keep in mind the methodological distinction that accounts and experiences are by no means identical.

Theological discussion of conversion, both learned and popular, is a third way the language of conversion enters historical discussion. The theological use of conversion has the potential to be the most capacious. It does not necessarily require specific experiences or verbal accounts. When Abraham Calov, a seventeenth-century Lutheran orthodox theologian, described conversion in his *ordo salutis*, we cannot assume he was thinking about actual conversion experiences or narratives of conversion among ordinary lay Christians.[24] In this sense the language of conversion could be highly abstract, describing an order or process of faith that would not be transparent to the individual. Undoubtedly, theological conceptions of conversion could affect how Christians interpreted their experiences and described them in their accounts, just as these experiences and accounts could shape how theologians conceived of conversion, both positively and negatively. But it is useful to remain alert to the distinctions.

Seeing this triad of experience, account, and theology as interrelated and yet distinct can help us better understand conversion in context. Each had the ability to interact and at times even correspond closely with the others. But experience, account, and theology are not identical, and we should be wary of trying to harmonize them unduly. One of the problems in understanding August Hermann Francke and conversion has been the tendency of scholars to assume that his own account of conversion written in 1690 or 1691 was not only an accurate description of his experience from three years earlier, but also the key to uncovering his subsequent theology of conversion and his normative expectations for others.[25] It would be obtuse to rule out any correspondences, but instead of creating an artificial harmony among these three aspects or establishing one experience as normative, we might learn more by turning our attention to the range of what Francke's contemporaries would have heard and read about conversion in testimonies, sermons, and theological tracts.

An important approach of this book will be to examine when and how accounts of conversion became widespread in Pietist communities and what these communicated to their audience. Understanding reception is key to comprehending the distinctive history of conversion and conversion narratives in German Protestantism—one that differs from history of conversion in Britain and North America in some important respects, and one that also challenges the portrayal of Pietist conversion in German historical and literary studies that sees Francke's account as normative.

The issue of Pietism and conversion narratives raises questions about early modern autobiography. Scholars of Puritanism, for instance, have often dealt with conversion as part of spiritual autobiography.[26] In German literary studies, Günther Niggl identified a central if uneven role for Pietist conversion narratives in the rise of the secular autobiography, a direction that Magnus Schlette continues to pursue.[27] Yet this larger trajectory toward a secularized, individualized understanding of autonomy can misconstrue the development of conversion narratives in Pietism, for most of them were neither written in the first person nor strictly autobiographical, despite the supposedly formative quality of Francke's first-person account. Of course, it is true that autobiography should not be limited to first-person accounts—and many autobiographical materials from conversations, letters, and other testimonies might be quoted or paraphrased in third-person accounts. Some, like Johann Caspar Schade, probably wrote autobiographical accounts in the third person, but the deliberate move to third-person representation in Pietist accounts of conversion in the mid-eighteenth century—especially accounts describing the experience of laypersons—undermines a clear development of conversion narratives toward "self-authorization" or the autonomous self.[28] In Pietism, first-person accounts remained largely the province of clergy and theology students, who presumably had the theological training to discern true conversion. Furthermore, an emphasis on the close connection of conversion narratives with a development of the autonomous self can also neglect both the fundamental role of advocates and Pietist communities in shaping conversion and even what determines an authentic experience. Conversion in German Pietism was as much about the community in which it occurred as it was about individual interiority.

This book examines how conversion and especially the portrayal of conversion experiences became problematic for many German Pietists. It begins with the autobiographical narrative of August Hermann Francke and its reception, which despite its significance and rhetorical force played much less of a role in eighteenth-century German Pietism than is often assumed (chapter 1). The book traces how diverse cultures of conversion developed within church Pietism, especially within the sphere of Halle's influence (chapter 2), and it examines the way Pietists at Halle and elsewhere began to interpret conversion increasingly in light of death and dying (chapter 3). Following Francke's death, the end of the 1720s and the early 1730s marked a series of changes and controversies. As a result, the so-called repentance struggle (or *Bußkampf*), a key part of some conceptions of religious conversion, became more rigidly defined and controversial. At the same time, heightened expectations around conversion engendered division among Halle's theologians (chapter 4). The emergence of Pietist periodicals in the 1730s meant that narratives of conversion could reach new audiences, yet at the same time these periodicals shaped markedly how German Protestants would encounter conversion experiences (chapter 5). Revivals, perhaps, played less of a role in German Pietism than in cognate movements in Britain and North America of the eighteenth century, but at the court of Dargun in Mecklenburg during the 1730s and 1740s a particularly successful—and controversial—revival emerged, in which the rigid application of the *Bußkampf* reached its apogee (chapter 6). Portraying distinctive aspects of Pietist conversion amid a dramatic context of crime and execution, the execution narratives became the most widely published genre of conversion accounts of the mid-eighteenth century; however, they elicited vigorous opposition from enlightened theologians, and some unintended consequences further discredited Pietist depictions of conversion (chapter 7). The decline of these models at the end of the eighteenth century allowed others to reemerge, in particular that of August Hermann Francke, which was "rediscovered" and subsequently became paradigmatic for German Pietism in the nineteenth and twentieth centuries.

The focus here is on church Pietism, especially that connected to the wider tradition of Halle Pietism. Church or ecclesial Pietists chose to stay within the confessional structures of the Protestant churches, yet the boundaries between church and radical Pietists were often fluid. The understanding and practice of conversion among church Pietists was much more diverse than has often been assumed—there was no "typical" Pietist conversion—and radical Pietists, such Johann Henrich Reitz, influenced how church Pietists understood conversion.[29] However, the range of radical Pietist understandings of conversion exceeds the scope of this book, as does a full portrayal of conversion among the Moravians. These deserve further treatment elsewhere.

Conversion Narratives in the Post-Reformation Period

At the end of his life, Martin Luther penned an autobiographical *Rückblick*, in which he describes his theological breakthrough. Some treat this account of his so-called *Turmerlebnis* as a kind of conversion narrative, but in fact there was no tradition of spiritual autobiography in Protestant Germany for the first century after the Reformation.[30] Luther's *Rückblick* was a description of his discovery of fundamental theological insights rather than an account of a conversion experience. The path to evangelical truth, consequently, did not require imitation or emulation of Luther's experience; rather the emphasis was on the apprehension of theological truths. The Lutheran understanding of conversion after the Reformation did not encourage any particular kind of conversion experience.

Luther and his followers tended to emphasize repentance, of which conversion was one aspect. They were wary of conversion experiences, especially ones that might imply human preparation for grace.[31] At times, conversion or *Bekehrung* could be understood as a synonym for repentance, as it was for instance in the *Apology of the Augsburg Confession*.[32] The linkage of ongoing repentance and conversion remained strong throughout the sixteenth century. As Paul Althaus summarized the views of Luther and the Lutheran tradition, "Conversion or daily repentance is nothing other than the event of baptism realized continually in life."[33] Although conversion had a place within Lutheran dogmatics, Althaus argues, it cannot be conceived as part of a chronological schema or temporal moment.[34]

Lutheran devotional literature in the late sixteenth and early seventeenth centuries bears out the intertwining of *Buße und Bekehrung*, of repentance and conversion, which tended to preclude conceiving of conversion as a specific event rather than an element of reoccurring repentance. In a series of sermons from 1575 on "Repentance and Conversion to God," Tilemann Heshus used the two terms almost synonymously, with *Bekehrung* as an aspect of the ongoing process of repentance that continues throughout one's life.[35]

The best-known Lutheran devotional writer of the seventeenth century, Johann Arndt, also closely linked *Buße und Bekehrung*. In his oft-reprinted spiritual classic, *Von Wahrem Christenthumb* (Of True Christianity)—which he revised and expanded between the publication of the first book in 1605 and the final edition of four books in 1610—Arndt criticized Protestants who identified themselves as Christians, attended to the church's rituals, and yet appeared to deny Christianity with their immoral lives and lack of repentance. Arndt urged them to a thorough repentance that would recall them to their creation in the image of God. Throughout the first book, Arndt often employed conversion as a synonym for repentance. In his chapter on "true repentance," he described conversion in this way: "Repentance or true conversion is a work of God, of the Holy Spirit, through which the human being recognizes his sin and God's anger towards sin, thereby awakening regret and sorrow in one's heart."[36] In numerous places in *Von Wahrem Christenthumb*, Arndt employed *Bekehrung* as largely synonymous with *Buße*,[37] though occasionally he also made conversion an aspect of the larger category of repentance, emphasizing by it the turn from the world and sinfulness toward God.[38] After the initial publication of the first book of *Von Wahrem*

Christenthumb in 1605, Arndt employed language of *Bekehrung* with greater frequency in later revised editions. In doing so he also emphasized much more explicitly that the work of repentance and conversion came from God and was not based on human efforts, thereby seeking to avoid the charges of synergism that followed the publication of the 1605 edition.[39] By discussing conversion almost always in the context of repentance, Arndt was following a Lutheran tradition of linking the two. However, while Arndt never spoke of a distinct conversion experience, he did emphasize experience as a critical aspect of piety and, indeed, theology. In doing so, he points toward a new direction for understanding conversion and conversion experiences in German Protestantism.

Johann Arndt, of course, was not the only one to emphasize repentance in the first half of the seventeenth century. Karl Holl describes a vigorous tradition of repentance preachers in Germany who were, like Arndt, critical of contemporary Christianity.[40] One of the problems that Arndt and others faced in a highly confessionalized society, in which almost all citizens were compulsory members of the church, was to distinguish the "true" Christians from those who professed Christianity yet through their actions denied Christianity in practice. Sifting the true from the false was no easy task, and some like Theophil Großgebauer would suggest a specific conversion experience as an identifier—and in doing so departing from the post-Reformation tradition.

Großgebauer's *Wächterstimme aus dem verswüsteten Zion* (Watchman's Voice Out of Zion Laid Waste) represented the apogee of Lutheran reform literature prior to the later Pietist movement.[41] Disappointed with the effectiveness of the traditional Lutheran practices, which, as the subtitle of his work noted, did not lead to "conversion and godliness," Großgebauer proposed a range of reforms from church discipline to the reform of the office of ministry.[42] Großgebauer considered himself an orthodox Lutheran, and many of his criticisms of the church and proposed reforms are echoed elsewhere in Lutheran reform literature of the seventeenth century.[43] One issue on which Großgebauer differed from his fellow reform theologians, however, was conversion and regeneration. In his *Wächterstimme*, Großgebauer broke with Lutheran tradition and argued for a datable conversion experience. The hour of conversion could be fixed, and it ought to be as important to a Christian as the hour of one's birth.[44] It followed that baptism was no guarantee of conversion and regeneration, contrary to what many preachers and laity believed.[45] For Großgebauer, conversion became a dramatic moment, occurring, he wrote, "not without great struggle and conflict, one that causes greater pain than when a child comes into the world, borne by his mother."[46]

Rather than linking *Bekehrung* so strongly to repentance, Großgebauer identified conversion with true regeneration, understanding it as an event that typically occurred once one had reached the age of discernment.[47] On two points, then, Großgebauer departed from the traditional Lutheran understanding of conversion and regeneration. First, rather than conversion being understood as a lifelong process, it became a dramatic moment in the life of the Christian that one ought to be able to recall vividly.[48] Second, Großgebauer broke with Lutheran tradition on baptismal regeneration. Although for him baptism remained a signal event in the life of a Christian, he no longer identified it with regeneration.[49] Although controversial, especially because of its Reformed overtones,[50] this opened new possibilities for conversion experiences within Lutheranism, especially as Pietists such as Spener came to understand regeneration as repeatable.[51] Some historians have argued that Großgebauer's understanding of conversion and regeneration directly influenced August Hermann Francke's famous conversion experience in 1687.[52] Großgebauer's call to identify the hour of one's conversion did not lead directly toward a tradition of conversion narratives. In fact, suggestive as the *Wächterstimme* is, Großgebauer did not claim to have had such an experience and did not leave any descriptions that suggest the practice of narrating conversion in the community in which he was active.

The lack of conversion narratives in German Protestantism and especially Lutheranism is striking in contrast to Britain and North America, where a tradition of narrating conversion was established by the mid-seventeenth century. In part, this could be connected to the requirement that prospective members of gathered congregations narrate their spiritual autobiography aloud to the congregation or to the minister when they applied for full membership, a practice absent from the German Protestant context, but it was also the Puritan emphasis on identifying one's status before God that further encouraged a tradition of narration.[53] Perhaps some of these Puritan narratives influenced Großgebauer, who was familiar with English devotional literature.[54] A forerunner may be seen in the narratives of lay visionaries such as Hans Engelbrecht or Anna Vetter, who combined autobiographical reflection with their experience of divine visions that authorized them to criticize both clerical and civil authorities.[55] But narratives that turned on a conversion experience were rare. In his well-known collection of sermons, *Der Seelenschatz*, Christian Scriver recounted a number of folksy stories of conversion, but these were far removed from the confessional Puritan conversion narratives of British Puritanism.[56]

An equivalent tradition of introspective, spiritual autobiography was slow to develop in German Protestantism until the rise of Pietism at the end of the seventeenth century.[57] There were nonetheless a number of texts that had something of the character of a conversion narrative before the late 1680s and early 1690s, when the distinct Pietist narratives began to emerge. For instance, Johann Jacob Fabricius, a dissenting Lutheran preacher who was on the fringes of the early Pietist movement, published an autobiographical account in 1669 that has elements of a conversion narrative.[58] In another case, a seafarer named Christian Bullen published a short autobiographical account of his turn from sin to Christ as part of his appeal to both clergy and laity in northern Germany to embrace repentance.[59] In another instance, Friedrich Breckling, in an autobiographical fragment, described a very different conversion-like experience of turning away from his previous alchemical and philosophical interests to commitment to Christ over a period of time that lasted several months. Breckling told how beginning in 1655 he was "awakened to a living faith" through reading scripture, Tauler, Luther, and Stephan Prätorious, and was "brought again to his God and creator, turn[ing] from all external things, human beings and creatures to Christ and His kingdom, spirit, unction, light and word in us."[60] There are others as well. Gottfried Arnold's *Unparteyische Kirchen- und Ketzerhistorie* contains a number of biographical descriptions of the spiritual lives of dissenters that have elements of a conversion story, including Quirinius Kühlmann's "conversion" to the ideas and thought of Jacob Böhme.[61]

One of the first conversions recorded in early Pietism is that of Johann Jacob Schütz (1640–1690), a lawyer in Frankfurt am Main. He was one of the initiators of the famous *collegia pietatis*, and scholars now recognize him along with Philipp Jakob Spener as the cofounder of the Pietist movement in the city.[62] In the 1660s, while a student in Tübingen, Schütz experienced a crisis about his Christian faith. He found no comfort in the Lutheran doctrines of his youth, considered the Bible absurd, and doubted the existence of God. Through contact with Spener in Frankfurt, Schütz gradually found his way back to Christianity, first through the writings of the mystic Johann Tauler and then in direct encounter with the scriptures through which, in Spener's words, Schütz uncovered "the divine power of Scripture through the very reading of it."[63] Deppermann stresses that Schütz's conversion was a lengthy process, without the dramatic turning point or breakthrough typical of later forms of Pietism. The overcoming of "atheism," however, would become a theme in the conversions of learned Pietists.[64] Schütz himself left no account of his conversion; we learn of it primarily through Spener, who for a time considered Schütz's conversion to be a model for how those wrestling with atheism could come to true faith.[65]

Early Pietism in Frankfurt was not, however, marked by an emphasis on conversion experiences. Despite his early enthusiasm for Schütz's conversion, Spener never thought that a specific conversion experience was necessary for a Christian life.[66] The gradual separation of Schütz from the established church in the 1670s and the division of the Pietist movement may have contributed to Spener's unease with the exemplary character of Schütz's conversion. Indeed, as Schütz moved toward separatism in the late 1670s, he seemed to imply that pious but committed churchmen like Spener were themselves in need of a Pauline conversion experience.[67] Schütz discussed the conversions of some Christians among the radical Pietists in Frankfurt;[68] however, in the published biographies of Frankfurt Pietists from his circle, conversion is not a central theme.[69]

The most notable spiritual autobiography to emerge from the Frankfurt circle of Spener and Schütz was that of Johanna Eleonora Petersen, who published her account in 1689 as an appendix to one of her theological tracts. Here she portrays the work of divine grace in her life and the difficult trials she has undergone in following Christ.[70] The account, later expanded by Petersen in 1718, has become one of the best-known texts of Pietism and is frequently reprinted.[71] Particularly significant for a Pietist text, it was first published at the midpoint of the author's life rather than after her death; however, while it details several decisive experiences, it cannot really be understood as a conversion narrative.[72] It rather reflects the early Pietist movement around Spener, in which conversion experiences were not expected. Spener composed his own *Lebenslauf* in the early 1680s, but he did not include any conversion or similar experience.[73]

What these texts do point to among German Protestants is what Ulrike Witt describes as a *Biographiseriung des Heilwegs*, a biographical depiction of the path to salvation, in which one's experiences become constitutive for understanding the progress of faith.[74] These biographical and autobiographical depictions of spiritual journeying became more common toward the end of the seventeenth century; however, given the diversity of the stories, the variety of ways that any turn (or turns) were portrayed, and the lack of explicit identification of a conversion experience, they did not constitute a tradition of conversion narratives. It was only with Francke's conversion in the late 1680s that conversion would become one of the key elements of Pietist narration, and to this we now turn.

1

AUGUST HERMANN FRANCKE'S CONVERSION

No other conversion experience in Pietism has received as much attention among historians as August Hermann Francke's conversion narrative. His account, considered paradigmatic and a model for Pietist conversion in the historiography, is the most widely analyzed and reprinted narrative of conversion in Pietism. Indeed, its characteristic features of repentance, tears, falling to one's knees, and then a subsequent dramatic turn from unbelief to an assurance of faith, in which doubt vanished "as quickly as one turns one's hand," have become a cliché in the depiction of conversion in Pietism.[1]

Francke was, of course, one of Pietism's most dynamic and successful figures, and no discussion of Pietist conversion experiences can avoid addressing his compelling *Lebenslauff*. But the influence and reception of his account also raise significant problems for the interpretation of conversion in Pietism. Prior to his death Francke's account had not been published, and among his contemporaries it was not well known, contrary to many interpreters' assumptions. Francke himself, it appears, did not intend it as a standard for others, and only much later in the course of the eighteenth century did it become the prototype of Pietist conversion. The disproportionate focus on Francke's account in the literature belies the diversity and development of conversion experiences in Pietism, and it tends to distort how Francke himself understood the conversion experience in general and the way that their depiction developed in Halle during his lifetime. To be sure, Francke's account had a literary quality that later readers would find attractive, and, as Anne Lagny argues, the experience it describes was "essentially communicable."[2] Yet Francke remained hesitant to disseminate his own and most other accounts of conversion. This chapter discusses the context of Francke's conversion and its ambiguous significance for conversion for Francke, Halle, and church Pietism more broadly.

Francke's Conversion

Francke composed his conversion narrative in late 1690 or early 1691 in one of the most tumultuous moments of the Pietist movement in Germany. His *Lebenslauff* holds the distinction of being one of the earliest Pietist accounts that the author self-consciously styled as a conversion narrative. It begins by recounting his youth, spiritual development, and education, and culminates in the dramatic episode in Lüneburg in 1687 that Francke explicitly identifies as his *Bekehrung* (conversion). Although Francke frames it largely in terms of his intellectual development from his childhood on, the narrative departs from the typical learned biography of his day in its repeated focus on his fitful spiritual progression, which reaches its apogee in Lüneburg, where the conversion process and the narrative itself conclude. Günther Niggl shows that the biographical detail and attention to his studies suggest something of the learned curricula vitae of his day, but the narrative arc focuses on the conversion story, a literary form that had few if any precedents in German Protestantism.[3]

Francke began with his childhood, but it is not as a wastrel or dissolute youth that he depicted himself. From an early age, according to his account, God instilled in him a "love of scripture and especially the office of ministry," so that his parents always planned to have him study theology. Francke described a period in which, following the typical willfulness of children, he turned away from God, but then, through the pious example of his sister, he found himself "revived." He came to hate the ways of the world and to dismiss "useless companionship, games, and other ways of passing the time," seeking instead more edifying activities, conducting his devotions, praying devoutly, and dedicating his life to God.[4]

This initial turn at age eleven or twelve was one of many in his account that illustrated God's providential guidance and Francke's early moves toward conversion. But these first attempts proved to be efforts he could not sustain. To be sure, through his grounding in scripture he was spared many of the temptations of youth, but his greater challenges were less these crude sins than his drive for academic success and intellectual pride. Beginning at the University of Erfurt at sixteen, he found his mind drawn to the "world and its vanity" while at the same time reckoning that he had departed from the "true Christianity" he had begun in his childhood. Francke emphasized, at times immodestly, his academic skills and prowess in mastering the subjects he engaged. But he employed this authorial strategy not so much to accentuate his intellectual growth as to heighten a sense of the problematic quality of his faith. By no means did Francke depict himself as devoid of any elements of faith whatsoever. While studying at the University of Kiel, he described how the "good spark" had flared up many times and that he had even resolved to separate himself from "the world and its vanity," seeking to live according to God's Word and to change fundamentally.[5]

Yet once again, the "great mob" pulled him back into a morass that was, he notes, worse than his previous dereliction. Looking back on his spiritual condition, he observed,

> Therefore, I was with all my studies nothing more than a great hypocrite, who, it is true, went with others to church, confession, and the Lord's Supper, who sang and prayed, even led good discussions and read good books, but in fact had none of the true power from these things, that is, the power to deny ungodly being and worldly lusts and to live in a chaste, right, and godly manner.... I grasped my theology in my head and not in my heart, and it was much more a dead knowledge than a living recognition.[6]

This pattern would recur several times in the coming years. Francke described his academic accomplishments while studying in Hamburg with the Hebraist Esdras Edzard, but he reports that when he left Hamburg he had "sunk ever more deeply into love of the world" and that this once again prevented him from following divine impulses toward conversion. Moments of recognition did spur Francke to seek God earnestly, but he reports that such moments were insufficient: "My seeking [of God] consisted rather more of outward rather than inner things. I sang and prayed much, read a great deal in scripture and other spiritual books, and even came in tears to confession, but all the time there remained stuck in my heart the conviction that praise, riches, and striving for the good life was no sin."[7] Consequently, to others Francke appeared to be a pious, studious young man, highly respected and appreciated by many, but in his own judgment he was something quite different: "I was nothing other than a mere natural human being, who had much in his head but was far removed from the righteous being that is found in Jesus Christ."[8]

The narrative shifts as Francke described his studies at Leipzig, where he enrolled in 1684. Unlike the earlier passages that described the continual tension between his academic progress and his spiritual deficiencies, here he addressed two specific controversies in which he was involved: the founding of the Collegium Philobiblicum and his translation into Latin of two works by Miguel de Molinos. To a certain extent, these sections constitute a digression within his explication of his conversion. Rather than condemning the lukewarm character of his faith, as Francke had done before, he now defended his actions and his orthodox perspective. Writing of the founding of the Collegium Philobiblicum, a group devoted to biblical studies, he described it as work motivated partly by Spener's urgent desire that he and his colleagues give more attention to devotional questions in their study of scripture, an approach many Leipzig professors supported, at least initially.[9] He argued that similar *collegia* had a long tradition at the university, and that there was nothing religiously untoward in the edification they sought. The Collegium would come to play a decisive role in the explosive growth of Pietism in Leipzig in the late 1680s. In the case of the Roman Catholic Quietist Miguel de Molinos, Francke distanced himself from identification with his thought while urging his fellow students and teachers not to condemn Molinos without having considered his works carefully. They should, he added, act in accord with the spirit of 1 Thessalonians 5:21—"Test everything; hold fast to what is good"—a verse that would become a favorite of many Pietist activists.[10] These passages reassured readers of Francke's Lutheran orthodoxy and reinforced his contention that his chief topic—his narrative of his conversion process—belonged securely within the boundaries of the Lutheran Church and its theology.

The year 1687 figures prominently in the account. By then Francke had become a lecturer at Leipzig, but the disjuncture between his outward appearance and his true inner condition increasingly distressed him. He recognized the profound misery that bound his soul, and he sought to free himself from it. Yet he described himself "as one who is mired in deep muck and perhaps can reach out with an arm but is unable to find the strength to pull himself free." Francke depicted himself as having "set one foot on the threshold of the temple and yet [being] held back by the deeply rooted love of the world from going completely inside." The ascent to the threshold was not entirely fruitless: "I loved godliness very much and spoke about it without deception, even earnestly, and announced to good friends my intention to live to the glory of God."[11] His friends noticed "a distinct change" in him. Nonetheless, Francke remained convinced that the "way of the world still had the upper hand with me."[12] Later that same year, God, whom Francke consistently recognized as the author of his conversion, led him to Lüneburg to continue his exegetical studies, during which the final phase of his conversion took place.

The episode in Lüneburg is the best-known part of a longer conversion narrative and has its own publishing history; however, the *Lebenslauff* portrays it not as an isolated event but as a product of Francke's prior struggles, when his alternation between intellectual pride and spiritual longing set the stage for what would occur in Lüneburg. Soon after arriving in the fall of 1687, Francke received a request to deliver a midweek sermon at the local church, a common request for a young visiting theologian. The invitation provoked a profound personal crisis. As he began to prepare the sermon on John 20:31—"But these [signs] are written that you may believe that Jesus is the Christ, the Son of God, and that believing you may have life in his name"—he questioned whether he could preach at all if he had doubts about his own faith. The earlier struggles issued in a new level of despair, driving Francke to shed tears, something he described as not typical of him. Although he found fleeting comfort in 2 Corinthians 4:7, Francke reported that his atheistic mind swiftly employed the tools of "corrupted reason" to banish the power of scripture from his heart. A visit to a devout churchman failed to allay his misgivings; indeed this conversation about the ways to discern true faith only deepened his anguish, convincing him that he had no such faith. Well-intended reassurances from a fellow theology student also brought no consolation. Bereft, Francke felt only intensified distress. Finally, on a Sunday evening a few days before he was to preach, Francke fell to his knees in his room and implored God to save him from his doubts and unbelief: "I cried to God, whom I still did not know nor trust, for salvation from such a miserable state [asking him to save me], if indeed he was a true God."[13] This time the result of his despairing appeal to God was different.

> He immediately heard me. My doubt vanished as quickly as one turns one's hand; I was assured in my heart of the grace of God in Christ Jesus and I knew God not only as God but as my Father. All sadness and unrest of my heart was taken away at once, and I was immediately overwhelmed as with a stream of joy so that with full joy I praised and gave honor to God who had shown me such great grace. I arose a completely different person from the one who had knelt down.[14]

One striking aspect of this account is the role of experience in combating the doubts sowed by reason.[15] In his doubt, Francke questioned the truthfulness of Christian scriptures: "Who knows if the Holy Scripture is God's Word; the Turks have their Koran, the Jews their Talmud; and who is to say which one of the three is correct?"[16] Reason (*Vernunft*) could not resolve this crisis of faith. Only the powerful conversion experience itself proved the truthfulness of Christianity; it afforded Francke a surety that had previously been lacking. In his account, the experience itself effected a certainty of faith.[17] He believed that it enabled him to know the joy Luther had known: "Now I experience that it was true what Luther said in his preface to the epistle to the Romans, 'Faith is a divine word that changes us and gives us new birth from God (John 1:12) and kills the old Adam, makes us completely other men in our hearts, minds, and thoughts and all our powers and brings the Holy Spirit with it.'"[18]

With his crisis of faith resolved, Francke was able to tell his friend of his "redemption" and joyfully devote himself to preaching, the task that had precipitated this latest bout of despair. Francke dates this as the moment of his conversion: "And this is the period to which I can point as that of my true conversion. From this time on my Christianity had a place to stand, and it was easier for me to deny the ungodly ways and the worldly lust and to live chastely, righteously, and godly in this world."[19] Here his spiritual struggles reach a resolution, and this episode concludes the *Lebenslauff*.

Francke composed the account about three years after the experience in Lüneburg; however, though the intervening years had included many dramatic events within the Pietist movement in Leipzig and elsewhere, Francke does not describe them, even those in which he had been intimately involved, but rather only vaguely intimates that "then the world came quickly to hate and to be hostile to me." To reinforce the watershed character of the conversion, Francke repeatedly invoked in the concluding paragraph of the account the phrase "from this point on" (*von da an*), signaling to the reader that this decisive moment in his spiritual autobiography overshadowed other momentous events in his biography to which he only alludes.[20]

Much of the scholarship on Francke's conversion narrative has sought to identify the intellectual roots of his unprecedented experience. Herbert Stahl emphasized his study of Luther and Molinos.[21] Erhard Peschke, probably the most influential interpreter of Francke in the twentieth century, found the origins of Francke's conversion in his reading of Molinos and Arndt.[22] However, both interpretations are problematic. Although Francke willingly placed himself in the tradition of Luther and Arndt, neither theologian advocated the kind of conversion experience Francke depicts here. Francke's desire to distance himself from Molinos in the conversion account itself makes the link to him less compelling as well. Even if Francke was disingenuous about his dependence on Molinos, the active struggle that he depicts here is quite different from the utter passivity advocated by Molinos as the pathway to higher levels of contemplation.[23]

More likely is Wallmann's argument that through Scharff, the devout churchman Francke encountered in Lüneburg, Francke came into contact with Großgebauer's ideas of conversion. These ideas certainly track Francke's experience more closely than does anything in Arndt, Luther, or Molinos, and Francke later credited Scharff for having introduced him to Großgebauer.[24] More recently, Matthias has proposed the influence of the Erfurt theologian Johannes Musaeus on Francke's views of conversion.[25] Moreover, as critical comments by Spener indicate, English conversion narratives circulated among Pietists in Germany at the time that Francke composed his narrative, and these may have influenced him as well.[26]

Dissemination and Reception

Scholars of Pietism have been far less interested in the reception and diffusion of Francke's conversion story than in its place in Francke's development and its influence on Pietism itself. But Francke's conversion narrative presents several interpretive problems, especially in its reception. It is often assumed, for example, to have been well known among Pietists, but there is little evidence for this assumption, and Francke himself rarely mentioned the account. A brief review of the transmission and reception of Francke's conversion narrative is therefore in order.

We know that Francke likely composed his conversion narrative in Erfurt in late 1690 or early 1691.[27] For a short period thereafter, he appeared ready to circulate copies of it. He sent at least one copy to his friend Kaspar Saggitarius in Jena, and in March 1692 Francke wrote to Spener that he was enclosing an account of the "beginning and continuation of his conversion," in order that it might aid an individual who had been struggling with "atheism," though Francke explicitly requested that Spener send it to others without divulging his identity as the author.[28] This early eagerness to share the account, however, does not appear to have lasted long. Beyond the early 1690s, there are few indications that Francke let others read his account or even that he spoke about it to anyone other than his most intimate friends. Given that Francke published liberally and eventually had at his disposal one of the most dynamic printing enterprises in Germany, the decision not to print his carefully composed conversion narrative must have been deliberate.

Of course, print publication is only one means of dissemination. Would others at Halle have known the details of his conversion experience during his lifetime through some other means? One possibility would have been through the wider circulation of manuscripts. Yet there is scant evidence for this. Indeed, Francke's 1692 comment to Spener that it be shared anonymously indicates that even then he did not envision its becoming even a quasi-public document. Matthias has shown that extraordinarily few copies of the conversion narrative circulated in Germany, and at one point in 1726, toward the end of his life, even Francke appeared unable to locate a copy of it in Halle.[29]

Another possibility is that Francke disseminated word of his conversion experience through discussion, lectures, and other forms of oral communication. Henningsen argues for this kind of oral tradition, which, he believes, made the account well known to students and others in Halle.[30] It is, of course, difficult to demonstrate that something was *not* a subject of discussion, but aside from instances from the early 1690s or the period just prior to his death (to which we will return), the evidence for oral transmission is very thin. Henningsen, for instance, cites a dialogue by Francke from 1701, and yet the passage that Henningsen ties most closely to Francke's autobiography alternates between first- and third-person narration; moreover, the central passages are in third person, making it doubtful that readers would have inferred that Francke was describing his own experience.[31] Albrecht-Birkner cites an intriguing example from 1704 that suggests some circulation of Francke's conversion story in Halle, but this appears to be an isolated example.[32]

When Francke did refer to his conversion, he was remarkably terse. A peasant on Canstein's estate, Jacob Schneider from Mehro, relates one such instance. He had undergone a complex experience of conversion and he felt a sense of closeness to the Pietists. After hearing Francke preach, he related how he went to Francke and asked, "'How did [you] come to possess such grace?' He laughed and said, 'I became a different human being.'"[33] As far as we know, Francke did not explicitly draw on his own conversion experience in his sermons, even when he preached about conversion.[34] And although he appears in a number of narratives counseling students wrestling with conversion, none mentions that Francke related his own story of conversion to them, an odd omission if we assume that Francke wanted to use his experience as a model for others.[35]

For the more than thirty years—from the mid-1690s to the mid-1720s—as the *Franckesche Stiftungen* developed, there is, in sum, very little evidence that Francke talked openly about or otherwise disseminated his conversion experience. None of this suggests Francke denied having a conversion, and we know that he did occasionally speak of it in generalities, as he did with the peasant from Mehro. Nor does Francke ever distance himself from the description of his youthful conversion, as for instance John Wesley appeared to do with his famous account of his "heart strangely warmed."[36] At the very end of Francke's life, it appears that he returned to his conversion experience. In a letter to Walbaum just a few months before he died, Francke recounted his Lüneburg conversion in some detail.[37] Furthermore, in notes he likely made during the last year of his life, he gives an account of his Lüneburg conversion in which he introduces several elements that did not appear in the *Lebenslauff*. He used the word *Bußkampf* to denote his anxious distress prior to conversion, and he drew a contrast between Lüneburg as his spiritual birthplace and Lübeck as his physical birthplace, a comparison he said he had often made.[38] In the final weeks before his death, Francke appears to have spoken more openly of his spiritual development and conversion. Both appeared in his description of an emotional prayer in the orphanage garden.[39]

The flurry of publications that commemorated Francke after his death in 1727 give some insight into the reception of the conversion account in the late 1720s. Several accounts made no mention whatsoever of the Lüneburg experience. A colleague from his Leipzig days, Paul Anton, emphasized in a memorial sermon how God "drew his chosen instrument to him powerfully during [Francke's] very young years," but he makes no reference in the biographical section of the sermon to a special event in Lüneburg.[40] A memorial sermon by an unnamed preacher from Halle described how Francke used his own experience to guide youth, but instead of directing attention to an experience at Lüneburg he stressed a version of an event Francke recounted in the *Lebenslauff*, when at around the age of eleven or twelve he came to hate the "vain nature of youth" and began praying daily in his room.[41] The sermon portrayed the event as follows:

> And in this our late [Francke] could especially call with joy on his own experience, that he knew the way and had traveled it himself, as he, God's name be praised, had related many times that God's spirit had already worked on his soul in his tenth year, when after the regular school hours, he went alone into his room, threw himself down before God, and pleaded with him that he would make him a vessel of his mercy. And as he gained from such little faithfulness such a great measure of grace, which was daily multiplied in him, he thus also sought to proclaim to others at every opportunity that they should attain such blessed means, grace and mercy, from God. In this way, God has especially blessed [Francke's] foundations in Glaucha where now for many years, children of ten to twelve years can, with their own words and from their own hearts, call on the Father in spirit and truth, which before had been alien to those who were masters in Israel.[42]

The sermon is exceptionally revealing. The preacher gave no indication of being an intimate of Francke's, but he was nonetheless an admirer, and for him the signal event in Francke's biography was this early experience, which, he wrote, "[Francke] had related many times."⁴³ Such a pious story, moreover, had an obvious relevance for the school children at Francke's orphanage, which may explain why the preacher chose an event from Francke's childhood, but it is also telling that the sermon did not refer to the Lüneburg conversion. For this German preacher, Francke's spiritual biography could be told without any mention of Lüneberg.

In the *Personalia* that accompany Johann Georg Francke's funeral sermon for A. H. Francke—a document that Matthias describes as the "official description of Francke's life"⁴⁴—the narrative takes Francke to Lüneburg and then pauses to tell the story of his spiritual development. Here the story begins with the ten-year-old Francke who, sensing "the powerful divine pull on his soul," made it his practice to withdraw from the unspiritual world to his chamber, shut the door, and pray on his knees with hands lifted up to God. The narrator attested that Francke had told this anecdote of his early youth many times.⁴⁵ According to the narrative, this "first fire" was never entirely extinguished and remained the foundation for his later, completed conversion. Francke had alternated for years between pious aspirations and the pull of the world, but the earlier "divine preparation" finally came to fruition in Lüneburg. Through continual prayer, Francke experienced there the "powerful *Bußkampf*" that culminated in a breakthrough (*Durchbruch*) and joyfulness, leading Francke, as the narrator notes, to name Lüneburg as his "spiritual place of birth."⁴⁶ This was the first published account of Francke's Lüneburg experience.

The *Personalia* balanced the story of A. H. Francke's youthful turn to solitary prayer and his later Lüneburg conversion. Other accounts made the earlier experience decisive for Francke's spiritual development. The rector of the university, Michael Alberti, for example, accorded far more weight to the earlier experience, which he recommended as a model for everyone who wanted to study theology and serve in the church. In his address, the Lüneburg experience appeared only as a brief capstone "in which the grace flowing forth from the evangelical wellspring of Christ poured out and anointed him *anew*."⁴⁷ One of Francke's students, Georg Friedrich Rogall, told Francke's spiritual story without any mention of the Lüneburg experience; he simply portrayed Francke's faith as the outcome of a costly struggle.⁴⁸ Johann Ulrich Schwentzel, preacher at the Moritzkirche in Halle, compared Francke to the wise King Solomon and describes his spiritual experience following the pattern of the *Personalia* by expressly beginning with the story of the ten- or eleven-year-old Francke's being drawn to God. He describes Francke's later spiritual struggles with markedly less detail, entirely omitting mention of Lüneburg. He chose, in other words, to emphasize not a definitive conversion experience but rather the ongoing possibility of conversion, which was the title of a popular sermon by Francke himself.[49]

The memorial sermon of Francke's son-in-law and longtime coworker Johann Anastasius Freylinghausen marked a break from the pattern of these other accounts in the late 1720s. Whereas the *Personalia* gave the first public account of the Lüneburg experience, Freylinghausen's sermon gave a much more detailed accounting, making it the decisive experience in Francke's life. Freylinghausen, who must have had a nearly complete version of the latter portion of the narrative at his disposal, draws liberally on Francke's account to accentuate the singular nature of the Lüneburg experience. He concludes, "See, dear ones, this experience of the divine work of grace, of a truly thorough and heart-changing conversion as well as [experience] of faith, lay above all as the foundation of your former teacher's office and work."[50] In comparison to the *Personalia*, Freylinghausen here elevates the Lüneberg experience, paraphrasing Francke's account and portraying Lüneberg as the turning point.

Francke's son Gotthilf August Francke followed the example of Freylinghausen. During the fall of 1727 he read the latter portion of Francke's conversion narrative aloud to students at Halle, telling them that this was something for which he had long searched and had only recently found. His words strongly suggest that the conversion narrative had been discovered only recently, and that it had not been part of the regular repertoire of writings on which preachers and biographers would have drawn when they wrote and spoke about his father. If this is correct, the use of the Lüneberg conversion narrative was something new.[51]

Large parts of Freylinghausen's sermon and other documents published around the time of Francke's death would be incorporated into the anonymously edited *Concise Yet Thorough Report of the Quite Noteworthy and Edifying Life of . . . August Herman Francke* (1728), which both made Francke's conversion known to a wider public outside Halle and inserted into the narrative a strong use of the rhetoric of *Bußkampf*.[52] After reading one of these accounts, probably the *Concise Report*, Countess Johanna Sophie von Schaumburg-Lippe wrote to Francke's son, "The supplement of our dear and late Professor Francke's *Lebenslauf* has given me indescribable joy, because I had long devoutly wished that one could have a detailed account of the wonderful dealings of God with his loyal servant. I am thankful beyond all imagination for it. It particularly made a powerful impression on my disposition to see that this dear man also had to go through the spiritual struggle of unbelief before he could attain the strength and proper conviction of the truth. Oh, what depth the Lord's riches have!"[53] For the countess, the reports of Francke's spiritual struggle (*Anfechtung*) and conversion appeared as a new feature of his biography. Clearly, the publications around his death had an impact on the public picture of Francke.

Yet we should not overemphasize their importance. The *Concise Report* and Freylinghausen's sermon appeared in only one edition. And in 1729, when Christian Gerber published a biography of Francke in his collection of spiritual biographies, he made no mention of the Lüneburg experience.[54] Though not one of A. H. Francke's intimate friends, Gerber nonetheless emphasized his long-standing friendship with him dating back to the early days of the Pietist movement, and proudly noted in the preface to the biography that he had received a letter from "his great friend" just two weeks prior to his death. Gerber, whose collection *History of the Regenerate in Saxony* included a number of conversion narratives, could hardly have been opposed to sermons or treatises that related the conversion stories of prominent individuals. Either he was unaware of the Lüneburg account, or he did not see it as the decisive moment in Francke's spiritual biography. Gerber's account further undermines any assumption that Francke's conversion story was widely known and used by Pietists even in the years immediately after Francke's death.

The numerous memorial writings that appeared in the late 1720s suggest that while some contemporaries knew the broadest outlines of Francke's conversion story, most had no knowledge of the full narrative, and none presented it as normative for others. In some depictions, the memory of Francke as a ten-year-old who withdrew to pray and found his life changed was just as important—perhaps more important—than memories of his adult conversion. It was the younger Francke's lecture to the students and Freylinghausen's sermon that began to emphasize the unique and normative character of the Lüneburg experience, and it is unclear how these local discussions would influence later views.

Even as Francke's autobiographical narrative became known to a wider audience in the late 1720s, it did not have a rapid diffusion in the print world, and its rarity must have limited its influence. Until the end of the eighteenth century, the only German printing of Francke's autobiographical narrative in German came in 1733 in Johann Jacob Moser's Pietist periodical *Altes und Neues aus dem Reich Gottes*.[55] A Latin version appeared in Boston the same year, but this had virtually no impact on European readers.[56] Francke's 1727 letter to Walbaum recounting his Lüneburg experience appeared in a journal of practical theology in the 1750s, but there is little evidence that the Lüneburg experience altered the public impression of Francke during most of the eighteenth century, even among Pietists. When Jean Pierre Niceron's *Mémoires* appeared in translation in Halle with a short biography of Francke, it contained only the vaguest reference to the topic, noting that in Lüneburg "his taste for piety, which he had had from his childhood on, was solidified and notably strengthened. Afterwards he used to name Lüneburg his spiritual fatherland, just as Lübeck was the city of his bodily birth." The Halle-based editor felt compelled to supplement or correct many other aspects of Niceron's biography of Francke, including one "major omission," as he called it, but he felt no need to expand or explain the sparse accounting of Francke's Lüneburg conversion.[57]

Only at the end of the eighteenth century did this public image of August Hermann Francke begin to change. August Hermann Niemeyer and Georg Christian Knapp, codirectors of the so-called Francke Foundations or Institutes, appeared to rediscover the narrative of Francke's conversion in the archives and commented on it in print. Niemeyer found his great-grandfather's account moving, if somewhat psychologically and theologically naïve.[58] More enthusiastically, Knapp described the account's "great relevance," and he went on to publish the narrower conversion account in the journal *Frankens Stiftungen* along with other biographical materials.[59] In the nineteenth century, the Lüneburg story took on a featured role in biographical accounts. J. A. Kanne made Francke's conversion and his falling to his knees a central feature of his extended profile in 1817.[60] One popular telling of the story, that of Heinrich Ernst Guericke, quoted extensively from Francke's autobiography and detailed the Lüneburg conversion.[61] An 1830 biography published in Philadelphia made liberal use of the autobiographical account.[62] Schmid quotes at length from Francke's story, and though he says that it had been a "blessing" for many, he does not make it normative for all Pietists.[63] Krämer especially makes it a pivotal moment in Francke's biography, but his analysis focused on Francke's inner development rather than the Pietist movement as a whole.[64] It is really only with Albrecht Ritschl's monumental history of Pietism, published in three volumes between 1880 and 1886, that Francke's experience in Lüneburg takes on a larger role; Ritschl argues that it marked a clear departure from Spener and became "the norm for others."[65]

It was, in fact, nineteenth-century historiography that pulled the Lüneburg conversion experience into the spotlight in Francke's biography, expanded on it, and made it an indispensable feature of Pietism, in some cases judging it to be normative for eighteenth-century Pietist experiences. As we can now see, this emphasis was a departure from common practice during most of Francke's lifetime and the rest of the eighteenth century, when the details of his Lüneburg experience were not well known, much less deemed a model for conversion. When historians make it paradigmatic, they reinforce a historical reconstruction that had little to do with how believers in the eighteenth century understood the narration of conversion.

2

EARLY PIETISM AND THE DIVERSE CULTURES OF CONVERSION

The compelling nature of Francke's conversion account has led some scholars to assume that it served as a template for conversion in early Pietism, especially in Halle. Typical perhaps is Kurt Aland, who argued that Francke's experience became the norm for a "conversion experience that could be temporally determined." Aland believed that "what was true for him was turned into a rule; compulsion and artificiality entered in and the *Bußkampf* became a *Bußkrampf*."[1] Aland's play on words in which *Kampf* (struggle) becomes a *Krampf* (cramp) captures the disdain later critics shared about Pietist conversion, but his reading distorts a proper understanding of the diversity of conversion in early Pietism and vastly overstates both the influence of Francke's account and the experience and role of the *Bußkampf* (repentance struggle). Certainly, conversion was an important topic for early Pietists, but they portrayed and interpreted it in widely divergent ways. Some Pietists, such as Spener, became outright opponents of conversion narratives in the early 1690s, and an ambivalence about conversion experiences marked much of the early movement.

Erfurt

One the earliest centers for conversion narratives in German Pietism was Erfurt in the early 1690s, the place where most scholars agree Francke composed the account of his conversion. Most of the narratives we have are considerably shorter than Francke's more literary account, and they depicted experiences that occurred in Erfurt itself rather than resembling Francke's retrospective account of an earlier time. The narratives illustrate one of the earliest conversionist impulses in Pietism, in which individuals strove to recount their experiences, but the diversity of the Erfurt narratives signaled the multiple directions that conversion could take in early Pietism.

When Francke arrived in Erfurt in spring of 1690, the Pietist movement was in turmoil. Although Francke had left Leipzig on his own in the fall of 1689, the government of Saxony subsequently expelled many Pietist adherents from Leipzig in 1690 for their conventicles and other unauthorized activities. Thanks in part to exiled Leipzig students, the movement spread quickly to many cities of central and northern Germany, from Erfurt to Lübeck.[2] With the support of Joachim Justus Breithaupt, an early Pietist, Francke received a call to the church of the former Augustinian monastery (Augustinerkirche) in Erfurt.[3] Francke's activities energized the Pietists in the city and attracted new followers to his sermons and conventicles, but his popularity also drew the ire of orthodox opponents who were able to have Francke dismissed by September 1691.

One of the conversion narratives from this period came from the lawyer Georg Heinrich Brückner, who described a pious upbringing in Gotha but related how he had repeatedly squandered these good beginnings with worldly diversions. His struggles between piety and pleasure continued through his university studies and his career as a lawyer in Erfurt, until Breithaupt and Francke challenged him to abandon his self-indulgence; otherwise, "the divine nature cannot find room within us." Brückner read Miguel de Molinos, whose call to stillness and rejection of all self-regard hit him hard. He prayed on his knees asking God "to infuse an upright essence and adorn my heart."[4] Then, as he was reading a chapter of Johann Arndt's *Wahres Christentum* on how the eternal good is manifested to the soul in a single moment,[5] he wrote that "it erupted like a lightning bolt in my heart and a true breakthrough [*Durchbruch*] occurred in me, through which I was profoundly moved. For I thought that I wanted to ascend to heaven and discovered that the kingdom of heaven is to be found within us." Following this sudden *Durchbruch*, Brückner supplemented his Bible reading through study of edifying works by Sebastian Franck and Jacob Böhme. But the most powerful influences he identified were the spiritual conversations he had with others, which led him to conclude that "as often as I retreat to the stillness of my heart, I immediately obtain divine strength and emotion."[6]

Brückner identified his experience as a *Bekehrung*, and it resembles Francke's account in some respects. Like Francke, Brückner struggled for assurance of faith. He prayed fervently, and he experienced a sudden moment of illumination that marked a fundamental change in his spiritual life. In both cases, pious clergy enter the picture. Like Francke, Brückner also described an ascetic turn away from worldly diversions. Unlike Francke, however, he does not suffer from atheistic doubts about the truthfulness of Christianity; rather, he seeks the presence of God. Perhaps the strongest contrast is the nature of the struggle. For Francke, the time leading up to his breakthrough is a dramatic struggle—which many interpreters identify with a *Bußkampf*—full of tears, pleading with God, prayer, and repeated kneeling, before finally he is able to stand up again in faith.[7] Brückner styled his conversion much more after the Quietist Molinos, emphasizing stillness and detachment rather than struggle as the prelude to a breakthrough. Though Francke acknowledges Molinos, he also distances himself and his conversion from him.[8] In the wake of their conversions, both turn first to scripture but then to very different kinds of literature: Brückner to the heterodox spiritualists Sebastian Franck and Jacob Böhme, and Francke to Luther's *Preface to Romans*.

Other written accounts from the same period in Erfurt also display some of the features of a conversion narrative. The merchant Nikolaus Fratzscher describes, for instance, how despite his outwardly pious appearance he remained a hypocrite in his heart until Breithaupt and other "faithful servants of God" convinced him of his error and taught him how to seek Christianity within.[9] In something like a repentance struggle, Fratzscher pleaded with God to set him on the "right path of Christianity" but reported no dramatic breakthrough; rather, he told of gaining "firm confidence to the dear Father in heaven" and a desire that he complete the "good work" begun in him. Fratzscher describes his experience as merely the "beginning of my conversion."[10]

In another account from the same period, the cooper Hans Ludwig Nehrlich describes traveling from his small town to Erfurt to learn about the new teachings associated with Francke and Breithaupt. According to his contemporaneous account, he discovered—after meeting with Pietists in Erfurt—that this was not a new doctrine but rather "the pure and unadulterated and ancient doctrine." Nehrlich tells a story not of deep repentance followed by a sudden breakthrough, but rather of God's leading him to Erfurt and to an illumination in the company of Pietists that he compared to Simeon in the Temple: "I comprehended rightly the truth of this doctrine, and my heart was quite moved, that I will now gladly say with the old Simeon: Lord, oh Lord. Let now your servant go in peace."[11] Some see this as a conversion, and Nehrlich's recollection more than thirty years later reinforces the importance of his 1691 experience, but his emphasis on the providential intervention that brought him to Erfurt and on illumination as the fruit of his experience, as well as the absence of any reference to repentance, distinguish his account from later conversion narratives.[12]

In addition to these accounts, we also have several retrospective stories of conversions in Erfurt at that time, including those of Johann Hieronymus Wiegleb and Johann Anastasius Freylinghausen, both of whom later became associates of Francke in Halle. Written toward the end of their lives and long after the events, the narratives contain details suggesting that these men may have based their narratives on accounts composed much closer to the original time. Wiegleb, for instance, described how he fell into despair regarding his "sinful depravity" while a student at Jena, and how he traveled to Erfurt in 1691 to see Francke, to whom he revealed his anxiety. Francke, he wrote, became the "blessed instrument" of his transformation by directing him toward faith in Christ, who alone could rescue him from his sinfulness and repentance. After praying as Francke directed, Wiegleb described how he finally could grasp Jesus through faith: "My heart was full of peace and joy in the Holy Spirit. The forgiveness of all my sins was confirmed to me, and I was freed from the rule of sin over me."[13] Freylinghausen also looked back later to a pivotal experience in Erfurt in the early 1690s. As a young theology student, he went to Erfurt to seek out Francke and Breithaupt. After one of Breithaupt's biblical colloquies, he felt spiritual unease and sought Breithaupt in his study, bemoaning his own inability to understand the "mystical descent." Breithaupt counseled him to pursue the path of contrition, which led Freylinghausen into a "restless, anxious, and legalistic state" that lasted nearly half a year and from which he only gradually emerged as the light of Christ illumined his "disturbed conscience."[14] One might glimpse echoes of what is later described as a *Bußkampf* in Freylinghausen's "sorrow for my sins" and struggle to come to a true recognition of Christ's work on his behalf, but neither Freylinghausen nor Wiegleb described these events as a *Bekehrung* or located them within the model of conversion supposedly typical of Pietist experience.

No set pattern of conversion marks these accounts, and they contain no consistent description of the experiences as instances of *Bekehrung* or conversion. What is striking, though, is the practice in Erfurt of recording conversions and similar religious experiences in writing.[15] From Wiegleb and Freylinghausen we have only later reflections, but the details in their accounts, compared to other episodes in their autobiographies, suggest that earlier narratives from their time in Erfurt may have influenced their narrations. There were likely other accounts written in Erfurt in the 1690s that no longer survive, and there are others from the same period written elsewhere. For instance, Martha Margaretha von Schönberg, an important figure later in

Halle, described her conversion in a short narrative following one of Francke's sermons in November 1691 after he had been dismissed from Erfurt.[16] And probably the best-known conversion experience in early Pietism, that of Johann Caspar Schade, was also composed around 1693.

Why record these experiences? Clearly, these Pietists initially wanted to share their accounts with someone, but there is no evidence that they wanted to print them and make them available to a larger public. In a 1693 letter to Spener, to whom he had sent a copy of his *Lebenslauff*, Francke observed that he could share the piece with others "struggling with atheism" but only anonymously.[17] Wendland's assertion that Francke had always intended it for publication has little basis.[18] It is more likely that the Erfurt Pietists intended their accounts to circulate only among a small circle of like-minded Christians.

The growth of the movement around Francke and Breithaupt provoked a reaction in Erfurt. Some of the clergy felt alienated by what they considered the Pietist disregard for parish boundaries and church rituals. Students were especially drawn to Erfurt for the lectures of Francke and Breithaupt, and the students gathered with residents of the city in conventicles and other devotional meetings that alarmed both civic and ecclesial authorities.[19] Nehrlich's account, with its play on the name "Erfurth Er führt" (Erfurt: He leads) indicates the perception of Erfurt as a divinely ordained Pietist destination in late 1690 and early 1691.[20] The authorities placed ever-greater restrictions on the Pietists in the city and dismissed Francke from his position in September 1691.[21] Breithaupt left for Halle shortly thereafter, possibly to circumvent his own removal from office.[22]

Their departure signals an end to this conversionist phase in Erfurt, but it is worth reflecting briefly on the episode's implications. The surviving evidence suggests that something was happening in Erfurt that led people to write conversion narratives. Such accounts from early Pietism are not plentiful, and their appearance at this time—along with other accounts that recall the same period—point to an innovative atmosphere in Erfurt. The best known of all Pietist conversion narratives, Francke's account, also dates to Erfurt during this period. Second, the accounts describe diverse experiences, none of which referred to a *Bußkampf*, and the narratives also differed in their structure: Brückner's account, for instance, differs from Francke's not only in its trajectory but also in the theological underpinnings, even though he gave Breithaupt and Francke credit for their aid in his transformation. His story also shows how conversion could sometimes be linked to heterodoxy.

Wiegleb and Gotha

After this early phase in Erfurt, Pietists continued to interpret their conversions in a variety of ways. Wiegleb and others from Erfurt settled in nearby Gotha, the residence of the Duke of Saxe-Gotha, where Francke grew up. His mother and sister still lived there, and he retained strong ties to the city, which became a center of early Pietism. Wiegleb, the assistant rector or principal of the town's *Gymnasium* (secondary school), also appears to have brought a conversionist bent with him to Gotha. The widely read 1693 exposé of Pietist practices, *The Extensive Description of Mischief*, which combined reports of Pietist excesses with exaggerations and unfounded rumors, described emotional scenes and unconventional conversion practices in Gotha. During one conventicle led by Wiegleb, for example, a young man from Erfurt fainted amid his "fervor for conversion" and had to be carried out of the gathering, an occurrence that reportedly drew praise from Wiegleb according to the disdainful author.[23]

The exposé further asserted that Wiegleb and others made slips of paper—some with "critical" phrases, some with "good" phrases, and finally some with the "best" phrases—and had the participants draw lots for them. They allegedly judged those who drew the "critical" slips of paper as unconverted, those with the "good" as half converted, and those with the "best" slips as "illumined" and fully converted.[24] The accusation invites some skepticism, and defenders of Wiegleb from Gotha disputed its veracity, noting that an inquiry had disproved the allegations.[25] In the eyes of opponents, however, Pietist conversion was not a sober turn to repentance or a praiseworthy change in morality—the opposition could have endorsed conversion as profound repentance and good ethics[26]—but an outburst of dangerous enthusiastic fervor combined with claims of implied perfectionism and the ability to know God's will by drawing lots that almost magically revealed spiritual status. Like many caricatures, though, the portrayal might have contained a grain of truth, however much distorted.

Wiegleb cared about conversion—no one could quarrel with that—but sometimes his language could, to a determined critic, suggest unorthodoxy. A confession of faith that he and three others composed in 1693, *Confessio Oder Glaubens-Bekäntniß*, spoke of a powerful experience of rebirth in which the individual was "reborn through the Word as a living seed," so that "he watches and prays according to the counsel of Christ and seeks to go about and walk in the power of the Lord, indeed to lead therefore his whole life through the assistance of the Holy Spirit in this rebirth." What disturbed the anonymous critic of Wiegleb and his fellow authors of the *Confessio* was less the idea of a conversion or the implication that the baptized Christian could lapse from the baptismal covenant, but the implicit notion of perfectionism in the suggestion that converts could avoid sin.[27]

Later, Wiegleb became entangled in several disputes about conversion at the Gotha *Gymnasium*, where it appears he fostered a conversionist atmosphere. One report describes the intense pressure that one student placed on another in 1694 to open himself to conversion, a tactic for which the author of the account criticized the Pietists for overemphasizing the conversion experience.[28] Other documents suggest the conversionist atmosphere and Wiegleb's place within it. One student reportedly said that the pressure to convert drove him to melancholy and fear that he had sinned against the Holy Spirit, which left him suffering "in hell."[29] Probably the most damaging story from Gotha was of a failed conversion in the summer of 1695. The young student Johann Wendel Meidinger sought to hang himself out of despair over his unconverted state. The circumstances of the suicide attempt remained controversial, but the father of the student, himself a village pastor, indicted the conversionist tactics Wiegleb fostered at the school as well as the Pietist literature circulating there.[30] For his part, Wiegleb allegedly sought to deflect blame by securing a deposition from the young Meidinger that praised the Pietists, especially Wiegleb, and blamed his distress on himself.[31] The only sure conclusion is that conversionism was rampant in Gotha and that some saw the Meidinger case as a warning against untoward pressure to convert.

Wiegleb continued to preach for conversions in Gotha, and in his *Haupt-Summa der Christlichen Lehre*, a 1697 adjunct to Luther's small catechism, he wrote of conversion as a defining moment in the life of faith. However, although Wiegleb emphasized the necessity of repentance before coming to Christ, he presented no schematic description of conversion but rather emphasized only that conversion is God's work.[32] The Gotha accounts also give no hints of any pressure to write conversion narratives or precisely date the experience. Determining who belonged to the converted or regenerate could become divisive, even among Pietists. Later, Wiegleb reported that a colleague in Gotha had doubted whether Francke's own sister, who lived in Gotha, truly belonged to the regenerate.[33] But the most contentious issue may have been Wiegleb's implied view that the converts could hope for perfection.[34]

Johann Caspar Schade

The absence of any normative pattern of conversion narrative in early Pietism is illustrated by Johann Caspar Schade's 1693 autobiographical account that was published after his death in 1698. Although historians have tended to neglect it when discussing the topic, Schade's narrative was the most widely published conversion narrative in early Pietism. Schade composed it following a severe illness when he concluded that he did not want to depart from this life without leaving an account of what "God has done for his soul." He framed his account in the light of Psalm 25:10, "All the Lord's paths are loving and faithful" to emphasize God's providence from the moment of his conception and throughout his life. The phrase recurs as a refrain throughout the account. Despite the difficulties of his childhood, including the loss of both parents at an early age, Schade affirmed that God had turned every event to his benefit. He portrayed himself as a pious child who wanted to preach and pray even as a babbling youngster, and he praised God that he had not fallen into all of the "common sins and passions" of youth. He faced temptations, and he lapsed into "vices and infractions," especially "jesting and foolishness" that caused his teachers, who had high hopes for him, to despair. But God never let him go entirely, and Schade praised God for rescuing him: "Praised be your mercy to me, that you have called me back from corruption and given me a better mind and another heart, and that you did not allow me to remain all too long in this foolishness and incomprehension but rather allowed a gracious light to rise up that led to repentance."[35]

In one respect, this outburst of praise functions as the turning point of the narrative. Immediately after the adoration of God, he praises Christ: "For as my sin became greater, the richer [your] mercy and grace was to me, together with your patience and forbearance, as proof and example of the love to all sinners and will for their conversion." Noting that "when I am converted, I should strengthen my brethren," Schade began to exhort young people to turn away from the temptations and sinful ways. Yet the narrative does not end at this point; rather, it continues by describing God's providential guidance through his academic studies in Wittenberg, which protected him, for instance, from the "harmful misuse of human wisdom and quibbling arts of disputation, from famously wrong subtleties in wisdom and divine doctrine ... [and from] the common if at the same time crude sins that are in fashion in such places."[36] God's providence continued, leading him along "loving and faithful" paths to Leipzig and August Hermann Francke's circle, in which Schade became a leader.

Yet Schade complicated the trajectory of conversion by describing a period of intense spiritual struggle (*Anfechtung*) in Leipzig, when the opponents of the Pietists attacked him publicly and he inwardly suffered bouts of trial, sorrow, and unbelief. He fell, he said, into a "profound disbelief of all divine things, so that I judged that I could neither believe nor pray any longer." This was different from Francke's lament that he lacked faith. For Schade, the episode of spiritual travail that ends the narrative revealed rather how God never abandoned him and continued to protect and guide him despite his unbelief. He never declared definitively that he lacked faith altogether, but rather "judged himself neither able to believe or to pray any longer." But the temporary absence of faith did not cut him off from God, who "held his hand over me so that neither Satan and reason could fell and enchant me nor also could anyone dare amid so many accusations, out of which hate has grown, to allow themselves to lay a hand on me."[37]

At the time, Schade may have believed he lacked faith, but in retrospect the narrative recounts how God worked in him all along. In the end, there is no triumphal breakthrough for Schade. Rather, he said only that God's protection enabled him to respond to his opponents in love and prayer, something that he has continued in "love and supplication to the present date."[38]

His account presents a model of conversion different from Francke's. Schade had a relatively early conversion in adolescence in which God changed him in heart and mind; however, his later life was not free from spiritual struggle, and there is no breakthrough in the end but rather the simple recognition that "God had turned all of these things to my benefit." His emphasis on God's providential guidance could easily imply that the *Anfechtung* at the end of the narrative was not a stage through which one passed once and for all but an ongoing possibility of the spiritual life even after conversion. It is hard to draw any schematic picture of Schade's conversion, and it does not fit what is sometimes described as the typical Pietist triad of conversion: divine stirring (*Rührung*), repentance struggle (*Bußkampf*), and breakthrough (*Durchbruch*) to conversion.[39] Early interpreters of Schade's narrative interpreted it less as a model for conversion than as a resource for Christians afflicted with *Anfechtung*.[40]

One might be tempted to treat Schade's account as anomalous or atypical, but such a conclusion cannot account for its status as the most widely printed and distributed conversion account of early Pietism. It first appeared in print as part of Spener's funeral sermon in 1698. In 1700, August Hermann Francke published it as an appendix to a new edition of Hieronymus Weller's *Marter-Buch*. In 1701, Gottfried Arnold published it as part of his *Leben der Gläubigen*.[41] By 1720, the editor of Schade's collected works noted that his *Lebenslauf* had appeared in thirteen editions.[42] Rather than pointing to Francke's unprinted and largely unknown conversion narrative as exemplary for early Pietism, we should point to Schade's account, which Pietists after 1698 found compelling.

Some commentators have drawn on a later third-person narrative found among Schade's posthumously published works to interpret his conversion in what they see as a more typically Pietist fashion.[43] There are indeed similarities between the earlier and later narratives. Both, for instance, deal with atheistic doubts and describe the spiritual struggles of a theology student or young minister. But there are also a number of differences. First, the later, third-person account presents a pattern of conversion that does not fit neatly with the earlier *Lebenslauf*. The governing theme of the *Lebenslauf*—Psalm 25:10, "All the Lord's paths are loving and faithful"—is missing. Two other biblical passages structure the account. Crucial episodes of the earlier account are absent in the later one, which contains no reference to the attacks from clergy hostile to Pietism that helped precipitate the spiritual crisis described in the earlier document. The third-person account also introduces new themes, such as the importance of the sacraments or the problem of competing religious traditions. More significantly, the later, third-person account presents a sudden moment of conversion, a center around which the plot of the narrative turns. Such a dramatic moment is missing in the more widely known and earlier autobiographical account. In addition, the third-person account presents an extended description of growth in the Christian life that appears nowhere in the *Lebenslauf*. In contrast to the *Lebenslauf*, the third-person account avoids any mention of place, time, or other specific individuals that would allow the reader to identify this account with a particular person or community.[44]

Moreover, even if we were to accept the third-person account as a more accurate description of Schade's conversion, it was not well known and could not have had the same impact as the many editions of the *Lebenslauf*. It was not the account that others, such as A. H. Francke or Philipp Jacob Spener, who knew him well, chose to publish about Schade. Schade may have drawn on his spiritual experience for the third-person account, and perhaps he did intend it as a model for others. He explicitly addressed a reader. But there is little reason to believe that Schade considered the third-person account a more accurate description of his experience than the autobiographical account. It is true that the former comports more easily with current assumptions about what Pietist conversion should have been, but even the most generous reading of the two accounts as compatible leaves us with the problem of identifying any narrative written for a specific purpose—and audience—with the actual experience of an individual. Especially, if assumed to be compatible, the two accounts underscore further the malleability of memory in recalling events.

Reitz and *Historie der Wiedergebohrnen*

The same year that Schade died and his autobiographical account appeared, the radical Pietist Johann Henrich Reitz published the first volume of the most significant collection of spiritual biographies in Germany. Reitz gave his collection a baroque title that conveys his intent: *History of the Regenerate, or Examples of Godly Christians, Who Are Known and Named as Well as Unknown and Unnamed, of the Male and Female Sex, in All Estates, How These Same Are First Drawn by God and Converted, and After Much Struggling and Fears, Are Brought to Faith and Peace of Their Conscience.*[45]

Reitz sought to present the diversity of "God's progress with the souls of his children" and did not intend the stories to be a rule for religious experience, but he did believe that nothing could be "more useful, more salutary, more evangelical" than to hear believers and regenerate individuals confess "their struggle, their path, their faith, their fear and birth-pangs, their past thoughts, speech, and behavior, and what God's grace has effected in them and what Satan, the world, and their flesh has meant to them or what has nettled and tempted them," and to collect these and make a story or narrative, a *Historie*.[46]

The first volume consists almost exclusively of conversion narratives translated from English. The source of these narratives was long unknown, but Hans-Jürgen Schrader identified them as originating with Vavasor Powell's *Spirituall Experiences, of Sundry Beleevers* (1653). Powell was a seventeenth-century Welsh preacher with pronounced millennialist leanings. The accounts in the first volume, all but two from the British context, are conversion narratives that follow a relatively consistent pattern Rudolf Mohr describes as (1) humiliation and distress for one's sinfulness, (2) conversion, and (3) growth in faith.[47] This initial volume accents the spiritual experiences of women—all but the last two narratives were accounts of women—and Reitz dedicated the volume to three women and praised female godliness.

Yet the first volume is in some ways unrepresentative of the subsequent volumes in the collection. Though women remain prominent, their narratives do not stand out as they do in the first volume. Furthermore, the biographies that Reitz published are not exclusively conversion narratives. Many of those from German settings, such as those from Johann Arndt or Julianna Baur von Eyseneck, portray no conversion at all. Others, such as the one from Jacob Böhme, feature conversions that are highly unconventional, if they were conversions at all. For instance, in the account of Böhme, Reitz identified as a series of "conversions" the threefold illumination that Böhme's biographer Abraham Franckenberg had described.[48] Reitz also draws on

Hans Engelbrecht's well-known autobiography to portray his vision of God and illumination as a kind of turning point, though neither Reitz nor Engelbrecht name it a conversion.[49] In the early volumes, there are few narratives from German Pietists. Christian Hoburg's biography depicts a conversion-like event that followed Hoburg's reading of Schwenckfeld's *Himmlische Arzeney (Heavenly Medicine)*, which "fully changed" his mind and led him to turn away from the world and his old friends. Emphasizing the inner word, Hoburg decided that one must experience the Holy Spirit in one's heart and be born again in the "Spirit of Christ."[50]

The second volume included biographies and autobiographies mainly from Britain, beginning with Edward VI (1537–1553) and extending to Elizabeth Moore, a poor woman who died in 1660. Reitz reprinted a few from France and the Low Countries, including an account of Pascal's life,[51] but only a handful came from German-speaking areas. Reitz often cast as a vision or illumination the narratives that depicted a transformative experience, much in contrast to the tendency of Powell's narratives translated for the first volume to depict an explicit conversion experience.[52] Gichtel's account portrays an early moment of illumination as a conversion but does not use conversion language to describe formative moments later in life.[53]

Some accounts in Reitz come closer to the putative pattern of a "Pietist" conversion. For instance, Samuel Schumacher from Zürich described a long period of despair and fear that he had committed the unforgiveable sin against the Holy Spirit, which led up to a change of heart while hearing a sermon in Lützelflüh.[54] Yet many others were more idiosyncratic. The story of a soldier named Peter Leideneck recounted his life-changing experience as a prisoner of war, which included a sudden ability to read. A divine vision even instructed him how to escape; however, unlike Schumacher, he suffered a series of setbacks and spiritual crises after his conversion that afflicted him whenever he compromised with the world, especially to please his unregenerate wife.[55]

As Dorothea von Mücke has emphasized, Reitz sought to present the diversity of the ways individuals were led to God. Reitz's conversions allowed for "comparison and self-reflection" but avoided a "template of conversion."[56] The accounts represented a range of confessions and geographic origins, suggesting that conversion was not limited to one area, much less one religious affiliation. For Reitz, a conversion experience was not an essential element in the biography of the regenerate. Moreover, the language of conversion was rarely consistent and often casual. It could both elevate the theme of illumination and valorize the breakthrough after a struggle with sin and repentance.

Gottfried Arnold

Reitz's was the best-known but not the only collection of this sort in Pietist circles. Gottfried Arnold published two volumes of spiritual biography in 1700 and 1701. The first, dealing with the early church, was a German edition of Georg Major's *Vitae Patrum*, for which Martin Luther had written a foreword in 1544. A number of the stories recounted conversions, though many reflect somewhat crude tales of individuals who turned from lives of sinfulness and converted suddenly to Christianity. The life of Apollonius, for instance, shows how he converted a murderer and taught him to live a Christian life. Another story gives an account of the prostitute Thais, who converts under the influence of Paphnutius, the fourth-century desert father. Thais dies "blessedly on the path of repentance." Most of these stories were short, though some, like the one about Ephraem Syrus, provide insights into a more extended process of conversion in the wake of a false accusation and subsequent imprisonment that issued in repentance and a new life in Christ. August Hermann Francke wrote the foreword to the book, but he was at pains to warn against considering the stories as models rather than using them as guides to following the only true exemplar, Jesus Christ.[57]

Arnold followed the *Vitae Patrum* the next year with another volume of spiritual biography and autobiography, *Die Leben der Gläubigen*, a book marked especially by its accent on Catholic piety. He reprinted Teresa of Avila's *Life* along with accounts of Angela of Foligno, St. John of the Cross, Catherine of Genoa, Jeanne de Chantal, and Nicolaus von Flüe. Alongside these Catholic lives, Arnold also printed biographies of Arndt and Luther. Britain provided the largest number of conversion narratives, which included Bunyan's *Grace Abounding* along with the maudlin child conversion stories of Janeway's *Token for Children*. Arnold published relatively few examples of German accounts, though he reprinted Schade's autobiography and an account of a young woman from Frankfurt, Elisabeth Kißner, which detailed her spiritual travail before her death. Though her story included struggle (*Kampf*), spiritual trial (*Anfechtung*), and bouts of uncertainty, it is not so much a conversion account as it is a tale about the deathbed struggles of a pious young woman who yearned to depart from the world.[58] Arnold concluded the *Leben der Gläubigen* with the conversion story of a young nobleman condemned to death for a killing a man in a duel. It differed markedly from the conversion narratives at Erfurt, though it is an early example of the kind of execution story that would become popular in the 1730s.[59] Like Reitz, Arnold saw no need for a specific conversion, and when he did include recognizable conversion narratives they conformed to no one pattern and employed no consistent vocabulary to describe conversion.

The diversity of spiritual biography at this time is further reflected in Francke's 1697 publication of a new edition of Hieronymus Weller's *Creutz-Schule*, a collection of martyr stories and spiritual reflections. In the preface, Francke recommends these as examples from the early church that could "convert" some from their "dead works" but especially could show the pious their need for prayer and fasting and the inevitability of suffering.[60] When Francke republished Weller's collection in 1700 he added three contemporary biographies, but only Schade's has the character of a conversion narrative.[61]

Ambivalence Regarding Conversion Narratives

Whence the reticence about conversion narratives? There is no question that conversion, at least as an ideal, was important for Pietism from its early days in Leipzig, Erfurt, Gotha, and Halle.[62] One of Francke's early tracts, *Short and Simple Yet Thorough Instruction to True Christianity* (1695), described the importance of converting "body and soul" to become a righteous Christian.[63] We recall as well the importance of narratives in Erfurt. But the events in this and other German cities did not create a tradition of narratives. Pietists seemed oddly uneasy with public accounts of conversion experiences.

One source of the unease came from Philipp Jacob Spener himself. In 1690, around the time when some Pietists began to compose the stories of conversion, Spener questioned whether it was necessary to delineate the "time and hour," a specificity that some had inferred from English Puritan authors. Spener did not question the validity of such conversions, but he worried that such "descriptions of conversion," too, could strike others as normative and lead to either unnecessary scruples or spiritual pride.[64] As the leading figure of Pietism in the 1690s, Spener's warnings may have dampened enthusiasm for the narratives. And after Reitz and Arnold published their collections, Spener made known his objections:

> The accounts of conversion, rebirth, and renewal, which are based on one's own experience, have this weakness that often Christian hearts, whose nature is right, begin to doubt the truly divine beginnings and fall into deep struggles, because they have not gone through such paths, and consequently want to force themselves to do this or that, which God has not effected in them. [This happens] when the authors do not

properly protect the reader and testify that God may have dealt with them in this fashion, but they cannot say that he would deal with all his children in the same way, much less indicate that their encounter would be a rule for others and therefore that everyone must experience things as they have.[65]

Like many other Pietists, Spener believed that God worked in many ways to elicit faith. He argued that the "weakness" of the narratives was their tendency to impose a set of expectations that veiled God's boundless mercy. It is hard not to see his comments as a criticism of collections like those published by Reitz and Arnold.

An ambivalence about conversion narratives lay at the heart of German Pietism, even at Halle. Francke, who seemed to encourage their composition—though not their publication—in the early 1690s, dropped the subject once he arrived in Halle. Albrecht-Birkner did not identify conversion or conversion experiences as an important issue in his controversies with his parishioners in Glaucha during the 1690s.[66] To understand conversion at Halle, we need to clear away some misconceptions. Conversion was indeed a theme and a spiritual goal at Halle, but neither Pietist practice nor Pietist publication can be shoehorned into a single pattern. To ignore the diversity is to misread both Francke and the conditions in Halle and to elide the problematic character of Pietist conversion.

Question of the *Bußkampf*

In the historical literature, Francke's Halle came to be known as the place of origin for a highly schematic and rigid understanding of conversion, for which Francke's religious experience provided the template. Typical of such a view is Kurt Aland's insistence that at Halle, Francke's experience became the norm, which required a "conversion experience that could be temporally determined."[67]

The idea of a single compulsory mode of conversion at Halle continues to mark much of the literature on Pietism and conversion.[68] Conversion remained a major topic for Francke after he was forced to leave Erfurt, but his conversion narrative was not well known before his death, and Pietists who underwent conversion and wrote about it did not feel the need to conform themselves to a fixed model.[69] They occasionally used the language of the *Bußkampf*, but more often they felt no need to mention it.

Chief among the scholars who have stressed the schematic and normative character of Francke's view of conversion at Halle is Erhard Peschke, who analyzed in detail the theology undergirding it. Drawing on Francke's sermons and other publications, he divided conversion into stages that largely followed the example of Francke's narrative. Peschke particularly attends to the characteristic repentance struggle or *Bußkampf*.[70] For Francke, according to Peschke, the unconverted first felt divine stirrings (*göttliche Rührung*) in their hearts. These opened them to the further work of the Holy Spirit that led them—normally, though not inevitably—into the repentance struggle (*Bußkampf*) in which the heart was conflicted, distressed, even shattered. A deep humiliation ensued; this led to the breakthrough (*Durchbruch*) to grace and faith, which Peschke identified as the "decisive conclusion of the process of conversion, the act in which all waiting is rewarded, all *Anfechtungen* overcome, and bitter struggle crowned with victory."[71] It is a dramatic and compelling story, but it minimizes the variety of settings and the diverse character of the descriptions even in Francke's own work. Peschke outlined Francke's view of the "stages" that led to conversion.[72] This approach depicted a Francke who was theologically consistent throughout his life. But Francke's sermons and other writings were largely occasional and not always consistent, and we should avoid the temptation to read a structure back into his writings that Francke may not have intended.

Peschke's approach has won a number of adherents in the community of scholars who study Pietism. Petra Kurten's analysis of Francke's conversion theology follows a similar three-stage understanding of conversion, with the *Bußkampf* at its center.[73] Ulrike Witt and others have adopted this tripartite scheme in order to understand conversion at Halle during Francke's lifetime.[74] I would like to propose an alternative reading.

From his earliest surviving sermon to one that he preached more than thirty years later at the end of his career, Francke preached about conversion.[75] The topic appeared in sermons, lectures to students, comments on preaching, and devotional publications. He wanted his readers and hearers to undergo the experience.[76] A heartfelt conversion that produces a fundamental inner transformation and not merely an external change in behavior was part of Francke's understanding of true Christian piety, a theme he reiterated time and again. But one can overemphasize both its centrality and its schematic nature. It is also important to give attention to change through time.

In much literature on Pietism, the *Bußkampf* is virtually identified with Francke's understanding of conversion. Peschke expressed this point of view when he argued that Francke "demands the *Bußkampf* as an unconditional presupposition of the conversion process."⁷⁷ Peschke's judgment has won widespread acceptance among historians of Pietism.⁷⁸

The *Bußkampf* is not a fiction; Francke employed the term throughout his writings. He did not use the word in his conversion narrative, but, to give one example, it appeared in his 1696 sermon on the penitential Psalm 51, in which Francke made struggle or striving—*Kampf*—the overarching theme. Citing 2 Timothy 2:5 in Luther's translation, "Und so jemand auch kämpft, wird er doch nicht gekrönt, er kämpfe denn recht,"⁷⁹ Francke drew on David's sixfold penitential struggle in the Psalm to admonish his parishioners: "But you who have heard this, what is the condition of your hearts? What do you say to this? Have you also experienced such a repentance struggle [*Bußkampf*] in your hearts?" He continued, "The longer I live in this city, the more my heart groans and is appalled that I must gaze on the impenitence of most. Oh Halle, Halle! Oh Glaucha, Glaucha! Just convert yourself. Go into yourself, so that you will be beset with grace from the Lord your God."⁸⁰

Yet as prominent as the *Bußkampf* could be for Francke in a powerful sermon like this, he could preach a penitential sermon a little more than a year later titled "On the Work of Conversion" where he described conversion without any recourse to the notion of *Bußkampf*, stressing instead the need for true repentance and a heartfelt change in one's heart.⁸¹ Francke emphasized that conversion was the work of God, dependent on divine initiative and action, not on any human works, but it was of course incumbent on the convert to recognize this work of God in his heart and confess it openly. True repentance or penitence (*Buße*) was mandatory, and without *Buße* or *metanoia* there was no real conversion.⁸² But Francke felt no need in this sermon to call on the idea of a repentance or penitential struggle, and in emphasizing true repentance and conversion he reflected a long-standing Lutheran connecting of the two.

In other works, he was also silent about the *Bußkampf*. His *Short Instruction on the Possibility of a True Conversion to God* (1709) did not mention it, even though the *Short Instruction* referred to an order of conversion set by God. Francke refers now and then in this text to the "struggle" against wanton sin or the need to recognize the "order of God" and not to neglect "serious wrestling" in conversion. The reference allows us to infer a kind of *Bußkampf*, but it does not function here as a precise theological concept or a stage in an invariable ordering of conversion. Often when Francke employed *Bußkampf*, as he did in an unpublished 1712 sermon on the *Durchbruch* to authentic Christianity, it functioned simply as a way to describe the necessity for repentance—a repentance at times even synonymous with the *Durchbruch* itself.⁸³

If we look beyond Francke to some of his allies at Halle, we find again no preoccupation with the *Bußkampf*. Johann Anastasius Freylinghausen, one of Francke's closest coworkers and his future son-in-law, wrote the *Foundation of Theology* in 1703 as an early popular theology from a Hallensian perspective.[84] Freylinghausen included a substantial section on repentance and conversion, but a reader would never know that either a *Bußkampf* or a datable experience was supposed to be part of "the divine order" in conversion.[85] Freylinghausen differed from his seventeenth-century predecessors in that he makes repentance an aspect of conversion rather than conversion an aspect of repentance, as it was, for instance, in Johann Arndt. The change highlights individual conversion. He also mentioned the need to persevere in the "struggle of repentance," but he was talking only about a consequence of conversion, not a necessary stage in the process.[86] His later work on the order of salvation, *Ordnung des Heyls*, published in 1713 for a lay audience, also fails to mention the *Bußkampf*.[87] Breithaupt could use the term occasionally, but it was not a clear stage in the path to conversion.[88] As Stoeffler has argued, the *Bußkampf* also plays no significant role in the works of many of Francke's other colleagues.[89] The *Bußkampf* did come to dominate some Pietist conceptions of conversion, but these came later and should not be identified with a supposedly fixed Hallensian mode of conversion.

Halle and a Culture of Conversion?

As one pushes more deeply into the question of a supposed culture of conversion at Halle, some red flags appear. First, as Markus Matthias cautions, Francke's talk about conversion did not lead to "psychological indoctrination" at Halle. Matthias points out that demands for conversion are entirely missing in the personnel records of the *Franckesche Stiftungen*, where one would expect to find them. In the *Album der Waisenkinder*, which describes the characteristics of the children in the orphanage, the issue of conversion is absent before 1730, and even afterward it rose to the surface for only a limited time.[90] Clear distinctions among the "converted" and the "unconverted" do not appear in the Halle records from the period of Francke's lifetime. Nor are there notable accounts of revivals or clusters of conversions in the city while he lived there. One minor revival among some of the children at the orphanage in 1718 appears to have been the exception rather than the rule.[91] For these and other reasons, W. R. Ward argued that "Francke was basically a preacher of reform rather than revival," and that Halle Pietism was "not itself revivalist" when compared to the European evangelical awakenings.[92]

Second, the accounts of conversion experiences from Halle are less frequent than one might expect. In his public talks, whether in sermons or lectures to students, Francke did not draw on such accounts, whether of his own conversion or those of others, in order to encourage repetition. At one point, he seemed to suggest the utility of such collections. In a 1699 sermon he commented favorably on the recent publication of Johann Henrich Reitz's *Historie der Wiedergebohrnen*: "Recently a little book has appeared, translated from the English into our German language, in which many examples of conversion are portrayed and in each one the marks noted, by which each one knew that his conversion was truthful and from God. It is to be wished that we would all follow such examples and learn to examine our conversions, in order that one not deceive oneself with the great mob and be fooled by mere imagination."[93]

But Francke does not appear to follow his own admonition or call for the publications of models. Gottfried Arnold published two collections of spiritual biographies at Halle, the *Vitae Patrum* (1700) and the *Leben der Gläubigen* (1701), both of which contained some conversion accounts.[94] But these do not set a precedent for further publication in Halle and may have represented not Francke's agenda but Arnold's. Francke's dedicatory preface to the former volume praises pious lives, but it does not mention conversion. Halle spawned no widespread practice of composing conversion narratives either for publication or for manuscript circulation within its networks.[95]

Francke could state forcefully the need to recognize the moment of conversion, so it is strange that he so often failed to mention it. A recognition of such a moment implies some form of verbal narration or accounting, whether written or oral. At one point Francke said in a lecture to students that "when one has experienced [conversion], it does not occur as if he had encountered it as in a dream and he would not know what had happened to him. Oh no! If a true change and conversion of the heart has taken place, he thus would indeed know the time and place that it had happened; he would know the length of time that it took."[96]

But at other times Francke could be much more ambivalent about the requirement that one identify the moment of one's conversion. Such knowledge could be useful in unmasking hypocrites who bore no "marks of conversion and regeneration" and who denied that anyone can know the status of their own conversion. But when it became a requirement, it could push sensitive souls into despair about their faith, even when they exhibited marks of belonging to the "children of God." What is necessary, Francke concluded, is to follow the requirement of 2 Corinthians 13:5 that "one examine oneself whether one is in faith and whether Christ is in us."[97] But Francke shied away from making a universal claim that would obligate everyone to have a particular kind of religious experience.

Third, important as conversion could be for Francke, it did not appear as part of his reform proposals or descriptions of Halle institutions. Bill Widén has argued that one understands Francke best when one reads his pedagogical writings. Widén observes the absence of significant reference to conversion in Francke's most significant published pedagogical proposal, the *Kurtzer und Einfältiger Unterricht, Wie Die Kinder zur wahren Gottseligkeit, und Christlichen Klugheit anzuführen sind* (1702).[98] Francke here accentuates the education (*Erziehung*) of young people, not their conversion. His goal is to form them through education and Christian instruction, not to convert them.[99] Francke's major programmatic piece, the "Grosser Aufsatz" written in 1704 and revised periodically over the next twelve years, confirms Widén's argument. There, Francke wrote of pedagogy and to a lesser extent of mission, but he said almost nothing about institutionalizing practices of conversion, although he wanted a corps of converted teachers and preachers.[100] He could be critical of too much conversionist zeal with younger children.[101] And he warned his students against "inopportune obsession for conversion" of others.[102] Francke valued conversion, but he valued other things as well.

In the controversies surrounding the Halle Pietists and the orthodox Lutherans prior to the later 1720s, moreover, conversion and conversion practices never formed a major point of contention. Hans-Martin Rotermund has argued that Valentin Ernst Löscher, an opponent of Pietism during Francke's lifetime, did not see conversion as a peculiar characteristic of Pietism, nor did he oppose the supposedly Pietist ideal of the *Bußkampf*.[103] Likewise, Martin Greschat notes that while Löscher and the Pietists understood conversion and regeneration somewhat differently, Pietists hardly had a monopoly on conversion. Orthodox Lutherans who opposed Pietists had no desire to deny that conversions were possible. Greschat does point to the polemical use of "converted" and "unconverted" in the debates between Halle and its orthodox opponents, but the issue was whether Halle exercised a special agency as an instrument of divine providence. Hallensians who saw themselves in this way had no compunction about describing their detractors as "unconverted."[104] A similar dynamic is found in the Pietist-orthodox debate on the need for a converted ministry, in which the Pietists could be scathing about the perils of an unconverted ministry.[105] In practice, though, Pietist language functioned here not to set requirements for individuals but to mark collective affiliation. Candidates for the ministerial office at Halle were not required to bring forth warrants of their conversion. Indeed, Friedrich Wilhelm, an advocate of having the Halle theologians certify candidates for ministry, forbade "spiritual examinations" as part of the process.[106]

How might we reconcile Francke's talk about the need for conversion and the relative paucity of conversion narratives and practices at Halle during his lifetime? First, Francke's high expectations did not result in a broader culture of conversion. He mixed his calls for conversion with demands for serious self-examination that would distinguish true converts from hypocrites (*Heuchler*). In a sermon from 1722, for instance, Francke warned his congregation, "There are very few among you who are truly converted to Jesus Christ. I speak, indeed, the truth. The fruits are witnesses to this, that only very few properly have the spirit of Jesus, and [that others] therefore are mired in the most shameful self-deception, since they nonetheless comfort themselves in the grace of Christ."[107]

Francke went on to identify self-deception as a hindrance to repentance and conversion. Many who were convinced that they had repented could easily, like the Pharisees, deceive themselves. At points, Francke seems to undermine any self-confidence about the ability to gauge sufficient repentance, for the Christian "must not trust his own heart" but rather turn to prayer, asking that God alter his "deceiving, doubting, evil heart," thereby allowing him to recognize the seriousness of "true repentance."[108]

Such statements easily could have had the effect of undermining the certainty of one's experiences, perhaps even calling into doubt an earlier experience or a *Bußkampf*. In other sermons, Francke insistently posed the problem of self-deception. Insincere conversions, he preached in 1719, often accompany illness or bodily distress. Conversion in these cases would "often only be seeming, so that not only others but [the individual] himself would be deceived by it and form a fundamentally false opinion of the state of his soul."[109]

Francke may have distrusted the truthfulness or durability of some conversion experiences. Brückner and Fratzscher, for example, were part of Francke's circle in Erfurt who composed their narratives at roughly the same time that Francke wrote his account. There can be little doubt that he knew of their compositions, for contemporaneous copies are preserved in the archives of the *Stiftungen*. But he would also have known eventually that these two converts moved in heterodox directions that he opposed and that would have undermined the veracity of their claims. Other contemporary accounts might also have given Francke pause. In 1703, the tack maker Johann Georg Rosenbach published an account that had some features Francke might have recognized—a prolonged period of struggle during repentance, tears, falling to one's knees, and prayer.[110] But while Francke initially sympathized with

Rosenbach, he grew disenchanted with his heterodox and separatist views, especially when the convert criticized infant baptism, questioned the Lutheran doctrine of the Eucharist, and frowned on regular preaching and church services.[111] Despite a conversion experience that tracks many elements of what one usually associates with a Hallensian model, Rosenbach's conversion seemed to confirm him in his heterodox views. The heterodoxy, or even apostasy, of several "converts" might have made Francke wary of publicizing conversion experiences, implicitly recognizing what Karl Morrison has called the "radical instability of meaning" in conversion narratives.[112]

But even when Francke may have been confident of the veracity of a conversion account, he was not always anxious to publicize them. His own account is a good case in point. There is no indication that Francke ever doubted the signal character of this event; the few clues we have point to its importance for him throughout his life, whether he was talking with a pious peasant or reviewing his own biography.[113] But after a short period when Francke considered circulating his conversion narrative, he seems to have lost interest in even sharing it, much less publicizing it. The public was likely unaware of it until his death.[114] Francke might have shared Spener's cautions about the unintended consequences of too much publicity when it came to conversion.[115]

He seems to have sympathized, at least implicitly, with Spener's reservations. A lively publishing climate prevailed in Halle. Francke easily could have collected narratives that circulated informally, but he showed no interest after leaving Erfurt. He appears to have been reluctant to use specific stories to illustrate his understanding of conversion. In one rare case, he related to students the story of a noble woman in Berlin whom Schade rebuked for superficial repentance prior to her true conversion, but he followed up with the caveat that one should not draw a method of conversion from this example or seek to imitate Schade's approach.[116]

Conversion was a prominent theme at Halle, but no singular method of attaining or explaining it prevailed there during Francke's lifetime. The reluctance to publish models of conversion underscores this absence, and the mostly private accounts of which we are aware exhibit a range of patterns that *could* include a *Bußkampf*-type experience but often did not. In Halle, however, other forms of spiritual biography that later emerged would be much more widely disseminated and read.

3

CONVERSION IN LIGHT OF DEATH
Von Schönberg and Henckel's Last Hours

A different kind of narrative emerged in Halle that would become distinctive for Hallensian Pietism: the narrative of the death and dying of the pious subject in the so-called *Letzte Stunden*. These thanatographies, as they are sometimes known, had a particular bearing on the understanding of conversion.[1] Though they often included accounts of conversion, they shifted the focus away from the conversion experience itself to dying and the end of life.

A. H. Francke and Martha Margaretha von Schönberg

An early example is Francke's 1703 funeral sermon for Martha Margaretha von Schönberg.[2] Von Schönberg was the daughter of a noble family, and she became involved with the Pietist movement at the end of the 1680s. In late 1691, she heard one of Francke's sermons in the city of Halberstadt not long after he had been dismissed from his position at Erfurt. According to her own autobiographical account, his sermon and a personal conversation afterward set her on what is often seen as the classic pattern of conversion: a stirring (*Rührung*) initiated by the sermon, followed by a period of struggle and repentance, culminating several weeks later in a experience in which "God, according to his eternal love and overwhelming mercy, sealed in my heart in a powerful and uncommon manner the certainty of his dear grace and love in Christ Jesus and the forgiveness of all my sins in the week before Christmas."[3] In a number of respects, von Schönberg's account fits others from the circle around Francke in the early 1690s.

She remained tightly connected to the Pietist movement throughout much of the 1690s, becoming a close friend of Anna Magdalena von Wurm, who would later marry Francke, as well as other prominent women in the Pietist movement. In 1699, she moved to Halle and became a governess in the Gynäceum, an advanced school for girls in Halle, for four years until it was dissolved in 1703, when she then joined Francke's household.[4] Ulrike Witt points out that despite her ostensibly exemplary conversion, her letters reveal that she never reached the kind of continuing assurance or definitive *Durchbruch* she had hoped to achieve.[5] Her spiritual doubts and struggle became intense when she fell ill in 1703. Her severe *Anfechtung* became a matter of deep concern among her friends in Halle, especially for Anna Magdalena Francke. Although her piety in life had seemed exemplary, the end of her life did not appear to be that of the expected *sanften und seligen Todes,* or gentle and blessed death of one who was dying in the confidence of faith that she described earlier in her conversion narrative.[6] Only at the very end of her life did Schönberg transcend her struggles and testify movingly to the strength of her faith.[7]

Witt sees von Schönberg's lack of a definitive *Durchbruch* and spiritual distress in dying as an interpretive problem for Francke and the Hallensians. If her early conversion were true, why such doubt and uncertainty? Her experience could threaten to undermine confidence about the path to salvation at Halle.[8] Witt might possibly over-interpret the evidence when she suggests that Schönberg's struggles present a fundamental challenge to the practice of conversion in Francke's circle, but von Schönberg is instructive for understanding the public portrayal of conversion at Halle. In his funeral sermon, Francke drew on her spiritual life as an edifying example. He identified a threefold struggle of faith: the penitential or repentance struggle (*Buß-Kampf*), the daily struggle of suffering (*Leidens-Kampf*), and the final struggle of dying (*Todes-Kampf*), of which the last "is the noblest, upon which it is utterly dependent that it be fought correctly."[9] It is striking that while he discussed von Schönberg's 1691 conversion briefly,[10] Francke gave narrative focus to the sermon by describing the final spiritual struggle, the *Glaubens-Kampf* at the end of her life. Rather than seeing this as something "dangerous and evil," Francke saw in the experience of this "spiritual Israelite," as he called Schönberg, an example of "a beautiful struggle and subsequent glorious victory."[11] Of course, Francke employed her final trials to impress on his listeners the need to assess their own spiritual condition and their ability to fight in faith as she has done.[12] However, as he emphasized, the victory in which she has prevailed is the final struggle of faith.[13] No one is crowned without struggle.¹⁴ In some respects, this telling of her story relativizes the earlier conversion; her struggle and perseverance unto death become the warrants that confirm its veracity.¹⁵ In turn, Francke reinterpreted the trials and spiritual distress of von Schönberg in her final illness. In these last struggles, it is not so much resistance to the temptations of the devil or victory over the lack of faith, but rather the purification of the soul through which one is made fit for salvation. Referring to her struggles, Francke cited the passage from Isaiah 48:10: "Behold, I have refined you, but not with silver; I have chosen you in the furnace of affliction."¹⁶ These themes of "refinement" (*Läuterung*) and "furnace of affliction" (*Ofen des Elends*) would become important tropes in subsequent Halle narratives about pious Christians. They signal a shift away from the assurance granted in the conversion experience itself to the experience of dying, a change especially exemplified in Erdmann Heinrich Henckel von Donnersmarck's *Die Letzten Stunden*.

Henckel von Donnersmarck and *The Last Hours*

The most prominent collection of biographical narratives to emerge from Halle during Francke's lifetime were those published by Erdmann Heinrich Henckel von Donnersmarck under the title *The Last Hours of Some Persons Who Cherished Protestant Doctrine and Died Blessedly in the Lord in This and Recently Passed Years*. Henckel published the first volume with seventeen accounts in 1720. Two additional volumes followed quickly in 1721 and 1723, and a final volume appeared in 1733. Altogether, the four volumes comprised fifty-one biographical narratives.¹⁷ Editions were frequently reprinted, and Henckel's *Last Hours* enjoyed wide popularity as edifying texts through mid-century.¹⁸

As the title suggests, these accounts were in most cases preoccupied with the final hours of pious individuals; however, while this focus on the death and dying of the individuals in the last weeks and days is dominant, the collection is in fact broader. As the Halle theology faculty noted in the preface, "Insofar as the title is concerned, it is indeed called the 'last hours of life,' but it should not therefore be understood as though there was only the intention of narrating the very last events in the life of the individuals portrayed here. In point of fact, it is necessary as well to touch on the previous noteworthy events in a life story, because they tend to throw light on the last hours of life and one can therefore draw a more complete judgment about the entire course of the life."¹⁹ A number of the spiritual biographies, though certainly not all, contain conversion narratives. As the most extensive collection of spiritual biography published in Halle during Francke's lifetime, *The Last Hours* exemplifies the Halle Pietist approach to conversion before the elder Francke's death.

Henckel (1681–1752) belonged to a prominent line of Silesian nobles who had chosen exile in part because of their Protestant convictions.[20] In 1691, his family settled on the estate of Pölzig in Thuringia. He studied in Halle, among other universities, and became an avid Pietist as well as a frequent correspondent with August Hermann Francke. Henckel and his family retained Silesian connections and were closely involved with the Pietist revival among Protestants there. There is no record that Henckel himself had experienced a conversion.[21] The difficult death in 1717 of his young wife, Lady Louise Sophie, likely provided the impetus for Henckel's collection of spiritual biographies. The day after her death, he wrote movingly to Francke about her spiritual struggles.[22] He later expanded this, and the detailed description of her final days became one of the accounts in the collection's first volume.[23]

Despite a pious youth and God-fearing faith that carried into her married life, the countess experienced a series of spiritual struggles and deep doubts as illness overtook her following the birth of her second child. Henckel described seven bouts of spiritual anxiety as her physical condition worsened. The questions raised are similar in some respects to those of von Schönberg. How could she be reckoned among the children of God if she had such doubts and spiritual anxiety at the end of her life? Of course, one could portray this as a conversion on the brink of death, but deathbed conversions were often criticized by Pietists, not least by August Hermann Francke, for their potential insincerity and opportunism. Moreover, such an approach might seem to impugn her previous Christian character in a way that her Pietist husband and friends were unwilling to do. Rejecting these approaches, Henckel instead portrayed her final difficulties as a progressive form of purification and refinement in which his wife's struggles paralleled those of Christ and through which she was made fit for salvation with him. In the account, brief moments of encouragement alternated with severe struggles, which only deepened as the account progressed. He described one such moment as follows:

> This refreshment was, however, like the previous ones, only a preparation for a more difficult and more severe struggle: for afterward she was thrown into a very great, indeed ineffable anxiety, and as her own words expressed it, [she was] led with the Lord Christ to the Mount of Olives and made part of his sufferings to a great extent. Meanwhile, the Lord,

who according to his marvelous counsel had led her to this battleground, granted her again one strength after another, in order to prevail and to overcome, yes even to thank him so heartily that he had dignified her with such suffering out his grace, so that she may be made akin to the image of his Son.[24]

After the seventh of these spiritual trials in which her faith was again severely tested, the countess at last found sure comfort and assurance. Now she was finally convinced that she had received the "crown" from the hand of the Lord—a reference to the oft-cited 2 Timothy 2:5—signifying that she would soon see the "holy patriarchs, prophets, and apostles of the Lord, and so many chosen of God, and yes, her dear Savior Jesus Christ."[25] Her struggles over, she testified movingly to her family and friends, and as her husband reported, she took blessed leave from all struggle and the Savior "led her into unending peacefulness."[26]

Henckel stressed the salutary nature of her spiritual anxiety at the end of life not only for herself, but also as witness for her friends and family and implicitly for anyone who read this account. The framework for the account is already presented in a letter Henckel wrote Francke immediately after his wife's death, in which he mentioned the sevenfold struggle and the notion that these trials fashioned her in "the image of the Savior."[27] One model was Francke's 1703 funeral sermon for von Schönberg. Henckel adopted Francke's language of refinement and purification in the dying process, and he quoted long passages from Francke's sermon in the prologue to the narrative, though without attribution.[28]

A number of the other accounts in the *Letzte Stunden* emphasized the value of the struggle of faith or *Glaubens-Kampf* in the process of dying as well. Henckel presents the case of von Schönberg in the second installment, largely based on Francke's sermon mentioned above. But Henckel also added considerable material recounting her last days, emphasizing not only the depth of her struggles and spiritual anxieties on the eve of death, but also the heights of her triumph at the end, and he did this in far greater detail than in the original sermon.[29]

In a variety of other cases, for edifying effect, Henckel elaborated the dramatic spiritual struggles during the "last hours."[30] In some cases, these accounts portrayed not just struggles but conversions that took place on the brink of death. One, for instance, was the story of a young man who repeatedly ridiculed his pious brother's attempts to persuade him to abandon carousing and gambling and to bring him to Christ. A severe illness gave him pause to reconsider his spiritual condition. At first, he bargained that if he were restored to health, he would leave off his vices and improve his life. But his illness continued to worsen, and as Henckel described it, his increasingly dire situation drove him to express full repentance, leading to a genuine conversion before death.[31]

More common representations in Henckel of deathbed conversions were accounts in which outwardly pious individuals recognized the limits of their previous piety in sickness and death. For instance, Christine Sophie Martini (1694–1719) grew up in a Pietist milieu. Her father, Justus Töllner, was a close associate of Francke's, and she married the Pietist rector of the Glaucha school, Christian Martin Martini. In Henckel's description, she led a "Christian and praiseworthy life" and her short marriage was exemplary. As her health deteriorated after delivering a daughter, she fell into a period of deep repentance and doubt about her soul. From her sickbed, she admonished her friends and family to take heed of her example and apply themselves more zealously than she had done to the practice of Christianity.[32] As all of Henckel's subjects did, Martini successfully navigated her final spiritual struggles to a good and Christian end; however, this account and several others like it suggest that external piety earlier in life may not accurately represent one's actual spiritual condition, and that conversion may still be necessary, even in the final days before death.[33]

In still other cases, Henckel recounted the pious deaths of many individuals who experienced little struggle or only mild bouts of spiritual anxiety. For instance, he described Louise Sophie von Wurmb as a model of piety throughout her life, and aside from a moment of "deep anxiety and exhaustion" he largely depicted her death almost joyfully as a paragon of Christian faith.[34] As Henckel explained, "For although one could see that she was in the midst of dying, she never complained about the slightest pains, even at the end. Rather, she spoke movingly and calmly all the time with great joyfulness and a smile on her face. The spirit of God always placed the most beautiful thoughts in her heart and the most edifying words in her mouth."[35] Henckel gave a glowing description of the exemplary nature of Wurmb's life and death, but it and other accounts like it were significantly shorter than the stories of those whose life and death were spiritually much more fraught.[36] Henckel appeared far more interested in exploring the lives of people in spiritual turmoil than in describing lives that are placid and faithful.

In a number of accounts, Henckel presented a distinct conversion experience well before the death. Typical was an early account of Samuel Elard, a theology student living in Berlin at the time of his death in 1701. The prologue described the necessity of both a struggle both prior to and after conversion: "A twofold struggle is necessary for the human being who will be saved: the repentance struggle [*Bußkampf*] and the struggle in faith [*Glaubenskampf*]." The account presented conversion relatively briefly. Traveling to Halle with the hopes of receiving his doctorate, Elard realized the "blind and sinister" nature of his previous student life. Though he had portrayed himself "honestly and well" before the world, Henckel wrote, he had become convicted of his inner unrighteousness, "for in Christ Jesus nothing counts but a new creature and each and every one, who will become saved, must go through the narrow gate of repentance and must have Christ living in his heart through faith. As soon as he recognized this through God's grace, he made it his serious task to go out from the lavish, courtly, and easy nature of the world and in contrast to penetrate in and to God." While this in some ways reflects the typical *Bußkampf* model of conversion we associate with Halle, it was presented in this narrative as only the first "necessary" step of salvation. Elard's early conversion, though, afforded him little subsequent certainty. Severe doubts continued to plague him even as he was considered a model Christian among his friends. Henckel quoted Elard's diary, in which Elard described his doubt and fears that "all grace was denied to me" and compared himself to the five foolish virgins of Matthew 25 who were excluded from the marriage feast. Elard recovered from this and other bouts of despair, but similar alternations of despondency and hope continued to beset him up through his final illness and death. Like Francke in his funeral sermon for Schönberg, Henckel shifted here from conversion to the subsequent struggle of faith in which one is made fit for salvation. Henckel's narrative focused on this continuing *Glaubenskampf* in Elard's life, which lasted until his final days when he ultimately triumphed over doubt and Satan.[37]

Less common was the portrayal of conversion found in the narrative of Hermann Peter Berghaus, which became the definitive turning point of the account. Henckel included here Berghaus's autobiographical account, in which he described the progression and completion of his conversion in Jena. The conversion marks the fundamental turning point in Henckel's narration of Berghaus's spiritual life, and he referred to it explicitly as such in his final illness. In the narrative of his dying days there is little of the explicit struggle found in other accounts. He is depicted as welcoming his physical infirmity with joy because God allowed him to "to taste his love so emphatically" through his illness. Unlike Elard or many others in Henckel, he neared death without spiritual anxiety or struggle. He regretted only that at times his weakness prevented him from conducting his devotions.[38]

But this structure of a narrative revolving around a conversion account was highly unusual in Henckel's *Letzte Stunden*. Over half the biographical accounts featured no discussion of a conversion experience at all. It was not merely that Henckel's genre focused on death and left little room for earlier conversions. Nicholas Lange's biography had no lengthy description of his death and rambled on for two hundred pages without mentioning a formative conversion experience, though it does include brief descriptions of Lange's role in the conversions of two women.[39] Even in cases where conversions were described or alluded to, they did not usually have a dispositive function; rather, they represented a preliminary moment that set the stage for the crucial experience of dying and death. Indeed, Henckel's final narrative describes in detail the conversion of a young theology student; however, despite an experience that tracks many elements of the "typical" Halle model, including a kind of *Bußkampf* and an explicit *Durchbruch*, the young man finds no certainty and remains spiritually in turmoil until his death nine years later.[40] In one narrative, Henckel warned that converts sometimes became comfortable and over time lost their ardent desire for "the pure milk of the Gospel," therefore endangering "what they have earlier achieved," intimating the instability of conversion.[41] To be sure, Henckel repeatedly declares the importance of conversion, especially in the prologues, but his treatment of it as a definitive experience is ambivalent, especially in the biographical narratives themselves.

Henckel's *Letzte Stunden* comprised the largest collection of spiritual biographies to emerge directly from Halle. August Hermann Francke's influence is apparent in the way Henckel composed many accounts, drawing on funeral sermons and other writings.[42] In several narratives, Francke appears as an actor whose charisma and piety exercised a decisive role in the subjects' lives.[43] Witt argues that Francke had a direct hand in shaping the accounts.[44] If so, these spiritual biographies afford a close look at the presentation of conversion from a Hallensian perspective in the 1720s and early 1730s. Certainly, no rigid model of conversion emerges from these accounts. Many made no mention of conversion at all, an omission that indicates that an exemplary Christian death was fully possible without a distinct conversion experience. And when conversion accounts were recounted, the structure of the experiences were quite diverse, and only occasionally conformed to schema of *Rührung*, *Bußkampf*, and *Durchbruch* that later historians consider "typical." Many conversions occurred without any indication of a *Bußkampf* at all.[45] Furthermore, terms like *Bußkampf* were not fixed in Henckel.[46] More tellingly perhaps, conversion did not necessarily play a decisive role in these narratives. There remained an ambivalence about their durability and consequently their long-term certainty, something that could only be judged definitively from the perspective of death and dying, a moment that took on increasing prominence in these Pietist spiritual biographies. Indeed, Henckel imbued these dying moments with special spiritual significance, a feature that many later conversion accounts in Pietism would also reflect.

Other characteristics of Henckel's accounts are worth noting. Ulrike Witt has conducted a careful social analysis of Henckel's biographies, revealing some telling features. Given the high representation of women in other accounts of spiritual biography, including that of Reitz, it is perhaps not surprising that a majority of the accounts deal with women—thirty of the fifty-four individuals portrayed are girls or adult women.[47] Nevertheless, the makeup of Henckel's collection is revealing. Of the adult women, a majority came from the nobility; the rest were largely bourgeois, many of them married to clergy; there were no women from artisan or peasant classes.[48] In contrast, the men all came from the bourgeoisie; however, they did not represent a broad swath of the burgher classes but were drawn heavily from clergy and theological students, who together made up sixteen of the nineteen adult male narratives.[49] In some respects, then, female accounts represent the dominant form of lay narratives in Henckel, whereas masculine accounts are overwhelmingly represented by pastors and theology students with university education, a clerical composition that will be present in many of the later male conversion narratives as well. Witt notes that most of the women portrayed in Henckel would be associated with the contemplative Mary rather than active Martha, much less a visionary Deborah. The male narratives divide somewhat differently. She distinguishes those who militantly pursued their Pietist goals from the mostly younger theologians without institutional positions who, like many of the women in Henckel, found themselves in an ongoing state of spiritual anxiety and doubt as they pursued their salvation. It was a "divine sorrow" that was not just a "transitional step on the way to conversion" but a permanent condition.[50] Witt attributes this in part to their common lack of opportunity to engage the "world" in activity grounded and stipulated by their religious convictions.[51] This imposed social inactivity might have indeed frustrated many, but the frustration also indicates the inability of these models of conversion and religious experience to provide continuing assurance.

A further dimension of Henckel's narratives is their confessional context. Almost all the narratives derive from a Lutheran Pietist milieu. Radicals or heterodox individuals have no place in the collection. The strong presence of ordained Lutheran clergy and theology students is a further indication that the collection reflected a defined ecclesial community. In fact, one of the few narratives without a specific Pietist context reinforced the Lutheran character. It described the deathbed repentance and conversion in Paris of Count Heinrich I von Reuß, one of whose last temptations is the effort by a priest to bring him into the Catholic fold.[52] Luther is cited frequently throughout the collection, and repeated reference is made in the prologues and biographies to explicit Lutheran practices of baptism, confession, and communion.[53] Thus, while the biographies highlight individual lives and their various paths in seeking salvation, they also locate these within an ecclesial community.

Finally, dying and death provide a particular if not peculiar perspective for this collection's approach to spiritual biography. These biographies suggest that it is only from the point of view of death that a life is most profitably assessed. In some respects, this widened the understanding of an exemplary Christian death to include those whose final days were not simply those of a gentle and blessed death that had been the model of Lutheran death and dying through the seventeenth century.[54] Instead, in Henckel those whose last days were fraught with spiritual anxieties and struggles can also be seen as models of piety. Here, the struggles prior to death are not portrayed as a lack of faith but as a process that prepares one for salvation, often through purification or refinement and formation in the image of Christ. This interest in the spiritual features of the dying process gave new impetus to the deathbed conversion. As much as Pietists, including Francke and Henckel, criticized the postponing of conversion until severe illness or impending death, they nevertheless allowed the possibility of such conversions.[55] The depictions in Henckel—even with explicit caveats—may have had the unintended consequence of encouraging such patterns. Indeed, even as Christina Sophia Martini exhorted her friends and family not to postpone their repentance until the last moment as she had done, the laudatory description of her conversion may have sent quite another message for those wishing to imitate her.[56] Especially in execution narratives, the prospect of death gained even greater prominence in the narratives.

The accent on death in Henckel's work had a narrative function as well, since such accounts could only be composed by a third party. Witt points to the use of autobiographical materials throughout Henckel, and indeed he often incorporated autobiographical statements, letters, and diaries within his narratives.[57] These autobiographical elements lent veracity to the depictions and indicate a level of self-reflection on the part of Pietists, but the framework of these narratives was not, finally, a first-person account. Indeed, one of the trends of conversion narratives in the church Pietist context was away from the self-narrated conversion account toward one composed by either a Pietist layperson or a minister.

Henckel's *Letzte Stunden* became popular devotional reading among German Pietists, and the volumes were repeatedly reprinted and expanded. From letters and other documents, we know that they circulated widely in

Pietist groups, and the form of the *Letzte Stunden* became a popular genre within Pietism, taken up within the new Pietist periodicals such as the *Sammlung auserlesener Materien zum Bau des Reichs Gottes* or Johann Jacob Moser's many editions of execution narratives titled *Seelige Letzte Stunden*.[58] Some Pietists composed and circulated *Letzte Stunden* in manuscript form as well.[59] Though they contained many accounts of conversion, they were not in the narrow sense conversion narratives. Nevertheless, they frequently touched on the experience, and as the most prominent collection of spiritual biographies emanating from Halle during Francke's lifetime, Henckel's *Letzte Stunden* had an important impact on the ways church Pietists portrayed conversion.

4

THE *BUSSKAMPF* AND CONFLICTING VIEWS OF CONVERSION AFTER FRANCKE

During his lifetime, only a few insiders knew the details of A. H. Francke's conversion experience. Francke himself, according to Matthias, reportedly had a hard time in the 1720s getting his hands on a copy of his own autobiographical account. But following his death in June 1727, a series of sermons, lectures, and publications memorialized his life and included for the first time public discussion of his conversion experience. In September 1727, Francke's son, Gotthilf August, told the assembled theology students in Halle that he had just discovered a copy of Francke's autobiographical conversion account and read it aloud to them nearly word for word.[1] In a memorial sermon for his father-in-law, Johann Anastasius Freylinghausen presented a condensed version of Francke's conversion experience, in which he referred to Francke's struggles in Lüneburg as a *Bußkampf*, a term Francke's original autobiography did not employ.[2] Freylinghausen's description of the conversion was incorporated into the anonymously edited *Concise Yet Thorough Report of the Quite Noteworthy and Edifying Life of . . . August Herman Francke* (1728), which set his conversion into an even stronger rhetoric of *Bußkampf* and made Francke's conversion known to a wider public outside Halle.[3] After reading one of these accounts, probably the *Concise Report*, Lady Johanna Sophie von Schaumburg-Lippe wrote to Francke's son of the "indescribable joy" she felt in learning about Francke's struggles.[4]

The public dissemination of Francke's conversion experience coincided with a new interest in publishing conversion narratives in German Pietism, and certainly the conversion account of Germany's then most prominent Pietist would have made an impact. But the growing interest in conversion narratives and their publication also generated controversy about conversion itself, not only between Pietists and their opponents but also among Pietists. A greater rigidity with regard to conversion experiences began to emerge in some quarters, part of what Matthias describes as a process of Pietist "confessionalization."[5]

Until the late 1720s, conversion may have been most closely associated with Pietism, but it does not appear to have been highly controversial in debates between the orthodox and Pietists or among Pietists themselves.[6] August Hermann Francke's nuanced view of conversion may have allowed for a level of flexibility, even ambiguity, in its interpretation that avoided or, at least, forestalled controversy. But stricter understandings of the pattern or mode of conversion had the potential to cause disagreement. After Francke's death, a number of conflicts rose suddenly to the surface, including issues associated in one way or another with conversion.

Testimoniumstreit

One of these was the so-called *Testimoniumstreit* (testimonial conflict) that emerged in Halle and pitted Francke's son and his allies against other Halle theologians. Pietists since Spener had long been concerned with the quality of the clergy in the churches and had sought improvement in the training and approval of candidates for ministry; if there was one group for whom Francke considered conversion essential, it was those going into ministry leadership positions.[7] King Friedrich Wilhelm I of Brandenburg-Prussia shared many of the Pietists' concerns about the quality of ministry, a matter reflected in royal edicts on preparation for ministry. The Halle theology faculty first gained a role in credentialing the Magdeburg clergy in 1719; however, as Friedrich Wilhelm made clear, they were not to exclude anyone without careful consideration, and they should not conduct a "spiritual examination"—a likely reference, according to Bach, to gauging the candidate's stage of conversion.[8] In the late 1720s, Friedrich Wilhelm expanded Halle's authority first to Pomerania and then to all of Brandenburg-Prussia, with the exception of East Prussia, for which credentialing fell to the theology faculty at Königsberg.[9]

The testimonial system was controversial, not least because it required most clergy to study in Halle for some period. Even staunch Pietists outside Halle blanched at this requirement because of the burdens it imposed.[10] Within Halle, it also provoked the opposition of several Pietist theologians, including Joachim Lange, Johann Jakob Rambach, and Johann Heinrich Michaelis. Here the expectation that the candidates be able to narrate in writing "the details of their conversion," and that the faculty examine carefully their Christian nature and "their own exercises and experiences in an active Christianity," drew particular scorn from Lange and Rambach.[11] Rambach archly questioned, "Where are the students to be found, who can not only teach [dociren] their own conversion, but also have enough experience in being led inwardly by God? Indeed, God must perform a miracle and convert hundreds of students by force."[12] Breithaupt sought to minimize the spiritual scrutiny of the candidates when he responded to the criticisms, arguing that "one can attest to nothing more than their civil righteousness. It is an exaggerated, fallacious conclusion, which our colleagues suppose to be the intent of the edict. For it is not the fundamental conversion but rather the degree to which the candidates possess spiritual insight."[13] The candidate's state of conversion did not, in fact, turn out to be a central factor in the testimonial system as it evolved in the 1730s, but conflict over testimony shows how laden with conflict any proposals for greater scrutiny of conversion could become, even in Halle.[14]

Conflict over the Bußkampf

Another notable conflict erupted between Count Nicholas Ludwig von Zinzendorf and advocates of a rigid form of conversion based on the Bußkampf. A godson of Spener raised in a Pietist milieu, Zinzendorf had been sent to Francke's elite Paedagogium Regium for schooling, and in his six years there he became well acquainted with forms of piety in Halle. Influenced by religious refugees who settled on his estate in the early 1720s, Zinzendorf became the leader of a new movement that was at first closely associated with German Pietism but came to have its own distinct identity, and is today known as the Renewed Unity of the Brethren or the Moravians.[15] Zinzendorf's community at Herrnhut had undergone a powerful revival in 1727, and, according to Uttendörfer, in the wake of this momentous event, conversion experiences and divisions according to spiritual status were common.[16] Zinzendorf, who could recount several powerful experiences in his youth, had himself never experienced a "typical" conversion, at least not one that included a Bußkampf.[17] Indeed, at a pastoral conference in Sorau in 1729, a Halle-trained minister named Johannes Mischke—an exile from Silesia—challenged Zinzendorf as to whether he had even experienced a conversion.[18]

The exact character of Mischke's challenge is difficult to reconstruct since it is filtered through Moravian sources, but the charge of an insufficient conversion did seem to unsettle Zinzendorf, who struggled with his own state of conversion for some time afterward.[19] Eventually, he developed an understanding of conversion that was adamantly opposed to the *Bußkampf*, largely on the grounds that any struggle or *Kampf* had already been accomplished by the work of Christ on behalf of sinners.[20] Disagreement about the nature of conversion and especially the *Bußkampf* may have contributed to the growing split between Zinzendorf and the Hallensians in the early 1730s. Count Stolberg Wenigerode, whose court promoted one of the stricter understandings of the *Bußkampf*, subsequently questioned the depth of Zinzendorf's "awakening."[21] Not all Hallensians embraced the *Bußkampf* as essential, and Mischke's Silesian background (with its strong emphasis on revival) may have been as important as his education in Halle for his view of conversion.[22] In fact, many of the most ardent advocates of conversion in the 1730s and 1740s had Silesian backgrounds, including Johann Adam Steinmetz.[23] Furthermore, later Moravian polemics tended to portray August Herman Francke and the Hallensians as obsessed with the *Bußkampf*.[24] Indeed, the language of *Bußkampf* appeared in Moravian sources in the early 1730s with reference to the children's revivals of 1727, indicating that a clean division between Halle and Herrnhut on the *Bußkampf* may be difficult to assert for the early 1730s.[25]

Until the late 1720s, the *Bußkampf* had not been especially controversial, and its meaning was not always fixed as a precise stage in the process of conversion. In many cases where individuals invoked it prominently, it could have radical connotations.[26] But as the *Bußkampf* began to take on a specific meaning within the conversion process, it also increasingly became a point of contention. New Pietist periodicals were beginning to publish with greater frequency conversion narratives that encouraged Pietists, at least in some circles, to delineate much more clearly how they understood conversion and to justify the publication and dissemination of these narratives.

One example is Samuel Lau's 1732 pamphlet *Scriptural Answer to the Question Whether It Is Necessary to Know the Time of One's Conversion (Schriftmäßige Beantwortung der Frage: Ob es nothwendig, die Zeit seiner Bekehrung zu wissen)*.[27] The pamphlet is significant for the way it demands a datable conversion for most true Christians and presents a highly schematic view of the experience. It was not particularly sophisticated in its argumentation, but it marked the beginning of a larger literary debate on the implicit schematization of the *Bußkampf* and the necessity of being able to distinguish whether one is converted. Lau also made the case for more discussion of conversion experiences, signaling a growing public interest in conversion narratives.

True Christians, Lau argued, ought to be able to distinguish the time of their conversion with some specificity. Of course, Lau was not the first to press this point; as early as Großgebauer this had been an issue in German Protestantism, and August Hermann Francke often made the same suggestion.[28] Lau puts a sharper point on the issue, however, when he argued not only that knowledge of the time of conversion was desirable as an indication of one's converted status, but also that the inability to name the time indicated the absence of a true conversion.[29] Of course, Lau allowed for some exceptions—a few saintly souls, for instance, never fell away from their baptismal covenant and needed no additional conversion experience, and a few troubled souls enjoyed an outpouring of grace but still wrestled with their conversion.[30] Nor did he mean to require the delineation of a precise time down to the day, month, or even year. Lau allowed for some chronological flexibility, but he nonetheless expected that one be able to describe an identifiable period in which one experienced a change in heart and the conviction of being drawn to God.[31]

Of course, to know the time of conversion presupposed an ability to recognize its marks, and Lau described in some detail stages of a true conversion that corresponded to what others have described as the typical Hallensian model: a *Rührung*, followed by a *Bußkampf*, which, when successfully overcome, leads to the final *Durchbruch* or breakthrough to grace.[32] The *Bußkampf* took on signal importance here. The intent was to make conversion more certain by identifying its invariable features. Successful negotiation of a *Bußkampf* and *Durchbruch* then became a warrant for valid conversion. Of course, Lau recognized that not all experience the *Bußkampf* in the same manner. Some experienced "divine sorrow" more forcefully than do others in whom the manifestations were more mild and drawn out, but the *Bußkampf* in one form or another appears essential. A gradual conversion is possible, Lau admitted, but the temptation is to return all too easily to the "vomit of one's sins" (*Sünden-Koth*). What is impossible, he argued, is that such a gradual conversion would pass without making a deep impression on the convert: "Unnoticed and without sensing anything at all, it is thus certainly impossible to be converted." Being able to identify the *Bußkampf* and other steps became a bulwark against self-deception, in which one naturally inclines toward a dangerous optimism and complacency. The *Bußkampf* and *Durchbruch* do not terminate spiritual progress. Lau allowed for advance in faith after conversion; he described the spiritual state of the converted as a series of stages in which the faithful are "children," "youth," or "fathers," but at each stage one can, because of conversion, consider oneself truly faithful and certain of the effects of the Holy Spirit.[33]

Lau insisted that clergy in their sermons and pastoral writings press for precisely this form of conversion. Francke frequently discussed the need for the clergy to help their parishioners distinguish true from false conversion, but Lau went further: the clergy should not only speak about this in general terms but should demand identifiable experiences of conversion of every Christian. These need not be uniform. Not everyone must experience the same intensity in the *Bußkampf*, but "I can insist with very good reason [that one identify] the time when these souls sensed their wretchedness, developed a desire for Christ, and were reborn in Him as a new creature, since no one is ever converted unless he has truly experienced this in himself."[34] The duty of ministers is to demand of their parishioners an accounting of their experience; they must be able to put the experience into words.

It would be obtuse to argue that Lau was not shaped by August Hermann Francke's understanding of conversion and the *Bußkampf*. Lau had spent several years at Halle; however, as important as this Hallensian background may have been, Lau did not cite Francke in his pamphlet.[35] The emphasis on the *Bußkampf* and schematic understanding of conversion in Wernigerode had a more distinctive and rigid character. Rather than coming directly from Francke, Lau's view may have derived from Lau's colleague in Wernigerode, Johann Liborius Zimmermann, who was a close friend of Lau's during their student days in Jena. Zimmermann described his own conversion as a student by claiming to have undergone both a *Bußkampf* and a *Durchbruch*. Later as court preacher in Wernigerode, Zimmermann became a strong exponent of a conversion with the *Bußkampf* at its center.[36] Zimmermann's conversion did not occur under direct Hallensian auspices; only afterward did he study briefly in Halle before becoming a court preacher at Wernigerode. There he developed a close relationship with Count Christian Ernst and Lady Sophie Charlotte. Zimmermann drew on his own experience in order to nurture the conversion of the countess, and he had a strong impact on the revival in Wernigerode.[37] In fact, Zimmermann, who was called to a chair in theology at Halle in 1731, may have brought a more revivalist understanding of conversion with him to Halle.[38] His death just a few years later limited his influence in Halle, and his replacement by Siegmund Jacob Baumgarten would certainly have represented a less ardent position on conversion.[39]

Lau's tract is significant because it elicited the first substantive public debate around the *Bußkampf* and the idea of a datable conversion. In 1732, an anonymous tract appeared in response to Lau, titled *Theological Answer to Two Questions*.[40] It did not directly refer to Lau, but its contents and comments by others nonetheless indicate that it was a response to Lau's original tract.[41] The author of the text is unknown, but it likely originated from someone close to Christian Friedrich Bauer, pastor in Friesdorf and later professor of theology in Wittenberg.⁴² This text was not especially polemic in tone, but it reveals the differences between the moderate orthodox position and the more aggressive conversionist ideas pursued by Lau and some other Pietists in the early 1730s. The tract took aim at two key elements of the view of conversion advocated by Lau: the *Bußkampf* and the ability to fix temporally the moment of conversion. The first part of the pamphlet criticized the absence of a warrant in either scriptures or the confessional documents for the notion of the *Bußkampf* as part of a fixed schema of conversion. At stake was not *Buße* or repentance but rather whether true repentance can occur without grace and faith and therefore function as a precondition for conversion. Accusing the conversionists of veering perilously close to works righteousness with their demand for struggle in repentance, the author charged that their views were more Roman Catholic than evangelical Lutheran, and perhaps even worse than Catholic.⁴³ Furthermore, the author denied that conversion invariably required a degree of regret and sorrow in one's repentance. Drawing on 2 Corinthians 7, especially verse 9, Pietists had long argued that a "godly grief produces a repentance that leads to salvation," thereby emphasizing the profound sense of repentance necessary in the Christian life.⁴⁴ By explicitly connecting repentance here to the *Bußkampf* as Lau did, a measure of "godly grief" seemed to be a necessary element of the *Bußkampf* and therefore of true conversion.⁴⁵ This demand for the "highest degree of sorrow" in the *Bußkampf* could lead an individual, on the one hand, to "to seek in his repentance extraordinary paths and violent movements in repentance in an enthusiastic manner." The case of the radical Pietist Johann Georg Rosenbach became paradigmatic of this "enthusiastic" outcome. Furthermore, such a demand could lead "to the most dangerous doubt of the truthfulness of one's repentance" in gauging whether "one has reached the proper degree of sorrow or not."⁴⁶

The bulk of the tract was given over to criticism of Lau's contention that it was possible and even in most cases necessary to identify the time of one's conversion. The author again criticized the biblical and confessional foundations of Lau's understanding of a datable conversion experience. What emerged was a different understanding of conversion and its experiential component. To be sure, the author affirmed that it was possible to have a powerful conversion experience that one would mark and remember. St. Paul illustrated such an extraordinary case.⁴⁷ But should Paul's example be the norm for most Christians?

In contrast to the model of sudden and dramatic conversion, such as Paul's, the author described conversion as a long process often without dramatic turning points—a process whose beginning one may often not recall. Instead of insisting on an appropriate level of struggle in repentance and an ability by the convert to identify conversion as marks of a truly heart-changing experience, the author stressed the results and fruits of conversion:

> He, who is then convinced in his conscience, that he not only regrets heartily all his sins as often as he recalls them, but also now views them with remorse and hatred, may not doubt in the least his conversion. One who is truly converted will and must necessarily sense a change between his present and former condition when he compares them. Yet as this change is thus not sudden and does not happen all at once, therefore one can be certain of the same [i.e., conversion] regardless of whether he can determine the actual time that it began.[48]

Experiences of God are diverse, and they cannot be reduced to such marks as degrees of repentance—a *Bußkampf*—or memorable moments of "the joyfulness of faith." The desire for such experiences can lead to "fanatical" exercises of repentance or induce a misleading security that would obviate the need for real conversion. This leads to a dangerous hypocrisy: "I am fully convinced that through this unfortunate proof many deceive themselves in a highly dangerous manner, and through their lies and deceptions, spiritual pride, falsity, envy, enmity, unrighteousness, defamation, vices, and various types of ruling devilry, nevertheless hold themselves above others as the dearest children of God. However, more careful examination of the current signs and fruits, either of belief or unbelief [of these individuals], would easily convince one how far removed they are from that." Consequently, the author urged that this view of conversion not become a topic for public discussion, especially in sermons, and he argued against making conversion experiences normative for a congregation. This would increase the uncertainty surrounding conversion by encouraging self-deception and engendering enthusiasm.[49]

The tone of the pamphlet was not especially polemical, though it revealed sharp disagreements. Its anonymity may have been an attempt to avoid *ad hominem* polemics that personalized the issues or identified them with a particular party. The author did not mention Lau by name, nor did he engage in broad attacks on church Pietists as did some other respondents to Lau.[50] Notably, neither tract mentioned August Hermann Francke. The *Theological Answer to Two Questions*, however, did draw on two moderate Pietists to bolster its position against Lau—Philipp Jakob Spener and Johann Franz

Buddeus (1667–1729). Spener's critical comments from 1690 on the identification of a moment of conversion in English accounts were particularly useful in countering Lau, and the author quoted Spener with delight.[51] Likewise, the author drew on Buddeus's comments on the variety of God's ways in effecting conversion—a contrast to the schematic path proposed by Lau—and emphasized repeated self-examinations and recognition of the fruits of faith as the surest ways to avoid self-deception, thus deemphasizing the need to identify a moment of conversion in the past.[52] Buddeus, who taught at Jena after leaving Halle in 1705, is sometimes seen as a mediating figure between Pietism, Lutheran orthodoxy, and Enlightenment. But he remained personally close to many Pietists; furthermore, Lau's friend and colleague in Wernigerode, Johann Liborius Zimmermann, cited Buddeus as a central figure in his own conversion at Jena in the mid-1720s.[53] The use of Pietist authorities to argue against Lau may have been a strategic ploy to discredit the Pietists by exposing their disagreements. Certainly, most other authorities cited were undisputed representatives of the Lutheran orthodox tradition.[54] But the inclusion of these two figures may also signal a willingness not to reduce the issues surrounding conversion to a simple opposition of Pietists against the orthodox.

Both show a concern for achieving certainty about conversion, but their conclusions run in diametrically opposed directions. Lau argued that by identifying a clear schematic and especially by being able to identify a period of conversion, Christians would gain greater certainty of their salvation. Though he recognizes the possibility of gradual conversion, he suggests indirectly that a powerful conversion experience with a dramatic *Bußkampf* and *Durchbruch* would give greater assurance. By emphasizing that one be able to describe the "period" of one's conversion and that this requirement be publicly discussed, even in the pulpit, Lau encourages the framing of the conversion experience in narratives.

The anonymous response finds greater certainty of conversion through the ongoing fruits of faith. Both Lau and the anonymous author affirm the need for conversion, and it would be a profound misreading to claim that authors who opposed the need for a strict *Bußkampf* model had no interest in conversion. Rather, the two groups advanced understandings of conversion that led in different directions. Lau's emphasis on experience and the ability to describe one's conversion reflected a culture in German Pietism that would be increasingly open to the circulation and publication of conversion narratives, and in some cases led to extreme emphases on the *Bußkampf*. His opponents would see the misplaced preoccupation with specific experiences of conversion as an occasion for hypocrisy and self-deception and an inducement to enthusiasm.

The following two chapters examine two consequences of Lau's position: first, the diffusion of the published narrative, in which conversion experiences found verbal expression within church Pietism; and, second, the controversial case of Dargun, in which Pietists sought to apply the *Bußkampf* consistently.

5

PIETIST PERIODICALS AND THE
CONVERSION NARRATIVE

Whereas August Hermann Francke remained reticent when it came to the publication of conversion narratives, particularly his own, the new Pietist periodicals of the early 1730s avidly published stories of conversions in letters, reports, and other devotional vehicles. The circulation of such accounts among a wider audience marked an important step in the public discussion of conversion in German Pietism. The most prominent of the new periodicals was the *Sammlung auserlesener Materien zum Bau des Reichs Gottes*, founded by Immanuel Traugott Jerichovius in 1731 and continued under various titles by Johann Adam Steinmetz from 1735 until 1761. The magazine included numerous conversion narratives in each issue.[1] A second, similar periodical also aimed at a church Pietist audience was *Altes und Neues aus dem Reich Gottes und der übrigen guten und bösen Geister* (1733–39), initiated by the prolific and peripatetic Pietist from Württemberg, Johann Jacob Moser.[2] Moser printed the first edition of A. H. Francke's autobiography, and he had a keen interest in describing the "work of conversion." His introduction to the first number of the periodical identified this "work" as a main goal of the publication.[3] Radical Pietists also published the *Geistliche Fama* (1730–44), which included some conversion narratives, though they were fewer in number and represented a much wider confessional context.[4] The *Sammlung auserlesener Materien* and its successor publications, along with Moser's *Altes und Neues*, call for special attention because they constituted the most important periodicals of church Pietism. They introduced an approach to the public portrayal of conversion that fit neatly with Lau's call for converts able to describe the moment of their rebirth. No single form of conversion prevailed in these descriptions, but these two periodicals especially reveal distinctive elements of conversion narratives as they gained wider currency within German Pietism.

The preoccupation with conversion appeared in the early numbers of the *Sammlung*. In the second issue, for instance, Jerichovius included an account of Philipp Jacob Spener's supposed conversion. His choice of Spener was surprising, given that Spener had never identified a moment of conversion in his own *Lebenslauf* and had questioned whether Christians could always recognize the "moment" and whether preachers could—or should—make evangelistic use of conversion narratives. In a relatively brief account, Jerichovius claimed that Spener underwent an identifiable conversion experience. According to a report from "the former amanuensis of the late man," the death of Spener's patroness in his youth shook him and became the "occasion for his conversion," after which he no longer allowed himself to be led astray and remained "true to God."[5] As far as conversion narratives go, it was tame, portraying nothing like a "typical" Hallensian conversion with a *Bußkampf* or *Durchbruch*. As later accounts in the *Sammlung* would indicate, Jerichovius was open to a variety of forms of conversion, but it was important to him to be able to say that Spener experienced a conversion of some kind. Jerichovius's report drew objections, and in a subsequent reprinting of the early numbers he removed the language of conversion from his description of Spener's youth.[6] Nonetheless, the incident signaled his desire to publicize conversion as a typical Christian experience.

Many of the narratives published in the early issues of *Sammlung* had been composed earlier and were only now being circulated. The majority of these early accounts were in the first person, though later they increasingly became third-person accounts. Almost all were printed after the death of the convert. Some were quite short, comprising only a few pages. For example, in an early issue, Jerichovius published the brief and undramatic autobiography of Gottlieb Joachim Krimmer, who described a pious childhood and youth but whose good inclinations could not resist the "lusts of youth." His "actual conversion," as he described it, occurred through an encounter with Professor Buddeus at the University of Jena, as well as through the sermons of a pious preacher in the city. This awakening, described without any suggestions of turmoil, much less of a *Bußkampf*, formed the center of interest in the narrative and became in Krimmer's account the basis for his later successful pastoral work in Uhlstedt and Strassfurt.[7]

Paired with Krimmer was a short account by an anonymous nobleman drawn to Berlin during the height of Johann Caspar Schade's influence in the 1690s but unable to meet Schade's expectations. For the following seven years, he struggled. The world considered him an honest and pious man, but his heart was not righteous before God; he had, as he put it, only "a half of Christianity": "Thus I often was led into a lamentable state, until finally my sweetest Savior, through his Spirit as well as through the reading of the works of the blessed Professor Francke, the letters of other children of God, and through the powerful words of comfort of Mr. Bäumler, allowed me to experience the power of the Gospel, which Moses and all the moralists could not provide."[8] From the perspective of more than twenty-five years later, he identified this period as the crux of his spiritual life. Pietist literature, letters from pious friends, and the influence of a minister all played a part in his conversion.

Johann Porst

Some of these autobiographical accounts, such as Johann Porst's narrative that appeared in the *Sammlung* in 1733, were more detailed. In the mid-1690s, Porst moved to Berlin to join the Pietist movement and went on to become one of the most prominent Pietists in the city.[9] He was confessor to the queen of Brandenburg-Prussia and was eventually appointed dean of the Nikolaikirche, a post Spener had held. Porst died in 1728 as one of the leading churchmen in Brandenburg-Prussia. Though rich in biographical detail, his printed funeral sermon included no mention of his long conversion, and subsequent biographical accounts of Porst made little reference to it.[10]

His conversion narrative published in the *Sammlung* was written in the first person, and internal evidence suggests that he composed it soon after his conversion in July 1698. Framed as a testimony to God's providential guidance toward a certain conversion, Porst's narrative emphasizes his close childhood connection to the Lutheran Church and its sacraments.

He described his first communion at thirteen as a signal event, and by his own account he was zealously pious as a child, always taking his Psalter or other books with him as he herded animals and even acting as a kind of lay preacher: "When I came among the other herders, I preached to them, fell with them on my knees and conducted prayer sessions with them." The local parish pastor recognized his intellectual gifts and furthered his education. He secured for him the opportunity to advance his studies at the *Gymnasium* in Hof. Here, however, Porst describes falling away from his youthful piety and "simplicity" into the ways of the world as his learnedness increases. In his godlessness he no longer thought about prayer, and God's Word became an "annoyance." His return to true faith in God occurred fitfully over the next ten years. Leaving Hof for the University of Leipzig, he asked God for forgiveness, but he lacked assurance: "I knew nothing of God and his community of grace, but rather remained in my sins, dead and deep in the darkness." In retrospect, Prost was able to recognize providential moments when, for instance, he found a position as tutor in the household of a family in Leipzig or later became a tutor and ministerial candidate in Neustadt an der Aisch. But even as he took on preaching duties, he concluded, "Indeed, I preached quite often, in the city as well as the countryside. Yet that which I preached, I myself did not do."[11]

He continued to experience "stirrings to repentance" periodically, but a turning point did not come until 1695 when he was moved deeply while reading one of Spener's sermons on Revelation 2:9, which he encountered when preparing for his own preaching:[12]

> Before, in, during, and after this contemplation I was stirred by God in such a manner, that I made the firm resolution to change my life and to say good night to all love of the world. Yet I lacked examples not only of those who carry themselves as true Christians but also of a faithful and experienced guide. Because I had been deeply moved by Dr. Spener's sermons of repentance, a desire developed in me so that I wished for nothing else than to see and hear this man, to ascertain whether in fact he himself lived in such a way as he taught from God's Word.[13]

A feature of this and many other subsequent accounts is the reading of Pietist literature as an impetus toward conversion. Porst was so taken with Spener's works that he longed to meet him in person. In another providential event, an acquaintance from a nearby city was called to a ministerial position in Berlin and agreed to take Porst with him in hopes that he might secure a position tutoring there. In Berlin, Porst associated himself with the Pietist movement around Spener and Spener's younger colleague Johann Caspar Schade.[14] Yet even there, though outwardly pious, Porst considered himself a hypocrite and remained, as he put it, "mired in his hidden sins." He entered into a period of struggle in which he came to despair of "God, heaven, hell, the devil, resurrection, and all other articles of faith," but through the guidance of the Holy Spirit his struggle ushered in a new awareness of his sinfulness that led to a radical conversion and disillusionment with the established church:

> And because God truly revealed to me my wretchedness and the corruption of the entire mass of Christians, a great hatred grew in me, especially against all godless and unconverted preachers, that these did

not sufficiently put before the people their abomination but rather through their absolution sealed their sins. At that point I fell far to the other side in that I completely rejected preaching, studying, and all such tasks, and I determined often that I would like to become a peasant, and learn to plow and to chop wood. And because I was of a fiery constitution, I fell into a severe obsession for conversion, wanting to punish and reform everything. And if God had not held his hand above me, I would have easily fallen into all manner of disorder.[15]

This stage in Porst's conversion—in which he goes too far in a radical direction—is unusual in such accounts. He is overzealous and appears to reject many of the practices and institutions of the established church—preaching, confession (and implicitly communion), and the ordained ministry. Particularly intriguing is his indictment of "falling into a severe obsession for conversion [*Bekehrsucht*]" in which he ardently wanted to convert others, punish everyone, and reform everything. Only providentially through God's hand, he noted, was he prevented from falling into "all manner of disorder," presumably more radical streams of separatist Pietism, suggesting now that true conversion required a wise moderation.

For a full three years Porst wrestled with his status before God, asking whether he "was a child of God or a child of the devil." One sign of his hardened heart, he averred, was the lack of tears. Despite continuing anxiety about his soul, he never "shed even one single tear for his sins." Between 1695 and 1698 he was close to the dynamic, young, controversial Pietist in Berlin, Johann Caspar Schade, whose criticism of lax practices in the confessional upset quite a few Christians in the city.[16] But none of these events enters his narrative, only general remarks about his false starts and God's patience with him.

The final portion of his conversion begins with his preparation for Easter in 1698. He was deeply moved by a Good Friday sermon in which Schade called for repentance. Porst wrote that when he returned home from church, "I fell on my knees and beseeched God, that I might be made certain of the forgiveness of my sins and of the reconciliation with him." Thrown into turmoil, Porst feared he remained spiritually dead. He attended another devotion with Schade on Saturday afternoon in preparation for communion on Easter; following Schade's discussion of the passion in light of the story of Joseph and his brothers (Genesis 45), Porst had a powerful experience: "There my brother Jesus introduced himself to me. Oh, where should I begin to tell what transpired in me! Jesus Christ revealed himself to my soul." At this moment, Jesus spoke directly to Porst. Now at last the tears overflowed, though he tried to hide them from his neighbors in church: "I wrapped myself in my cloak; then the tears flowed in streams and streams. The more Jesus revealed himself to me, the more my heart melted away." Moments of powerful spiritual illumination continued until the next morning, when Porst took communion at the early Easter service; although by then the intensity of the experience had begun to abate, Porst was still overjoyed. He praised Jesus: "Oh, how you sweeten all sorrow, how you crown all struggles in repentance with magnificent victory; how you so effortlessly pour out on my soul effusive comfort, peace, and joy."[17]

Nevertheless, even after this powerful Holy Week experience, he was not yet fully assured of salvation. Finally, in July 1698, he resolved to discover "his election and entry into the book of life." He read the article on *Gnadenwahl* but found little certainty there.[18] Then he picked up a songbook and began to sing one of Spener's hymns.[19] As he came to the verse "Then guide my spirit to that place in order that I may read that my name is inscribed there," he recorded the conclusion of his long-awaited conversion: "Then was my spirit lifted into eternity because I truly saw my name inscribed in the book of life, and I received assurance that for eternity it should never be blotted out. Then my soul once again was flooded with a rush of tears, and I was assured in divine fashion of my salvation."[20] This attainment of certainty marks the conclusion of the narrative and underscores the importance of assurance in his spiritual search. There are other striking features: his tears, for example, illustrate the somatic dimension of his experience and indicate to him the earnestness of his thorough repentance. His use of ecclesial rites and devotions to frame the beginning and ending of his narrative accents the importance of the church. Confession, communion, organized worship, and the proclamation of the Word of God deeply informed both his pious childhood and his final conversion. The depiction of his overzealousness in the middle of the account—during which he rejected all ecclesial practices—highlights the significance of the church at the end. It was a public sermon that set him on the path to the final conversion, and it was in the church sanctuary—a point Porst emphasized—while preparing for Holy Communion, that he received his revelation from Christ. Alongside these ecclesial features were distinctive Pietist elements. Having a Pietist minister was indispensable. Schade was one of the most ardent Pietists in Berlin, and Porst highlighted his influence. Likewise, it was not just any hymn that finally brought him certainty but one composed by Spener. Throughout, Porst's narrative emphasized the clergy, who influenced him through devotional books, songs, and public preaching. Porst also believed, of course, that he must be personally assured of his salvation. Church services, communion, and other practices—

even those conducted by good Pietists—were not sufficient; individual experience and conviction mark the true Christian. But the church and ordained clergy loom always over the narrative.

Porst's account does not fit easily into a simple schema of conversion. Features of the Hallensian model show up—Porst discussed *Rührungen* and described *Kämpfe in der Buße*, which sound almost like a *Bußkampf*—but this experience required an extraordinary length of time and his quest took unusual twists and turns. Moreover, Porst cautioned against false conversion. From his later vantage point, he could identify spiritual deficiencies in his middle period—the lack of tears, for instance—but he also criticized his fall into *Bekehrsucht*, when he, too, avidly sought to convert others, an indication that he wrongly considered himself converted at that point. Pietists and non-Pietists alike criticized *Bekehrsucht* in conversion practices; Porst discussed the topic at greater length elsewhere.[21]

Johanna Sophia von Dennstädt

A different first-person account published in the *Sammlung* was that of Johanna Sophia von Dennstädt (ca. 1703–1729). Daughter of a family from the lower nobility with strong ties to Pietism, Dennstädt describes a pious childhood, including visions in which Christ spoke to her. She squandered these godly beginnings in part, she complains, because her tutor praised her so much that "there arose in me a high self-regard." Even her own near-fatal sickness and the later death of her father, she writes, were not able to bring her to a "true conversion." For several years, she remained in this state. At times she felt as if she were being prodded in the right direction, and she felt a deep desire for the Eucharist. Yet she failed to receive the kind of spiritual direction that would lead toward true conversion, so she turned away from scripture to the vanities of the world.[22]

When she was fifteen, a "righteous" preacher came to her town; after hearing his sermon, her sister repeated it to Johanna Sophia, an act that "blessed me with God's prevenient Grace."[23] This drove her to prayer, but again she lacked spiritual guidance, had no knowledge of regeneration, and remained in turmoil. Once again through her sister she received one of Francke's printed sermons, *Der Unterschied der Selbstrechtfertigung und der wahren Rechtfertigung* (The Distinction Between Self-Justification and True Justification), on the parable of the Pharisee and the tax collector. This sermon "penetrated into my marrow and bones." She added a telling commentary: "All these phrases were nothing other than thunderclaps in my heart, even spears and nails. I read these amid countless tears and found instruction on how I should properly attack it. Then my inner distress was revealed to me by God, which caused much anxiety and sadness."[24] Though her narrative presents this experience as progress, her distress did not end. At times, she had atheistic doubts; at other times, she entertained blasphemous thoughts. Nevertheless, she noted that "the mercy of God did not allow me to sink too far. From time to time the true savior quickened my heart with a sweet vision of grace." The struggles continued. At one point she was drawn to the radical followers of Gichtel, but their view of scripture repelled her. Again through her sister she received a tract by Francke that moved her heart; but not until she visited Halle in 1720 and encountered Francke, his wife, and his colleagues in person did she record real spiritual progress. After spending half a year in Halle, she wrote, "The evangelical Spirit began to gain ground in my soul, although indeed quite a few spiritual struggles [*Anfechtungen*] were not lacking." Two years later, in 1723, Dennstädt moved with her mother to Halle, where, she wrote, "I reveled with great joy in my heart in hearing the Word of God and especially the paternal exhortations of the dear Professor Francke, who now rests in God."[25]

Her story reveals ongoing struggles but no definitive turning point. She connected the secondhand sermon of the visiting preacher with God's prevenient grace and Francke's writings with right instruction. She referred often to her lack of conversion and omits mention of any *Durchbruch*. Only after being in Halle in person did she seem to undergo a decisive change, but she described this rather vaguely as "the Evangelical spirit gaining more and more space in my soul"—a state that, she allowed, continued to be subject to continuing spiritual struggles or *Anfechtungen*. Her vagueness about her implied conversion stands in contrast to her vivid descriptions of her earlier struggles. From her letters to Francke in the 1720s it appears that Dennstädt remained a spiritual seeker, but they also make clear that it was less conversion that she sought after reaching Halle than a fuller mystical experience with Christ. Her letters to Francke in the 1720s are effusive, even florid, when they depict her desire for closeness to Christ.[26]

Again, it was communal participation—nurture by a "righteous" clergy and the reading of Pietist literature—that moved her forward. The emphasis on the sacraments, which is pronounced in Porst and some other accounts, is absent from her narrative, but her rescue from the followers of Gichtel, the inspiration of church sermons, and "the evangelical spirit"—a theme implying confessional adherence to the Lutheran Church—signal that her gradual conversion took place within a churchly Pietism. She valued Halle as a place with a community of true believers, almost as a place of pilgrimage, much as Porst valued Berlin.

Characteristics of Periodical Conversion Narratives

Among the other first-person autobiographical accounts in the *Sammlung* was one by Johann Hieronymus Wiegleb, who recounts his 1691 conversion in Erfurt under the influence of Francke, the "blessed instrument" in God's work with his soul. His conversion forms the highpoint; the following thirty-nine years as schoolteacher and clergyman in Gotha and Halle fill only a scant few pages.[27] In later issues, first-person accounts become increasingly rare, and the ones that appear nearly always come from men with formal theological training. According to the issues of the *Sammlung* from 1731 through 1734 and its immediate successor, *Fortgesetzte Sammlung auserlesener Materien zum Bau des Reichs Gottes* (1735–37), seven out of the ten first-person conversion accounts were of clergy, teachers with theological training, or theology students. Of the remaining three, a woman, Johanna Sophia von Dennstädt, wrote only one. Twenty-nine other accounts were third-person narratives.[28] In the successor publications *Verbesserte Sammlung auserlesener Materien zum Bau des Reichs Gottes* (1737–43) and *Closter-Bergische Sammlung nützlicher Materien zur Erbauung im wahren Christenthume* (1745–61), first-person accounts gradually faded from view. In the *Verbesserte Sammlung*, only four accounts were first person while twenty were in the third person. In the *Closter-Bergische Sammlung*, five out of the seventeen accounts were in the first person, and only two of these were originally German; the others came from translations of previously published English accounts, in which first-person accounts were much more often the rule.

Johann Jakob Moser also published numerous "accounts of God's conduct in the work of conversion" in his competing periodical, *Altes und Neues aus dem Reich Gottes und der übrigen guten und bösen Geister* (1733–39).[29] Here the familiar features emerge, though less strongly than in the *Sammlung* and its successors. Of the twenty-five conversion narratives that Moser published, eleven were in the first person and fourteen in the third person. Over the seven years of its publication, the proportion did not shift. As in other periodicals, male first-person narratives outnumber female first-person accounts—there are only two by women—but unlike the case in the other periodicals, the theologically trained constitute four of the nine men's accounts, a significant but still less dominant proportion.[30] In addition to being the first to publish in 1733 Francke's autobiographical conversion narrative,[31] Moser also published the self-description of Heinrich Schubert, a Hallensian Pietist celebrity among the faithful in Potsdam, though his account appeared anonymously.[32] Moser published narratives from people of more socially diverse backgrounds, including, for instance, uneducated laymen, who make only rare appearances in Jerichovius's and Steinmetz's publications.[33]

Third-person narratives are a hallmark of conversion accounts in these periodicals, and the form alters the depiction. Rather than presenting self-reflection, the third-person narration ostensibly allows another to comment. The first-person account is more immediate, featuring the voice of the convert, whereas third-person accounts distance reader and convert. Both kinds of narratives can be edited, revised, reshaped, or even fictionalized to evoke a tone, emphasize a value, or reinforce a range of views, and in any verbal account we should not collapse the distance between an event and its narration.[34] The voice of the narration, moreover, does not establish a fixed autobiographical character; some writers presented their own conversion in the third person, as perhaps Johann Caspar Schade did.[35] In other cases, editors changed the grammatical voice from first to third person but largely followed the diction of the original account.[36] In still other instances, the author may include substantial autobiographical excerpts in a third-person account. Nevertheless, the choice of narrative voice represents an evaluative judgment. Particularly in German Pietist narratives, which often stress authority figures—usually Pietist clergy—the emphasis on third-person narration has significance.

Some third-person accounts simply continue the tradition of the *Letzte Stunden* popularized by Henckel, in which conversion comes to fruition in the moment before death. For instance, in the *Sammlung* a clergyman subtly implied conversion in the story of a countess who overcame doubts and unbelief in her final sickness.[37] In another more obvious deathbed conversion, the *Sammlung* in 1734 described a milkmaid who avoided the daily prayer sessions organized by her mistress and slept through church services. Though diligent in her duties, she had displayed a quick temper. She promised many times to change, but not until her final illness did she undergo conversion: "For in the last night before her passing, this maid fell into an internal struggle, so much so that externally she flailed about with her hands to ward off her enemies. Shortly thereafter, she achieved victory and cried out with these words: God has strengthened me so that thus all three times I have overcome [my struggles]."[38] The narrator recorded the milkmaid speaking in Low German, the dialect of northern Germany, as on her last day she expressed her faith to the minister and others around her. The change to dialect reinforced the authenticity of her recorded words.

Accounts of conversion overflowed with instances of final illness and death. The dramatic circumstances lent these accounts poignancy and power, as they related the turn to faith and the hours before death. Yet their narrative power might also induce readers to postpone their own conversions until the end of their lives and, as several Pietists worried, to ignore doing anything about their spiritual state until then. To counter such possibilities, the editors included stories of ambiguous or failed conversion attempts—one powerful counselor at court lived an honest and irreproachable life, but when he became ill he fell into a crisis about salvation, called a minister, and bewailed his unconverted state:

> Oh, God have mercy on me, an abominable sinner, and let me experience mercifulness for Christ's sake! A year ago, as I was sick, you heard my prayer when I told you that, from the bottom of my heart, I wanted to convert. Oh, how have I deceived my soul! You have often stirred and convinced me with your Word during sermons, but I never had the strength to reach a real breakthrough [*Durchbruch*]; it always remained merely a good intention. Oh, God, how have I deceived my soul![39]

The minister consoled him with words of Christ's mercy, but the court counselor felt no comfort: "Oh, let no one save his repentance until his deathbed! For it is difficult then. I want to forewarn everyone with this." The clergyman prayed with him but his turmoil continued, and even though he thanked God for the opportunity to confess his sins even at this late moment he remained doubtful. No joy or certainty surfaced, as they had in other accounts. Rather, the testimony of the dying man became an admonition to others. Citing his final words as the threefold repetition of *Herrlichkeit*, a reference to the last petition of the Lord's Prayer, the account holds open the possibility of conversion for unconverted readers; however, the tone remains ambivalent.[40]

Unsure or failed conversions made frequent appearances. In *Altes und Neues*, a village pastor appeared to recognize that he was dying yet did not take his conversion seriously as he put his affairs in order. In his sermon for Busstag (Day of Repentance), he expressed deep regret for his sinfulness, but before he could finish he collapsed in the pulpit and died. His truncated repentance in his final moments could have allowed for a glimmer of optimism about his fate, but the title of the selection seemed to imply a pessimistic conclusion:

"The Curious End of a Preacher Who Had Been Wanton in His Conversion and Died."[41]

The *Fortgesetzte Sammlung* reported a failure that was not merely "curious" but rather "ill-fated." The parish pastor described a schoolteacher who was diligent in his profession and not subject to such vices as drinking or gambling but nonetheless was avaricious and all too easily "allowed himself to be drawn into strife and discord." His contentious behavior forced a transfer to a new position, but he resisted a change of heart, according to the pastor, and rebuffed attempts to convert him. When he fell gravely ill, he began to worry about the status of his soul: "He had read in a book about a conversation between Christ and a faithful soul, and he found that what was described there did not correspond to his own soul, for he had not yet experienced any of the blessedness which believers in Christ Jesus possess and which he had often heard about in my sermons." Over the next days, the pastor (and narrator of the account) sought to prod him toward conversion, and while he appeared to make some progress—at one point he reported a vision of Christ—he remained distrustful of the minister, sometimes even lashing out. A few days before his death, the pastor found him in complete desperation and turmoil. He assured him of the divine offer of grace, but to no avail. As if to signify the futility, the narrative reported that he turned his back on the preacher and, in bed, began to flail at the wall with his arms without saying another word. He remained silent for two days. His final words, according to the narrator, were "For me it is too late." The pastor allowed that in his silence his heart could have been changed, but he expressed no certainty of this. As the title suggested, the narrative reinforced not the promise of divine mercy but the peril of postponing conversion, a point reinforced by the schoolteacher's turning his back on the Pietist preacher.[42] To underscore this, other narratives celebrated the advantages of an early conversion before one had to confront the possibility of death in severe illness.[43]

Third-person accounts presented a number of voices. In an early number of the *Sammlung*, the editor told of receiving an account from a widow, who in her own words described the remarkable conversion of her servant. The narrative did not follow a typical pattern. As the widow recounted the case, the young woman fell into a crisis about her failure to believe the truth of Lutheran teaching on the real presence in the Eucharist. Convinced of her unbelief, the maid spent five weeks in torment, but when the widow sent her on an errand into the countryside the servant had three successive insights that brought her to conversion. First, seeing the stalks of grain bowing over in the wind and then returning upright, she comprehended that God would forgive her sins and raise her up. Second, as a flock of sheep passed by, she realized that she was herself a lost sheep and that a conversion to God would open heaven to her. Finally, a wild poppy helped her understand that her heart was like the poppy's center, bound with black filaments that indicated the devil's hold on her, while the red petals signified that she "has been washed in the blood of Christ." When she returned home she told the widow, who enthused about her conversion: "Nothing, according to the will of God, had to remain hidden to this simple soul any longer. For the spirit of God had made her wiser than all her teachers, and everything was now alive and robust to her."[44]

Many third-person accounts quoted extensively from testimony of the converts, sometimes describing them as *Buß-prediger* (preachers of repentance) because of their moving testimony. For instance, the *Sammlung* described Christoph Cubehn, a hunter from the village of Ziethen, whose dying turned him into "an actual preacher of repentance." A letter from the pastor of the village, from which the editor quoted liberally, recorded the man's sudden illness, spiritual struggles, and conversion, but the heart of it recounted his testimony from his deathbed to friends and family, urging them one by one to follow him in his struggle and convert. When one friend glibly promised to repent but could not enumerate his sins, the dying man rebuked his insincerity: "You are a treacherous and false man. There is in your heart no truth or sincerity." He appealed to his fellow villagers to take advantage of the pastor's sermons: "You live in splendid times, for you can enjoy the pure, unalloyed presentation of the Word of God; yet you allow it to go in one ear and out the other." Throughout most of the account, the village pastor sat at his bedside, offering words of comfort but also engaging the dying man in spiritual dialogue. While the layman's words carried special weight because of his conversion, the narrative also reinforced the authority of the Pietist pastor. In a telling moment in which the pastor expressed doubt about his successes in the parish, the hunter assured him that if he continued to strive as he had, God would reward him.[45] As the man weakened, the pastor's voice in the narrative strengthens, and it is his words that conclude the account.

An overwhelming number of the third-person accounts reached the public after the death of the person featured in the narrative. In many cases death was an integral part of the narratives, providing the occasion for the long-awaited conversion that had earlier eluded the convert; in others it afforded the opportunity to depict the dramatic perseverance or completion of an earlier conversion; and in a few accounts an untimely death precluded a true conversion, a somber warning to those who would postpone conversion until their last moments. Discussing conversion in light of death stretches back to

Henckel's *Letzte Stunden* and the tradition of Pietist funeral sermons such as von Schönberg's. Even accounts that mentioned death only incidentally did not ordinarily appear in public until after the death of the chief character. The perspective of death provided an element of certainty and lent stability to the depiction of conversion. One could write without the fear that the convert might relapse and appear to falsify the original experience or require its reinterpretation. Furthermore, after death the converts could not contradict the published account or draw on their conversion experiences to justify heterodox views. Death pervaded German Pietist conversion narratives.

The Role of the Pietist Clergy

Pietist clergy and theological students often starred in these dramas. They were the frequent subjects of first- and third-person narratives; they appeared as key actors in the accounts of others; and often they were the recorders who described the conversion experiences of others. Their predominance among first-person narratives established the Pietist clergy as models of male conversion. In third-person accounts they often failed to seize center stage, but they still affected the outcomes.[46] Pietists expected a converted ministry; the preaching of the converted clergy carried more weight—so argued a number of Pietists[47]—for their spiritual experience made them worthy guides able to direct others to conversion. The narratives of Pietist clergy reinforced their spiritual authority by depicting their own conversion and, in a number of cases, their ability to convert others. For instance, Heinrich Schubert's autobiographical narrative, which appeared anonymously in *Altes und Neues*, portrayed a gradual conversion that began in the kitchen with his mother's prodding and concluded with an encounter with Francke at Halle nearly two years later in 1713; however, the narrative itself concludes with a description of his work as a court preacher in Ebersdorf and a claim about his "fruits" in bringing others to conversion.[48]

Pietist clergy often appeared in the accounts as experts in converting others. Leopold Franz Friedrich Lehr (1709–1744), for example, had a youthful conversion and a providential encounter with August Hermann Francke, who happened to visit his hometown and "prayed over him and blessed him with the laying on of hands."[49] His father's pious death a few years later laid the foundation for his conversion; its completion came through his encounters as a student with Pietists in Jena and then Halle, where he completed his studies.[50] The conversion account in the biography concludes with his departure from Halle. As he embarks on his career, the narrative describes his success with his parishioners and others. Lehr was the author of a Pietist hymn, often associated with conversion, titled "Mein Heiland nimmt die Sünder an." In fact, stories circulated of a "truly great sinner" in southern Germany who had been impervious to attempts to convert him but turned to God on his deathbed after reading and discussing Lehr's hymn.[51]

After Lehr became a *Diakon* (assistant pastor) in Köthen in the early 1740s, he was deciding whether to accept a call to another position. On a walk in the countryside Lehr encountered a shepherd weeping because, as the man explained, he had heard that Lehr might leave: "Now, I have become so old and have not yet converted myself. God has now begun his work in me. If only he [Lehr] could stay just long enough until I would be truly converted."[52] His plea moved Lehr to stay. The shepherd perceived Lehr, the converted Pietist pastor, as necessary for his own conversion. In a number of different ways, the biography of Lehr highlights Pietist clergy and theologians as exemplars of conversion and actors or agents of conversion within the accounts of church Pietism. Laity did not extend such respect to all ordained clergy. In fact, a number of accounts portrayed the dangers of an unconverted ministry—they faced the possibility of damnation and discouraged true seekers.[53]

This influence need not be as personal as Francke's laying his hands on the young Lehr, though charismatic Pietist clergy starred in many narratives as partners in pastoral conversations or as preachers.[54] Printed sermons and other literature circulated as inexpensive pamphlets, and converts referred to them frequently. Johanna Sophia von Dennstädt said that Francke's sermon penetrated her "marrow and bones," and Pietists disseminated sermons like this by the thousands in cheap editions.[55] Porst credited an edition of Spener's repentance sermons as a means of his conversion, just as others would credit the reading of Pietist sermons.[56] Printed collections of Pietist hymns also propagated Pietist views, and converts cited them—both sung and read—in conversion stories.

Clergy wrote many of the stories themselves. Though most of the third-person accounts remained anonymous, clergy often left signs of their authorship in other accounts by referring to their official roles even as they remained unnamed. Often among the best-educated members of a community, with duties that included pastoral oversight of their parishioners, they recorded and disseminated—not surprisingly—the spiritual experiences of others. Yet this meant that unconsciously or not, clergy selected the stories and likely edited them to present views of conversion that fit their beliefs. Editors of the periodicals often took pains to present these as accurate accounts, even the anonymous ones. They stressed that the accounts followed the "original" or came from a manuscript in the author's own hand. In a note to one account, the editor of the *Sammlung* emphasized the godliness of the author as well as the fidelity of the printed account to the original: "We had received this current report in writing already two years ago from a true widow, as Paul says in 1 Timothy 5:5, of which we purposely would not change the least bit."[57]

Such protestations raise suspicions that not all accounts saw the light of day in an unembellished form. A note appended to one story in *Altes und Neues* suggested that some accounts were not always accurate: "The editor assures [the reader] that the contents are indeed true and not, as is often the case on such occasions, amended and made more boastful."[58] In a few instances, when we can compare multiple printed accounts or have a manuscript at hand, the stories generally appear faithful.[59] Lächele argues that some accounts appear to be edited in order to favor one party or another.[60] Likely much more important than minor editing were the principles of selection that determined which accounts made it to the printer for inclusion in the periodicals and collections. The choices of editors reflected decisions about the forms of conversion they wanted their readers to see.

Church and Confessional Identity

The narratives enfolded the experience of conversion into the church practices of Lutheran Pietism. Individual and inward, conversion also occurred in church communities usually linked to the established church, and the authors reminded their readers of that connection. The omnipresence of ordained clergy reinforced the church connection, especially in their function as preachers. But the narratives also depicted other rituals and practices of the church, above all the Eucharist. For Krimmer, Porst, and Dennstädt the Eucharist anchors the stories, even if it is not depicted as sufficient for conversion. It appears throughout third-person accounts as well. The author of Engel Utstiem's narrative described the peasant girl's "heartfelt conversion" as beginning with a catechetical discussion of Lutheran doctrine in preparation for the Eucharist: "From this hour forth all her own sins and all the vanity of the world became her greatest burdens, whereas the Word of God and her Lord Jesus became her greatest pleasure, if not her strength and life amid the work in the household and in the fields." The author marveled at the effect that the ritual practice of the Eucharist in the church evoked for the young woman: "Especially it was for her as if the heavens opened anew each time she was in church and heard the chanting words of institution in a clear voice as the bread and wine were consecrated."[61]

When the author described her exemplary death a few years later, the Lord's Supper appeared again. The author recounted that she recalled gratefully the instruction she received before the communion that led to her conversion: "Then with a genuinely heartfelt hunger for her redeemer, she received the sacrament of the Lord's Supper, his real body and blood. Through this, the Lord effected, according to his free grace, such a joyful faith in her that she spent several hours in quietude contemplating the great faithfulness and love of her great savior."[62] In Utstiem's narrative the Eucharistic piety is manifestly Lutheran, and the servant girl also set out on her path of conversion by meditating on the Lutheran doctrine of the real presence.

Ritual observance alone was insufficient; Pietists had long criticized the unthinking reliance of baptized Christians on the sacraments and regular participation in church services as evidence of true piety. The narrators often portrayed Christians who conformed externally but deceived themselves about the state of their souls. In one of the few dialogue formats, Jacob Schneider, a peasant from Mehro, described his spiritual condition before his conversion: "I lived my life in such blindness, relied upon the fact that I went to confession, to church, and to the Lord's Supper, in which I was very diligent, and led an otherwise honest life."[63] Although the narratives portrayed a few "atheists" who spurned Christianity prior to their conversion, most depicted nominal Christian churchgoers.[64] Yet these narratives make clear that true conversion did not entail separation from the church or even indifference to its practices; rather, the result was often to bring them more closely into the fold of the established church, especially a parish church with Pietist leanings and leadership.

Conversion narratives in these publications could reinforce confessional identity in other ways. Sometimes conversion rescued the convert from radical or heterodox influence. Porst had to pass through a radical stage in which he rejected established church practices and harangued the unconverted. The final, more moderate stage of his conversion came to fruition within the liturgical and sacramental framework of the Lutheran Church. Dennstädt leaned toward the radical followers of Gichtel, but she rejected their view of scripture and returned to the established church. A narrative from Denmark described a woman who met exiled separatists from Sweden who made a deep impression on her, but the narrator credited the Holy Spirit with rescuing her from their errors and added that a traveling German court preacher and Halle Pietist literature brought her fullness of salvation.[65] Conversion partially reintegrated her into the ecclesial community of her village.[66] Other narratives told how converts escaped heterodox influences. Jacob Schneider described how he was able to avoid the errors of Johann Wilhelm Petersen's universalism as well as the separatist tendencies of radical Pietists in Brandenburg.[67] Pietist context was almost always essential to conversion, but this context did not exclude confessional or ecclesial identity but often reinforced it.

In the *Sammlung* and its successors and in *Altes und Neues*, the German narratives were overwhelmingly Lutheran. Jerichovius included biographies of persecuted Protestants who faced threats of exile or prison unless they converted to Catholicism, but he praised them for remaining faithful to their faith.[68] In one account, the title mentioned a *Bekehrung* because the conversion was to Protestant truth, but such stories were not precisely conversion narratives, even though their proximity to conversion narratives in the *Sammlung* imparts a confessional character to the other accounts.[69] One later issue of the *Fortgesetzte Sammlung* included the conversion of a Catholic on his deathbed, but the point was that he turned from a dissolute life of whoring and drink to heartfelt belief and trust in Jesus Christ.[70] There was no explicit turn from Catholicism to Lutheranism in the narrative, and not all the authors portrayed Catholics unsympathetically.[71] Nevertheless, the extended struggles followed a pattern typical of Pietist deathbed conversions, and it was his Lutheran wife who decisively urged him toward his final conversion.

The authors also included a few Reformed narratives with little confessional commentary.[72] The collections departed most visibly from the Lutheran confessional context through the inclusion of narratives from Britain. Beginning with the *Verbesserte Sammlung* in 1737, Steinmetz included an increasing number of narratives translated from English.[73] These mark not only a more ecumenical view but also a wider international perspective on conversion experiences.

Conclusion

These Pietist periodicals mark a new level of publicity for conversion narratives in church Pietism, which aside from Henckel's *Letzte Stunden* tended not to publish such accounts widely. The *Sammlung auserlesener Materien* and *Altes und Neues aus dem Reich Gottes* circulated the accounts to a wide range of readers in German Pietism, who read them privately and also discussed them in prayer groups and conventicles. The form or pattern of conversion is hardly uniform. Relatively few conformed closely to the pattern supposedly set by August Hermann Francke's own narrative or advocated by Lau, with the distinct steps of *Rührung*, *Bußkampf*, and *Durchbruch*. In many cases, there was no definitive *Bußkampf*, at least in the strict sense of the term. Heinrich Schubert, the leading representative of Halle Pietism in Potsdam, portrayed his conversion without a classic *Bußkampf*; instead, he depicted it as a gradual process that began in his mother's kitchen and reached completion in Halle.[74] Many other accounts reveal little in the way of *Bußkampf*. The servant girl's vision of the poppy or Dennstädt's insistent searching cannot easily be understood as classic descriptions of a *Bußkampf* conversion. A number of accounts referred to the *Bußkampf*, but they did not view it as a fixed step in conversion and employed it as a synonym for a general *Anfechtung*.[75] A few accounts did feature a typical Halle pattern of conversion. In 1739, the *Verbesserte Sammlung* brought the first-person account of a young, unmarried woman whose conversion proceeded along the classic *Bußkampf* model—precisely what one would expect in the supposed Franckean model of conversion—but among the published conversion narratives in these publications, the extended, first-person narration by a woman that followed a *Bußkampf* model was an anomaly, not the rule.[76]

The published accounts featured the clergy, whether as converts, preachers, providers of spiritual counsel, and advocates—even agents—of conversion. They also wrote many of the accounts, shaping them to their interests. Pietist clergy emerged as paradigms of male spirituality and arbiters of true conversion, which often occurred within a confessional context and church community.

Almost all the narratives appeared after the converts had died, and the events leading up to death figure more centrally than they do in Henckel's earlier narratives. The *Sammlung* and *Altes und Neues* portrayed failed conversions as warnings to their readers and often appeared after the convert's death. Some circulated in manuscript for some time before being published.[77] Postponed publication removed the danger of falsification.

These periodicals established a public tradition of conversion narratives in German church Pietism that until the 1730s had been much more modest than is often assumed. It presented a range of conversion models but also cast them in an identifiable confessional and clerical context. The next chapter will examine the ways strongly conversionist ideas could shape a Pietist movement and place the *Bußkampf* itself center stage.

6

CONVERSION IN DARGUN

The revival that began at the court of Dargun in Mecklenburg during the 1730s constituted one of the most prominent expressions of the *Bußkampf* model of conversion in the history of German Pietism. By most standards, Dargun was small and inconsequential, located far from the commercial and governmental centers of Mecklenburg-Schwerin, a duchy itself of only moderate influence in eighteenth-century Germany. Yet, for a time in the 1730s and 1740s, Dargun played an outsized role in Pietist debates about conversion. Influenced by Samuel Lau and others from the Pietist stronghold in Wernigerode, Duchess Augusta of Mecklenburg and her specially chosen Pietist ministers inculcated a culture of conversion that reached far beyond the court itself and shaped the direction of Mecklenburg's territorial church. Practices of conversion and the ideas that lay behind them caused years of controversy in Mecklenburg and beyond. Even within the larger ambit of Halle Pietism, the emphasis on conversion in Dargun proved divisive, above all for its rigid insistence on the *Bußkampf* (repentance struggle). The discord it evoked sheds light on the larger place of conversion within eighteenth-century Pietism and reveals that the story of a rigid model of conversion was hardly as straightforward as some historians have portrayed it to be.

Early Pietism in Mecklenburg and Duchess Augusta

Mecklenburg and the university at Rostock had been the home to several powerful streams of reform within Lutheran orthodoxy during the seventeenth century, but Pietism never found a strong foothold there. During the Pietist controversies of the 1690s, Mecklenburg turned in an increasingly anti-Pietist direction. The theology faculty at the University of Rostock became known as a bastion of orthodoxy in the fight against the Pietists.[1] Duke Friedrich Wilhelm I codified opposition to Pietism in 1708 in the so-called *Emendations* to the 1602 church order, which condemned Pietist practices.[2] By the early eighteenth century, many of the clergy in Mecklenburg had studied in orthodox Rostock and increasingly shared the anti-Pietist convictions of their teachers and sovereign.

Elements of Pietist influence and sympathy remained in Mecklenburg, ranging from quiet adherents of August Hermann Francke to the more radical Pietism of such preachers as Leonhard Christian Sturm and Ludwig Gerhard.[3] Overall, however, the Pietist movement in Mecklenburg during the early eighteenth century was small and relatively unobtrusive within the territorial church.

Some of the strongest support for Pietism there emerged, unexpectedly given its marginal status, at the court of the Duchess Augusta in Dargun. Augusta (1674–1756) was the unmarried daughter of the last Duke of Mecklenburg-Güstrow. His death without a male heir in 1695 threw Mecklenburg into turmoil over succession. In the extended negotiations to unify the two Mecklenburg duchies, Augusta and her widowed mother enjoyed an unusual amount of autonomy for the rest of their lives in return for support of a greater Mecklenburg-Schwerin.[4]

Questions of religion had long interested Augusta, and like her sisters—Christine, Countess of Stolberg-Wernigerode; and Louise, queen of Denmark—she had Pietist sympathies.[5] Augusta took up the study of Greek and Hebrew in order to read the scriptures in the original languages, and she carried on an avid correspondence on religious topics, including an important exchange of letters with Johann Wilhelm Petersen.[6] After her mother's death in 1718, her court relocated from Güstrow to Dargun, whose modest palace and lands Augusta received as an apanage for the duration of her life.[7] The political crisis in Mecklenburg surrounding Duke Carl Leopold, whose authority in the duchy was reduced by an imperial commission in 1719, severely weakened the government, limiting its oversight of the *Landeskirche*, the territorial church, which in turn strengthened the autonomy of the Duchess Augusta in religious affairs in Dargun, particularly regarding the right to make appointments in the schools and churches.[8]

Augusta took an early interest in the condition of religious life in the churches surrounding Dargun during the 1720s. She was active in distributing Bibles in Dargun and nearby villages, an enterprise undertaken by many Pietists, foremost the Canstein Bible Institute in Halle.[9] According to Wilhelmi, she also sought to improve the quality of the schools. Her correspondence reveals a form of piety which reflects that of many noble Pietists of the early eighteenth century.[10] Augusta clearly had an affinity for some elements of Halle Pietism. When looking for a new *Pagenmeister* in 1722, she asked the pastor in Recknitz with close connections to Halle, Simon Ambrosius Hennings, to seek a suitable suggestion from A. H. Francke.[11] Her court preacher, Georg Friedrich Stieber, had studied in Halle and corresponded occasionally with Francke, and he supported, for instance, many of the Pietist practices proposed by George von Horn, the new *Pagenmeister* from Halle.[12] Despite meeting Francke personally at least once, Augusta herself maintained few direct ties to him or others in Halle. She once objected to von Horn's prayer sessions, saying that she did want any "Hallensian gangs" at her court, though her complaint was less about Francke-style Pietism than what she considered the improper gatherings of women and men together in prayer sessions at court.[13] During the mid-1720s, a number of courtiers developed an avid interest in the Danish-Halle missions to India, one of Halle's most prominent endeavors.[14]

By the mid-1720s, it appears that the duchess and some members of her circle began moving in an increasingly heterodox direction away from church Pietism.[15] She reportedly developed an ardent interest in the doctrine of the *apokatastasis*, which became a topic in her correspondence with her sister and Johann Wilhelm Petersen in the mid-1720s.[16] Similarly, we know she supported the production of the radical Pietist Berleburg Bible from its beginnings, and her secretary and later *Hofrat*, Jacob Christian Hellwig, developed in the 1720s and 1730s close ties to some radical Pietists.[17] Simon Ambrosius Hennings, a confidant of Augusta and pastor in Recknitz, frequently corresponded with Francke and others in Halle on her behalf, but by the mid-1720s Hennings also seemed to be drawn toward more radical views.[18] Several reports indicate that in the early 1730s Augusta seriously considered calling the deposed preacher and radical Pietist Victor Chistoph Tuchtfeld to one of the parishes over which she held the right of patronage.[19] During the early 1730s, she also reportedly evinced interest in the events in Herrnhut under Count Zinzendorf.[20] Whether Augusta was as spiritually labile as some have suggested is difficult to ascertain, but it is clear that even into her mid-fifties she remained open to religious innovation.[21] When her nephew Christian Ernst, Count of Stolberg-Wernigerode and staunch ally of Gotthilf August Francke, visited Augusta in Dargun, he suggested filling clerical vacancies with Pietist preachers from Wernigerode. Under Samuel Lau and Johann Liborius Zimmermann, his court had been the site of an exciting revival, and Christian Ernst urged her to import two young preachers to Mecklenburg, both of whom had participated in the revival in his lands.[22]

The New Preachers and Conversion

Until the 1730s, the topic of conversion attracted little attention in Dargun, and clergy there discussed it primarily in relation to the conversions of Jews or Hindus in India to Christianity, rather than to the transformational conversion of nominal Christians.[23] The arrival of the two new preachers, Jakob Schmidt and Henning Christoph Ehrenpfort, brought a new emphasis on individual conversion to the parishes near Dargun. Appealing to her rights of patronage, Augusta had little trouble winning congregational approval for the candidates she presented. Schmidt became preacher in the village of Levin and Ehrenpfort in Groß-Methling, both near Dargun.[24]

The letters Schmidt and Ehrenpfort dispatched to their allies in Wernigerode signaled that they perceived themselves almost as missionaries communicating a new form of piety that contrasted strongly with what they found in Mecklenburg. Schmidt's letter to Lady Sophie Charlotte just a few months after their arrival in 1733 recounts the new preachers' early successes, including the sickbed conversion of a member of the court who, after many struggles, "grinned with joy as soon as he heard of the Lord Jesus, and would even have preached this to her highness the Princess had he the strength in his body." A few sentences later, Schmidt described an old lady who came to him after his sermon, telling him that she had come to doubt her previous faith, but through God's grace it was now finally strengthened. She had heard many preachers before, she told him, but "they had all preached out of the Old Testament," implying, at least in Schmidt's telling, that his was a New Testament message that had been absent.[25] Because they are clearly subjective assessments we must take them with a grain of salt, yet they represent the sense of mission in building the "Kingdom of God" (*Reich Gottes*) that these outsiders to Mecklenburg possessed.

Augusta was pleased with the newcomers. When the Röckenitz pastorate immediately adjacent to Dargun opened up in 1734, she transferred Ehrenpfort there and installed August Hövet, her former *Pagenmeister*, as pastor in Groß-Methling.[26] Schmidt reported that even in such a short time Ehrenpfort could count several conversions, and the groundwork was laid for many more.[27] Initially, the other Pietists at court, who perceived the Holy Spirit at work in the revival, received the new clergy enthusiastically.[28] Wilhelmi reports that Schmidt may even have been initially sympathetic to Hellwig's millenarian und universalist ideas.[29]

Before long, however, there were complaints.[30] Augusta integrated the new clergy into the life at court, inviting them to preach and giving them opportunities to establish prayer meetings.[31] When Ehrenpfort's sermons in

Röckenitz began to draw more and more members of the court, the court preacher Stieber took offense and objected, especially when Augusta sought to appoint Ehrenpfort as *Hofdiakon*.[32] Stieber's complaints did not sit well with Augusta, and she seized the occasion to dismiss him, replacing him with another pastor from Wernigerode, Carl Heinrich Zachariae, a leading proponent of the *Bußkampf* theology but nonetheless a relatively orthodox Lutheran on most doctrinal issues. Zachariae had been *Diakon* in Wernigerode and worked as a close associate of the court preacher Samuel Lau.[33] Furthermore, he had a close relationship to the Count and Countess of Stolberg-Wernigerode, with whom he remained in frequent correspondence.[34] Arriving in the fall of 1735, the new court preacher became the leading figure of the Dargun Pietists, advocating a vigorous theology of conversion based on the *Bußkampf* but also drawing lines more clearly to exclude radical Pietist tendencies.

The intense prayer meetings and the new clergy's emphasis on conversion appeared alien to many in Dargun and the surrounding villages. In the minds of many locals, kneeling during prayer or meditating on images of Christ's crucifixion were practices redolent of Catholicism; the resulting rumors even drew some curious Catholics to Dargun.[35] Many in Mecklenburg had little sensibility for the emotional conversion experiences that occurred in these circles, and wild rumors about these conversions gained credibility not only among the common people but also among the non-Pietist clergy. Yet the new clergy enjoyed a fair amount of success with their revivalist methods and could count increasing numbers of conversions, most prominently that of the duchess herself.

Augusta's conversion occurred sometime during the early period of the revival, before the end of 1735. In a letter to G. A. Francke, Schmidt noted briefly in September 1734 that the duchess had progressed spiritually and that she more and more trusted the new preachers, even though she was "surrounded by great hindrances."[36] There are no contemporary reports, and aside from a brief autobiographical reference that she included in a letter to her nephew, King Christian VI of Denmark, our knowledge of her conversion comes largely from a third-person narrative composed in 1741 that is part of a larger collection:

> Princess Augusta had struggled for many years with her own righteousness. In doing so, she had considered herself the equal of the world, was admired by all, believed in the power of her own exercises and efforts, and she stumbled onto the doctrine of the return of all

things [*apokatastasis*], all of which, however, did not kill the old Adam. My Lord, [Count Christian Ernst of Stolberg-Wernigerode] gave her Francke's writings, which produced in her a desire to have a preacher recommended from Wernigerode. My Lord sent her two, Ehrenpfort and Schmidt. When she heard the two preach, her unrest grew ever greater, until God made the words of Revelation 3:15–18 alive to her, through which the entire condition of her soul was revealed to her, drawing her fully away from everything. She learned to call out and cry earnestly for grace until, one early morning, she lay exhausted from her struggle, beseeching God for grace. Before she could expect it, God gave her peace in an effusive amount, so that her heart was full of God's praise. When she lay down again, she thrashed around so much in bed that, had God not especially protected her, she would have broken her neck. This became then a new basis for her praise of God and made her especially courageous in mocking with joy the devil in all his power and cunning. From this time forward, the world repulsed her.[37]

This rather uneven account contains many of the typical patterns of Dargun conversion narratives. The author refers to Augusta's heterodox ideas as hindrances to her progress toward salvation. The providential intervention of Count Christian Ernst brought her in contact with Pietist texts that in turn led her to request preachers shaped in this tradition. After their arrival in Mecklenburg these Pietist clergy revealed to Augusta the true condition of her soul, and following a series of spiritual struggles she received confirmation in her heart of divine peace. From this point forward, Augusta's opposition to the "world" made her an advocate of conversionist practices and ideas. It is striking how closely Augusta's conversion fit the *Bußkampf* model of conversion—an initial stirring, a deep period of repentance, and finally a sudden breakthrough to an assurance of grace and peace, all datable at a specific place and time.

The arrival of Carl Heinrich Zachariae in 1735 marked a new phase in the movement in Dargun. Court preachers were among the most prestigious clergy in Mecklenburg, and Zachariae's prominence allowed him to take leadership of the movement in a way that the pastors in outlying villages could not. By this point, opposition to the Pietists in Dargun had begun to take root. Zachariae's task was therefore twofold—first, to counter opponents outside Dargun; and second, to reinforce the movement internally and purge heterodox ideas that Zachariae perceived to be threatening true religion at court.

Opposition to Dargun in Mecklenburg

Outside Dargun, Zachariae faced a growing challenge. By the spring of 1735, the stories of dramatic conversions and other practices in Dargun and nearby villages caused alarm in Mecklenburg. Duke Carl Leopold, who had an ambivalent relationship to the Pietists, wrote from Wismar asking Jacob Sigismund Suckow, pastor in Neukalen and *Praepositus* in the area, to investigate.[38] Suckow began conducting inquiries and collecting reports critical of the "new priests," as they were called, and their suspect conversion practices. Though the reports were partisan and largely based on hearsay and rumors, they reveal a great deal about how outsiders perceived the revival and how novel the conversion experiences appeared to many in Mecklenburg at that time. Many of the statements Suckow and others gathered illustrate the divisiveness that the new demands for conversion could evoke in the parishes. Both clergy and laity gave supernatural explanations for individual experiences, and the clergy especially suggested that the newcomers had introduced heterodox ideas to the duchy.

Critics charged that the conversionist clergy sharply divided pastors and laity into converted and non-converted camps, which in their eyes challenged traditional Lutheran practices and devalued the sacraments. Numerous times, they cited examples of the new Pietist preachers warning their parishioners that if they should take the Eucharist without being truly converted, it would not aid them in any way.[39] The clerical critics were especially incensed that the conversionist preachers allegedly defamed their colleagues in Mecklenburg, calling them unconverted and "wolves" among the sheep.[40] Predictably, they decried the emphasis on personal conversion and the necessity of the *Bußkampf* as a new form of Pelagianism and a variant of popery.[41] Lay complaints paralleled these clerical charges but focused more on the fracturing of the parish community and the inclusion of some and exclusion of others. The emphasis on conversion as the sole way to salvation and the corresponding devaluation of both the Eucharist and baptism troubled many, especially as the new construal of conversion seemed to call into question the salvation of departed family members who had not experienced an explicit conversion.[42] Many were troubled by what they saw as the hidden and exclusive nature of the prayer meetings and gatherings organized by the clergy.[43] The laity were especially sensitive to reports that converts received material benefits while those who held back were disadvantaged in their trade.[44]

Whether distorted or exaggerated, some of these accusations are not unexpected, given the extent to which the "new preachers" emphasized conversion. The revivalists might not have expressed themselves as crudely as the critics would report, but the number and range of critical remarks do suggest that many parishioners interpreted the emphasis on conversion as a break with past religious rhetoric and practice. Indeed, the critics did not doubt that conversion experiences were taking place, but they saw them as evidence of heterodoxy and enthusiasm that were, for many, tinged with magic and the illicit manipulation of supernatural forces.

Opponents often connected visions to the experience of conversion. In one case, a critic reported that Ehrenpfort had supposedly said of a highborn person at court "that she had had Jesus with her visibly in bed the entire night," implying both enthusiasm and shocking impropriety.[45] Others in the throes of conversion reportedly fell into ecstatic states and had visions of relatives in heaven.[46] One case described a sergeant who, during his *Bußkampf*, went out into the churchyard in "fear and trembling," but then as "a spirit in the form of a child appeared to him he immediately became calm," signifying his progress in conversion.[47] Other rumors spoke of visitations by the angel Gabriel; some more darkly told of the devil's taking the form of a dog in order to lead the converted astray.[48]

One popular explanation among the critics for the flood of conversion experiences was the employment of powders or elixirs with magical or pharmacological powers that allegedly induced powerful religious experiences. Critics described these variously as "Quaker powder" (*Quacker-Pulver*, also *Quäcker-Pulver*), "conversion powder" (*Bekehrungs-Pulver*), or an "elixir" (*Trunck*). Sometimes they were mixed with beer.[49] The pastor Pauli from Gorrendorf reported stories that "those in Dargun und Levin make use of *Quacker-Pulver* and that the people really become frantic from it, especially those in Röckenitz."[50] In Schorrentin, the pastor reported, "It is to be presumed that these evil people use the so-called *Quacker-Pulver* and administer it to the people." Allegedly, it was only necessary to sprinkle some of it on the seat of a chair, and when someone sat down, "as soon as it becomes warm, it strikes into the blood and causes anxiety and pain, so that one becomes frantic"; anxious people in such a state were ripe for exploitation.[51] These were not just rumors among the common people; clergy also took them seriously. In his official inquiry conducted with the senior of the Güstrow clergy, the pastor from nearby Alt-Kalen, Suckow specifically asked a woman he interviewed "whether those who wished to convert were supplied with a powder or elixir from the aforementioned priests," to which the woman replied yes, though significantly she couldn't name the person who had told her this. When he continued and queried, "How then did these people act or gesture after being given this powder or elixir?" she responded, in Low German,

"They are said to become completely mad so that they also have to hide their heads in fear."[52]

Stories of a Quaker powder with power to induce ecstatic religious experiences date back to at least the middle of the seventeenth century in Germany, and opponents repeatedly accused Pietists of pharmacological mischief.[53] In Rostock, a 1707 dissertation purportedly revealing the mysteries of so-called Quaker powders was so popular that it was reprinted several times between 1707 and 1745.[54] In some respects, Quaker powder or elixirs provided a rational, scientific explanation for extraordinary religious states, which outsiders to the movement were otherwise at loss to explain. At the same time, the implication was often one of magic and satanic influences.[55] Stories of a "Quaker powder" may have been part of timeworn anti-Pietist narratives that were easily deployed in this context, but the Dargun Pietists may have inadvertently encouraged these explanations with their frequent use of medicines from the apothecary in Halle, particularly the *essentia dulcis*.[56] Yet, even given small amounts of mercury present in the *essentia dulcis*, it is unlikely these medicines produced the psychopharmacological effects their opponents claimed.

Other explanations of conversions claimed illicit, supernatural, or quasi-magical forces at work. Suckow circulated the story that a painting in one of the conventicle rooms in Dargun had magical qualities. He queried a local official "whether then the new priests had painted something like a calf on the wall, and when a conversion was proper, this thing would begin to bellow." The official vaguely responded that "it was generally discussed here and there," but he could not be more specific. Follow-up questions, which detailed more occult connections to the painting, referred to "crows and devil's feet [*Teuffelsfüßen*]" in the room—items suggestive of the occult—but the inquiry elicited only a general acknowledgment of rumors.[57] Others alleged that the "new priests" encouraged outrageous practices of meditation to induce conversion. One woman told Suckow, "People have said that when they want to be newly converted that they should lay their heads on the oven and were to pray so long until they could no longer name God and Jesus and collapse into unconsciousness, something many have encountered."[58]

A maelstrom of such stories and rumors surrounded the revival in Dargun and the nearby parishes in the mid-1730s. It is hard to know whether critics like Suckow believed the more outlandish rumors or simply propagated them to discredit the "new priests," as he frequently labeled them, but some of the tales gained credence far beyond the immediate vicinity of Dargun.[59]

In some areas, popular anxiety about the new movement led to resistance against Augusta's policy of installing Pietist pastors to parishes over which she held the right of patronage. The pastoral election in Jördenstorf in the summer of 1736 illustrated the difficulties she faced. As patron, she had sole authority to nominate candidates, and by presenting a slate of only likeminded Pietists she was able to skew the election in her favor.[60] Dissatisfied with her proposals, the parishioners, spurred on by local nobles, petitioned to postpone the election, but after some hesitation Carl Leopold allowed it to go forward.[61] As the clergy and officials assigned to carry out the presentation sought to conduct the election, they encountered stiff resistance at the doors of the church from the assembled villagers, who prevented them from entering. Some estimated that five to six hundred people were present in the churchyard, and as the party neared the church, cries of "We don't want any Quakers here! Split the heads of these knaves and Quakers in two!" were reportedly heard.[62] Some in the crowd attacked the party and injured one of the clergy badly. Fighting back the mob, the duchess's guards were able to bring the clergy and the officials to safety in the parsonage, but the election itself was abandoned. Two hours later, when they finally withdrew from Jördenstorf, some of the people in the crowd called after them, "There go the Quakers and the converted," warning them never to return.[63]

The duchess and her allies blamed the local nobles for stirring up resentment, and although they certainly played a role in fomenting the discontent of the villagers, the cries of "Quakers," "knave," "converted," and (in some eyewitness accounts) "sorcerer" (*Hexenmeister*) signal how closely many in Jördenstorf had tied the revival in Dargun not only to heterodoxy and the arch-enthusiasts of their day—the Quakers—but also to elements of magic and witchcraft.[64] The events at Jördenstorf thwarted Augusta's intended appointment; unable to get her way, the duchess elected to leave the parish without pastoral leadership for thirteen years.[65] Moreover, the violence of the anti-Pietists in Jördenstorf served to rally prominent supporters of Pietism in Prussia and Denmark to her side.

At the height of these controversies, Zachariae, the newly installed court preacher at Dargun, moved to counter what he considered heterodox influences of radical Pietists. In particular, he sought to isolate two longtime allies of Augusta, Privy Counselor Hellwig and Pastor Hennings from Recknitz, both of whom he held responsible for heterodox beliefs at court. In a letter to Wernigerode from January 1736, Zachariae described Hellwig and Hennings as conniving to undermine religion at the court and provoking opposition to the *Bußkampf*-oriented conversion of the Pietists from Wernigerode. He singled out for criticism their allegedly heterodox ideas about the *apokastasis panton*.[66]

Once Augusta's closest adviser, Hellwig, who had at least initially been collegial with Ehrenpfort and Schmidt, now found himself increasingly marginalized at court.[67] He withdrew from church services in Dargun and eschewed most religious matters until Augusta finally dismissed him in 1738. In the same way, Augusta severed her once-close connections to Pastor Hennings in Recknitz, whose ideas on the *apokatastasis* were anathema to the conversionists; her Wernigerode allies referred to him as "that wretched universalist."[68] Zachariae's letters make clear his intent to purge the remnants of heterodox ideas in Dargun.

The Dargun clergy faced still more challenges from the orthodox establishment in Mecklenburg. In early 1736, the consistory in Rostock summoned Schmidt to Rostock to investigate his views of conversion. Schmidt successfully defended himself by drawing on the 1602 church order that stressed *Buße und Bekehrung*. Though obviously self-serving, Zachariae's account of the hearing leaves the impression that the orthodox Rostock consistory was unprepared to deal with the new form of conversion theology advocated by Schmidt.[69] That would change over the course of 1736, when the opponents sharpened their theological criticisms and focused on what they saw as the theological deficiencies of the *Bußkampf*. A disputation questioning the orthodoxy of the *Bußkampf* appeared in Rostock in the summer, and then a Hamburg newspaper reported on the disputation's publication and connected it to the reports and rumors coming out of the revival at Dargun. These made the controversies surrounding Dargun a public affair with implications far beyond Mecklenburg.[70]

Dargun as a Public Pietist Controversy

Until the summer of 1736, events in Dargun were little known beyond Mecklenburg. In 1735, a short notice had appeared in the *Fortgesetzte Sammlung zur auserlesenen Materien zum Bau des Reichs Gottes* commending the power with which the Word of God was being preached in and around Dargun.[71] Schmidt, Hövet, and Ehrenpfort each published a sermon in 1735 in defense of their views, but these early works seemed to generate little controversy, perhaps because of their relative obscurity.[72] But a 1736 notice in the widely distributed journal *Hamburgische Berichte von neuen gelehrten Sachen* was a different matter. It reported on the publication of the disputation, which voiced specific criticisms of the *Bußkampf*, but then went on to connect these to the rumors surrounding the revival in Dargun in a way the academic disputation had not. Describing the advocates of the *Bußkampf* as "riffraff," the article accused them of spreading this pestilence throughout Germany, infecting even the pious and the well educated with their poison. The article claimed that Dargun was full of "sectarians" who peddled all kinds of false teachings, including supposedly Quaker practices of self-castigation: "There many lie and howl day and night on the ground, and sometimes do nothing else for days and even years than cry, sigh, scream, macerate their bodies, and similar things that are displeasing to God and man as they seek to find their way to a true and scriptural understanding."[73] The article helped inflame a local dispute into a much larger controversy.[74]

Until this point, Zachariae had not taken a pronounced public role in the defense of the movement in Dargun. Ehrenpfort had published a short treatise on *Das Geheimnis der Bekehrung* in the first half of 1736, with one of its not-so-subtle points being that conversion was a mystery to much of "corrupt Christianity" in his day, an indirect rebuke to the orthodox Mecklenburg clergy who seemed to know so little about it.[75] The disputation in Rostock and the Hamburg newspaper account spurred Zachariae into action. He composed a response and published the most extensive defense of the *Bußkampf* that any Pietist had written in 1736, *Der in Gottes Wort und unsern Symbolischen Büchern wohlgegründete Buß-Kampf* (The *Bußkampf*, Well-Founded in God's Word and Our Symbolic Books).[76] Zachariae's goal, as the title suggests, was to ground the Pietist teaching of the *Bußkampf* in scripture and Lutheran tradition, and to free his understanding of *Bußkampf* from any association with radicals. He took aim at Burgmann's disputation and the article in the *Hamburgische Berichte* with arguments that echoed those of his mentor, Samuel Lau, in a number of places. Like Lau, he drew on Lutheran tradition, but Zachariae adopted a more polemical tone.

Zachariae built his argument on Luke 13:24, "Strive to enter through the narrow door; for many, I tell you, will try to enter and will not be able." The narrow door or gate (*enge Pforte*) was a common theme among the Dargun Pietists, one that their critics also mentioned.[77] For Zachariae, the "striving" referred to the struggle that took place in repentance, and he insisted that without it one could not achieve salvation. He amplified the idea of striving and struggle in repentance with numerous passages from the Old and New Testament, and linked it as well to the Lutheran tradition of repentance and conversion, *Buße und Bekehrung*. Zachariae pointed to the confessions to justify the idea of a struggle in conversion, but he appealed especially to the writings of Martin Chemnitz, who had written explicitly of such a *lucta* (struggle).[78] The Burgmann disputation had been particularly keen to connect the *Bußkampf* to various heterodox teachings and movements, including radical sectarians, theosophists, indifferentists, perfectionists, and the so-called terminists, who restricted the opportunity for repentance to a limited period of time.[79] Indeed, the disputation argued that, rightly understood,

Bußkampf was not necessarily an objectionable term, and he even agreed with one of Lau's descriptions of it.[80] Nevertheless, the author of the disputation sought to link the use of the *Bußkampf* in Mecklenburg to as many heterodox movements as possible, thereby incriminating Dargun with aspersions of heterodoxy.

Unwittingly, the disputation's wilder accusations served Zachariae's purposes of defending the orthodoxy of the Dargun movement. He had no problem decrying sectarians, theosophists, perfectionists, or terminists, who in many cases held views that he saw as hindrances to true conversion.[81] That the Burgmann disputation spent so much time on the alleged sectarian and heterodox associations of the *Bußkampf* to a certain extent obscured the major point of contention: the conviction of Zachariae and others in Dargun that a conversion experience was the sole path to salvation, and more specifically that a *Bußkampf* was required as proof that the conversion was true. While the disputation aggressively criticized the form of conversion associated with the Dargun clergy, it provided no alternative. Its discussions of conversion in the Lutheran tradition were theologically impoverished, lacking the subtlety of the anonymous and less polemical response to Lau several years earlier.[82] It suggests something of the limitations of the provincial theologians at Rostock in opposing Zachariae and others in Dargun that the most telling criticisms of the Dargun movement came from other Pietists.

One of the misconceptions of the Dargun controversy was that it was primarily a conflict between the Pietists and their perennial opponents, the Lutheran orthodox. Peschke portrayed the controversy in Dargun as the incursion of Halle Pietism into the largely orthodox territory of Mecklenburg.[83] Certainly, the conversionist theology of the new Dargun preachers represented a challenge to the practices of traditional Lutheran orthodoxy espoused by the faculty in Rostock and by many of the duchy's clergy, but they were not the only ones who took umbrage at the form of conversion that Zachariae and the others in Dargun advocated.

Russmeyer's Criticism of Dargun and the *Bußkampf*

One of the most severe critiques of the Dargun movement came from Michael Christian Russmeyer, professor of theology at the University of Greifswald and a representative of a moderate form of church Pietism. Though he did not study at Halle—for that matter, neither did Zachariae—Russmeyer did study at Jena under Buddeus and was part of the Pietist network that included Halle. In the mid-1710s, he apparently sought to join Halle's missionary activity in southern India.⁸⁴ When he encountered opposition at the University of Greifswald to his Pietist proclivities, he turned for advice to A. H. Francke and other Pietists.⁸⁵ He pursued a number of Pietist practices at the university, including the *collegia pietatis*.⁸⁶ Although Peschke treats Russmeyer as a representative of the Lutheran orthodox position, almost nothing ties him to Lutheran orthodoxy apart from his opposition to Zachariae.

It is unclear how Russmeyer came to learn of the revival in Dargun. Located in eastern Mecklenburg, Dargun was relatively close to the border of Pomerania, and by the mid-1730s he may have heard first- or secondhand reports in nearby Greifswald.⁸⁷ In 1736, he published a sermon that subtly questioned a rigid understanding of the conversion process.⁸⁸ He reported later that the Dargun clergy denounced this printed sermon from their pulpits.⁸⁹ By 1737, he had received a detailed report from Hempel, the former court physician at Dargun, about the revival there. Zachariae's aggressive defense of a *Bußkampf* theology, coupled with what Russmeyer considered rigid and potentially hypocritical expectations of conversion in Dargun, led Russmeyer to respond in print.

His tract, *Die Sonderbare Krafft Christi, die Heucheley zu entdecken* (1737), did not name Dargun or cite either Zachariae's or Ehrenpfort's writings by name, but no one could miss the target of Russmeyer's criticisms. The main part of the text criticized the potential for self-deception and hypocrisy in contemporary Christianity. Too many nominal Christians cultivated the appearance of godliness, he argued, but often they, like the scribes and Pharisees of the New Testament, lacked true piety. His criticisms were wide-ranging, but he made it clear that people who overemphasized the necessity for conversion and entertained an assurance that they belonged to the "converted" stood in danger of hypocrisy. Just in case someone happened to miss the message, he made the charge bitingly clear in his appendix. Without naming names, he included a scathing criticism of the practices associated with Dargun. He quoted an anonymous report by court physician Hempel, who, Russmeyer assured the reader, was "no enemy of the aforementioned preachers" but nonetheless was deeply troubled by some of their practices.⁹⁰

Russmeyer did not categorically object to the *Bußkampf*. Showing his Pietist roots, he revealed that he had undergone just such a conversion: "I myself have experienced this path, but it never occurred to me that it should be a universal path for all conversions and that whoever follows this is converted. The wisdom of God is manifold." Russmeyer objected to the rigidity with which the conversionist clergy employed the *Bußkampf*. He cited cases in which these clergy had allegedly judged previous conversions too superficial because the seemingly converted "had run through the *Bußkampf* too quickly and were counseled that they should start from the beginning again."[91] Russmeyer objected that neither the Bible nor the confessions required a *Bußkampf*—on this matter some of the orthodox critics were right—but he wanted not so much to discredit conversion experiences as to recognize their diversity, a point on which he quoted from the writing of August Hermann Francke.[92] Russmeyer acknowledged that an extended *Bußkampf* was possible, but he disliked—indeed, deplored—the schematization of the conversion process that he saw in Dargun, which included not only an extensive *Bußkampf* but also a sensible breakthrough to "joyfulness in faith" and a "love kiss of Jesus" that seals one's rebirth.[93] Even these teachings he did not reject out of hand, but he feared that the rigidity and lack of scriptural warrant portended perfectionism, neglect of the doctrine of baptism, and even enthusiasm.[94] Russmeyer feared further that the notions prevalent at Dargun might lead some people to falsely believe themselves to be converted and others, perhaps truly converted, to despair of God's grace. Russmeyer affirmed some of Burgmann's criticisms, but he kept his distance from other orthodox complaints about the Dargun party.[95]

Russmeyer's publication drew an indignant response from Dargun,[96] but other Pietists also found the Dargun movement problematic. In an unpublished opinion in 1737, the theology faculty at Halle affirmed the *Bußkampf* as in keeping with scripture and the Lutheran confessions, but they explicitly did not interpret it in a temporal sense, rejecting the idea that a long *Bußkampf* necessarily ensured a true conversion.[97] An anonymous treatise by one of Gotthilf August Francke's allies appeared in 1738 and sought to mediate but also took issue with the schematic understanding of the *Bußkampf*.[98] We know from correspondence that Francke worried about the public dispute between Russmeyer and the Dargun clergy, and as the controversy intensified, he became exasperated with the intransigence of the "friends in Dargun."[99] Through an intermediary, Francke sought to have Count Christian Ernst of Wernigerode intercede with Zachariae to quell the controversy.[100]

Others with more radical Pietist roots also took issue with Zachariae. Hellwig, dismissed from his position at court and criticized in print by the Dargun clergy, published his own exposé, in which he argued that the obsession with the *Bußkampf* bordered on the magical and suggested works righteousness.[101] This earned him a blistering reply from Dargun that attacked his orthodoxy.[102] Other moderate Pietists such as the Halle-educated Stieber, who also was ousted from his position at court, continued to voice criticisms in public and in private about the events in Dargun.[103]

Dargun gave rise to dozens of polemical publications in the 1730s and 1740s, and their breadth illustrates that this was no simple conflict between

"Pietists" and "orthodox." It was also a controversy within Pietism about divergent understandings of the *Bußkampf*. Nor can it be cast as a break between Hallensian and other forms of Pietism. Pietists on both sides could cite August Hermann Francke in support of their opinion. One could argue that Russmeyer was closer to Halle than was Zachariae, who had few personal connections to Gotthilf August Francke or others there.

Certainly, some orthodox opponents skillfully exploited the divisions between Pietists. Erdmann Neumeister, a Lutheran minister in Hamburg and one of the most adept anti-Pietist publicists of the 1730s, showed almost palpable glee in his preface to Hempel's account of the revival at Dargun.[104] Neumeister was probably the informant who kept the *Hamburgische Berichte* well supplied with stories critical of the Dargun conversionists. Indeed, Hempel, the former court physician, designated the publication of his report as a Judas trick.[105] Neumeister drew also on Pietist critiques of Dargun, a reminder that its schematic conversionist theology also offended even clergy and others with ties to Halle. In contrast, the orthodox in Mecklenburg showed little sophistication in dealing with the Dargun Pietists.[106]

The Continuing Revival in Dargun

Despite the controversy and occasional interference by the consistory, Zachariae and the others were able to continue their revivalist activities in Dargun. Augusta never wavered in her support, and her protection meant a great deal. The Mecklenburg consistory in Rostock cited Ehrenpfort, Hövet, and Schmidt to appear before it again in 1737, and the consistory secured an opinion against them from Leipzig. Nevertheless, the attempt to sanction the Dargun clergy turned into a fiasco. Augusta contested the procedure in the *Hofgericht* in Güstrow, which ruled in her favor. The Dargun Pietists elicited favorable judgments from the theological faculty of the University of Königsberg and the law faculty of the University of Frankfurt. Moreover, Augusta put Duke Carl Leopold, who continued to wield some authority in religious matters, and his brother Duke Christian Ludwig in Schwerin, under internal and external pressure to rule in favor of the Dargun party.[107] Both Christian VI of Denmark and Friedrich Wilhelm I of Brandenburg-Prussia weighed in on behalf of the Dargun clergy and criticized their treatment by the consistory.[108] Lacking both strong intellectual leadership and political support in Mecklenburg, the consistory effectively capitulated and dropped the matter.[109] Its failure illustrates the weakness of the territorial church in Mecklenburg that allowed Augusta and her clergy to pursue their revival.

Amid opposition from many quarters in the late 1730s, Zachariae and his colleagues continued the revival with little interference. The opponents in Jördenstorf kept Augusta from installing Pietist clergy from outside Mecklenburg in additional parishes, at least temporarily, but she filled other positions in the area around Dargun with loyal Pietists.[110] In the summer of 1736, for instance, Zachariae sought the recommendation of a *Hofkantor* from Count Christian Ernst, bringing to Dargun the Halle-trained Jacob Rudolph, who became a mainstay among the Pietists at court.[111] As *Pagenhofmeister* she also installed a Pietist theological student, Ludolph Balthasar Leonhardt, whom she later placed in a pastorate.

The Mecklenburg opponents of Dargun may have overplayed their hand. In a report from the court of Schwerin in late 1736, one commentator observed, "The *Politici* are too intelligent and do not believe everything blindly about which the wicked preachers gossip; rather, they have come to recognize the source from which this sort of thing comes. I can assure you that at this court, almost no one pays attention to it." The comment made it clear that that several members of the court, including the heir to the duchy, had visited Dargun and come away impressed.[112]

Augusta and her allies also began to find supporters among the native clergy, who were put off by the intemperate and wild accusations from the opposition. Laurentz Henrich Berner, pastor from nearby Cammin, had led the delegation at the abortive pastoral election in Jördenstorf, where he was badly beaten by the mob. Although initially suspicious of the "new preachers" in Dargun, he became curious when he heard that "they lived just as they preached." After the violence in Jördenstorf he gave them full-fledged support, reporting that the blows he received "freed him from human fear" and led to his full conversion and a sense of peace in God.[113] He subsequently became such an ardent advocate of the conversionist theology that his parish complained to the consistory.[114] Like Berner, other Mecklenburg clergy also overcame their reservations and aligned themselves with the Dargun movement, sometimes following a conversion experience.[115] Across the border in the towns of Demmin and Anklam, both part of Prussian-controlled Pomerania, the Dargun preachers had allies as well.[116]

The revival in Dargun and surrounding villages expanded during the later 1730s despite the continuing print controversy and the stubborn opposition from some of the orthodox clergy in Mecklenburg. One visitor from Wernigerode at the end of the 1730s reported that 40 of the 150 members of the *Hofgemeinde*, the court parish, belonged to the converted. Nearby parishes also had substantial numbers of converted *Kinder Gottes* (children of God). Converts in the nearby village parishes of Levin, Röckenitz, and Groß Methling were fewer, but the number was "growing daily."[117] The visitor also noticed a high number of converts on the estates of nobles associated with the Dargun, citing one case in which only one of twenty domestic servants remained unconverted. Even most of the field hands belonged to the circle of the converted.[118]

Constructing Conversion at Dargun

A collection of conversion narratives from 1741 provides a glimpse into the ways that conversion was understood at Dargun in the late 1730s and early 1740s. A lively exchange between Dargun and the court of Wernigerode led a visitor from the Harz in late 1741 to compile a series of forty-two accounts that he—or more likely she—gleaned from conversations with converts.[119] Most of the narratives were only a paragraph or so, though a few were longer, especially those describing the piety of the highborn, including Duchess Augusta. The collection comprised twenty-six accounts of women, sixteen of men, from Dargun and the adjoining areas. They ranged from simple coachmen to Augusta's *Hofmeister*, von Moltzahn. All portrayed a dramatic episode or period of struggle that led to a successful conversion. Written in the third person and notably condensed, these are hardly transcripts of conversations, but they do have the character of stories recounted to the visitor; furthermore, the author occasionally refers to details told "to me."[120] These accounts signal an expectation at Dargun that the "converted" be able to tell the story of their conversion. At one point, the author marveled at how a thirteen- or fourteen-year-old boy could "recount his conversion so accurately, how he had been awakened, what happened to him in repentance, and in what way he came to peace," though she recorded little of his narrative.[121] Other visitors at this time noted the readiness of converts in Dargun to tell their story.[122]

In contrast to many of the accounts in Henckel's *Letzte Stunden* or periodicals like the *Sammlung auserlesener Materien*, the perspective of death did not predominate; rather, they represent a more immediate point of view focusing on the process of conversion itself.[123] They tell little about the converts' life before or after their conversion. In these accounts, conversion begins with an *Erweckung* (awakening). Elsewhere in German Pietism, *Erweckung* can sometimes be a synonym for conversion, but here it refers to the initial stirrings (*Rührungen*) in which the process begins. The author refers, for instance, to a cook's wife who was "awakened" first in Stettin but whose conversion was only completed in Dargun when she "came to peace."[124]

After awakening, most of the converts entered a difficult period of repentance and struggle. Here, the author does not employ the term *Bußkampf*, but *Anfechtung*, struggle, and repentance are all features of this stage. At times, the author describes this middle step in great detail, as (s)he does with the story of von Moltzahn, brother of Augusta's *Hofmeister* and later an advocate of Dargun's style of revivalism. The sermons he heard in Dargun "penetrated to his core," and although several times he nearly reached his goal, these promising starts and their "sweet sensations" seemed to evaporate quickly. Finally, following an emotional prayer session with his household tutor, he retired to his room. Falling on his knees and praising God for his grace, he then "stood up, confessed the hymn 'die sanfte Bewegung, die liebliche [Kraft],' and thereupon he received seal upon seal that he was an heir of God and had the forgiveness of all his sins."[125] This breakthrough marks the last step of the conversion process.

Throughout the accounts, converts cited sermons, hymns, Bible passages, and conventicle sessions as the occasions or triggers of their experiences. The author described a woman at court who "had long sought her righteousness," but upon hearing Schmidt preach twice she saw "her own condition vividly depicted" and it propelled her into a crisis:

> God blessed her, though, in that she entered into a truly salutary bowing down and a great work in her soul. She did not flag in her struggling, begging, and beseeching until she was truthfully and lively convinced of the grace of God. Since she endured, as if she had lain in true fear of hell, God blessed her with a verse from an old, beautiful hymn of penitence, where among other phrases appears "and when the entire host of hell would completely devour me."[126] At this point, as a lowly worm, she grasped Christ in his righteousness and poured herself into it. Since then all distress disappeared. She enjoys the peace of God and does not know how she can praise God enough for all the goodness and blessing that he has presented to her.[127]

Whereas the sermon in this instance launched the process of repentance and conversion, elsewhere a sermon could provide the final impulse to a breakthrough. Lady von Örtzen had begun her conversion many years before in Halle, but not until she came to Dargun and heard Zachariae's sermon did she realize her full conversion. In other cases, Bible verses were pivotal. Several narrators cited Matthew 11:28–29, "Come to me, all you that are weary and are carrying heavy burdens, and I will give you rest. Take my yoke upon you, and learn from me; for I am gentle and humble in heart, and you will find rest for your souls." Others drew randomly from the Pietist *Sprüchkästchen* that contained Bible passages and short remarks designed to facilitate full conversion.[128]

The purpose of this collection is not entirely clear. Given the specific details about highborn individuals and the rather clumsy prose, print publication was unlikely. The author might have intended the accounts as demonstrations of the growth of the "Kingdom of God" and compiled them for edification within the closed networks of Pietists associated with Dargun and Wernigerode. The numbering of the accounts and the precise enumeration of the ones related to the Dargun movement elsewhere suggests not merely an interest in individual stories but in the collective movement. Clearly converts from coachmen to court officials in the region were practiced in telling the details of their conversion, though there does not appear to be a strong tradition of written autobiography, even among the literate.[129]

Most of the more extensive conversion narratives stem from the hand of the Pietist clergy in Dargun, who circulated them to allies in Wernigerode. Sometimes these appeared as parts of letters, other times as separately composed conversion accounts. One example is the story of a cowherd, whose account Zachariae composed and sent to Wernigerode in 1740.[130] This was, however, not a transcript of the cowherd's own words, as some other narratives claimed to be, but a carefully structured account that quoted from the cowherd freely but also portrayed his conversion as paradigmatic for the Dargun movement.

Written from Zachariae's perspective, the account opens with the cowherd's arrival at Zachariae's house from a village several days' journey from Dargun. He sought to meet Zachariae. Initially, the court preacher was skeptical and refused to see him, but the cowherd persisted; after several others vouched for his earnestness, Zachariae agreed to meet him. After asking him to state his reason for coming, Zachariae recorded this conversation as part of the narrative:

> COWHERD: I came here and must convert myself to God—otherwise, I cannot be saved.
>
> ZACHARIAE: How did you arrive at that? You are certainly baptized, and baptism is powerful. Isn't that true?
>
> COWHERD: Yes. But we live so godlessly, and in this way we cannot become saved.
>
> ZACHARIAE: You would, of course, have your pastor in the community who can reveal to you the condition of your soul.
>
> COWHERD: Among us, they are all godless. They swear and curse.

> ZACHARIAE: You certainly have the Bible. We know of no other conversion than that which is in the Bible.
> COWHERD: I cannot read.
> ZACHARIAE: Conversion is a divine work of grace and we cannot give it to you. You must request it from God. God would find you in your community just as he would find you here, for God is tied to no place.
> COWHERD: I have asked God day and night. Yet I do not know how.
> ZACHARIAE: Do you have no faith?
> COWHERD: No. I have no faith.

Zachariae took the opportunity to explain the distinction between understanding the true doctrine of faith and having faith in one's in heart, and began instructing the cowherd in the "order of salvation." He praised the Lutheran Church for its true doctrine but stressed that a living faith "must be effected in our hearts." Testing him again for ulterior motives, he questioned the cowherd further:

> ZACHARIAE: Are you perhaps searching only for alms? Do you otherwise have worldly intentions?
> COWHERD: No. I have my own bread and I am satisfied with it.[131]

The cowherd repeated over and over again, "I must convert myself; otherwise I will not become saved!" Finally convinced of his earnest intent, Zachariae continued to instruct him about the order of salvation and how to ask God to help him recognize "his miserable sinfulness, because otherwise he could not attain true repentance." Though the cowherd could repeat little more than "Dear Jesus have mercy on me. Dear Jesus help me. Dear Jesus convert me. Dear Jesus show me my sinfulness," Zachariae noted that he could see positive steps in the young man and urged him to attend the regular church service the next morning, where one of his colleagues was preaching. Impatient, the cowherd hoped that he could be "finished" and return on his long journey home, whereupon Zachariae responded, "My friend, conversion does not work like shoeing a horse, so that when you give it a pair of horseshoes it can run off." The court preacher sent him to some pious members of the community to lodge for the night und urged him to hear the sermon the next morning.[132]

According to Zachariae, the next day's sermon had a powerful effect on the cowherd. He was moved to tears and exclaimed that he had "never heard such a sermon" before and wondered whether it was possible that anyone would remain unconverted in Dargun with such preaching. In the afternoon he visited Zachariae again and announced, "God has forgiven my sins. This has never happened to me before. In the room where I slept, I prayed, and during my prayer it was as if God spoke directly to my heart telling me that all my sins were for forgiven. I am very happy. Now I know that I will be saved when I die. Yesterday I was still a sinner and did not know it. Now I want to take communion." At first, Zachariae professed not to trust the suddenness of his conversion and questioned him about the depth of his repentance and the state of his faith. Others also probed the extent of his distress, clearly worried that the young man had not experienced a thorough *Bußkampf*. One of them asked him "whether he had experienced the distress of sin in his heart." The cowherd responded that it indeed had felt "as if two millstones lay upon his heart." The questioner continued, "So the distress of sins was in fact a great distress?" He responded, "O yes! Sometimes it appeared as if it were gone but then it appeared again." The individual continued and asked about the current state of his heart and whether he still felt distress. The cowherd replied, "No, for my sins are forgiven; it is as if the stones have fallen from my heart." He added, "Now I know with certainty that I will die saved." His questioner pressed further "whether he would have died saved before." The cowherd responded, "O no!" Another asked, "What did he contribute?" He responded, "I contributed nothing, but I have gotten something." When asked what that was, he responded, "I have gotten my salvation."[133] The probing questions of Zachariae and others, almost an interrogation, continue at length in the narrative, but the cowherd's responses proved to be satisfactory.

Having established the certainty of the man's conversion, the narrative recounts the hostility and ridicule he had felt in his village from friends, family, and even his pastor, and it describes his remarkable, providential trip to Dargun during the deep winter. After this rapid conversion, he stayed on in Dargun for another five days, during which time he developed an intense desire to learn to read. He began to distinguish his letters and quickly could sound out syllables and words using the Bible and other pious texts. According to Zachariae, he learned to read before leaving Dargun, a skill the cowherd credited to the same grace that granted him conversion. When he left the town, friends gave him a Bible and Arndt's *True Christianity*, and according to Zachariae's postscript, he managed on his return trip to spark a revival in an entire household.[134]

With the exception of the relatively brief *Bußkampf*, the conversion corresponded to the Dargun model. There is no reason to doubt the first-person quotes from the cowherd, but it is evident that Zachariae carefully selected this account to develop in detail and likely also chose statements from the cowherd carefully and selectively. More than the limited insight it gives us into the spiritual life of the cowherd, the structure and form of the account tell us how Zachariae wished to portray a conversion at Dargun. At the beginning, he is questioning, even skeptical, signaling that the Dargun clergy are not driving the young man toward conversion or pressuring him. Moreover, he uses the dialogue to establish his solid Lutheran credentials on baptismal regeneration, adherence to scripture, and the validity of "evangelical Lutheran" doctrine. Against charges that clergy and converts in Dargun teach that one can effect one's own conversion, Zachariae elicited from the cowherd the acknowledgment that one does not bring about conversion by oneself—it comes from God. And although the cowherd is now assured of salvation, Zachariae quotes him as saying, to the pastor's satisfaction, that original sin still inheres in him, thus forestalling any charges of perfectionism. In questioning the cowherd several times about whether he was seeking alms or other gain, Zachariae seemed to be responding to criticisms that the converted at Dargun sought material rewards.

While Zachariae portrays himself and others as wary of quick conversions and initially skeptical about the man's swift progress, the portrayal interprets the unexpected rapidity of the conversion as a sign of God's gracious action. The cowherd's ability to learn to read in an improbably short time also reinforced the miraculous nature of God's work. The account exemplifies, however, some of the implicit tensions in the Dargun revival. Zachariae expected that conversion would normally be arduous and lengthy, but here he met a young man who traveled to Dargun intending to be converted and achieved his goal in less than a day. When Zachariae referred the man to his village pastor, he was, consciously or not, insulating himself from charges that he denigrated other clergy, yet the account also glorifies the powerful preaching of the Dargun clergy and their authority to adjudicate a claim that one had been converted. The young man is told that he cannot bring about conversion himself, but from an outside perspective he made the first step when he chose to go to Dargun. He is also told that God can find him anywhere, suggesting no need for him to come to Dargun, but the account implicitly depicts Dargun as a place where conversion is more likely to happen.

Zachariae carefully composed—or perhaps better, constructed—the account, but he did not intend to publish it in print. Though the clergy in Dargun engaged in lively polemical exchanges through their tracts and treatises, they published very few conversion accounts and none at all of living persons. Nevertheless, the account of the cowherd did become well known in the circles of Pietists connected to Dargun and Wernigerode. When a court official from Saxon-Saalfeld, Anton Heinrich Walbaum, visited Dargun a year later in 1741, he referred by name to the "cowherd who was converted here some time ago" and clearly had learned of his conversion from correspondence and conversation with people in Wernigerode.[135] These and other accounts circulated widely in manuscript form in Pietist networks, most often through descriptions in letters but also through manuscript narratives.[136]

Manuscript dissemination within closed networks allowed Pietists to exchange conversion narratives that would have been far too sensitive for print publication. For instance, at the request of Gotthilf August Francke, Jacob Rudolph relayed to him the conversion story of the hereditary prince of Mecklenburg, Friedrich (1717–1785).[137] Because he would become the ruler of Mecklenburg-Schwerin, Friedrich's embrace of Pietism encouraged the Pietist clergy who followed such cases closely. As a young man, Friedrich was close to his great aunt, Augusta, and a report from 1736 indicated that the nineteen-year-old had been a frequent visitor to Dargun and held the "friends" there in high regard.[138] But while drawn to the Pietists and their understanding of repentance and conversion, he was unable to shake entirely the vices of dancing and gambling; consequently, some in Dargun doubted, according to Rudolph, whether "he had experienced a true justification."[139] Friedrich's father, Christian Ludwig, strenuously opposed his son's Pietist tendencies, and others at court in Schwerin laughed at Friedrich's pious behavior. Rudolph described a lengthy conversation from late 1743 or early 1744 during a visit to Dargun when the young prince poured out his heart to Carl Friedrich von Moltzahn, the chamberlain. Friedrich explained how just a few weeks before he had experienced "in the enjoyment of Holy Communion" the assurance of God's grace "with divine joy and sweet comfort in his heart." Now, he told von Moltzahn, he understood what one in Dargun meant by "true conversion to Christ" and could say "Ja und Amen" to it all.[140] Beyond this, Friedrich's long discussion with Moltzahn was less a description of conversion than a confession of his adherence to the movement and its ideals, especially the centrality of conversion. Indeed, Friedrich's conversion had significant consequences for Mecklenburg. After becoming ruling duke in 1756, Friedrich "the Pious," as he became known, steered Mecklenburg in an increasingly Pietist direction and ensured that Augusta's legacy continued well into the second half of the eighteenth century.

Compared to the number of manuscript conversion accounts in circulation, the number of print conversion narratives was small. Only two found their way to print between 1735 and Augusta's death in 1756. Like the narratives of Pietists elsewhere in Germany, these published accounts portrayed converts whose death was an integral part of the narrative structure. This stood in contrast to most of the manuscript narratives from Dargun that were composed shortly after the conversion experience while the convert was still living. They rarely included any mention of severe illness or death.

The earliest published conversion narrative from Dargun told the story of a brutal double murderer, Christian Friedrich Ritter, who was sentenced to death by being broken on the wheel in 1738. After sentencing, the clergy in Dargun mounted a veritable crusade to bring Ritter to conversion. Ritter at first angrily mocked the Pietist clergy, but then under their strenuous intervention he progressed from being an incorrigible criminal woefully ignorant of Christian faith to a model for others seeking true conversion. Like the cowherd, Ritter learned to read in nearly miraculous fashion in order to grasp God's Word on his own. He perfectly exemplified the Dargun model. The account culminated in his final breakthrough shortly before the execution to full assurance of forgiveness. He died under the blows of the executioner as a paragon of Christian faith.[141]

The accounts of condemned and then converted criminals were among the most popular published narratives in German Pietism. Ritter's account fits the pattern of these accounts. It was reprinted many times and without doubt was the most widely known conversion narrative from Dargun.[142] Almost certainly written by one of the Dargun preachers, the narrative portrayed their heroic perseverance during the time of Ritter's conversion. The extended length of the narrative allowed sufficient space not only for a vivid depiction of the course of Ritter's conversion but also for showing how the clergy worked within Lutheran confessional assumptions. Consequently, the Ritter account appeared to have had a different audience from that of many of the manuscript conversion accounts, whose function was primarily internal and devotional.

The only other printed narrative from Dargun, in 1747, described the conversion of Zachariae's ten-year-old son and his exemplary death the next year. It was a classic description of the *Bußkampf* in which the young boy agonized about his spiritual state. At one point he felt some joy and confidence in God, but "he did not want to take it as assurance, however, because he had not rightly experienced repentance. Thereupon he felt great distress and fear." Talk about conversion in the parsonage only intensified his despair, especially when his father rejoiced about recent converts in the community. His father's expectations of the *Bußkampf* were daunting. Even as he viewed his son's distress, he remarked that it "remained to be seen" whether he would reach conversion. Eventually, after days of despair, the boy felt a sense of assurance and "true peace in his soul." Members of the household were initially dubious, but the boy was so confident in the gift of grace, asserting "that he would gladly give up his head before he would deny or conceal it," that their doubt turned to celebration.[143] The editor appended an account of his illness and death the next year that reinforced the validity of the boy's conversion. Even when gravely ill and conscious of death's approach, the boy remained sure, according to the narrative, of his faith and his desire to be united with Christ.[144]

Modern readers find disturbingly coercive elements in both of these accounts. Wilhelmi describes the young Zachariae's conversion as indicative of the "the entire monstrosity of the *Bußkampf.*"[145] These two published accounts are much more emotionally fraught and dramatic than most manuscript accounts. Whether they give much insight into the spiritual lives of the two protagonists may be doubtful, but both nonetheless present ideal types of conversion in Dargun during the 1730s and 1740s. They reveal a great deal about the expectations at Dargun and the ways the Pietists there wanted conversion to be understood by others.

Whereas prior to the 1730s dramatic conversion experiences were relatively unknown in Mecklenburg, by the mid-1740s the Pietists in Dargun could claim some success in bringing about a broader acceptance of conversion. They could count not only the ducal heir but also a number of native clergy among their adherents. Yet conversion experiences remained both controversial theologically and tainted with elements of magic even among the pastors and the ducal government.

Beatus and Late Opposition to Conversion

The conversion efforts of a cantor in the town of Malchin not far from Dargun illustrate the continuing potential for magical interpretations, which could have tragic consequences. Small groups of Pietist adherents appeared in several areas of Mecklenburg in the 1740s, including Malchin, where in 1743 a woman in jail awaited her imminent execution. Possibly inspired by the story of Christian Friedrich Ritter's conversion in Dargun, the cantor of the main church, Wilhelm Wolrath Beatus, visited her regularly. Shortly before her scheduled execution she expressed a sense of repentance, accepted Jesus Christ, and exhibited a "miraculous joyfulness" about her coming death. On the day scheduled for her execution, "she admitted everything freely and expressed her desire to die."[146] For unrelated reasons, however, her execution was delayed, which drew the displeasure of the townspeople, who suspected that her recent conversion influenced the postponement, and they blamed the cantor for the delay. He continued to visit her, asking her to meditate on the hymn "Mein Heyland nimmt die Sünder an" in order to sustain her conversion, and he gave her a slip of paper with the lyrics written on it.[147] According to Rudolph, the ebullient praise emanating from the cell during meetings with the cantor aroused more suspicion, and one of the guards now claimed to have seen the cantor hand her a piece of paper that she supposedly ate. As a result, the authorities banned Beatus from further visits.

The authorities executed the woman, but things took a turn for the worse for Beatus when Friedrich Wilhelm Crüger, senior pastor in Malchin, produced a young woman who claimed that Beatus had once forced her to pray before certain paintings in his house, denied the baptismal covenant (i.e., baptismal regeneration), and surreptitiously snuck a piece of paper with magical words into her buttered bread, which had caused her to become nauseated. Pastor Crüger called for an investigation of the cantor by the ducal authorities.[148] Beatus was arrested and taken to Duke Carl Leopold's residence in Dömitz, where he heard the charges the young woman had made and was interrogated about the practice of eating slips of paper as well as other suspicious practices in Pietist conventicles, including allegations of sexual impropriety.[149] Shortly thereafter, the ducal authorities arrested three more members of his Pietist circle in Malchin, one young man and two young women, and brought them to Dömitz. When Beatus did not confess, his interrogators tortured him, but he still refused to admit guilt. After outside legal opinions finally arrived in favor of the cantor, the imprisoned Pietists were released.[150]

The failed case proved embarrassing for Carl Leopold. As a result of the accusations, Beatus had lost his position in Malchin, and the torture left his hands crippled.[151] Remorseful, Leopold granted Beatus a monthly stipend and later appointed him rector of the school in Dömitz.[152] Rudolph wrote later that the incident was widely known in Mecklenburg.[153] The open ridicule of Carl Leopold even appeared in a satiric Low German poem.[154] Popular stories about the torture circulated well into the next century.[155]

Beatus's case brings into focus many of the superstitious rumors that surrounded conversion in Dargun. In the 1740s, the most prevalent appear to be allegations of *Zettelfressen*. There is no question that certain devotional practices among Pietists in Mecklenburg involved slips of paper, such as Bogatzky's *Schatzkästlein*. Rudolph describes his own use of rolled-up slips of paper with Bible verses printed on them. At prayer meetings, he would dump these from a tea tin onto the table. Participants then drew them at random and looked up the corresponding passages in the Bible, though Rudolph acknowledged that rumors were so widespread that when some new participants saw the slips of paper, they feared at first they would have to eat them.[156]

In Mecklenburg, some rumors alleged attempts to convert the unsuspecting by sneaking a piece of paper with magical words into their bread and butter.[157]

Accusations of *Zettelfressen* among Pietists date back to at least the early 1700s and continued periodically throughout the eighteenth century.[158] It is not difficult to imagine that non-Pietists might conflate unfamiliar Pietist devotional practices with older folk traditions such as giving animals pieces of paper to eat in order to protect them.[159] Some of the stories had a fantastical nature. One told of a young man who received a piece of paper from a Pietist in Mecklenburg, but instead of swallowing it as instructed, he kept it hidden in his mouth to examine later. When he put it in his hand, it turned into a toad and hopped away.[160] It is difficult to judge whether Crüger, the anti-Pietist pastor in Malchin, believed the plausibility of such rumors or just capitalized on them to attack Pietists. Certainly, Carl Leopold and his learned jurist, Gottfried Rudolf Ditmar, took the charges of *Zettelfressen* seriously enough to arrest Beatus and others and to torture Beatus.

The debacle of Malchin further injured Carl Leopold's reputation, but it also brought into disrepute some of the wilder charges made against Dargun. Occasionally allegations resurfaced of a *Quacker-Pulver*. In 1747, the credulous *Geheimrat* Ditmar recorded another case of a girl who claimed that two spinster women in Wismar had sought to convert her to the "Dargun faith" by hiding a black powder in her buttered bread.[161] This appears to be one of the last allegations of this sort that the Mecklenburg authorities took seriously.

Consolidation?

By 1747, revivals and conversions were no longer such unusual events in Mecklenburg. When the long-term pastor from the town of Sternberg, David Franck, reported to his superintendent on the recent revival in his parish, he showed little defensiveness, putting it in continuity with his three decades of pastoral experience in the town. This was a marked change from the wild accusations that surrounded the first revivals a dozen years earlier.[162] By no means did Augusta and her Pietist clergy succeed in winning the allegiance of a majority of the clergy in Mecklenburg, but gradually they accumulated more and more support within the territorial church. In letters to fellow Pietists, the Darguner enumerated the names of Mecklenburg clergy who had "been converted in office" and chose to ally themselves with the Pietists.[163] The Pietists also elevated "converted" candidates to preaching and administrative positions within their sphere of influence. After violent opposition had thwarted the election of her candidates in Jördenstorf in 1738, Augusta left the pastorate unfilled until 1748, when she finally succeeded in nominating three "believing candidates" of her choosing, ensuring that Jördenstorf would receive a Pietist minister.[164] Opposition never disappeared entirely in the duchy, but as Schmaltz notes, by the late 1740s the consistory lost any desire to interfere in most matters, especially in ministerial appointments.[165]

On her deathbed in 1756, Duchess Augusta noted with delight and many tears that God had granted her the opportunity to witness the election of Leopold Flörke in Altkalen. She must have seen it as a triumph that a young man with close ties to the Dargun movement had replaced Joachim Friedrich Sarcander, who from the earliest days of the revival had been one of the movement's most implacable foes.[166] Augusta also expressed pleasure that her former *Pagenhofmeister* Christian Buk had become pastor in the town of Schwaan after Pietists at court in Schwerin had engineered the removal of his chief rival from consideration.[167] With her death, the court of Dargun came to an end—and with it the duchy's most ardent center of Pietism. Her sustained efforts over two decades played no small role in the long-term success of Pietism within Mecklenburg during the mid-eighteenth century.

Pietists always remained a minority, but with the conversion of the ducal heir they gained a powerful advocate in Mecklenburg, and after his father's death in 1756, Friedrich the Pious, as he became known, sought to take the duchy in a Pietist direction, continuing Augusta's legacy. When the University of Rostock resisted his appointment of the Pietist theologian Christian Albrecht Döderlein and his control more generally, Friedrich secured a charter and established the University of Bützow along Pietist lines in 1760 with Döderlein as its first rector.[168] Modeled on Halle, the University of Bützow and its *Pädagogium* never lived up to its expectations, yet during Friedrich's reign it influenced the training of clergy for Mecklenburg until his successor reunited it with the University of Rostock in 1789.

Conclusion

Why did the movement in Dargun succeed in a territory with a long history of opposition to Pietism? First, the instability of Mecklenburg's government during the reign of Carl Leopold (1713–47) left the territorial church severely weakened. Removed from most ducal authority in 1719, Carl Leopold retained much control over religion in the duchy. The clergy remained doggedly loyal to him despite his own religious inconstancy, flirting as he did with both

Catholicism and radical Protestantism. The movement did not lack for opponents—whether they were capable is another matter—but it is striking how little leverage the duchy's superintendents or consistory, despite their misgivings, could exercise over Augusta's new clergy. The decline of the university in Rostock, particularly the reduced prominence of the theology faculty, left the duchy without authoritative voices to counter Dargun's understanding of conversion. Outbursts such as the one at Jördenstorf in 1738 may have signaled deep resistance to elements of the Pietist program, but the failure to carry out an election that Carl Leopold had approved only underscored the weakness of the territorial church during this period.

Second, Augusta's successes illustrate the changes in religious practice that someone in her position could put in place. For more than two decades, she exploited the weakness of the territorial church and pushed through Pietist reforms. When she encountered resistance, she skillfully drew on her connections to some of Europe's rulers to support her, including Christian VI of Denmark and Friedrich Wilhelm I of Brandenburg-Prussia, who intervened on her behalf with the duchy's consistory. Internally, Augusta took advantage of her patronage rights in the parishes under her control to seek candidates who fulfilled her expectations. As with Schmidt, Ehrenpfort, and Zachariae, she imported candidates from other parts of Germany but also promoted clergy from Mecklenburg who affirmed her Pietist agenda. At the parish level, her triumphs show how a powerful patron could manipulate the tradition of clerical election in Mecklenburg to install favored candidates.

Augusta's efforts went beyond simply appointing favored candidates. She also devoted resources to creating a more intense religious culture in the parishes under her control. In many villages, she installed teachers with Pietist credentials and showed her favor by supplementing their salaries. A report from 1739 tells us that of twelve local schoolmasters, the duchess had appointed six "believing" Christians and built houses for some of them. In other cases, where she "couldn't get rid of the old unconverted" schoolmasters, she appointed her favored teachers alongside them and simply paid the additional salary.[169] Overall, Augusta increased the availability of teachers and improved and quality of instruction in the schools around Dargun, even as a chief aim remained religious edification.[170]

Augusta showered advantages on her chosen clergy. Non-pastoral burdens on the rural clergy in the eighteenth century were considerable, and her financial support allowed them to devote more of their time to their pastoral duties. In one village parish, known for its destitution, she offered her new preacher a salary supplement of 150 Reichstaler at time when the salary of a Rostock professor amounted to 200 Reichstaler—a remarkable contrast to the typical remuneration of the rural clergy. In addition to providing increased salaries, she built parsonages and sometimes even provided fine carriages and horses.[171] These financial advantages allowed the clergy to devote more time to their work in the parishes and at court. Many of the Pietist clergy from outlying areas preached during weekly services in the court chapel, and others led prayer meetings at court as well as in their parishes. The clergy supported by Augusta had the means to hire theology students as tutors and assistants in their far-flung parishes. In a letter to G. A. Francke, Schmidt describes how in one parish village a theology student sparked a revival.[172] These committed theological students would have reinforced the revival in and around Dargun, just as the rich regimen of prayer meetings, preaching, and other church services all contributed to an intensive form of religious culture.

Third, amid these conditions, the Dargun clergy applied a form of conversion-oriented Pietism that fit the demands of rural parishes and especially the *Hofgemeinde*. The introduction of conversion strategies focused on the *Bußkampf* marked an abrupt departure from previous practice in Mecklenburg and at first drew opposition from many quarters, especially the established clergy. And while these "new measures" also sparked distrust and division, stimulating rumors about *Quacker-Pulver* and other magical deceptions, they also succeeded in introducing new ways of framing religious experience in Mecklenburg and making this form of conversion an accepted part of religious life. Their adherents persisted as a minority among both the clergy and laity in Dargun, though they wielded real influence on the parishes.

One reason for their success was their ability to tie their Pietist beliefs to other practices of the church. They valued clerical leadership, and as the examples of Ritter and the cowherd show us, the clergy were both agents and judges of conversion, often deciding when a *Bußkampf* had been sufficient or a testimony of assurance justified. These clergy wove conversion into the confessional structures of the Lutheran Church in Mecklenburg. Preaching, communion, and hymnody permeated the conversion narratives. Especially after Zachariae arrived in 1735, the Dargun Pietists drove out ideas they considered heterodox or unfriendly to their cause. Their opponents accused them of sectarianism, but the Dargun Pietists saw themselves as orthodox Lutherans who strengthened rather than weakened a confessional church.

These successes of Dargun Pietism reveal, further, that a single-minded emphasis on conversion and the *Bußkampf* remained controversial in German Pietism, even in circles related to G. A. Francke and Hallensian Pietism. The rigid schema of conversion in Dargun divided Pietist from Pietist as much as it did the Pietist from the Lutheran orthodox laity and clergy. Few would have been opposed to conversion as a general category of religious experience, but the new Dargun model, deploying concepts drawn from A. H. Francke and especially Samuel Lau, drew stiff opposition. While their orthodox opponents in Mecklenburg discredited the Pietists as dupes or agents of fanaticism, superstition, and even magic, moderate Pietists like Russmeyer excoriated the Darguner for their inflexibility and divisiveness, but the critics could not undo what the Dargun Pietists had begun. Dargun stands as a testimony to both the divisiveness and the power of a conversionist piety in an eighteenth-century German duchy.

7

EXECUTION NARRATIVES

Conversion experiences of condemned criminals became the most popular form of published conversion narratives in the eighteenth-century German Pietist movement. Combining vivid descriptions of crimes with edifying tales of redemption, these accounts were particularly popular in the 1730s through the 1760s. Pietists published them in pamphlets, reprinted them in periodicals, and then anthologized the narratives into collections arranged by criminal category.[1] There, pious Christians could read tales of wicked acts and vicious criminals who would yet find otherworldly redemption in a glorious conversion. In some respects, these are curiosities—often with a grisly tinge. They are exceptional stories of conversion but also significant for what they tell us about conversion narratives and about larger patterns of authorial practice. With their narration by a third person, the Pietist clergy as converting agents, clear schematic patterns of conversion, and death as their centerpiece—an event that conveniently precludes relapse—they illustrate the development of Pietist conversion narratives in the eighteenth century, sometimes to the point of caricature. Some critics even alleged that such stories became an inducement to suicide by proxy.[2] Perhaps more than any other genre of conversion narratives, they raise acute problems of authenticity and subjectivity in the interpretation of experience. As vivid depictions of conversion they became widely popular, but their publishing success also may have brought about their demise because they discredited the "drama of conversion" in the later eighteenth century as tastes changed and criticisms abounded.[3]

Pamphlets describing the conviction and execution of criminals have a long history apart from Pietism, and often included statements of regret and repentance prior to the execution. One aim of the descriptions was to secure the criminal's recognition that the conviction and sentence had been just, an aim facilitated by the involvement of the clergy.[4] Clerical manuals outlined how the local clergy should visit the prisoners in jail in order to encourage their repentance and conversion but also for them to admit their culpability.[5] In most jurisdictions in Germany, the clergy also took part in the executions themselves, walking with the condemned to the gallows and praying and comforting them up to the moment of execution, sometimes attending to them throughout the gruesome process.[6] Engravings of executions often portrayed the presence of the clergy prominently (see figure 1).

In especially notorious cases, the printing of pamphlets was driven by the public's interest in the cases and printers' desire to make a profit.[7] The condemned often spent weeks and sometimes months imprisoned while the authorities sought outside legal opinions to confirm the judgment and manner of execution.[8] During this time, the clergy often labored with prisoners to induce conversion, access that afforded a vantage point for composing such accounts. Some, like Andreas Schmid, pastor in Berlin, composed journalistic accounts of the crime, trial, and execution, describing the twists and turns as evidence came to light and confessions emerged. Often they recorded statements of repentance and conversion, though these did not necessarily form the core of the narrative.[9] Several accounts in the early eighteenth century revealed the regret and repentance of the condemned through verses they ostensibly composed.[10] Song frequently accompanied the executions both as expressions of regret and as popular comment on the process.[11]

The clerical manuals instructed the clergy to secure repentance before exhorting the condemned to undergo conversion, and Lutheran theology especially taught that repentance was possible even for the most grievous sins.[12] Often, however, claims of repentance and conversion coming from the prisoners failed to satisfy Pietist expectations. Many—Pietists and non-Pietists alike—could be openly skeptical of such expedient changes of heart, calling them *Galgen-Reu* (gallows regret) or *Schächers-Buße* (robber's repentance).[13] Johann Jacob Moser, the best-known purveyor of execution narratives to the German public, cast doubt on easy conversions in which a prisoner merely "accepts the words of comfort from the preacher, sings and prays along with him, and prior to the execution directs a further lament to God, despite the fact that they who have eyes to see can find nothing that would lead them to conclude that the poor human being has come to a true recognition of God or that his heart has been powerfully touched not to mention changed."[14] He mentioned one narrative that Christian Gerber had circulated widely, charging that it lacked any marks at all of a "righteous conversion."[15]

Frontispiece to Johann Jacob Moser, *Selige letzte Stunden einiger dem zeitlichen Tode übergebener Missethäter* (Leipzig, 1742). Theol.oct.K3687. Württembergische Landesbibliothek, Stuttgart.

Pietists like Moser worried that the seemingly easy repentance in the face of violent death misled the sinful into a false security about their conversion. They believed that the exemplary narrative should demonstrate heartfelt conversion, often through detailed descriptions of the stages of conversion in which a rigorous struggle in repentance (*Bußkampf*) features prominently. The power of the narrative should both inspire the devout and gainsay doubters who questioned the prisoner's sincerity.

Andreas Lepsch

Beginning around 1730, Pietists began to compose such accounts for a larger audience. One early example was an account of the execution of Andreas Lepsch, who had been convicted of bestiality in Potsdam in 1730. The author, Heinrich Schubert, was one of Potsdam's best-known Pietist clergymen. Unlike most later accounts that featured lurid descriptions of the offense, this one includes only the briefest description of the crime, an indication perhaps of its shamefulness. The narrative opens with Schubert visiting the dejected Lepsch, who plainly resented Schubert's arrival at his jail cell as a harbinger of his death.[16] The court had not yet announced the sentence, but Schubert sought to convince Lepsch that execution would be just, for the crime was reprehensible, as the prisoner would have known were he not ignorant of the Bible and the catechism. He cited Leviticus 20:15, which prescribed the death penalty for bestiality and reminded Lepsch him of the condemnation in Deuteronomy: "Cursed be anyone who lies with any animal" (27:21). Schubert's initial strategy might have been to drive Lepsch to regret his predicament more deeply, but the minister also sensed an opening—an emotional "stirring" (*Rührung*) in his Pietist vocabulary—and offered Lepsch an opportunity: "Silently, I praised God for such stirring and closed my interview with a prayer, and asked him then if he would want to follow me, seeing that he must die and his sentence would soon be announced. When he answered with a moving yes, I advised him to throw himself down on his face before the majesty of God often and to pray: Oh God! I am cursed, but have mercy on me!"[17]

Schubert and three of his colleagues then swung into action, visiting him often in both the mornings and the afternoon, pleading for a readiness to accept conversion. They brought him communion, read to him from the Bible, prayed with him, and conducted a kind of short catechetical course to instruct him about the Lutheran path to salvation. In his account of the events Schubert quoted Lepsch liberally, but the narrative voice belonged to

Schubert, who wrote in the first person and framed the account to fit his Pietist view of conversion and redemption.

Schubert chronicled almost day by day Lepsch's progress over the next few weeks. Initially, Lepsch resisted this view of himself as utterly sinful. He never denied his crime, but he tried to defend himself, explaining "that he had never been a fornicator ... he had never allowed drinking to overwhelm him, he had never stolen the smallest thing from anyone, and that he had never been a quarreler nor inclined to cursing." Schubert agreed that others had testified to his normally fine behavior, yet the pastor remonstrated with him that Jesus knew the depravity of his heart better than anyone, reproaching him for his disregard of scripture and the misuse of the Lord's Supper. Faced with this pressure, Lepsch, according to the narrator, "surrendered and broke out in quite moving words, with which he testified that his heart and entire life had been evil. Afterwards, he frequently repeated that his whole life amounted to nothing and he had a fundamentally evil heart, and he added that indeed if he had been able to learn to read and had been better educated in godly words in his youth, it would have been far better for him, for he had grown up like a beast in great blindness and ignorance."[18]

This encounter illustrates that the execution conversion narratives often did not concern themselves with repentance for the crime itself. In many of them, the prisoner admitted to the crime quite easily. The accounts highlighted the "fundamentally evil heart" of all who remained unrepentant and the need to struggle against this condition. The criminal act heightened the narrative arc—and likely also its appeal to readers—but the repentance that these authors sought was not limited to the criminal; they also appealed to a broader audience whose hearts remained unconverted. Moser reproached those who felt themselves superior to these criminals yet remained unconverted: "In God's eyes, they are not one whit better at root than the most terrible Sodomites, murderers, adulterers, and blasphemers; rather, these criminals have only revealed in concrete outbursts that which, following its secret lusts, lies so well concealed in the power of every human heart."[19]

In the rest of the narrative, Schubert recorded the fitful progress that attended Lepsch's pathway toward conversion. As a Pietist might have expected, Lepsch's despair at first deepened as the clergy asked sharp questions that led him to see that nothing he could do, even prayer, had the power to reconcile himself to God. But this was no reason for despair: though he could do nothing, God had pitied the entire world and thus sent his son as redeemer, who in taking on human form and dying had atoned for all sins and reconciled the world to God. Through him alone, Schubert explained, is eternal salvation possible. Here Schubert described one of several turning points, informing the reader that "one could rightly sense how [Lepsch's] anguished and oppressed heart began, as it were, to draw air, and to gain the far-off hope that he, too, would be so fortunate as to have salvation. He was left in silence and told that he should also pray: Oh Lord Jesus, you died for me and have reconciled me with God, oh give me in grace true penitence and true faith."[20]

Schubert did not use the vocabulary of *Bußkampf* and *Durchbruch* that so often appeared in later accounts, but Lepsch's conversion followed a familiar pattern of profound repentance followed by the recognition of grace, though the breakthrough to grace did not occur in a single moment but rather gradually, through a series of steps. The official pronouncement of the death sentence one morning temporarily threw Lepsch in doubt, but Schubert noted that this dismay did not last long. By afternoon, with the aid of his colleagues—whose diligence Schubert praised—Lepsch had once again grasped, in Schubert's words, "that he would quite willingly submit in humility to his punishment and wished for nothing else than that his poor soul might be saved." The final breakthrough came when Lepsch's son visited his father on October 11, and his father remarked that his execution could not come soon enough, because he looked forward to seeing his savior. Though he had earned damnation, the savior had shown him holiness. Schubert concluded that "there one saw and heard with joy in one's heart how his redeemer was everything to him."[21]

Much of the remainder of the account relates the depth of Lepsch's conviction. In a series of questions and answers, the minister probed how Lepsch understood his newly won faith, seeking to show that his understanding of salvation was orthodox and that Lepsch trusted not at all in his own abilities but attributed everything to God's grace. The condemned man became a paragon of lay belief, carefully parsing Schubert's questions—demonstrating to the reader that he was not simply parroting responses—to provide the correct answers, but exhibiting a real and "great hunger" for God's Word and a desire for prayer.

The final act of the narrative came with the execution of the condemned man. Lepsch's crime was so shameful that he was to be burned alive. In none of the execution narratives was the conversion of the condemned seen as a mitigating factor in sentencing. Clergy typically encouraged the prisoners to accept their temporal punishments, just as they did in Lepsch's case. But the spectacle of execution also allowed narrators to demonstrate the depth of the new convert's faith. As the execution neared, Schubert anxiously questioned Lepsch. Finding him in tears the day before the execution, Schubert worried that Lepsch was losing his faith, but the prisoner reassured him that he had no fear and remained confident; the tears were God-given. On the day of execution, Schubert and his colleagues met with him early in the morning, prayed, read scripture, and gave him communion. On the way from jail to the court and from there to the place of execution, Lepsch expressed his certainty and reassured the soldiers guarding him that he would not escape: "I do not want to run away but rather want to die, for the Lord Jesus will not let me go." Even as he was bound and tied to the stake, Lepsch was not outwardly shaken. Schubert called out to him, "Andreas, how are you?" Lepsch responded, "Quite good!" Schubert questioned one last time, asking, "Who has your heart?" to which Lepsch responded, "My heart is with the Lord Jesus." The narrative concluded, "And thus was the pyre ignited and this pardoned sinner went to Christ his savior."[22]

Schubert's account was not the earliest, but in some respects it established a precedent for the Pietist execution narratives that would follow. Narrators partly borrowed from Henckel's *Last Hours*, in which the authors detailed the spiritual condition of the dying, though here execution rather than illness marked the individuals' end.[23] And unlike Henckel's accounts, in which portrayals of conversion varied greatly, the execution stories invariably featured a dramatic conversion experience that epitomized the redemption of an abject sinner and illustrated how even a hardened criminal could repent and find salvation. The intimate retelling of the story of conversion and its wealth of detail—the enumeration of precise days, the effect of particular Bible passages and hymns, and the description of temporary setbacks—lent a verisimilitude to the narratives that aimed to counter suspicions of a feigned conversion. Schubert portrays himself as skeptically probing Lepsch's faith only to be pleasantly surprised at his responses.

Christian Friedrich Ritter

A number of similar execution narratives appeared in the 1730s. One of the best known in the period was that was that of Christian Friedrich Ritter, a brutal double murderer in Dargun, which gained wide circulation. It was also the first published conversion narrative from the Dargun revival.[24] The account begins with the depiction of a wayward upbringing and a criminal past that culminated in a vicious crime near Dargun in 1738. Ritter's account included extended descriptions of the bloody murders themselves, which depicted precisely how Ritter stabbed and slashed at his victims. Ritter is quickly apprehended, tried, and, in accord with a judicial opinion secured from Rostock, sentenced to death by being broken on the wheel.[25]

After sentencing, the Dargun clergy made Ritter's conversion a priority. According to the published account, the four ministers associated with Dargun and two theological students visited him daily. Taken aback by his ignorance of Christian tenets, they first gave him elementary instruction, dividing the articles in the catechism among themselves in order to provide him with an intensive, short course on Lutheran beliefs. At first Ritter resisted; he sold the Bible they had given him and "hardened his heart against grace."[26] Even as they sensed progress, he rejected any need for conversion. Finally, one of the preachers awoke in him the first inklings of "true repentance," and this set him on the pathway of a *Bußkampf* conversion.

Visited frequently by the four ministers and two students, Ritter entered into a period of profound repentance: "He began then to cry out to God in a plain manner, that he might allow him to recognize his sins while still living and grant him true remorse for them." He began a remarkable transformation, leaving behind his old "impudent gestures and frivolous attitude" and expressing a fervent desire for faith. Like others in the throes of conversion whom we have encountered, he hungered for the Word of God so much that he learned to read in a remarkably short period of time. When he showed himself to be ever more devout and zealous in his faith, the duchess allowed him to attend public worship, and the narrator described how in church he would "fall on his knees and beg God fervently for a blessing from his words." He discussed intently Luther's catechism with the Dargun preachers and joyously thanked God "that he had brought him to this place and so faithfully and richly cared for the salvation of soul." Yet, while the narrator marveled at Ritter's praise of God and his ongoing repentance, he also revealed that Ritter had still not achieved complete certainty that God had forgiven his sins.[27]

As the execution neared, Ritter voiced his worry about the absence of certitude in his faith; however, after an evening of intense prayer on his knees pleading with God, he received assurance: "Thus was his soul so richly comforted, that from that point on he could believe with full certainty through the confirming grace of God that God had forgiven him of all his sins, accepted him as his own child in Christ, and made him an heir to eternal life. Here all anxiety, distress, and fear ceased, and his soul was well beyond all measure." With this breakthrough, his conversion was now complete. Ritter could face the horrors of his execution without fear, even speaking of it as his "wedding day," the day he would be united with his savior. Accompanied by the Pietist clergy, Ritter went to the place of execution without wavering and prayed powerfully before the onlookers before dying under the blows of the wheel.[28]

A number of characteristic features in Ritter's story echo Lepsch's account. This is not surprising, because the Dargun clergy reported that they made use of Lepsch's narrative: "At other moments, the heartfelt conversion of Andreas Lepsch, which the dear Pastor Schubert in Potsdam published, was read to him, bit by bit, and discussed with him. Such was so inspiring, that he could not hear or speak with others about it enough."[29] One can see why the execution narrative would have appealed to the Dargun clergy and other Pietists. Here even the most hardened criminal can repent and reach conversion. The narrator described in detail the repentance struggle (Bußkampf) that preceded the execution of the sentence. The final breakthrough portrays the Dargun process of conversion in dramatic fashion. Ritter's constancy, even when faced with an excruciating death, underlined the power of his conversion. Further, the narrative showcases the intervention of the Pietist preachers and the way they bind Ritter's conversion to orthodox Lutheran understandings of scripture and catechism, describing even regular attendance at church, which the manacled prisoner ardently desired. Not least, Ritter's inevitable death at the conclusion provides a finality and certainty to the account that many of the manuscript narratives from Dargun lacked. There is no chance of Ritter relapsing into sinfulness.

The Circulation of Execution Narratives in Published Collections

It is important that the authors of these Pietist execution narratives circulated them to a broader audience. This lent them significance beyond the local community in which they arose, and in several cases they became models of conversion. Lepsch appeared first as a pamphlet in Potsdam in 1730, perhaps in three different editions, and then Schubert appended it to his first collection of sermons, published in Magdeburg in 1733, giving it wider distribution.[30] Ritter's account appeared in pamphlet form in Magdeburg in 1739, and in 1740 the periodical *Verbesserte Sammlung auserlesener Materien* picked it up. In the same year, Moser published both Ritter's and Lepsch's accounts in a collection of execution narratives, titled *Seelige letzte Stunden*.[31] Moser's collection established the execution narrative as a specific genre, distinct from other conversion narratives.[32] It was the first of many editions Moser published, and in the following years several other authors followed suit; by mid-century, these execution narratives constituted the most widely published conversion accounts in the Pietist movement.

In his introduction, Moser defended his view of conversion and stated a rationale for collecting and publishing the accounts. Belonging to the larger genre of thanatography, Moser's book, in contrast to Henckel's, depicted exclusively the "blessed last hours" of condemned criminals. He argued that too many people underestimated the demands of true conversion and misunderstood an insistence on thorough conversion as somehow an instance of Pietist heterodoxy. For Moser, conversion remained a possibility for every person, even those who had committed the most despicable crimes. The power to convert remained in God's hand, of course, but the examples of these redeemed malefactors illustrated the availability of God's grace even to those in the direst of circumstances. Moser went so far as to suggest that "crude sinners" are more open to conversion because they more easily recognize their condition, whereas "he who is not aware of any crude sins that the world punishes, gladly believes that he is already converted and does not want to convert himself."[33] His depiction of "crude sinners" and graphic depictions of their misdeeds doubtless also appealed to a wider reading public.

Moser claimed a dual purpose for his collection. First, he wanted to encourage the civil authorities and the clergy to try to bring prisoners facing execution to heartfelt conversions. Moser worried that far too many nominal Christians comforted themselves with minimal expressions of repentance or a few pious phrases, which fell far short of the change of heart and mind and lively faith in Jesus Christ that salvation requires. His collection provided edifying case studies for the clergy and the condemned that illustrated how true conversions could occur. Second, and more important for the broader reading public, Moser wanted this collection to be an example for ordinary people who felt themselves superior to these "wretches" and yet were not truly converted.[34]

Moser's first collection was modest, comprising only four narratives. He wrote an introduction and reprinted the more extensive narratives of Lepsch and Ritter as well as two briefer stories of murderers, one from Württemberg and one from Denmark, that had not previously appeared in print. Moser's collection must have found a ready audience, for two additional editions appeared in 1742, one in Leipzig and one in Jena. In 1745, he published an edition with several additional accounts. In 1753, he published an expanded version that included thirty-one narratives of both men and women, which was again reprinted in 1767.[35] Others began publishing collections as well, and many other accounts appeared as single pamphlets. In 1752, for instance, Johannes Cleß published a guide to the conversion of "malefactors" that included several condemned conversion narratives, and in 1753, Woltersdorff began the publication of these narratives in a series titled *Schächer am Kreuz* (Thief on the Cross), which went through multiple editions.[36] These became the most frequently published genre of conversion narratives in mid-century

Pietism. The popular account of Ritter appeared in print at least nine times after his death in the eighteenth century, Lepsch's account as many as fourteen. In contrast, Francke's now-paradigmatic conversion narrative appeared once in German in 1733 and not again until late in the eighteenth century. Even if one includes other brief accounts of Francke's conversion, such as the *Kurtze Nachricht*, the contrast is striking.[37]

Moser's anthologies set a precedent for execution narratives in German Pietism. Their intense focus on the process of conversion set them apart from other "gallows literature" of the day.[38] They were not designed to evoke pity in the readers for the plight of these poor wretches. Nor were they really about the wages of sin and the dreadful consequences of crime. Above all, their point was to display the power of repentance and conversion in even the most hardened criminals, an emphasis that could undermine the intended deterrent effect of a public condemnation and execution of criminals.

Moser reveled in accounts that depicted dramatic transformations and reversals. In Ritter's case, the villain who cut off one victim's hand, slashed her in the face, and left her to die is transformed by the time of his execution into an ardent exemplar of faith who met his excruciating death joyfully, likening it to his wedding day.[39] In the case of Anna Regina Töpler, convicted of arson and murder, the account portrays a woman who was incorrigible from childhood and led by Satan to indolence, theft, and harlotry. Twice she tried to burn down her brother's house; she succeeded on the second attempt. Imprisoned for the latter crime, she did not deny her culpability, but initially "she behaved inhumanely, swore horribly, whooped, crowed, sang scandalous songs, roared just like the devil, and acted so dreadfully that one's hair stood on end when one walked by."[40] Even as her execution neared, she drove off the pastor who narrated her account with her foulmouthed retorts and ridicule. Then, as if coming out of a deep sleep, a dramatic change came over her and she began to undergo in a few short days a rapid conversion and transformation into a penitent, converted child of God who joyfully went to her execution, fully expectant of her salvation. She knelt down willingly for the sword "and thus occurred her blessed death with a stroke. Thereupon this sinner, pardoned in the blood of Christ and justified, with the great certainty of her salvation went into eternal glory."[41] Here, as in many other accounts, the crudest of sinners became the exemplar of a penitent and joyful Christian unafraid of death.

Many of the accounts in Moser detail conversion with meticulous attention to temporal sequence, psychological states, and religious feelings. Töpler's relatively swift conversion was not the norm. The longer narratives, especially, depict difficult and fitful moves toward conversion that happened over a matter of weeks and even months. Anne Marthe Hungerland underwent a long imprisonment from her conviction for infanticide to execution, and her "breakthrough" to assurance of her salvation lasted months, because of the "wrestling and struggling" she experienced as Satan sought to throw obstacles in her way. The intimate description of the twists and turns on the path toward conversion was a clear means of countering the charges of skeptics, who saw only a feigned *Schächers-Buße* at work.[42]

The conclusion of all these stories was never in doubt: all led to a conversion followed by an execution. Unlike some of the conversion accounts in periodicals that occasionally portrayed a failed conversion as a warning, all of the accounts in Moser and Woltersdorff were "successful" cases.[43] Moreover, by design, even the most dramatic and edifying cases of conversion inevitably culminated in the subject's death. The writers of these narratives, in fact, saw the hope of pardon as an impediment to successful conversion.[44] Nor did a "successful" conversion, no matter how celebrated, become grounds for commutation of the death sentence, not on the side of the authorities or that of the clergy. The narrators dismissed opponents who suggested that the hope for an easing of the sentence might be the reason for the newfound joyfulness.[45]

Death had been a feature of Pietist accounts of conversion ever since Francke's sermon on von Schönberg and especially Henckel's *Letzte Stunden*. Only from the perspective of death could one judge a conversion aright. In execution narratives, the prospect of death became a central feature of the plot, and almost always the execution at the *Rabenstein* (ravenstone) or gallows constituted a high point.[46] No doubt, as Kurt Tucholsky mordantly commented a hundred years ago, part of the popular appeal of these narratives was the pathos of the last moments.[47] For the Pietists, the trials of impending death and execution became final warrants for the validity of the conversion.

An important element of almost all narratives was the pious testimony of the condemned up to the moment of execution. Anne Marthe Hungerland willingly placed herself on the execution block and, referencing Stephen Martyr, cried out to the crowd, "Oh, I see the heaven open above. Lord Jesus! Take up my soul." The narrator continues: "She received among these the last of her words the happy stroke. All the words, which she spoke, she enunciated with great power and joyfulness all the while so movingly that most of the spectators broke out in tears." From the *Rabenstein*, Gertrude Magdalene Bremmel prayed at length, praised God, and admonished the assembled crowd before willingly stretching out her neck for the executioner's sword. Even as Else Klicken, convicted of infanticide, was bound and placed in a weighted bag to be drowned, she affirmed that she was "a child of

God and bride of Jesus," who had saved her through his death, much to the satisfaction of the narrator.[48]

Another minister described the case of Andreas Roosen during the last minutes before hanging. Roosen reinforced the authenticity of his conversion by praying confidently before hanging, and even climbing the scaffold ladder willingly before proclaiming loudly, "Jesus, into your hands I commend my spirit."[49] Only a few accounts dwelt on the physical suffering, leaving this to the imagination of the readers, but even in those cases, withstanding an excruciating death could become another example of hard-won faith and the sureness of conversion.[50] Death marked the end of the temporal story, demarcating the line between the worldly life and the eternal realm to come. Death also prevented any relapse, any chance that conversion could later be falsified by a return to sinful ways. In this sense, the execution narratives present a logical if extreme development of stories about people who died well.

The controlled circumstances of the execution conversion narratives allowed the authors to reinforce certain themes that also appeared in other Pietist accounts. More than in any other set of conversion narratives, these highlight the role of the clergy. In almost all cases, clergy framed and composed the narratives. While careful not to give themselves the credit for the work of conversion—after all, this belonged to God alone[51]—they often depicted themselves as instrumental, visiting the prisoners, sometimes in teams, challenging facile assumptions about their spiritual condition, teaching them the rudiments of the Bible and catechism, and urging them to repentance. After conversion, the Pietist clergy continued to encourage them, often it seemed spending hours and hours in their company, particularly in the last days before execution. Some accounts tell of three and four ministers who visited the condemned alongside several theological students.[52] The attention showered on the condemned must have sometimes seemed overwhelming. The unique access the clergy had gave them an intimate view of someone's spiritual progress, but it also allowed them to shape, as active participants, not just their accounts but also the course of the conversion. All this put high expectations on the character of the clergy, and in the foreword to his collection Moser appealed for converted ministers to take on such cases.[53]

The accounts tended to accentuate the importance of the church, and Moser's narratives especially emphasized a Lutheran, if Pietist, identity. His stories came from a wide geographic swath from southern Germany to Scandinavia, but thirty of the thirty-one are Lutheran, which, given the profusion of conversion narratives in the Reformed tradition, could hardly have been a coincidence and reveal confessional selection on his part. They also present a contrast to the ecumenical nature of the narratives in Reitz's *Historie der Wiedergebohrnen* or even the *Closter-Bergische Sammlung Nützlicher Materien zur Erbauung im Wahren Christenthum*, published by Johann Adam Steinmetz, who had close ties to Halle Pietism.[54]

Woltersdorff remained somewhat more open and included some Reformed narratives, but in both Woltersdorff's and Moser's collections the narratives had a Lutheran confessional flavor that emphasized Luther's catechism and a Lutheran understanding of the sacraments. Here, as in Mecklenburg, the elements that reinforced a confessional identity—a Pietist Lutheran one—were not incidental to the stories. By presenting a schematic depiction of conversion, Moser in particular located his stories in a Lutheran Pietist tradition that emphasized a stirring or awakening, difficult struggles during repentance, and then the breakthrough to grace and assurance of salvation. In other words, Moser's collection reinforces the conversion theology articulated by Samuel Lau in Wernigerode or Karl Heinrich Zachariae in Dargun, for whom an extended struggle became a warrant for true conversion.[55] Woltersdorff, by contrast, had a broader understanding of conversion; by emphasizing the quick conversion of the thief on the cross next to Jesus, he implied that conversion need not be the long, drawn-out affair Moser preferred.[56]

Gender in the Execution Narratives

The execution narratives paralleled other published accounts in many respects, but they differed in some respects, especially with reference to gender. The Pietist periodicals contained few conversion narratives of lay men; most male narratives were about clergy or theology students. In Moser's collection of criminals' conversions, the narratives of men outnumbered those of women two to one, and only one of the men's narratives concerned a clergyman. In contrast to the other published narratives, most of the criminal converts came from the lower social strata—soldiers, peasants, carpenters, or tobacco spinners. Only a few were from the middle classes or nobility, groups that provided the leading characters in the periodical narratives. Women in the execution accounts, most of whom faced charges of infanticide or child murder, were frequently servant maids or other domestics.

Moser may have selected the narratives of men from the lower classes to illustrate the powerful reversals brought about by conversion. In his accounts, conversion transformed brutal ruffians who murdered without compunction into model Christian men. The narrator of Andreas Roosen's account marveled at the way the converted swindler admonished and comforted his fellow prisoners as he prepared for the gallows: "What a wonderful change! Here a villain and robber became a preacher of repentance." Other criminals, too, became "repentance preachers" through their deaths. A soldier who had stabbed an officer in a drunken state but went through an exemplary conversion and execution became, in the eyes of the narrator who told his story, "more a martyr than a malefactor."[57]

The gendered language of the sinner as bride, a trope with deep roots in Lutheran baroque hymnody and especially in the Moravian movement, reinforced the sense of transformation of the converted when the condemned approached death.[58] As his execution neared, Ritter spoke frequently of his "wedding day" and his desire to see his "beautiful and sweet savior."[59] Another converted murderer, Johann Christoph Serpes from Züllichau, referred to his prison cell as his betrothal chamber and thanked God that he had made him the "bride of Jesus." The shroud that had been made for his execution became his bridal gown, to be worn when he had his union with Christ. The narrator described the mood of the clergy following the execution: "The hearts of the preachers were so full with joy that they had led this bride to the Lord Jesus, that they were hardly of the mind that they were returning from a bloody execution, but rather it was as if they had just come back from a cheerful wedding banquet."[60]

Bridal imagery appeared especially in accounts of women's experience. Anne Marthe Hungerland spoke longingly of her coming union with Christ, at which she would be a heavenly bride.[61] Anna Margaretha Renner, executed for infanticide, finally overcame her shame and sense of unworthiness and embraced her role as bride of Jesus. Looking forward to her execution as a marriage day, Renner paraphrased Genesis, stating "Bone of my bone, flesh of my flesh," words that were part of the Lutheran marriage ceremony.[62] Bridal imagery appeared most frequently in the execution narratives, perhaps because the ritualized context in which the executions were carried out—with attending clergy, prayers, and even choristers intoning hymns—lent itself to comparisons with rituals of marriage.[63] However, such imagery was not unknown in other conversion accounts.[64]

The prevalence of tears underscored dramatic changes in the protagonists' character. Crossing between the inner self and the outer body, the tears were appropriate natural symbols for the transition from the unconverted to the converted state.[65] For Anton Nadler, a delinquent who had shot dead a fellow criminal, the "flood of tears" springing forth in his prison cell signaled his turn to authentic repentance and then conversion. For Lepsch, tears were God-given signs of his assurance of salvation. For women, too, tears signaled a demonstrative shift in spiritual progress. In the narrative of Anna Regina

Tölper, whose foul mouth and irreverent behavior had driven off the clergy, a sudden transformation, accompanied by the "pouring out of tears," signaled the change of heart.[66] Affective weeping, of course, was by no means a purely feminine characteristic at the time, yet it is suggestive how Zedler tied this form of tears to "children, women, and the soft."[67] Tears were a feature of many conversion narratives, but for men especially weeping reinforced the transformation from depraved criminal to compliant Christian.

Reliability, Fictionalization, and Selection

How reliable are these accounts? Susanne Kord asserts that Moser's accounts were implausible and highly fictionalized in order to conform to a particular schema and uniformity of vocabulary.[68] The accounts raise difficult questions about subjectivity of the narratives and give very little access to the inner lives of the converted. In most cases, the authors were learned, Pietist clergy who undoubtedly framed the narratives in terms derived from their own theological and cultural convictions. The conversions took place in quasi-coercive situations in which the condemned were quite literally a captive audience and the objects of extraordinary clerical effort. Even if we grant that the authors quoted the condemned with some accuracy, we must also assume both a high level of both suggestibility in the remarks of the converted and selectivity on the part of the narrator. More starkly than perhaps any other conversion narratives, these illustrate the distance that Karl Morrison described between the events we call conversion and their verbal representations.[69] Given the charged atmosphere of the impending execution and the imbalance of power between the captives and the visiting clergy, these are hardly unbiased, but are they as fictionalized or falsified as Kord asserts?

Both Woltersdorff and Moser especially claimed to place a high premium on reproducing the accounts accurately, as if to provide in advance an answer to skeptics who questioned their authenticity. Woltersdorff states that the accounts are "unadulterated" and come only from trusted sources.[70] Moser also takes pains to assure his readers that the accounts are "reliable."[71] Where we can trace the development of an execution narrative from a locally published pamphlet to one of these collections, Moser and Woltersdorff both reproduced the wording of the originals with only small orthographic changes. Woltersdorff tended to include more of the supporting materials—longer prefaces and sometimes the exhortations of the clergy at the execution—whereas Moser featured the conversion itself.[72] In addition, Woltersdorff inserted his own commentary and explanations into the narratives in a distinct typeface but did not alter the original text significantly. Since a number of these accounts initially appeared in print almost immediately after the event in the communities where the execution occurred and often included public words by the condemned, they would have been susceptible to complaints that they had misrepresented the prisoner's words. This would have undermined their goal of representing true conversion.[73] Even the opponents of such narratives in the eighteenth century did not question their basic veracity, although they contested the interpretation and wanted to prohibit their distribution.[74]

Without question, the accounts are highly stylized and contain striking similarities across time and geographic areas. Yet the argument that Moser's execution narratives are fictional, or at best "unabashedly fictionalized" accounts, is not especially satisfying, given that Moser largely reproduced preexisting print narratives and did not rewrite them in any way.[75] As we trace the language of these accounts from local pamphlets to periodicals and collections, it is apparent that neither Moser nor Woltersdorff rewrote the accounts to fit a particularly literary model or that they even edited the language markedly. The similarities among the accounts that drew Kord's attention already exist in the local pamphlet literature. Accounting for these similarities is considerably more complex than asserting the heavy hand of an editor or author.

One explanation has to do with the peculiar culture of conversion that emerged in German Pietism after 1730. In such a culture, one finds an emphasis on particular patterns of conversion that other Pietists could replicate elsewhere. The execution narratives reproduced in Moser may be extreme in several respects, but they fit a larger pattern of schematic conversion that we might encounter in the Pietist periodicals or in movements at Dargun or Wernigerode. Further, we know that Pietists drew on other conversion narratives when "coaching" others through a conversion. The clergy at Dargun, for instance, used Schubert's account of Lepsch's conversion in working to convert Christian Friedrich Ritter, and Moser himself emphasized the exemplary nature of these stories for those awaiting execution.

From this point of view, the language and phrases that Kord points to as suspiciously similar across accounts may be hackneyed and unoriginal but are not necessarily fictional, at least in the sense that it was deliberately falsified. Take, for instance, the phrase Kord cites that appears in several of the accounts of women just prior to execution. Anne Marthe Hungerland was said to have placed herself willingly on the executioner's stool and to have cried out to the crowd "Oh, I see the heaven open above. Lord Jesus! Receive my soul!" just prior to the blow of the sword.[76] This phrase occurs in several narratives, suspiciously so for Kord, but the biblical reference to the martyrdom of St. Stephen (Acts 7:56), which has similar wording, was part of the catechizing of the condemned.[77] Framing these converted criminals as martyrs akin to St. Stephen may appear surprising, but it gives us insight into the way many of the Pietists viewed the converts.

Another reason for the similarity across accounts is the high level of selectivity. Moser did not publish every written conversion account he chanced upon, but rather only those that fit favored patterns of crime and exemplary conversion. He sought especially dramatic reversals of depraved criminals who were transformed into paragons of Christian faith and selected his portrayals accordingly. Women convicted of infanticide in Moser's collection were never just seduced or led astray; rather, he depicted them as deeply depraved. The account of Catharina Elisabeth Uhl described her as not only ignorant of basic Christian tenets but also as possessed by "a truly satanic malevolence of the will," which manifested itself in disobedience to her parents, anger and vengefulness toward neighbors, multiple sins of the flesh, theft, and in "a thousand other ways" as well.[78] Accounts without such a backstory or lacking an ideal pattern of conversion had less appeal for Moser and the other Pietist collectors of conversion narratives.[79]

Suicide by Proxy

The controversy surrounding cases of suicide by proxy illustrates that contemporaries did not perceive these execution narratives as fictional retellings. Suicide by proxy, or suicide murders, were instances in which an individual would commit a capital crime with the intent of being executed by the authorities, thus avoiding the religious consequences of suicide, for which repentance was not possible.[80] The Moser collection includes at least one clear instance of suicide by proxy, in which a household servant, Gertrude Magdalene Bremmel, killed an innocent child in her care in order to bring about her execution at the hand of the authorities.[81] Bremmel made no attempt to conceal the crime and immediately presented herself to the local official (*Vogt*) and confessed her actions, "freely and without any excuses." Later, according to the narrator, Bremmel acknowledged that her motive was the hope for salvation: "Thus she thought, when you just do what you have planned, you will be executed, and through the shedding of your blood, everything will be repaid, and you will be saved. Such thoughts were first aroused in her when she had previously seen an execution in person and imagined at that point that whoever dies in this manner cannot but become saved."[82] In the process of her conversion, Bremmel came to see this as an "abominable action" that she deeply regretted. The clergy had criticized the presumption of salvation that she hoped to achieve with her execution, but they worked fervently to bring her to a proper understanding of repentance and true conversion.[83]

Along with Dargun, Wernigerode, close by to Bremmel's home and where her trial and execution took place, was one of the centers of Pietism that strongly advocated an extended repentance struggle in conversion, and clerical views there corresponded closely with those presented in the Moser narratives.[84] Bremmel professed no intimate familiarity with Pietist beliefs prior to her incarceration; she claimed repeatedly that she had never understood true repentance and conversion before.[85] That she was deeply moved by the example of a previous execution in which a conversion was implied nonetheless signals she was not entirely unfamiliar with aspects of Pietist conversion attending executions.[86] Moreover, the center of gravity in the narrative is Bremmel's successful conversion and faithful death. In the end, she achieved what she had set out to do initially: to die in assurance of grace and salvation.[87]

The account of Bremmel's crime, conversion, and execution appeared in print several times in pamphlets. The Count of Stolberg-Wernigerode, whom the narrator described as witnessing Bremmel's execution and interacting with her briefly at the place of execution, sent a copy of the pamphlet to G. A. Francke in early 1745 "for his encouragement," describing it as an example of the "great mercy of God toward a child murderess, who was executed [lit. justified] here."[88] The pamphlet went through two editions in Wernigerode, and then both Moser and Woltersdorff picked it up in their collections of the 1750s.[89]

The influence of Pietist ideas of an exemplary conversion on Bremmel prior to killing the child is suggestive if inconclusive. Other sources indicate that both Pietists and non-Pietists worried that such narratives could spark imitation. In the preface to the 1753 edition, Moser added a paragraph that warned against such a "misuse": "May the Lord prevent, that no one would be so blind, foolish, and audacious to misuse these examples and commit an act punishable with the death penalty, so that he may die devoutly. Such [a decision] is beyond the powers of a poor sinner or a preacher, regardless how sincere and talented he may consider himself."[90] If he knew that misunderstandings were possible, though, why did he include Bremmel's story, especially given that she initially labored under just such a misconception? Presumably, the power of Bremmel's conversion outweighed the dangers of promoting her original motive, which she later came to regret profoundly. Other Pietists had worried about this as well. Even before the heyday of

Moser and Woltersdorff's collections, the former Halle theologian J. J. Rambach warned:

> There are examples of individuals who believe it to be something beautiful and glorious to die at the ravenstone. They imagine that such poor sinners are so beautifully prepared for death that they have so many thousand people as witnesses and observers of the end of their life, which they would not be able to have with a natural death in their sickbed. Indeed, these poor sinners are praised by everyone for their beautiful last moments, even from the pulpit. And through these strange fantasies, they are led astray to kill a child or someone else, in order that they could also take part in this honor.[91]

Later Woltersdorff also acknowledged the complaint that such conversion narratives could incite individuals to commit crude crimes, but he argued that such accusations misunderstood the content of the narratives.[92] Tyge Krogh suggests that this was a particular problem in Lutheran lands.[93]

Nor were these just worries of hypersensitive Pietists. Criticism came from other theological directions as well. The Enlightenment theologian Gotthilf Samuel Steinbart contended that the publication of narratives like those found in Moser were indeed an inducement to suicide by proxy, and he urged their suppression.[94] Steinbart recounted the case of a woman who was despondent about her chances of salvation were she not executed by the authorities and, according to Steinbart, resolved therefore to kill a child or a pious preacher, neither of whose souls she considered to be in danger, so that she could die at the hands of the executioner.[95]

Criticisms of the Execution Narratives

Steinbart's criticisms went beyond the issue of inducement to suicide by proxy; he developed a much larger criticism of the false expectations and heroic efforts to convert "arch villains" prior to execution, and he ridiculed the practices and publications that enabled this. "In this," Steinbart wrote, "the arch villains have a great advantage over other Christians. The worst knaves, rogues, and murders cannot miss the mark of heaven, when they do something so terrible that they must be sentenced to the gallows, sword, wheel. For as soon as a judgment in the case of a miscreant has been pronounced, the clergy rush to him." Steinbart continued that few could resist the efforts of the clergy in light of the horror of their coming execution: "For nothing occurs more naturally than the conversion of poor sinners, who in so many accounts of the last hours are trumpeted as special miracles of God's grace, to great injury of religion and piety."[96]

Steinbart mocked the typical pattern of conversion behind many of the narratives that appeared in Moser and Woltersdorff, describing for his readers how the clergy first pushed the condemned to recognize their utter depravity, brought them to regret their sins, and then bit by bit offered them the mercy of Christ and the hope of salvation. The result was, in Steinbart's eyes, a sham repentance and conversion that fooled no one who examined the matter closely: "An entirely ordinary mind can already perceive that through all this, a completely real change in the moral character of the wrongdoer has not occurred at all, much less could this wrongdoer be fundamentally reclaimed and sanctified."[97]

On a more practical level, Steinbart criticized the way these execution narratives undermined the deterrent effect that public executions were meant to achieve. "What was the logical consequence of this?" Steinbart complained. "The entire impression that public executions should have on the common people to frighten criminals and maintain public safety is lost. The unexpected view of the heroic joyfulness of an offender has a livelier effect on the spectators than the otherwise well-known elements of the execution, and hinders then the typical horror, which ought to shock the wicked." Steinbart blamed the printed accounts of the execution narratives for encouraging suicide by proxy and urged that they be suppressed. And while he does not go as far as some critics who would forbid the clergy to attend to the condemned at all, Steinbart did endorse preventing the clergy from accompanying the condemned to the place of execution and especially from urging them to displays of joyfulness at the moment of execution.[98]

Of course, a *moral* conversion had never been the goal of the Pietists. Though Steinbart grew up in a Pietist milieu in Züllichau, he moved in a rationalist direction by the late 1760s.[99] He criticized what he saw as "magical" expectations on the part of the Pietist clergy in the dramatic conversions. His connection of morality and conversion exemplified a typical Enlightenment criticism of Pietist conversion.[100] Kittsteiner sees in this the collapse of the theatrical "drama of conversion" and the end of a distinct form of conversion represented by the execution sermons.[101]

At the same time, the criticisms by Steinbart as well as others indicate that even skeptical contemporaries took seriously the reports of dramatic conversions at the gallows as eyewitness accounts and did not treat them as fictionalizations. Both the critics and supporters agreed that these accounts could shape how people acted and played a role in promoting Pietist conversion.¹⁰² Contemporaries on both sides of the issue agreed that these narratives could affect how the condemned and the spectators saw these conversions and executions. One side thinks it makes them more pious, while the other finds them a moral hazard.

By the 1770s, suicide by proxy had become a problem. Royal edicts in Denmark and Brandenburg-Prussia sought to counter it by limiting the involvement of the clergy in the rituals of executions, and in Denmark the authorities went so far as to substitute hard labor for capital punishment.¹⁰³ This in turn undermined a certain form of the Pietist conversion narrative that had reached a logical, though not necessarily inevitable, conclusion in the execution narratives by which Pietists had sought to constrain and control religious experience.

The demise of the popular execution narratives allowed other genres to reassert themselves as normative Pietist conversion narratives. While heretofore almost unknown, August Hermann Francke's conversion narrative was later rediscovered at the end of the eighteenth century. It offered a model of conversion that appeared much more fitting to contemporary mores than the gruesome and entertaining tales of the conversion at the ravenstone and gallows. By the early nineteenth century, Francke's conversion became the paradigmatic account of conversion in Pietism, a position it has held to the present day.

CONCLUSION

When August Hermann Niemeyer, the great-grandson of August Hermann Francke, and Georg Christian Knapp, codirectors of the *Franckesche Stiftungen*, "discovered" the conversion narrative of August Hermann Francke in the Halle archives in the early 1790s, they were struck by the force of the manuscript account. Neither appeared aware of the earlier published versions of Francke's autobiographical narrative in German or Latin, or other pamphlets such as the *Concise Yet Thorough Report*, which appeared around the time of his death.[1] Niemeyer was mildly critical of Francke's dramatic account, noting that had Francke been aware of "certain, more correct theological and psychological ideas" that had since come to light, he might have been spared some anxiety.[2] Knapp was more enthusiastic, and in 1794 he published the text of the conversion narrative that Francke's son, Gotthilf August, had read aloud to students in 1727 but never published.[3] The emotional tenor of the account may not have been entirely to Niemeyer's taste, but at least Francke's first-person narrative avoided many of the problems of the execution narratives.

With Knapp's publication, Francke's conversion entered the historiography in a new way, and by the early nineteenth century detailed descriptions of the Lüneburg experience dominated such accounts of Francke's life as J. A. Kanne's sketch in 1817 and especially Heinrich Ernst Guericke's 1827 biography.[4] The latter, in turn, became the basis for the 1830 *Memoirs of Augustus Hermann Francke*, which featured the conversion story and popularized it in the United States.[5] By the early 1830s, accounts of Francke's conversion appeared in the popular religious press in North America,[6] and it anchored biographical retellings throughout the nineteenth century. Leading interpreters of Pietism—Krämer, Schmid, and above all Albrecht Ritschl—made Francke's Lüneburg experience the lens through which to view both his life and the subsequent Pietist movement.[7] By the early twentieth century, Mahrholz, Wendland, and others made it one of the paradigmatic conversion experiences of Pietism, specifically of Halle Pietism.[8] And by mid-century, when Kurt Aland declared that Francke's conversion had become a "rule" for others, it had become a commonplace in twentieth-century literature on Pietism to treat Francke's autobiographical account as *the* exemplar of German Pietism.[9] In making these claims, scholars then and today are following a tradition stretching back to the nineteenth century. It is a tradition, however, that oversimplifies and to a certain extent distorts the complicated conversion experiences of eighteenth-century Pietism. Never published during his lifetime, Francke's narrative was familiar only to a small circle. It was not well known during most of the eighteenth century until Niemeyer and Knapp's publications of the 1790s. Relinquishing Francke's autobiography as the template allows other patterns of conversion in the eighteenth century to emerge more clearly.

But if the depiction of conversion in church Pietism, especially in the orbit of Halle, was not modeled on Francke's account, what was conversion for a Pietist? Some have fallen back on the eighteenth-century Pietist *Bußkampf* model, but this is problematic on multiple levels. The *Bußkampf* was no fiction; it was a term that many Pietist authors employed, though not at all uniformly. At times, it was just a synonym for the old Lutheran concept of *Anfechtung*; elsewhere it was an expression of a deep *Buße* (repentance) that was part of standard Lutheran piety. Francke's own employment of the word was not consistent, and it was not essential to his description of conversion. His autobiography does not use it, and some scholars have even argued that Francke's own path to conversion in his autobiography cannot properly be understood as a *Bußkampf*.[10]

In some instances, it took on a specific character within the order of salvation. This was the case in Wernigerode and especially Dargun during the 1730s and 1740s, and this view found continued expression in a number of the published narratives, including some of the execution stories. Nonetheless, the strict construction of the *Bußkampf* created disputes not only between Pietists and their orthodox opponents but also among Pietists themselves. In the 1730s, Pietists at Halle complained that their opponents misrepresented their practices of conversion.[11]

Rather than assuming a schematic model based on Francke or even a rigid model of the *Bußkampf*, patterns of conversion, especially in early Pietism, were highly diverse. Beginning with the first cluster of conversion narratives composed in Erfurt in the early 1690s, Pietists advanced a multiplicity of depictions. In an unpublished account from 1690 or 1691, Georg Brückner emphasized the influence of Molinos and described a Quietistic stillness as a prerequisite to conversion. Brückner's account featured an emotional *Durchbruch* (breakthrough), but this never became a necessary feature of early Pietist conversion stories.

The most common print conversion account in early Pietism, the autobiography of Johann Caspar Schade, also featured no triumphal "breakthrough," and it departed from the later "typical" Pietist conversion in that he continued to be plagued by spiritual travail (*Anfechtung*), even after his heart and mind had been transformed. This meant that the most frequently reprinted Pietist conversion narrative before 1730 did not fit many of the later stereotypes. Some have sought to supplement Schade's inconclusive autobiography with a third-person account found among his unpublished papers that conforms more closely to historians' expectations of what a Pietist conversion experience should be.[12] Yet this is a good example of how conversion experiences in Pietism have been misinterpreted. The preference for models that fit preconceived assumptions and the neglect of diverse portrayals have distorted how we interpret conversion in this period. Maybe the third-person account that Gottfried Arnold attributed to Schade and later published might be a better description of Schade's inner life than his more widely reprinted autobiography. However, this begs the question of why so many of Schade's closest associates, especially Spener and Francke, repeatedly chose to reprint his quite different autobiographical account.[13] This description of Schade's conversion would have been the reading fare of a broad audience, not the relatively obscure third-person account. By reading everything through one prism, historians run the risk of neglecting the multiple forms of these experiences. Even at Halle, Francke was loath to prescribe a specific pattern. In recalling how Schade brought a noblewoman to conversion in Berlin, Francke warned his students that such stories were "singular" examples that should not be imitated.[14]

Without question, Pietists yearned for conversion, wrote about it, and preached sermons designed to evoke it, but they privileged no single pattern. One can point to some examples that fit a "classic" Pietist conversion or contain elements of the *Bußkampf*, but these should not overshadow other different examples or cause us to forget that the autobiographies and biographies of many Pietists portrayed no conversion experience at all. Written in a radical Pietist context, Reitz's well-known *Historie der Wiedergebohrnen* (1698–1745) was not strictly a collection of conversion narratives, especially after the first volume.[15] After 1730, with the appearance of such Pietist periodicals such as the *Sammlung auserlesener Materien zum Bau des Reichs Gottes*, more conversion narratives began to appear in print, but they followed several distinct patterns.[16]

The problem of conversion goes beyond dispelling stereotypical portrayals. I have tried to show how uneasy Pietists were with depictions of conversion experience, especially the experiences of persons still living. For all their language about the need for conversion, many Pietists, including the ones at Halle, did not encourage people to memorialize conversion in verbal form, whether oral or written. To be sure, Francke and others in the early 1690s appeared to flirt with composing narratives of conversion, but this tendency quickly dissipated and no sustained tradition of publishing or even collecting conversion experiences emerged. Some Pietists, such as Spener, consistently opposed the circulation of conversion narratives. Others were more ambivalent—at times August Hermann Francke seemed to recommend them—but despite the strong rhetoric about conversion as a goal in his sermons and tracts, he appears to pull away from them in practice. But why?

The inherent instability of a subjective conversion experience was certainly one consideration, and this instability manifested itself on several levels. Most obvious was the problem of relapse: an apparently converted person could fall back into sinful behavior and beliefs. This was an issue in the mission field, as Bartholomäus Ziegenbalg learned with one of his most celebrated early converts,[17] but it could also be a problem for published collections, since a living individual could throw his printed narrative into doubt by reverting to a sinful life, forcing the editor to excise it from future editions.[18] Even more frequently, the narratives had to account for instances when seemingly converted people came to doubt their faith, questioning whether their assurance of salvation perdured. This was a major theme, for example, in Francke's funeral sermon for Martha Margaretha von Schönberg, and it became a leitmotif in the genre of the *Letzte Stunden*. The focus on the struggle at the end of life, moreover, had the effect of relativizing the decisive nature of prior conversion experiences.

Some, like Spener, feared that any fixed model of conversion in narrative form could have a distorting effect on ways that men and women construed their spiritual progress. Still others worried that a claim of true conversion could lead to mistaken beliefs, including the dangerous doctrine of this-worldly perfection. And others felt the need to be alert for heterodox or heretical pretenders who claimed that a profound religious experience authorized their unorthodox views. It also troubled Francke that some might deceive themselves by mistaking the initial inclinations toward conversion for true conversion.

In any number of ways, Pietists sought to constrain and regulate the depiction of religious experiences. The most common was to postpone any publication until after a convert had died. Only from the perspective of death could one assess the truth of a religious experience. Few conversion narratives appeared in print before an individual's death, so spiritual biography in Pietism became ever more focused on death as a definitive turning point, especially in the genre of Henckel's *Letzte Stunden*, or in the well-known spiritual biography of the ten-year-old Christlieb Leberecht von Exter, which Francke had published in 1708.[19] The execution narratives took the emphasis on death and the "last hours" to a logical conclusion.

In turn, the effort to shape and control conversion had other consequences. One was a shift to the third-person narrative voice. Pietists often transposed first-person narratives to the third person. Sometimes, this was merely a shift in grammatical voice in which an editor kept the rest of the text largely verbatim. We see this, for instance, in large portions of Zeigenbalg's narrative in a biographical sketch published after his death. The editor of the *Ausführliche Berichte* drew on the diction of Ziegenbalg's first-person account but rendered it in the third person with minor rewording and paraphrasing.[20]

This was often not merely a literary convention; it could also be an intervention that preserved autobiographical material while distancing the reader from the first-person account. In many cases, the editor shifted the narrative voice to that of a clergyman. In the execution narrative of Andreas Lepsch, for example, the minister Heinrich Schubert narrated Lepsch's conversion and spiritual development in his own voice. This allowed the narrator to frame the conversion within an ecclesial setting. Other clergy described themselves as facilitating the transformation. And still others used accounts of their own conversion to accentuate the clergy's ability to recognize their own true conversion and narrate their own spiritual development. Such accounts underscore the clerical imprint that conversion narratives often bore in Germany, the result of clerical distrust of unmediated lay reflection.

The rise of the *Bußkampf* in the 1730s was an attempt among some Pietists to ensure the validity of a conversion. By demanding an extraordinary level of contrition and repentance, these Pietists hoped to ensure that the conversions would be lasting and true. In certain circles, particularly in Wernigerode and Dargun during the 1730s and 1740s, conversion narratives took on a schematic character and standardized experiences became prerequisites of a true conversion. Yet, even in these settings, the unyielding demand for a *Bußkampf* had a destabilizing effect, dividing Pietists from one another and intensifying the opposition of the orthodox.

We can interpret the execution narratives as an extreme attempt to fix or determine the nature of Pietist conversion, and they represent many of the characteristics we have associated with it: the use of the third-person voice of a reliable Pietist narrator, an extended period of repentance, doctrinal fidelity, and not least the delay of the account until after the death of the convert, a literary strategy that rendered the experience unfalsifiable. To be sure, these were not "typical" Pietist conversions. No authors wanted their readers to imitate the entire arc of the story, and certainly they did not want them to imitate the crimes. Nor can we infer that most readers with whom these accounts were popular saw them as templates for their own spiritual lives. The lurid crimes and terrible punishments must have titillated some readers, even as they could rationalize the stories as testimonies to divine grace or a call to convert prisoners awaiting execution. Yet, in seeking to resolve the uncertainties around conversion in new ways, the portrayals of triumphant conversion in the execution narratives may also have encouraged suicide by proxy, which proved even more destabilizing to Pietist conceptions of conversion.

The ambivalence about conversion and the attempt to "fix" it reveals an ongoing distrust of religious experience among church Pietists. At least since Johann Arndt, German Protestants had emphasized *Erfahrung* (experience) as an essential part of true Christianity, and Pietists were, almost by definition, no exception. De Boor makes a powerful argument that the experience of conversion allowed Francke to banish his atheistic, rational doubts.[21] However, Francke did not impose that kind of experience on others, and for him as well as many church Pietists, an apparent experience of conversion alone remained insufficient. It needed to be qualified and evaluated, something best done by a pious clergyman or Pietist leader within a community, and this was only reliable from the perspective of death. It is not too much to say that many Pietists distrusted the subjective experiences that accompanied conversion. Opponents of the Pietists who concocted stories of Quaker powders or magical slips of papers had an even more intense distrust of religious experience.[22]

This wariness stands in tension with the repeated call to conversion so often found in Pietist writings. Francke offers an example: in his widely circulated *Short and Simple Yet Thorough Instruction to True Christianity* (1695), Francke urged his readers not to postpone their conversion.[23] This urgency reappeared in Francke's sermons and tracts throughout his career, whether in his famous open letter on preaching or his collected sermons. Conversion was the ideal, both for Francke and for many of his associates and allies, such as Johann Hieronymus Wiegleb or Johann Porst. But historians can easily misinterpret this ideal by assuming that it described the typical Pietist experience. Pietists could be much more skeptical in assessing a claimed conversion experience than they sounded when articulating their hopes. Aside from the obvious problem of relapse or false conversion, Francke continually warned against self-deception in assessing one's conversion. His warnings relativized the experience by reminding converts that their conversion could turn out to be deceptive.[24] This reticence stood in the background when Pietists moved away from autobiographical accounts in the first person or postponed publication of conversion accounts until after the convert's death.

Some of the uneasiness is captured in the term *Bekehrsucht*, literally an "obsession for conversion," a term both Pietists and their opponents used in the eighteenth century to depict untoward practices. It is no wonder that critics of Pietism would have used it for this purpose. It is more surprising that Pietists used the term in the same way. It could refer both to one who was overzealous in the drive to convert others as well to an individual who had an inordinate desire to be converted. The earliest reference I have encountered is Johann Porst's autobiography written in the late 1690s. Here, he described himself as succumbing to a "violent obsession for conversion" and being rescued from a lapse into "all manner of disorder" only by God's guiding hand. This divine guidance led to his true conversion, which was something quite different from what the *Bekehrsucht* had sought to precipitate.[25] Porst continued to criticize *Bekehrsucht* into the 1720s.[26] In Halle, Francke criticized *Bekehrsucht* in his *Idea studiosi Theologiae* (1712), in which he portrayed the ideal theology student as one who avoided "untimely obsession for conversion" in his interaction with his neighbors.[27] Francke's colleague Joachim Lange was similarly critical of *Bekehrsucht*, arguing that the common concern for the welfare of one's neighbor, which is part of the common priesthood, should not degenerate into a *Bekehrsucht* that often results in "more offense than edification."[28] Others closely involved with Pietist circles, such as Johann Jakob Moser, also warned against *Bekehrsucht*.[29] These examples indicate that even the most earnest proponents of conversion could entertain a profound ambivalence about the experience. During the Enlightenment, the opponents of Pietism naturally used the term to discount claims about conversion. Johann Joachim Spalding railed against the "hypocritical *Bekehrsucht*" and criticized the practice of composing conversion narratives.[30] But the Enlightenment critics were not raising the red flag for the first time.

The discussion around *Bekehrsucht* indicates that many Pietists could be uneasy about too much zeal regarding conversion. Porst's self-criticism offers an early example of this discomfort. In the 1690s in Gotha, the overzealousness of one of August Hermann Francke's acolytes, Johann Hieronymus Wiegleb, led, in the eyes of his detractors, to an attempted suicide. Even ardent conversionists like Wiegleb moderated their demands by the early eighteenth century.[31]

Exhortations to conversion did not necessarily entail a compulsory "method" of conversion.[32] There were pockets where Pietists created an almost coercive culture of conversion—Dargun is perhaps the best documented case—but these instances happened on the periphery of the main Pietist movements and often created division among the Pietists themselves. August Hermann Francke and most other German Pietists were not revivalists in the sense that we have come to understand the term from the British and North American context. When W. R. Ward, the great British historian of evangelicalism, observed that Francke was more a reformer than a revivalist, he captured something that many historians of Pietism often miss because they read his career predominantly through his conversion experience.[33] As Bill Widén has shown, Francke made very little mention of conversion in his main pedagogical works. Arguing that A. H. Francke was less concerned with the experience of conversion than he was with education (*Erziehung*), Widén suggested that Francke envisioned a pedagogical pathway to true Christianity.[34]

Francke could be quite sober about the prospects of widespread conversion. Writing in 1714 to Curt Friedrich von Wreech, who was among the captured Swedish army officers exiled to Siberia in the Great Northern War and deeply inspired by Francke's writings, Francke cautioned against hoping for a universal conversion or awakening, noting that the blows and humiliations of God unfortunately led only a few to turn to Christ.[35] Much of the Halle support of the Swedish exiles in Siberia was devoted less to sparking an evangelical revival than to building educational institutions in Tobolsk.[36]

The contrast between German Pietists and British and North American revivalists can be seen in the divergent ways they depicted conversion. There is little reason to doubt that British models of conversion narratives influenced German ones. Spener singled out the deleterious influence of "English" models just as the first German Pietist narratives began to emerge in the early 1690s,[37] and among the earliest depictions of the transformational, inner-Christian form of conversion in German were translations from the English.[38] German Pietists read these accounts, and they no doubt influenced Pietist thinking. But German Pietists remained much more reluctant to publish their experiences. The English Puritan John Bunyan published his autobiographical account in 1666 and revised and expanded it in later editions before his death in 1688.[39] There is nothing comparable among leading German Pietists. Johanna Eleonora Petersen's *A Short Narration of How God's Guiding Hand Has Guided Me Hitherto* (1689) has some similarities with Bunyan's account, in that it was published relatively early in her life and later included further additions, but Petersen's narrative was not a conversion narrative.[40] Later in the eighteenth century, the Methodists John Wesley and George Whitefield published accounts of their conversions in the 1730s when they were young men and most of their careers lay before them. Wesley may have later regretted his portrayal of his experience at Aldersgate,[41] but there is no equivalent among conversion accounts of leading German Pietists, which, if they found their way into print at all, only did so after the death of the author. Jonathan Edwards's *A Faithful Narrative*, an account of the revival and conversions in Northampton from 1737, has almost no parallel in the print culture of German Pietism.[42] Even at Dargun, the leaders of the revival chose not to circulate print descriptions of revival and conversions, though they shared much else through manuscript networks.[43] Moreover, though it is possible to make too much of it, most British narratives, even of relatively unlearned laity, appeared in first-person narration, whereas their counterparts in Germany published lay narratives in the third person. To be sure, German Pietists translated Edwards into German and read the Anglo-American conversion narratives, but they did not imitate them in print.

The focus in this book has been on the Hallensian tradition and its larger orbit, a tradition that informed church Pietism throughout the eighteenth century, but there were other paths of German Pietism, and in them, as well, conversion experiences were problematic. The Renewed Unity of the Brethren, or Moravians as they have become known in English, were a Pietist-influenced revival movement that paralleled and to a certain extent competed with the church Pietism represented by Halle. As a youth, the founder of the movement, Nicholas Ludwig von Zinzendorf (1700–1760), attended the elite academy at Francke's Foundations. He could report later that he had been reckoned among the *Erweckte* at Halle,[44] but Zinzendorf never had a decisive experience that one could characterize as a moment or definitive process of conversion.[45] There is some evidence that early Moravians standardized the expected experience, employing categories such as *Tote*, *Erweckte*, and *Bekehrte* to depict stages of spiritual development, complete with a *Bußkampf*, at least in some contexts in Herrnhut.[46] Yet, even as Zinzendorf struggled with the nature of his own conversion, he and the Moravians eventually opposed what they saw as the Halle conversion practices, especially anything smacking of the *Bußkampf*.[47] Martin Schmidt suggests that the Moravian antipathy to the *Bußkampf* may well have contributed to the polemical "invention" of a compulsory *Bußkampf* in the historiography on Halle Pietism.[48] Moravians encouraged their members to compose memoirs (*Lebensläufe*) that would portray their lives from a spiritual perspective. Originally, Zinzendorf intended that these accounts would be read aloud to the community after one's death, as part of the *Singstunde* for the departed.[49] These were autobiographical, reflective accounts that often contained observations by an editor about the end of their life. Mettele argues that Moravians after the 1730s relinquished any notion of a dramatic or decisive conversion experience.

Conversion was a process, with dramatic events perhaps, but it was a "a lifelong pilgrimage on precarious terrain."[50] In emphasizing the contrasts between Moravians and other Pietists, Mettele paints conversion and conversion narratives in Halle Pietism with too broad a brush, yet she has recognized significant differences. Moravian memoirs rarely had the character of a narrative whose plot turned on conversion, whether sudden or gradual, a characteristic she attributes to their inattention to sanctification and opposition to perfection. A number of the Moravian memoirs could be anticlimactic, sometimes even representing gradual disillusionment with the Moravian community, to which an unnamed narrator obliquely referred.[51]

Like Mettele, Bruce Hindmarsh emphasizes the role of community in the Moravian narratives and shows that in contrast to the early Methodist narratives, which highlighted "agonistic struggle," Moravian memoirs reflected a greater sense of self-effacement, childlike faith, and surrender.[52] Often the narrative high point of the Moravian autobiography was admission to the community and participation in the Lord's Supper.[53] Rather than referring to their *Bekehrung*, a term with which they would have been quite familiar, Moravians preferred *Erweckung* (awakening), which has a very different set of connotations than the fundamental reversal implicit in language of conversion or the dramatic inception of an altered life implicit in the biological metaphors of regeneration and new birth. The differences extend beyond opposition to language of the *Bußkampf*. Hindmarsh interprets these patterns broadly as "conversion," but as he points out, the Moravian understanding of conversion, in contrast to the one found in both early Methodism and church Pietism, was more aesthetic than it was agonistic.[54]

Unlike lay narratives of church Pietism, the Moravian memoirs were, despite some editorial interventions, predominantly dictated or written in the first person.[55] At the same time, Moravians shared with the church Pietists some complicated reactions to conversion narratives. Though different from the "last hours" that highlighted one's spiritual condition immediately preceding death, the Moravian memoirs also accented the dying hours. The memoirs had a quasi-liturgical function at the funeral service, which cast spiritual biography into the context of meditation on death or "going home," as Moravians phrased it. Like most Pietists, but unlike Methodists, Moravians avoided publicizing their accounts until after the individual had passed away. The Moravians, though, did not focus on an assurance of salvation that was a common theme of the church Pietist accounts.

Radical Pietists were diverse, and there is no one pattern of practice we can associate with their approach to experiences of conversion. Johann Henrich Reitz was closely allied with radical Pietists, but the biographies he reproduced in his *Historie der Wiedergebohrnen* represented no single tradition; moreover, as further volume and editions of his collection appeared, descriptions of conversion experiences became less frequent and less dominant.[56] Early published accounts by radicals such Johann Georg Rosenbach may have helped convince church Pietists to eschew the publication of narratives. Right after the publication of his *Wondrous and Gracious Conversion* in 1703, Rosenbach found favor with August Hermann Francke and his close ally Canstein. But as his views on infant baptism and the Eucharist developed in heterodox directions, they may have contributed to Francke's growing skepticism about published conversion narratives written by living individuals.[57] For many years, critics of Pietism viewed Rosenbach's autobiography as the exemplar of "enthusiastic" conversion, a reputation that would have reinforced the skepticism of church Pietists.[58] Other radical figures such as Johann Tennhardt published autobiographical accounts that detailed mystical experiences and illuminations that culminated in a call to preach repentance, much like the earlier model of Hans Engelbrecht or Jacob Böhme, accounts that did not portray a conversion experience.[59] In another stream of radical Pietism, the Inspirationist Johann Friedrich Rock described a series of "awakenings" and "blessed movements," but for him, as for Tennhardt, prophecy and not conversion was the centerpiece of his autobiographical narrative.[60]

The radical Pietist periodical *Geistliche Fama* (1730–44) reproduced some of the same conversion narratives that appeared in church Pietist publications, including Moser's *Seelige Letzte Stunden*,[61] but the editors of the *Geistliche Fama* could be highly critical of any form of conversion that merely appeared to conform to external expectations. They particularly disliked what the editor of the *Geistliche Fama* called "the learned hand of priestly edification" that shaped the narratives in the *Sammlung auserlesener Materien*.[62] The journal accented the variety of conversion experiences and the sole action of God in their production.[63] The editors assailed the attempts of an earnest clergyman to "convert" a pious yet dissenting shepherd who rejected the Lutheran Church's practice of communion. They took particular exception to the clergyman's imposition of church discipline and his appeal to the civil authorities after his attempts at persuasion failed.[64] Given that many conversion narratives highlighted the ordained Pietist clergy as agents who helped effect conversion and reincorporate the "converted" into the church—often symbolized by depictions of the communion ritual—it is hard not to see this as a criticism of church Pietist narratives.[65]

The discussions of conversion in the *Geistliche Fama* had an anti-clerical and anti-institutional bent, and the line between conversion and spiritual illumination was often blurred. This distinguished them from Moser's collections or the various editions of the *Sammlung auserlesener Materien*.[66] For radicals like the Schwarzenau Brethren who instituted believer's baptism, conversion experiences seemed to play only a minor role, in part because the ritual of baptism could function as a decisive marker in the life of an adult believer after repentance.[67] Some radical Pietists, like Johann Conrad Beissel, leader of the Ephrata community, developed a view of double conversion, in which water baptism confirmed the second conversion experience.[68]

Conversion was never the sole property of Pietists, and their radical, orthodox, and Enlightenment critics could all grant conversion a role in the Christian life. The debate among them was about distinguishing true from false conversion. When Johann Joachim Spalding (1714–1804), a leading theological figure in the German Enlightenment, published a sermon titled "Warning Against False Conversions," he noted in the preface the confusion sown among his parishioners about conversion.[69] He was concerned about not only the gullible souls who followed the *Schwärmer* but also the reasonable men and women who dismissed true conversion because they associated it with "either weak, enthusiastic minds or hypocritical hearts." In a passage that he surely intended as a criticism of conversionist Pietists, Spalding railed against those "who praise their own conversion, compose detailed accounts of it, and presume to be able to judge decisively whether others are converted or not. In doing so, they build completely on such bases and marks that are not valid according to the truth or before God." He especially disliked the association of conversion with powerful emotions, such as deep sorrow followed by preternatural joy in God's grace—a model of conversion in many published accounts.[70] Spalding viewed conversion as improvement in one's life and a change in heart and mind characterized by "purity of heart, a calm conscience, and agreement with God."

The response of Enlightenment theologians to conversion is beyond the scope of this book, but as Spalding's "Warning" suggests, understanding "true" conversion remained as troublesome for Enlightenment theologians as it was for many Pietists.[71] A number of Enlightenment theologians grew up in a Pietist milieu, but most came to reject a revivalist or dramatic experience of conversion in favor of an enduring change in heart, behavior, and mind, thereby devaluing the power of signal experience and attenuating any supernatural character in conversion.[72] At the end of this tradition, Kant questioned whether conversion could ever truly happen in a moment that would fundamentally alter one's life.[73]

Why does understanding Pietist conversion matter? Conversion has long been central to depictions of German Pietism. But it has often functioned as a caricature, one derived from the compelling story of August Hermann Francke's own conversion. This overlooks the experiences and descriptions of other, lesser-known Pietists. Accounts of conversion were highly contested, remarkably diverse, and ultimately much more interesting than a single template would suggest. The assumption that a standard model lies beneath Pietist thinking and practice may be appealing, but it distorts our interpretations.[74] Conversion experiences present a host of interpretive difficulties, yet caricatures aid modern historians no more than reliance on pharmacological or magical descriptions aided eighteenth-century readers.

Most Pietists simply did not make an experience of conversion a compulsory requirement of the Christian life. This explains why so many prominent Pietists, from Philipp Jacob Spener to Justus Joachim Breithaupt and Paul Anton to Joachim Lange, described no conversion experiences in their autobiographies, and why the composers of conversion narratives, such as August Hermann Francke, did little to publicize their own or urge others to narrate theirs. Ambivalence about conversion narratives continued throughout much of the eighteenth century and was constitutive of (and not merely incidental for) Pietism. It drove Pietists to constrain and shape conversion narratives in ways that separated Pietist narratives from those of evangelicals in Britain and North America.

It is partly for these reasons that German conversion narratives have always sat somewhat uneasily in broad narratives of the development of autobiography. Günther Niggl begins his landmark book on German autobiography with Francke's conversion narrative as the prime example of a new form of spiritual reflection and vocational autobiography, but he finds few successors to Francke's narrative. Later writers either "subverted" Francke's conversion model (Joachim Lange) or resurrected "schoolmasterly" versions (Friedrich Oetinger) on the path to secularizing Pietist autobiography.[75] Yet the secularizing teleology at the heart of Niggl's analysis may be misplaced, and one wonders whether the full, public impact of autobiographical conversion narratives like Francke's may have been felt only in the nineteenth century, at least in the subculture of evangelical Protestants, after his narrative became well known and these German Protestants became more comfortable with public portrayals of conversion.[76]

German Pietism may not have been the fertile ground for public, autobiographical retellings of conversion that one finds among evangelical communities in Britain or Anglophone North America in the eighteenth century. Hindmarsh argues that "the evangelical conversion narrative flourished, then, when Christendom, or Christian civil society, had eroded far enough to allow for toleration, dissent, experimentation, and the manifestation of nominal and sincere forms of adherence to faith, but not so far as to elide a traditional sense of Christian moral norms and basic theological and cosmological assumptions."[77] Perhaps in eighteenth-century Germany, Christian civil society had not yet eroded to the point that could allow for the level of toleration, dissent, experimentation, and open expressions of faith that Hindmarsh identifies in Britain. Despite some openings, German lands did not have the level of religious differentiation, at least among Protestants, that characterized eighteenth-century Britain. Conversion accounts in German Pietism remained confessionalized in many respects, and Pietist leaders tightly controlled how lay men and women expressed their faith publicly in narratives.[78] Given the Pietist emphasis on conversion as a goal, the lack of a strong, public tradition of autobiographical conversion narratives may have created a vacuum that allowed other depictions to fill the void. One of the tropes of German literature in the eighteenth century is the story of a hypocritical conversion, which figured prominently in Gottsched's satirical play *Pietisterey in Fischbeinröcke* and more influentially in Karl Philip Moritz's novel *Anton Reiser*. The relative scarcity of prominent Pietists, lay or clergy, who published their own autobiographical accounts—apart from the extremity of the execution narratives or the drama of death—may have ceded ground to Pietist critics to explain to a reading public what conversion experiences might mean.

This book has deliberately focused on the inner-Christian mode of early modern conversion that scholars identify as transformation or intensification, and which lies at the heart of Pietist conceptions of true conversion. While it is not identical with other forms of conversion, whether from another religion to Christianity or between Christian confessions, understanding the ways eighteenth-century Pietists depicted experiences of conversion or *Bekehrung* has relevance for these other forms as well. In this sense, the current division between *Bekehrung* and *Konversion* in much current German historiography can be unhelpful, and it also points to the limitation of discrete modes of conversion that do not overlap. Some Pietists interpreted conversions not merely as an intensification of something already present but an event at least as momentous as a Protestant becoming Catholic, or a Jew becoming baptized; in their eyes, the individual moved from a nominal, false Christianity to a true Christianity that signaled a fundamental change in their eternal fate.

Pietist perceptions of conversion colored the Pietist approach to other forms of conversion in the eighteenth century, whether it was among missionaries in South Asia, in which initial expectations of conversion to Christianity tracked Pietist expectations of a specific pattern of conversion, such as the case of Ziegenbalg and Kanapati Vattiyar, or in the Institutum Judaicum at Halle, where coworkers were often disappointed that their Jewish proselytes did not exhibit the Pietist patterns of conversion they expected.[79] It would be hard to conceive of demands for the conversion of Joseph Süsskind Oppenheimer in Württemberg before his execution apart from the larger context of expectations around Pietist conversion at that time. Or later in 1769, when Lavater called on Moses Mendelssohn to convert to Christianity, Pietist expectations of conversion, though here with millenarian overtones, were likely at work.[80] By no means should Pietist conversion be the norm for all other forms of conversion in eighteenth-century Germany, but conceptions of conversion were dynamic across discrete modes or categories that the distinctions of *Bekehrung* and *Konversion* obscure rather than illuminate.

The recovery of August Hermann Francke's conversion account in the late eighteenth century gave it a prominence it lacked for most of the eighteenth century, not only in Germany but abroad as well.[81] It may well be that nineteenth-century descendants of Pietism in the *Erweckungsbewegung* found Francke's story particularly amenable to their own views of conversion; certainly it avoided the most problematic aspects of many eighteenth-century conversion narratives.[82] In the nineteenth century, Francke's autobiography was recounted and reprinted more than it ever had been in the eighteenth. In both scholarly and popular accounts it came to be seen as the paradigmatic conversion narrative of Pietism, but that view belies a much more ambivalent and problematic relationship of Pietists to conversion in the eighteenth century, who prized it as a goal and yet struggled to define true conversion and come to terms with it in practice and depiction.

NOTES

INTRODUCTION

1. Scholars continue to debate the definition and parameters of Pietism. For an overview, see Strom, "Problems and Promises." See also Shantz, *German Pietism*, 1–11. A review of the debates is found in Lehmann, "Perspektiven."
2. Francke quoted in Erb, ed., *Pietists*, 105.
3. James, *Varieties*. There is a substantial literature on conversion. One of the best resources on current scholarship from diverse methodological perspectives is Rambo and Farhadian, eds., *Oxford Handbook*.
4. Carlebach, *Divided Souls*. On fears of Christian conversion to Islam in early modern Britain, see Degenhardt, *Islamic Conversion*, 1–9.
5. Duggan, "Compulsion and Conversion."
6. Corpis, *Crossing the Boundaries of Belief*; Lotz-Heumann, Mißfelder, and Pohlig, eds., *Konversion und Konfession*; Siebenhüner, "Glaubenswechsel."
7. Kieckhefer, "Convention and Conversion," 43.
8. Rambo, *Understanding Religious Conversion*, 12–14.
9. Shantz, "Conversion and Sarcasm."
10. Obst, "Elemente atheistischer Anfechtung."
11. Luria, "Politics of Protestant Conversion," 28.
12. See, for instance, the contributions in Bremmer, van Bekkum, and Molendijk, eds., *Paradigms*. One exception is the overview article by Breuer, "Konversionen."
13. Corpis, *Crossing the Boundaries of Belief*, 19; Lotz-Heumann, Mißfelder, and Pohlig, "Konversion und Konfession," 12.
14. Carlebach, *Divided Souls*. Conversion to Judaism from Christianity was far less common but not unknown. See, for instance, the collection by Mulsow and Popkin, eds., *Secret Conversions*.
15. This is especially notable in Siebenhüner's overview article "Glaubenswechsel in der Frühen Neuzeit."
16. A good example of this shift is Thomas Bertram's recent translation into German of Hertz's book *How Jews Became Germans*, in which he consistently employs *Konversion* and *konvertieren* rather than *Bekehrung* and *bekehren* to render the English "conversion" and "convert." See Hertz, *Wie Juden Deutsche wurden*.
17. Lotz-Heumann, Mißfelder, and Pohlig, "Konversion und Konfession," 17–23.
18. Most historians of Christianity continue to use *Bekehrung* for inner-Christian conversion; see, for example, Matthias, "Bekehrung und Wiedergeburt." Germanists continue to employ *Bekehrung* as well, although synonymous alternation with *Konversion* has become increasingly common. See, for instance, Schlette, *Selbst(er)findung*, 239, which identifies Francke's conversion explicitly as a *Konversion* but uses *Bekehrung* and *bekehren* more frequently. See also Kormann, *Ich, Welt und Gott*.
19. Herbst, *Wie finden Erwachsene zum Glauben?*, 173–74. Unless otherwise indicated, translations here are my own.

20. Morrison, *Understanding Conversion*, 28–29.

21. Pollack, "Überlegungen," esp. 36, 37, 47, 48.

22. The distinction between the event or experience of conversion, on the one hand, and a narrative description of it, on the other, is one of the central points in Morrison, *Understanding Conversion*, xi–xiii, 4–5.

23. Mahrholz emphasizes the unique insight afforded by autobiography. See Mahrholz, "Wert der Selbstbiographie."

24. On Calov on conversion in the context of *vocatio*, see Appold, *Abraham Calov's Doctrine of "Vocatio,"* 96–100.

25. See, for instance, Kurten, *Umkehr*. Kurten recognizes some of the difficulties but does not resolve them. See also Sträter, "August Hermann Francke," 27–28. Sträter sees his biographical experience as the "turning point and fulcrum" of engagement with Francke's theology.

26. See Morgan, *Visible Saints*; Pettit, *Heart Prepared*; and Caldwell, *Puritan Conversion Narrative*. For later British Protestantism, see Hindmarsh, *Evangelical Conversion Narrative*.

27. Niggl, *Geschichte*; Schlette, *Selbst(er)findung*. The classic work by Misch, *Geschichte der Autobiographie*, puts less emphasis on Francke and Pietist conversion narratives than on other spiritual autobiographies that did not function as accounts of conversion (vol. 4, pt. 2, 810–11).

28. Hindmarsh, *Evangelical Conversion Narrative*, 342.

29. The terms "church" and "radical" Pietism remain problematic but are established in the literature on Pietism. For a thoughtful analysis of the radical Pietism including a new typology, see Shantz, *German Pietism*, 147–78.

30. Harran describes Luther's *Turmerlebnis* as "the culminating insight—the moment of conversion—in a long process." See Harran, *Luther on Conversion*, 190. Gaventa also cites Luther's experience as a classic example of conversion. See Gaventa, *From Darkness to Light*, 10–12.

31. On the primacy of repentance in the Reformation understanding of conversion, see Steinmetz, "Reformation and Conversion." The process of conversion for the Reformers, Steinmetz argues, "is not completed until every aspect of the human personality is driven out in the light of God's severe mercy, judged and renewed" (28).

32. See, for instance, Wengert and Kolb, eds., *Book of Concord*, 209. More broadly, see Althaus, "Bekehrung," 4ff.

33. Ibid., 13.

34. Ibid.

35. Heshus, *Vier Predigten von der Busse und Bekehrung zu Gott*. As part of the larger process of *Buße*, see especially fol. 41v.

36. Arndt, *Von wahrem Christenthumb*, 1:33.

37. Ibid., 1:36, 70, 222–23.

38. In the sense of "conversion of the heart from the world to God." See ibid., 1:39.

39. The changes in book 1, chapter 21, between the final 1610 edition and the original edition in 1605 are telling in this regard. See Arndt, *Vier Bücher von wahrem Christenthumb* (1610), 1:222; Arndt, *Von wahrem Christenthumb: Die Urausgabe des ersten Buches* (1605), 181. Later in book 2, Arndt is keen to stress that conversion is effected only by God. Arndt, *Vier Bücher von wahrem Christenthumb*, 2:5. On Arndt's efforts to avoid synergism, see Schneider, *Der fremde Arndt*, 78–79.

40. Holl, "Die Bedeutung der großen Kriege," 324–25.

41. Großgebauer, *Wächterstimme*.

42. On Großgebauer, see Strom, *Orthodoxy and Reform*, 195–221.

43. See Leube, *Reformideen*.

44. Großgebauer, "Treuer Unterricht von der Wiedergeburt," an appendix to *Wächterstimme*, 95.

45. "Many rest in the thought, as they have so unfortunately been taught and guided, that they have been converted in baptism." Großgebauer, *Wächterstimme*, 72; also Großgebauer, "Treuer Unterricht," 85.

46. Großgebauer, *Wächterstimme*, 73.

47. For Großgebauer this was typically in adulthood, although he allowed the possibility of conversion or regeneration in childhood. See Großgebauer, "Treuer Unterricht," 74.

48. Großgebauer is quite clear that conversion takes place in an hour or even a single moment. Ibid., 93.

49. Ibid., 95.

50. The issue of baptismal regeneration was a major point of contention between Reformed and Lutheran believers. See Theodore Beza's 1586 comments to Jakob Andreae in Nischan, *Prince, People, and Confession*, 141.

51. On Spener's reception of Großgebauer and his understanding of regeneration, see Wallmann, *Spener*, 172–74.

52. See Wallmann, *Der Pietismus*, 110.

53. For an overview on conversion narratives and the gathered churches see Hindmarsh, *Evangelical Conversion Narrative*, 46–50. See also Morgan, *Visible Saints*; and Caldwell, *Puritan Conversion Narrative*.

54. On Großgebauer, see Strom, *Orthodoxy and Reform*, 195–221; and especially on conversion, see ibid., 213–15.

55. In contrast to most later conversion narratives, the turning point for Engelbrecht is a near-death experience and vision of ecstatic transport through which he becomes more enlightened than "any learned doctor." Engelbrecht, *Warhafftige Geschicht*, 27–29. Engelbrecht's story was widely recounted and reprinted well into the eighteenth century. Anna Vetter combined her visions with a kind of spiritual autobiography that also had some structural similarities with later conversion narratives, but as in Engelbrecht divine visions form the turning point and claim to authority. Vetter's autobiography and visions were published in Arnold, *Unpartheyische Kirchen- und Ketzerhistorie*, 2:280–94, esp. on her spiritual renewal, 2:282. See also Kormann, *Ich, Welt und Gott*, 158–73.

56. Scriver's tales often described a sudden conviction on the part of the individual against their previous life and a turn toward humility and holy living. See, for example, Scriver, *Seelen-Schatz*, 1:122, 138. Scriver includes similar stories of Jewish conversion to Christianity; see ibid., 1:136–37. These stories had a rhetorical value for Scriver, but he also emphasized that such abrupt conversions were unusual, and that most conversions were long, extended processes. Ibid., 1:177–78.

57. On this point, see Greyerz, "Was It Enjoyable?," 184. Recent literature on Germany has given a fair amount of attention to forms of autobiographical compositions, also referred to as self-narratives (*Selbstzeugnisse*) and ego-documents (*Ego-Dokumente*). See Greyerz, ed., *Selbstzeugnisse der Frühen Neuzeit*; Kormann, *Ich, Welt und Gott*; Greyerz, Medick, and Veit, eds., *Dargestellte Person*; Krusenstjern, "Was sind Selbstzeugnisse?"

58. Fabricius, *Kurtze und warhaffte Beschreibung*. Fabricius used the pseudonym Justus Kläger. On Fabricius and his autobiography, see Klueting, *Reformatio vitae*, 94. Despite the language of turning, Fabricius does not name this a conversion, but a later biographer, writing in the 1690s, does. See Holterhoff, *Memoria Johannis Jacobi Fabricii*, 2.

59. Bullen, *Vox Clamantis*, 98–99. Bullen did not describe this as conversion. Rather, for Bullen as in Arndt, repentance (*Buße*) und conversion (*Bekehrung*) remained largely synonymous. See ibid., 97.

60. The longer account is found in Forschungsbibliothek Gotha, Chart A 306, 184ff. A shorter account is found in the appendix to Gottfried Arnold, *Unpartheyische Kirchen- und Ketzerhistorie*, 2:1103, which was contributed by Breckling.

61. On Kühlmann, see Schmidt-Biggemann, "Salvation Through Philology," where Schmidt-Biggemann discusses Kühlmann's Böhmist conversion (262–64). See also Mahrholz, *Deutsche Selbstbekenntnisse*, 113–17.

62. Deppermann, *Johann Jakob Schütz*. See also Wallmann, *Der Pietismus*, 137–43.

63. Spener quoted in Deppermann, *Johann Jakob Schütz*, 60.

64. Deppermann, *Johann Jakob Schütz*, 60–61. On atheism as a theme in Pietist conversion, see Obst, "Elemente atheistischer Anfechtung"; and de Boor, "Erfahrung gegen Vernunft."

65. Deppermann, *Johann Jakob Schütz*, 61–62.

66. See Spener's remarks from 1690 in Spener, *Theologische Bedencken*, vol. 1, pt. 2, 197–98. For Spener's criticisms of conversion narratives, see below.

67. Deppermann, *Johann Jakob Schütz*, 194.

68. Ibid., 122–24.

69. On these, see ibid., 120–23. For instance, Schütz's account of Maria Juliana Baur von Eyseneck includes no conversion experience. The biography was reprinted by Arnold in *Leben der Gläubigen*.

70. Petersen, *Eine kurtze Erzehlung*, 235–95. On this account, see Albrecht, *Johanna Eleonora Petersen*, 222–23. Kormann devotes substantial analysis to the appendix (*Eine kurtze Erzehlung*); see Kormann, *Ich, Welt und Gott*, 113–47. That Kormann contrasts the *Eine kurtze Erzehlung* with her husband's much more secular autobiography, rather than with equivalent models of male spiritual autobiography (e.g., August Hermann Francke), undermines some of her conclusions on the nature of spiritual autobiography and gender.

71. A well-edited modern edition of the complete autobiography is Petersen, *Leben*, edited by Prisca Guglielmetti. See also Petersen, *Life of Lady Johanna Eleonora Petersen*, edited and translated by Barbara Becker-Cantarino.

72. Guglielmetti, "Nachwort," 96–97.

73. Spener, *Werke*, 1:1.

74. Witt, *Bekehrung*, 184. Here the depiction of the individual's spiritual experiences grants a kind of authority to their convictions; right doctrine, while not irrelevant, takes a secondary role.

CHAPTER 1

1. The most complete, modern edition of the autobiographical conversion of August Hermann Francke is Matthias's *Lebensläufe*, 5–32. Matthias also provides an excellent overview of the extensive literature on Franck's narrative (153–54). A partial English translation of the narrower conversion experience is found in Erb, ed., *Pietists*, 99–107. Translations for the first part of the *Lebenslauff* are my own; latter sections follow Erb, unless otherwise noted.

2. Lagny, "Lebenslauff et Bekehrung," 109.

3. Cf. Niggl, *Geschichte*, 8–9.

4. Francke, *Lebensläufe*, 5–6.

5. Ibid., 7, 10, 11.

6. Ibid., 12.

7. Ibid., 13.

8. Ibid., 14.

9. Ibid., 17.

10. Schneider, *German Radical Pietism*, 158; on its use among radicals and dissidents, see Gierl, *Pietismus und Aufklärung*, 502–8.

11. Francke, *Lebensläufe*, 23–24; Erb, ed., *Pietists*, 101 (my translation).

12. Francke, *Lebensläufe*, 24; Erb, ed., *Pietists*, 101.

13. Francke, *Lebensläufe*, 27–29; Erb, ed., *Pietists*, 104–5.
14. Francke, *Lebensläufe*, 29; Erb, ed., *Pietists*, 105.
15. De Boor, "Erfahrung gegen Vernunft."
16. Francke, *Lebensläufe*, 26; Erb, ed., *Pietists*, 103.
17. Francke, *Lebensläufe*, 144.
18. Francke, *Lebensläufe*, 30; Erb, ed., *Pietists*, 106.
19. Francke, *Lebensläufe*, 31; Erb, ed., *Pietists*, 106.
20. Francke, *Lebensläufe*, 31; Erb, ed., *Pietists*, 106.
21. Stahl, *Francke*.
22. Peschke, *Bekehrung und Reform*, 13–40.
23. On de Molinos, see Baird, "Miguel de Molinos"; and McGinn, "Miguel de Molinos and the *Spiritual Guide*."
24. Francke, *Collegivm Pastorale*, 2:579. See also Krämer, *Lebensbild*, 29–30. On Scharff and Großgebauer, see also Wallmann, *Der Pietismus*, 110.
25. Matthias, "Gewissheit und Bekehrung." In opposition to Wallmann, Matthias discounts the influence of Großgebauer through Scharff, but his argument relies largely on Großgebauer's theological departures from Scharff's more orthodox Lutheranism and assumes a rather linear transmission of ideas (12–13). Given that Francke later credited Scharff with introducing him to Großgebauer, it is entirely possible that Francke absorbed aspects of Großgebauer's ideas of conversion with which Scharff may have disagreed.
26. See Spener's critical remarks regarding the English conversion narratives in 1690— roughly at the same time that Francke composed his narrative in Erfurt. Spener, *Theologische Bedencken*, vol. 1, pt. 2, 197–98. This indicates that such narratives were well known to at least some German Pietists at this time.
27. Matthias has suggested the period of October 1690 to March 1691 as the most likely time of its composition. See Matthias, "Franckes Erweckungserlebnis," 77; Matthias, "Gewissheit und Bekehrung," 30; Francke, *Lebensläufe*, 73–75.
28. Spener, *Briefwechsel mit August Hermann Francke*, 91, 103.
29. Francke, *Lebensläufe*, 77.
30. "Francke told the story of his conversion over and over again." Henningsen, "Leben," 279.
31. Henningsen's ellipses and condensations in the relevant quote (p. 276) give it a coherence from which the reader would conclude that Francke is speaking about his own conversion. The original citation makes it more likely that only readers who already knew the outline of his conversion story might have seen the passage as Francke's self-description. See Francke, *Zweyfache Schriftliche Ansprache*, 44–50.
32. Albrecht-Birkner notes that one of Francke's lay opponents, Johann Martin Weidner, appeared to refer directly to phrases from his conversion account in 1704. She cites it as the oldest known example of the reception of Francke's conversion account. Albrecht-Birkner, *Francke in Glaucha*, 103. Weidner was long associated with members of Francke's circle dating back to Erfurt in the early 1690s, a time when Francke's conversion account likely circulated among friends, and Weidner's acquaintance with it may date from then rather than the early 1700s. Weidner appears to have been a contentious figure from his Erfurt days. See Albrecht-Birkner, *Francke in Glaucha*, 41–42. Having studied theology in Erfurt and then Halle, he later became a tailor, which did not affect his willingness to engage in ongoing theological controversies with leading Pietists. In addition to his conflict with Francke, he accused Justus Joachim Breithaupt of Pelagian tendencies. See his letter to Breithaupt from August 24, 1716, Universitätsbibliothek Kassel, 4 Ms. hist. litt. 15[408,2.
33. *Fortgesetzte Sammlung auserlesener Materien zum Bau des Reichs Gottes* (hereafter *FSAM*) 36 (1736): 472.
34. Albrecht-Birkner argues that it was his sermons and not his conversion story that was the model for conversion (*Bekehrungsanleitung*). Albrecht-Birkner, "Franckes Krisen," 97. There

are, however, hundreds of Francke's manuscript sermons that have never been analyzed that could provide greater support for this line of argument.

35. See Schubert's account, where he consults Francke in the midst of his conversion, in *Altes und Neues aus dem Reich Gottes* 4 (1734): 10. Francke's response is characteristically terse.

36. On Wesley's Aldersgate experience and subsequent interpretation of it, see Outler, ed., *John Wesley*, 51–53. See also Maddox, ed., *Aldersgate Reconsidered*.

37. Though condensed, the similarity of phrasing and flow suggests that Francke may have had a copy of the narrower conversion account on hand. Dated March 23, 1727, the letter was reprinted in the journal *Theologia Pastoralis Practica*. See Francke, "Erbauliche Briefe."

38. Krämer, *Beiträge*, 61.

39. There are two accounts of the prayer in the garden. The first appears in *Kurtze, iedoch gründliche Nachricht* (reprinted in Francke, *Lebensläufe*) and an account quoted by Niemeyer in "Uebersicht," 2:290–92. The latter account is much more circumspect about conversion. Which of the two is more reliable is difficult to ascertain. Though *Kurtze iedoch gründliche Nachricht* is earlier, its author is unknown and may have shaped its presentation in a particular direction. Selections in Niemeyer's article tended to be based on archival sources.

40. Anton, *Knecht des Herrn*, 13.

41. Matthias, *Lebensläufe*, 6.

42. *Die Glaubens-Kraft Eines Evangelischen Lehrers*, 6. The Francke Foundations or Institutes (die Franckeschen Stiftungen) were the complex of social and educational institutions that grew out of Francke's original orphanage begun in 1695. For an overview, see Obst, *August Hermann Francke*.

43. The fact that the story told here and that in the *Lebenslauff* differ in some details (the *Lebenslauff* mentions eleven or twelve years, this account ten) suggests that Francke did retell it.

44. Francke, *Lebensläufe*, 111. Johann Georg Francke (also Franck) was not related to August Hermann Francke.

45. The story of a decisive experience in one's early youth was common among many Pietist leaders. See the *Lebensläufe* of Joachim Lange and of Joachim Justus Breithaupt—Lange, *Lebenslauf*, 6–9; Breithaupt, "Breithaupts eigenhändig aufgesetzter Lebens=Lauf." Niggl sees Lange's autobiography (started in 1720 and published in 1744) as subverting the schema established by Francke's own narrative (Niggl, *Geschichte*, 11), but this would be doubtful if Francke's narrative was not well known and therefore lacked model character as argued below. Cf. Niggl, "Zur Säkularisation der pietistischen Autobiographie," 378–79. On Breithaupt's early experience, see Rieger, "Besessenheit und Pietismus." On the contrast with Francke's narrative, see Lagny, "Breithaupts Lebensbeschreibung."

46. *Personalia* in Francke, *Lehrer der Kirche*, 19, 20.

47. Alberti, *Wohlverdientes Ehrengedächtniß*, 5, emphasis added.

48. Rogall cites the passage from Francke, *Zweyfachen Ansprache*, 44ff., as autobiographical, but he does not use the word "conversion" to refer to this. Later he compares Francke's emphasis on *Buße* and *Bekehrung* to Luther, casting Francke's understanding of conversion in a traditional Lutheran context. See Rogall, "Paranesis publica," 188–89. It is unlikely that the *Personalia* would have reached Rogall by the time of his address.

49. Schwentzel, *Salomon*, 9–10. Schwentzel alludes to a sermon, probably Francke, *Kurtzer Unterricht von der Möglichkeit der wahren Bekehrung*. See Albrecht-Birkner, "Franckes Krisen," 90. Raabe and Pfeiffer identify eight editions of this sermon by 1740. See Raabe and Pfeiffer, eds., *August Hermann Francke*, 133–35.

50. Freylinghausen, *Amt u. Werck*, 45.

51. Gotthilf August Francke proposed reading his father's conversion narrative to the assembled students on September 18, 1727: "But since today an account has come into my hands that I have long sought after, in which the late man [i.e., A. H. Francke] had himself composed

[the account of his conversion] already many years ago, I would thus like to read it aloud." Archiv der Franckeschen Stiftung, Halle (hereafter AFSt), H N13, 763. Cited in Francke, *Lebensläufe*, 78.

52. Francke, *Kurtze, iedoch gründliche Nachricht*.
53. Letter from Lippe to G. A. Francke, November 19, 1728, Staatsbibliothek zu Berlin–Preußischer Kulturbesitz, Berlin (hereafter StBPK), Francke Nachlass, 2, 15/3.
54. Gerber mentions the visit to study exegesis with Sandhagen in Lüneburg but omits any mention of the conversion or spiritual struggle there. Gerber, *Zweyter Anhang zu der Historie der Wiedergebohrnen in Sachsen*, 264. Gerber must have composed the account after May 1728 because in it he described reading Francke's funeral sermon to his wife during her final illness at Pentecost (280). It may be that neither the *Concise Report* nor Freylinghausen's sermon had reached him by then.
55. *Altes und Neues* 3 (1733): 56–69.
56. Mather, ed., *Vita*.
57. Niceron, *Nachrichten*, 17:201. See also the preface by editor F. E. Rambach, who would have experienced A. H. Francke personally as a student and as a colleague of his father.
58. Niemeyer, "Uebersicht," 34.
59. Knapp, "Beyträge," 419. A reprinting of the narrower conversion account follows these comments.
60. Kanne begins the spiritual biography with the story of the ten-year-old Francke withdrawing to his room to pray but then draws heavily from the Lüneburg experience. Kanne, *Leben*, 175–83, esp. 180–81.
61. Guericke, *August Hermann Francke*, 30–44.
62. Brown, *Memoirs of Augustus Hermann Francke*, 29–33. This was largely based on the Guericke biography cited above.
63. Schmid, *Geschichte des Pietismus*, 156–59.
64. Krämer, *August Hermann Francke*.
65. Ritschl, *Geschichte des Pietismus*, 2:250–53.

CHAPTER 2

1. Aland, "Bemerkungen," 563.
2. Mori, *Begeisterung*.
3. Wallmann, "Erfurt und der Pietismus," 413.
4. Brückner, AFSt, H D84, fol. 17v.
5. See book 3, chapter 6: "Wie sich das höchste ewige Gut oft in unserer Seele eräugert in einem Augenblick." Arndt, *Vier Bücher von wahrem Christenthumb*, 1610. This passage actually stems from Johannes Tauler; see Wallmann, "Erfurt und der Pietismus," 419.
6. Brückner, AFSt, H D84, fol. 17v.
7. Francke, *Lebensläufe*, 29; Erb, ed., *Pietists*, 105.
8. Francke, *Lebensläufe*, 19–20. Francke translated Molinos into Latin, and it is likely through this translation that Brückner became familiar with Molinos.
9. Fratzscher's "Bericht" was from 1690. See AFSt, H D84, fol. 18r.
10. AFSt, H D84, fol. 18r.
11. AFSt, H D89, 233–34.
12. Lächele considers Nehrlich's experience in Erfurt as indeed being a conversion. See Lächele, "Einführung," 4. This text contains an autobiographical account composed by Nehrlich in 1723. In his later account, Nehrlich describes a long spiritual discussion with Francke, and he identifies a sermon by Breithaupt as especially moving. Perhaps this was the basis for the reference to Simeon in the Temple that the contemporaneous account cites (35–36).

13. *Sammlung auserlesener Materien zum Bau des Reichs Gottes* (hereafter *SAMR*) 7 (1732): 821–31. Notable in this account is Francke's directing him toward faith in Christ alone rather than toward further concern with his sinfulness and repentance (826–28).

14. Freylinghausen describes this transformation in his *Lebenslauf*, published upon his death: *Wohlverdientes Ehren-Gedächtniß*, 34–35. Freylinghausen briefly discussed the composition of *Lebenslauf* with A. H. Francke in a letter dated June 16, 1725 (AFSt, H C241, 39), and it is likely that the autograph *Lebenslauf*, which only appeared in print after his death, dated from this period. See also Paul, *Johannes Anastasius Freylinghausen*, 55–61.

15. Another autobiographical fragment from the same period is a confession of faith by Gebhard Levin Semler, AFSt, H D89, 92–93. On Semler, see Mori, *Begeisterung und Ernüchtung*, 46, 157.

16. The date of the narrative itself is unclear. Perhaps she composed it as early as 1692. Her handwritten account was reprinted in her funeral sermon, and another third-person version appears in the archives at Halle. The autobiographical account is reprinted with her funeral sermon, Francke, *Gedächtniß- und Leichen-Predigten*, 456–58; and in Henckel von Donnersmarck, *Die letzten Stunden*, 2:122–24. Her testament contains a third-person account, but nearly identical in form. See AFSt X/1/1. Von Schönberg's conversion narrative did not, however, mark the end of her spiritual struggles. See below; and Witt, *Bekehrung*, 167–84.

17. Spener, *Briefwechsel mit August Hermann Francke*, 91.

18. Wendland, "Die pietistische Bekehrung," 197–98.

19. Wallmann, "Erfurt und der Pietismus," 414–15.

20. AFSt, H D89, 233–34.

21. Wallmann, "Erfurt und der Pietismus," 415–17.

22. Lehmann, "Breithaupts Berufung."

23. The anonymous author of the exposé was very likely Johann Benedict Carpzov, *Außführliche Beschreibung*, 79.

24. Ibid.

25. Fergen, *Waarhafftiger Bericht*, 131–32.

26. See, for instance, on conversion, Olearius, *Geistliches Hand-Buch*, esp. 1369. Olearius's son, Johann Christian, one of Francke's early opponents, republished the *Geistliches Hand-Buch* in 1692, which shows that Pietists did not have a monopoly on language of conversion in the early 1690s during their battles with their orthodox opponents. See Winkler, "Christen als Minderheit," 405.

27. Wiegleb et al., *Confessio*, 7, 37–38. A further response to the critic of the *Confessio* indicates that perfectionism was largely the controversial issue at stake. See *Bescheidentliche Beantwortung*, 9–13.

28. In a document dated December 8, 1694, Johann Christian Graetzler described in two "acts" the attempt to convert him. Though his report has the character of a conversion account, it appears to criticize, even satirize, the conversionist attempts in Gotha, especially the intensive practices of prayer and the peer pressure of other students. Landesarchiv Thüringen–Staatsarchiv Gotha, Oberkonsistorium Loc. 17, Nr. 20, fols. 119r–120r.

29. See ibid., 171r. See also Rieger, "Eine pietistische Ausbildungsstätte?"

30. Landesarchiv Thüringen–Staatsarchiv Gotha: Oberkonsistorium Loc. 17, Nr. 20, fols. 172r–173v.

31. Ibid., fol. 187r–v. Cf. Rieger, "Eine pietistische Ausbildungsstätte?"

32. Wiegleb, *Haupt-Summa*, 32–36.

33. AFSt, H C243, 70.

34. Wiegleb, *Haupt-Summa*, 55–60, esp. 60.

35. Schade, *Lebenslauff*, fols. b4r, b6v.

36. Ibid., fols. b6v, b8r.

37. Ibid., fol. c3r.

38. Ibid., fol. c3v.

39. See Peschke, *Studien*, 1:42–47, 66–75. See also Kurten, *Umkehr*, 88–103; Witt, *Bekehrung*, 75–81; Kirn, "Penitential Struggle." Witt describes it as the "Triade des Heilsgeschehens." On the difficulties of the *Bußkampf* as normative, see below.

40. The anonymous author of a further biographical account, which appeared in the same publication as the original *Lebenslauf*, interpreted Schade's final *Anfechtung* as a comfort for those who were in a similar situation. See "Ausführlicher Bericht."

41. Spener, *Christliches Ehren-Gedächtnüß*; Weller, *Marter-Buch*; Arnold, *Leben der Gläubigen*.

42. See title page to Schade, *Geistreicher Schriften*, vol. 1.

43. Wendland treats the two accounts as mutually compatible. See Wendland, "Die pietistische Bekehrung," esp. 198, 222. Obst relies on the third-person account as the more accurate of the two. See Obst, "Elemente atheistischer Anfechtung."

44. It is possible that Schade drew on some of his own experiences in this account, but unless we presume that Schade repudiated his earlier *Lebenslauf*—something for which there is no evidence—it is more likely that Schade intended this not as an alternate description of his conversion, but rather as an exemplary account designed to help others find a "bridge and handhold" to rescue themselves from the "mud of unbelief and their blinded minds." Schade, "Merckwürdige und erbauliche Erzehlung," 410.

45. Reprinted in Reitz, *Historie der Wiedergebohrnen*. On Reitz and the publishing history of this collection, see Schrader, *Literaturproduktion und Büchermarkt*.

46. Preface to Reitz, *Historie der Wiedergebohrnen*, vol. 1.

47. Mohr, "Über die *Historie der Wiedergebohrnen*," 80.

48. Reitz, *Historie der Wiedergebohrnen*, 2:85. Cf. Franckenberg, *Gründlicher und wahrhafter Bericht*, 5–31.

49. Reitz, *Historie der Wiedergebohrnen*, 2:120–31.

50. Ibid., 3:63–64.

51. The account describes briefly what is usually identified as his conversion in 1654 as a turning point in which Pascal forsakes his scientific investigations. However, most of the narrative recounts a first-person confession of Pascal's from the end of his life. See ibid., 2:218.

52. An anonymous account of a pastor's widow from Ottweiler describes a vision of Christ, whose kiss reveals to her that he is her bridegroom and that her name is written in the book of eternal life. See ibid., 2:229–30. See also the biographies of Jacob Böhme and Hans Engelbrecht that Reitz republished in abbreviated form. Ibid., 2:82–89 and 2:120–31.

53. Reitz, *Historie der Wiedergebohrnen*, 3:192–215.

54. Ibid., 3:221–22. For an in-depth analysis of Schumacher's conversion experience, see Dellsperger, *Anfänge*, 44–52. Dellsperger points out that Reitz shortened Schumacher's account and made it less mystical.

55. Reitz, *Historie der Wiedergebohrnen*, 3:236–50.

56. Mücke, "Experience," 21.

57. Arnold, *Vitae Patrum*, 1:163–65, 1:309, 2:56–63, foreword to vol. 1. Francke here also emphasizes the diverse ways that God leads each individual. For an extended interpretation of Francke's preface and the issues of exemplarity such collections present, see Erickson, "Religious Conversion," 63–69.

58. Arnold, *Leben der Gläubigen*, 1143–58. Reitz presents the same story in a slightly condensed version. Kißner's deathbed struggles have some similarities with the later accounts of the so-called *Letzte Stunden* (last hours). See below.

59. "Georg Frederick von Hohendorffs Buß-Glaubens- und Todes Proceß," in ibid., 247–55. This account was later reprinted by Moser in his *Seelige Letzte Stunden 31 Personen*, 633–52.

60. Francke, "Foreword," in Weller, *Creutz-Schule*, fols. A5r, A6v, A7r.

61. Weller, *Marter-Buch*. The appendix included Schade's autobiography along with accounts by Berlin Pietists Johann Paul Astmann and Johann Fritschen. On Weller, see Kolb, *For All the Saints*, 152–53.

62. For Leipzig, see Eler's reminiscences in Reitz, *Historie der Wiedergebohrnen*, 7:146.

63. This tract was first published anonymously in 1695 and later appeared in many editions under Francke's name. See Francke, *Kurtze und einfältig iedoch gründliche Anleitung*, 4.

64. Spener, *Theologische Bedenken*, vol. 1, pt. 2, 197–98.

65. Spener, *Letzte theologische Bedencken*, 2:116.

66. Albrecht-Birkner, *Francke in Glaucha*.

67. Aland, "Bemerkungen," 563.

68. See, recently, Mettele, "Constructions," 20, who compares the diversity of Moravian patterns of conversion with the "single compulsory 'method'" at Halle.

69. Some scholars have long resisted the caricature of a compulsory method of conversion at Halle, among them Beyreuther, *Selbstzeugnisse*, 11–12; and Stoeffler, *German Pietism*, 14–15. More recently, see Matthias, "Bekehrung und Wiedergeburt," 61.

70. Although *Bußkampf* is often translated as the "penitential struggle," and occasionally "atonement struggle," given the broader implications of *Buße* in Lutheran Pietism I prefer "repentance struggle." It also does not imply that through acts of penitence or atonement one somehow earns conversion, a position Pietists would have rejected.

71. Peschke, *Studien*, 1:46.

72. See especially ibid., 1:66–75. It is noteworthy, though, that here Peschke does not really harmonize the distinct ways Francke classified individuals into different categories.

73. See Kurten, *Umkehr*, 88–103. Oddly, though Kurten recognizes the criticism of the dominant *Bußkampf* model of conversion at Halle, she does not really attempt to resolve the objections (69–77).

74. Witt develops her understanding of "Die Triade des Heilsgeschens" in *Bekehrung*, 75–81.

75. *Vom Reschschaffenen Wachsthum des Glaubens*, preached November 1, 1691, in Halberstadt, reprinted in Francke, *Predigten*, 1:33–34; "Die scharfe Augen Christi in Beurtheilung einer wahren und falschen Herzensbekehrung," preached July 26, 1722, AFSt, H M15b, 255–315. In the former, he concluded by admonishing his listeners to examine themselves truthfully regarding whether they belong to the unconverted, the penitent, or the faithful. In the latter, he discussed Christ's ability to discern among true and false conversions.

76. See, for instance, the discussion with students from July 4, 1709, in Francke, *Lectiones*, 4:293–99; on preaching and conversion, see *Vom erbaulichen Predigen*; on the theme of conversion in his biblical lectures, see Francke, *Observationes Biblicae*, esp. 397–99.

77. Peschke, *Bekehrung und Reform*, 113.

78. Among many examples, see Gawthrop, *Pietism*, 141; Hindmarsh, *Evangelical Conversion Narrative*, 164; and Herzog, *European Pietism Revisited*, 20.

79. More than modern translations, the King James Version comes closer to Luther's rendering and reads, "And if a man also strive for masteries, yet is he not crowned, except he strive lawfully." 2 Timothy 2:5. *Busz=Predigt über Ps. LI, v. 11, 12, 13. Darinnen Der Kampff eines Busfertigen Sünders vorgestellet worden Den. 5. Jun MDCXCV In der St. Georgen Kirche zu Glauche an Halle* (Halle, 1695), reprinted in Francke, *Predigten*, vol. 2.

80. Franke, *Predigten*, 2:37.

81. "Von dem Wercke der Bekehrung," preached on May 6, 1696, reprinted in Francke, *Predigten*, 2:46–47.

82. Franke, *Predigten*, 2:58–59, 61–64.

83. He writes, "Look: one may also call that a breakthrough [*Durchbruch*], a repentance struggle [*Bußkampff*], a work of repentance [*Buß-Arbeit*], yet it must first come to that, and one rejoices appropriately (and thanks God for it), when, with an individual, it has just come only so far that he properly recognizes his previous, miserable condition." AFSt, H M6, 33; Peschke, *Katalog*, Nr. 1069.

84. Freylinghausen, *Grundlegung der Theologie*. On Freylinghausen's theology of conversion, see Paul, *Johannes Anastasius Freylinghausen*, 186–204. Yet, Paul also tends to read a fixed notion of the *Bußkampf* into Freylinghausen.
85. Freylinghausen, *Grundlegung der Theologie*, 290–306.
86. Ibid., 304.
87. Freylinghausen, *Ordnung des Heyls*.
88. See, for instance, Breithaupt, *Der Ordinanden Examen*, where the *Bußkampf* is a synonym for *Anfechtung* and an example of the kind of profound spiritual experiences that good ministers should be able to draw in their interactions with the laity (fols. B7r–v). Cf. Paul, *Johannes Anastasius Freylinghausen*, 364–66.
89. Stoeffler, *German Pietism*, 50.
90. Matthias, "Bekehrung und Wiedergeburt," 67.
91. StBPK, Francke Nachlass, 21, 1/2, 63, Toellner to Francke in 1718.
92. Ward, *Protestant Evangelical Awakening*, 63, 72. A possible exception is a 1718 report by Toellner to Francke regarding an account of a "good arousal" among the orphans: "That indeed many have voluntarily declared orally as well as in writing, to convert righteously with God's help and also to come together in prayer after school and truly pursue sanctification earnestly." StBPK, Francke Nachlass, 21, 1/2, 63. Toellner makes no mention of the *Bußkampf*.
93. Francke, *Untergang*, 14–15.
94. Arnold, *Vitae Patrum*, and *Leben der Gläubigen*.
95. One exception might be the autobiographies that candidates for missionary work prepared before being sent abroad. See, for instance, Benjamin Schultze's 1718 autobiographical narrative in the Halle mission archive that recounts his long period of anguished doubt and spiritual despair in seeking God, though the converting turn in the narrative was largely intellectual and lacking language of *Bußkampf* or *Durchbruch*. AFSt, M 1 C 11, 51. However, not all of these autobiographical accounts in the mission archive portray a conversion prominently. Nicolas Dal's narrative from the same year described in a rather offhand manner how Francke's printed sermons became "the key to the door of God's kingdom of grace" after he encountered them, with no further elaboration. AFSt, M 1 C 11, 54. Both Dal and Schultze became longserving missionaries in India.
96. Francke, *Lectiones*, 3:384. Discussion from September 8, 1712.
97. Ibid., 4:295–96. Discussion from July 4, 1709.
98. Widén, *Bekehrung und Erziehung*, 5; Francke, *Kurtzer und Einfältiger Unterricht*.
99. On Francke's pedagogical methods, see Whitmer, *Halle Orphanage*.
100. Podczeck, *Schrift*, 82. Widén acknowledges this point, noting, "The precondition for successful teaching is naturally that the teachers and parents be living Christians." Widén, *Bekehrung und Erziehung*, 5.
101. On children and conversion, see Widén, *Bekehrung und Erziehung*, 5.
102. Francke called this an "unzeitiger Bekehrungsucht." See Francke, *Idea studiosi Theologiae*, here 470.
103. Rotermund, *Orthodoxie und Pietismus*, 114.
104. Greschat here gives examples of Francke and other Pietists lamenting Löscher's "unconverted" state and demanding that he convert, but this was less of a demand for a spiritual experience than it was for Löscher to affirm the teachings of the Halle Pietists and recant his criticisms of the Halle party. See Greschat, *Zwischen Tradition*, 293–307.
105. For an example, see the sermon by Francke on the problem of the unconverted clergy and their ineffectiveness. "Von dem Dienst untreuer Lehrer," in Francke, *Predigten*, 1:400–437. See also Strom, "Pietism and Revival," 191–93.
106. Bach, "Halle Testimonial System," 41.

107. A. H. Francke, "Die scharfe Augen Christi in Beurtheilung einer wahren und falschen Herzensbekehrung," AFSt, H M15b, 261.
108. Ibid., 300.
109. Francke, *Die Bekehrung Durch Leibliche Trübsal*, 33.
110. Rosenbach, *Bekehrung*, 1.
111. On Francke's relationship to Rosenbach, see Schneider, "Der radikale Pietismus," 141.
112. Morrison, *Understanding Conversion*, 4.
113. See, for instance, chapter 1, above, where I discuss a conversation from the late 1690s recalled by a peasant on Canstein's estate, Jacob Schneider.
114. Gerber's account, published two years later, is detailed but omits any mention of a conversion experience.
115. On the contrast between Spener and August Hermann Francke on conversion, see Wallmann, *Der Pietismus*, 109. On Spener's caution regarding conversation narratives, see Spener, *Letzte theologische Bedenken*, 2:116; and above.
116. Francke, *Collegivm pastorale*, 2:232–33. Francke concluded, "Thus it is not a method that one can prescribe as a rule and say: therefore, one should also do it like this in the future." He continued, "They are exemplars that are not imitable; [they are] singular exemplars of a personal kind."

CHAPTER 3

1. Literally these refer to accounts of an individual's death and became an important part of spiritual biography in the eighteenth century. For a list of those published by Pietists, see Lächele, "'Maleficanten' und Pietisten," 199–200. Many were composed only in manuscript.
2. Francke, *Der letzte und schöne Glaubens-Kampff des Israels Gottes*. Although preached in 1703, it was though likely published in 1704. See Raabe and Pfeiffer, *August Hermann Francke*, 311.
3. The autobiographical account is reprinted with her funeral sermon in Francke, *Gedächtniß- und Leichen-Predigten*, 457. It is also found in Henckel, *Die letzten Stunden*, 2:122–24. Her testament contains a third-person account that is nearly identical in form: AFSt, W X/1/1.
4. On von Schönberg's biography, see Witt, *Bekehrung*, 167–70.
5. Ibid., 172.
6. Ibid., 173–74.
7. See the description in his sermon, Francke, *Gedächtniß- und Leichen-Predigten*, 461–63. See also Witt, *Bekehrung*, 174.
8. Witt, *Bekehrung*, 174.
9. Francke, *Gedächtniß- und Leichen-Predigten*, 423–24.
10. Her conversion is mentioned in the main body of the sermon (Francke, *Gedächtniß- und Leichen-Predigten*, 441), and is then described in the biographical appendix to the sermon.
11. Ibid.
12. "Suppose we maintain that we are already awakened through God's Word and have already entered into the prescribed struggle [*Kampf*]; we should nonetheless be concerned that we may make proper use of the good example presented to us of this fighter [*Kämpferin*], who remained true until the end." Ibid., 446–47. See also 444–45.
13. See ibid., 444. The biblical reference is to Jacob in Genesis 32:28, "For you have striven with God and with humans, and have prevailed."
14. Ibid., 446. The allusion is to the Luther Bible, 2 Timothy 2:5, "Und so jemand auch kämpft, wird er doch nicht gekrönt, er kämpfe denn recht."

15. By reducing this to "the specific Hallensian schema of stirring [*Rührung*], repentance struggle [*Bußkampf*], and conversion [*Bekehrung*]," Witt oversimplifies Francke's approach to conversion in this sermon. See Witt, "Biographiensammlung," 198.

16. Francke cites this passage near the opening of the *Applicatio* of the sermon itself (441), and then in the *Personalia* applies it specifically to Schönberg: "This illness of hers was at the same time the furnace of affliction [*Ofen des Elends*], in which the heavenly father, holy and hidden yet at the same time also kind and dear, purified, refined, preserved, elected, and made her, his daughter, truly beautiful." Francke, *Gedächtniß- und Leichen-Predigten*, 460.

17. Henckel, *Die letzten Stunden*.

18. The last edition was published in 1757.

19. Henckel, *Die letzten Stunden*, preface, vol. 1, §XIV (unpaginated).

20. On the Silesian background of Henckel and his family's involvement with the Pietist movement, see Patzelt, *Pietismus*, 33–38.

21. According to Patzelt, despite their affinity for Francke and Freylinghausen, neither Henckel nor his brother, Wenzel Ludwig, experienced a "Pietist conversion" under their auspices. Ibid., 35.

22. Letter of Henckel to A. H. Francke, June 9, 1717, AFSt, H C433, 16.

23. Henckel, *Die letzten Stunden*, 1:160–210.

24. Ibid., 1:193.

25. Ibid., 1:205–6. In the Luther Bible, 2 Timothy 2:5 reads, "Und so jemand auch kämpft, wird er doch nicht gekrönt, er kämpfe denn recht." The King James Version reads, "And if a man also strive for masteries, yet is he not crowned, except he strive lawfully."

26. Henckel, *Die letzten Stunden*, 1:210.

27. AFSt, H C433, 16.

28. A longer passage from the funeral sermon (Francke, *Gedächtniß- und Leichen-Predigten*, 445–46) appears almost verbatim. See Henckel, *Die letzten Stunden*, 1:165–67.

29. Henckel's biography of von Schönberg follows Francke's funeral sermon closely, especially 1:121–29. The most striking difference in the two accounts is the much more extensive description of Schönberg's final illness in Henckel, 1:129–45. Cf. Francke, *Gedächtniß-und Leichen-Predigten*, 460–63.

30. Other spiritual biographies in which Henckel depicted a powerful *Glaubenskampf* included those of Samuel Elard (Henckel, *Die letzten Stunden*, 1:21–33), Anna Catharina Wiegleb (1:285–300), Christine Sophie von Sebottendorf (1:301–28), Countess Louise Bibiane zu Solms (2:24–41), Count Johann Friedrich zu Solms (2:42–63), Juliana Patientia von Schultt (2:64–80), Anna Elisabeth Porst (2:115–45), Lucia Ursula Stern (2:155–96), Christiane Magdalene Helmershausen (2:329–55), Johann Georg Schmalvogel (4:140–66), Princess Christiane Louise zu Ostfriesland (4:167–97), Dorothea Elisabeth Gerhardt (4:278–301), Marie Helene Wagner (4:301–16), Charlotte Magdaelne von Fragstein (4:316–48), and Martin Jakob Bäumler (4:364–435).

31. Petrus Laurentius Michaelis, Henckel, *Die letzten Stunden*, 2:1–23.

32. Ibid., 1:340.

33. Regine Margarethe Rumpus, ibid., 3:279–319; Margarethe Weidenheim, ibid., 4:1–24. In Weidenheim's account, Henckel closely associates the language of conversion with her final struggles (4:20).

34. Louise Sophie von Wurmb, ibid., 1:42–52.

35. Ibid., 1:50.

36. For similar accounts, see for instance Andreas Reinbeck, ibid., 1:55–62; or Georg Johann Hencke, ibid., 2:309–28, for whom Hencke describes neither a conversion earlier in life nor a spiritual struggle in death. The exception is Nicholas Lange, whose biography spans nearly two hundred pages but includes little in the way of spiritual struggle, conversion, or even an extended

description of his death. In contrast to the other narratives, this is a rather straightforward biography. See Nicholas Lange, ibid., 3:79–278.

37. Ibid., 1:21, 24–25, 29. Rather than the metaphor of the furnace of affliction or being transfigured through suffering, here the image is of triumph over Satan and being conformed to the suffering Christ on the cross. Ibid., 1:33.

38. Hermann Peter Berghaus, ibid., 3:329–32, 335, 337, 339.

39. Ibid., 3:156.

40. Henckel states plainly that the student had been converted in 1721 in Jena, writing, "There he passed through the narrow gate of conversion [enge Pforte der Bekehrung] with all seriousness and zeal and came to a divine change of heart amid much prayer, weeping, and wrestling." Ibid., 4:372.

41. Ibid., 3:57.

42. In addition to von Schönberg's account, Witt notes that the accounts of Juliana Patientia von Schultt and Anna Catharina Wiegleb were based on Francke's funeral sermons. See Witt, "Biographiensammlung," 194.

43. Francke appears as a decisive influence in the narratives of von Schönberg (see above), Johanne Eleonore Becker (Henckel, *Die letzten Stunden*, 1:121), the children Anne Elizabeth Fiedler and Marie Elizabeth Rausch (2:204), Johann Andreas Wiegleb (2:228), Margarethe Weidenheim (4:10–11), and Charlotte Magdalene von Fragstein (4:340).

44. Witt, "Biographiensammlung," 194.

45. See, for instance, the description of conversion for Johanna Ursula von Geusau. Henckel, *Die letzten Stunden*, 1:226; or that of Countess Benigna von Solms (2:87–88), neither of which incorporated a *Bußkampf*.

46. In the case of Lucia Ursula Stern, *Bußkampf* followed an initial conversion rather than preceding it. Ibid., 2:162–63. Cf. Witt, "Biographiensammlung," 206.

47. There were fifty-one narratives, but fifty-four individuals were portrayed. Witt, "Biographiensammlung," 190.

48. Ibid., 190–93. According to Witt, fifteen of twenty-seven women were from the nobility, and eight of these twenty-seven had been married to clergy.

49. Witt notes that nine of the male narratives were of clergy, another seven were of theology students, while five accounts were of children. Ibid., 192–93.

50. Ibid., 193, 214. Witt suggests that this is in part due to both the women and the men without theological appointments lacking the opportunity to express a "religiously grounded and stipulated activity in the 'world'" (214).

51. Ibid.

52. Henckel, *Die letzten Stunden*, 1:98, 99.

53. In numerous places, Henckel refers to baptism as "bath of regeneration," a phrase with distinctly Lutheran overtones that locates regeneration in baptism. See ibid., 1:9. A good example of confession and communion is the biography of Johann Andreas Wiegleb, who called A. H. Francke to his sickbed to confess his sins, and then immediately before his death partook of "Holy Communion with exceptional devotion" (2:228–29).

54. On this point, see Kümmel, "Der sanfte und selige Tod." Kümmel notes, however, that the actual portrayal of death in funeral sermons did not correspond to the ideal: "A literal death struggle [*Todeskampf*] was hard to harmonize with the ideal of dying and therefore was only seldom mentioned." Ibid., 201.

55. In the prologue to the story of Heinrich I von Reuß, Henckel affirms the possibility of conversion when the individual "is placed in the circumstances of death" so long as he or she "has not been completely given up to a perverted mind and the judgment of a hardened heart." See Henckel, *Die letzten Stunden*, 1:77; Witt, "Biographiensammlung," 197.

56. Henckel, *Die letzten Stunden*, 1:340.

57. Witt, "Biographiensammlung," 202.

58. See, for example, *Sammlung auserlesener Materien* 19 (1734): 333–47. Moser's first volume of execution narratives was published anonymously with the title *Seelige letzte Stunden einiger dem zeitlichen Tode übergebener Missethäter* (Leipzig, 1740). On this and subsequent editions, which all used *Letzte Stunden* in their titles, see below. Moser recommended the Henckel collection in his *Beytrag*, 273.

59. This was especially the case in Wernigerode. See the category in the archive titled "Lebensläufe und Letzte Stunden." Landesarchiv Sachsen-Anhalt, Abteilung Magdeburg, Standort Wernigerode (hereafter LASA Wernigerode), Rep. H. Stolberg-Wernigerode, Nachlass Heinrich Ernst I, B, Nr. 20. Collections of *Letzte Stunden* were also found in the manuscript holdings of the Wernigerode library; see Förstemann, *Stolbergische Bibliothek*, 140. Once in the possession of the University of Halle, these materials are unfortunately no longer available to researchers.

CHAPTER 4

1. Francke, *Lebensläufe*, 78. This was the so-called *Bekehrungsbericht*, which was an excerpt from the longer *Lebenslauff*; it focused on the conversion in Lüneburg. First published by Moser in 1733, this was the account that had the most significant literary influence. On its reception and publication, see above; and Francke, *Lebensläufe*, 78–80.

2. Francke, *Amt u. Werck*. The third-person description of the conversion is found on 36–46. The *Personalia* in the appendix explicitly refer to Francke's struggle as a *Buß-Kampf* (73). In some of his own autobiographical remarks from late in life, Francke referred to a *Buß-Kampf* as part of his conversion experience. See Krämer, *Beiträge*, 61. Similarities between Francke's remarks and Freylinghausen's account suggest that his son-in-law was likely familiar with the *Bekehrungsbericht* and the later notes reprinted in Krämer.

3. Francke, *Kurtze, iedoch gründliche Nachricht*, reprinted in Matthias, *Lebensläufe*.

4. Letter from J. Sophie von Schaumburg Lippe to G. A. Francke, November 19, 1728, StBPK, Francke Nachlass, 2, 15/3.

5. Matthias, "Bekehrung und Wiedergeburt," 67–70. See also Strom, "Conversion, Confessionalization, and Pietism."

6. Rotermund, *Orthodoxie und Pietismus*, 114.

7. See, for instance, the sermon by Francke on the problem of the unconverted clergy and their ineffectiveness, "Von dem Dienst untreuer Lehrer," in Francke, *Predigten*, 1:400–437.

8. Quoted in Bach, "Halle Testimonial System," 41. See also Paul, *Johannes Anastasius Freylinghausen*, 368–77.

9. Bach, "Halle Testimonial System," 42.

10. Bach details the opposition of Pietist church officials outside Halle, such as Lamprecht Gedicke and Johann Gottfried Hornejus, explicitly for the burden it presented to many candidates but also implicitly for the challenge the Halle testimonial system presented to traditional forms of patronage. Ibid., 43–45.

11. Quoted in Matthias, "Bekehrung und Wiedergeburt," 69; see also notes 127 and 128.

12. Quoted in Tholuck, *Geschichte des Rationalismus*, 30.

13. Tholuck, *Geschichte des Rationalismus*, 30–31.

14. Matthias notes that conversion "played no role" at all in the written testimonies that are extant. See Matthias, "Bekehrung und Wiedergeburt," 79.

15. On Zinzendorf and the early Moravians, see Vogt, "Nicholas Ludwig von Zinzendorf."

16. Uttendörfer, *Zinzendorf und die Mystik*, 110–11. See also Uttendörfer, who in describing this time, wrote, "Zinzendorf was in the middle of a revival [*Erweckunsbewegung*] and worked together with his colleagues not only for conversion but also for the purpose of an exact and strict sorting of souls according the Pietist schema of the dead [*Tote*], awakened [*Erweckte*], and

converted [*Bekehrte*]. There were likely few places where the Pietists ideals were implemented with such decisiveness, not only in an organizational sense but also inwardly, as they were in Herrnhut at this early time." *Zinzendorfs religiöse Grundgedanken*, 37. For the ongoing nature of these divisions at Herrnhut, see Aalen, *Theologie*, 316.

17. On Zinzendorf's early spiritual experiences in relation to conversion, see Geiger, "Zinzendorfs Stellung," 15–18.

18. Zinzendorf later wrote, "Herr Mischke said in a Sorau conference that I was never righteously converted." Büdingischer Sammlung I, "Note zum Vorwort," quoted in Aalen, *Theologie*, 319. Spangenberg also quoted a recollection from 1740: "On occasion, the blessed, departed Mischke, among others, said that I was yet unconverted and that I proposed unconverted servants of God." Spangenberg, *Leben*, 3:532. Zinzendorf dated the recollection of Mischke to 1729. Spangenberg noted an earlier criticism of Zinzendorf in 1727 specifically on the issue of the *Bußkampf*, but whether this derived from Mischke, as some assume, is open to question. See Spangenberg, *Leben*, 3:401. Mischke's relationship with the early Moravians was considerably more complicated than the issue of conversion or the *Bußkampf*. Cf. Teufel, "Die Beziehungen zwischen Herrnhut und Sorau."

19. See Zinzendorf's own comments from 1750 reprinted in Uttendörfer, *Zinzendorf's religiöse Grundgedanken*, 229. See also this comment from Uttendörfer: "In spite of that he decided on the basis of Mischke's influence in 1729 to make an attempt to experience a conversion according the Pietist pattern, and according to his own judgment this brought him further clarity as he wrestled with it." *Zinzendorf und die Mystik*, 111.

20. For an overview, see Geiger, "Zinzendorfs Stellung," 17–21; and Atwood, *Community of the Cross*, 48–49. For a more sophisticated investigation of Zinzendorf's theological development on this point, see Aalen, *Theologie*, 314–20.

21. Uttendörfer, *Zinzendorf und die Mystik*, 110; see also Reichel, *Senfkornorden*, 30ff.

22. For a description of Mischke's revivalist fervor in Silesia, see the observations of Bogatzky, *Von Bogatzky's Lebenslauf*, 105.

23. On Steinmetz, see Stievermann, "Halle Pietism."

24. Martin Schmidt suggests that "the compulsory requirement of a *Bußkampf*, which he [A. H. Francke] supposedly imposed on the children of the orphanage, is probably imputed wrongly to him and possibly represents a polemical invention of Zinzendorfs." Schmidt, *Wiedergeburt und neuer Mensch*, 205.

25. A report from the early 1730s uses the language of *Bußkampf* to describe the "awakening" of a twelve-year-old girl during the 1727 revival: "After a three-day *Bußkampf*, the twelve-year-old girl Susanna Kühnelein broke through into [new] life in the night and was so powerfully enkindled that she set all the girls in motion and in flames, who then spent most of the day (and previous night) in prayer and pleading, and therefore did not pause to eat so that they could proclaim the virtue of their redeemer." Quoted in Schmidt, "Kindererweckung," 116. Schmidt notes that later remarks in Herrnhut sources relativized the earlier *Bußkampf* language (117). Generally, the Moravians referred to these as *Erweckungen* (awakenings) rather than conversions, though they are not always consistent in doing so. Cf. ibid., 124.

26. See, for example, the criticism in Ebenfeld, *Entdeckung*, of Joachim Friedrich Blanckensee's printed conversion narrative, which put his conversion and *Bußkampf* in the context of the radical Pietism of Tennhardt, Gichtel, and Tuchfeld. Quoting Arndt and Spener, Samuel Walther, who published the *Entdeckung* under the pseudonym of Johann Ebenfeld, appears to have moderate Pietist sympathies. Blanckensee's original print autobiography is lost, an autobiographical version appeared in Reitz, *Historie der Wiedergebohrnen*, 7:117–44; but here the prominent language of the *Bußkampf* in the original title is missing. On Blanckensee, see Hinrichs, *Preussentum und Pietismus*, 144–45.

27. Lau, *Schriftmäßige Beantwortung* (1st ed.).

28. On Großgebauer and Francke, see above.

29. Lau, *Schriftmäßige Beantwortung* (2nd ed.), 2, §2.
30. Ibid., 14–16, §6, §7. Lau makes clear that both groups are relatively small in number, but that particularly the latter posed a significant pastoral problem.
31. Ibid., 5–6, §4.
32. Lau describes the process in detail. Ibid., 27–44, §13–20.
33. Ibid., 37, §17, 43–44, §20; 45, §2; 20–21, §9.
34. Ibid., 67, §33.
35. Lau matriculated at the University of Halle in 1724. See Juntke, ed., *Matrikel*, 257.
36. Jacobs, "Johann Liborius Zimmermann." On his own conversion and understanding of *Bußkampf*, see ibid., 135–42, 216–25.
37. Ibid., 157–59.
38. On the *Erweckungen* in Zimmermann's in Halle, see Jacobs, "Johann Liborius Zimmermann," 171–72.
39. On Baumgarten, see Sorkin, *Religious Enlightenment*, 115–63, esp. on conversion, 129–30.
40. *Theologische Beantwortung Zwoer Fragen*.
41. In subsequent editions, Lau responded to specific points made in the anonymous tract. Moser later described it as a direct response to Lau's book. Moser, *Beytrag*, 391–92.
42. The tract itself is preceded by a new translation of the book of Ecclesiastes that Bauer published with commentary in 1732 as *Erläuterter Grundtext*. Bauer's new translation is distinctive enough that the identification of the texts poses no problem. Which of the two appeared first in print is unknown, as is the motivation for the inclusion of Ecclesiastes with a tract on conversion. The proper translation and interpretation of Ecclesiastes was controversial among Pietists. See, for instance, the letter of Johann Jacob Rambach to A. H. Francke complaining about Johann Wilhelm Zierold's criticisms, March 3, 1725, StBPK, Francke Nachlass 17, 1/9, 44. Ecclesiastes may have seemed relevant to criticisms of fixing the time of conversion in that the biblical book construed much human striving as vanity, but the precise connection remains obscure.
43. *Theologische Beantwortung Zwoer Fragen*, 20.
44. For Francke's view of *göttliche Traurigkeit*, see the early catechism sermon summarized by Peschke, *Katechismuspredigten*, 177–81. Bogatzky describes wrestling with *göttliche Traurigkeit* in his autobiography, *Lebenslauf*, 49–50.
45. Lau makes the connection of the *Bußkampf* to "godly grief" especially clear in the preface to the revised edition, *Schriftmäßige Beantwortung* (3rd ed.), 9–14. On the criticism of a specific degree of grief, see *Theologische Beantwortung Zwoer Fragen*, 8–10.
46. *Theologische Beantwortung Zwoer Fragen*, 11, 17.
47. The author sees Paul's conversion as extraordinary, not typical. Ibid., 50.
48. Ibid., 49.
49. Ibid., 48, 66, 72–73.
50. In contrast, see, for instance, the review of the second edition of Lau's tract in the *Fortgesetzte Sammlung von alten und neuen theologischen Sachen* (the continuation of the *Unschuldige Nachrichten*) that rather crudely caricatured his position as following Spener, a mischaracterization that the author of the *Theologische Beantwortung Zwoer Fragen* would not have accepted. *Fortgesetzte Sammlung von alten und neuen theologischen Sachen* (1734): 876.
51. *Theologische Beantwortung Zwoer Fragen*, 42–46. The passage cited from Spener is in the *Theologische Bedencken*, vol. 1, pt. 2, 197–98. See above. In a comment added in later editions, Lau noted that Spener's criticism was based on the requirement of a "very precise indication" of the time of conversion and not the looser understanding of the time of conversion advocated by Lau. That Spener mentioned a *Durchbruch* Lau took as confirmation of his larger understanding of conversion. See Lau, *Schriftmäßige Beantwortung* (3rd ed.), 6–8, §4.
52. *Theologische Beantwortung Zwoer Fragen*, 14, 41.
53. Jacobs, "Johann Liborius Zimmermann," 142. Buddeus is sometimes seen as a mediating figure among Pietism, Lutheran orthodoxy, and Enlightenment, but he had taught at Halle

and continued to have close personal connections to many Pietists. On Buddeus, see Nüssel, *Bund und Versöhnung*.

54. Most were drawn from relatively early representatives of Lutheran orthodoxy, including Martin Chemnitz (1522–1586), Johann Gerhard (1582–1637), and Jesper Rasmussen Brochmand (1585–1652). Among later theologians, those from Wittenberg tended to predominate, including Johann Hülsemann (1602–1661) and Johann Andreas Quenstedt (1617–1688), which, given the likely Wittenberg origins of the pamphlet, is understandable. With the exception of a very brief reference to Löscher (in *Theologische Bewantwortung Zwoer Fragen*, 47), prominent anti-Pietists are not cited.

CHAPTER 5

1. These have been extraordinarily well analyzed by Rainer Lächele in two major publications, *Pietistische Öffentlichkeit und religiöse Kommunikation* and *Erbauungszeitschriften als Kommunikationsmedium*. The *Sammlung auserlesener Materien zum Bau des Reichs Gottes* was published from 1731 to 1734. After Jerichovius's death in 1734, Johann Adam Steinmetz took over as editor of the *Fortgesetzte Sammlung auserlesener Materien zum Bau des Reichs Gottes*, published between 1735 and 1737; the *Verbesserte Sammlung auserlesener Materien zum Bau des Reichs Gottes*, published from 1737 to 1743 (hereafter *VSAM*); and the *Closter-Bergische Sammlung nützlicher Materien zur Erbauung im wahren Christenthume*, published between 1745 and 1761 (hereafter *CSNM*). On the development of the series, see Lächele, *Erbauungszeitschriften als Kommunikationsmedium*, 40–94.

2. Walker, *Johann Jakob Moser*.

3. He noted, "The first, and I would gladly admit, the main part of my collection will be a variety of reports of God's guidance, especially in the work of conversion." *Altes und Neues* 1 (1733): 11–12. Francke's autobiographical account appeared in *Altes und Neues* 3 (1733): 56–69.

4. On the *Geistliche Fama*, see Zeller, "Geschichtsverständnis." The *Geistliche Fama* could be especially critical of conversion under the influence of the ordained clergy. See the critical comments of the "priestly edification by the learned hand" in the preface to the first number, a reference to the *Sammlung auserlesener Materien, Geistliche Fama* 1 (1733): 3r. See also the long discussion of true and false conversion, *Geistliche Fama* 11 (1733): 6–107.

5. "Merckwürdiger Anfang der Bekehrung des sel. D. Speners," *SAMR* 2 (1732): 216–18.

6. Jerichovius obliquely mentioned the objections in a brief note to the second edition and replaced *Bekehrung* with *Erweckung* in the title, and substituted the phrase *Gelegenheit zu seinem mehren Ernst im Christenthum* for the original text of *Gelegenheit zu seiner Bekehrung*. Cf. *SAMR* 2 (1732): 216–17; and *SAMR* 2 (1733 [2nd ed.]): 216–17.

7. *SAMR* 3 (1732): 335–39. The date of the narrative is unclear; it was composed some years after Krimmer came to Straßfurt in 1717. He died in 1730.

8. *SAMR* 3 (1732): 340–41.

9. Delius described him as "after Spener, the most important representative of Lutheran Pietism in Berlin." See Delius, "Briefwechsel," 89.

10. See Rau, *Göttliche Wohlthaten*; and Bachmann, "Johann Porst," in *Zur Geschichte der Berliner Gesangbücher*, 147–64.

11. *SAMR* 9 (1733): 74, 75, 77.

12. *SAMR* 9 (1733): 78. "I know your affliction and your poverty, even though you are rich. I know the slander on the part of those who say that they are Jews and are not, but are a synagogue of Satan." Revelation 2:9.

13. *SAMR* 9 (1733): 79.

14. On Schade, see above.

15. *SAMR* 9 (1733): 80–81.

16. Ibid., 82. Porst was the first of seventeen students in Berlin to sign a letter to the elector in support of Schade in 1697 during the height of the controversy. See Obst, *Berliner Beichtstuhlstreit*, 66. See also Murakami-Mori, "Berliner Beichtstuhlstreit," 62–94.

17. *SAMR* 9 (1733): 83–84.

18. Presumably from Article 11 of the Formula of Concord, "Concerning the Eternal Predestination and Election of God."

19. The hymn, "Es sei Herr, deine Gütigkeit," appeared in many hymnals, including Freylinghausen's famous collection, *Geistreiches Gesangbuch*. Spener specifically wrote the hymn to address the question of the *Gnadenwahl*. See Spener, *Bedenken*, 371. From Vol. 4, *Theol. Bedencken*, 320, dated 1697.

20. *SAMR* 9 (1733): 86–87.

21. See his twelfth "Betrachtung," titled "Von Versuchung der Kinder zur unzeitigen Bekehr-Sucht," in Porst, *Compendium*, 739–43. Giving a sense of his hesitation to force conversion and a particular method, Porst wrote, "To convert others is the work of God. Jeremiah 31: 18. To undertake this by one's own efforts is great foolishness. Perverse means and methods belong as well to that form of converting others. God converts through grace, others through anger; God [converts] through patience, others through vehemence; God [converts] through Word and Spirit, others through their own spirit; God accommodates the weakness of human beings, but others want to compel all things" (742).

22. *SAMR* 10 (1733): 219–21.

23. Lächele identifies this as an itinerant preacher. More likely, this was just a preacher from another parish who had been asked to preach in their town. Cf. Lächele, *Pietistische Öffentlichkeit*, 104.

24. *SAMR* 10 (1733): 220–22. Francke's sermon on Luke 18:9–14 from August 1713—*Der Unterschied der Selbst-Rechtfertigung und der wahren Rechtfertigung*—was first published in 1714 and appeared in multiple pamphlet editions; see Raabe and Pfeiffer, *August Hermann Francke*, 370–71. It was likely in this form that Dennstädt encountered it. The sermon was later included in a number of August Hermann Francke's sermon collections, including *Sonn- und Fest-Tags-Predigten*, 1302–38.

25. *SAMR* 10 (1733): 223–25.

26. See, for instance, letters from November 29, 1722, and February 20, 1725, StBPK, Francke Nachlass, 9/1, 29–30.

27. *SAMR* 7 (1732): 821–31. Notable in this account is Francke's directing him toward faith in Christ alone rather than toward further concern with his sinfulness and repentance (826–28).

28. This is using a broader definition of conversion narratives, including those in which a failed or near conversion is included for edifying purposes.

29. Moser, *Altes und Neues* 1 (1733): 11–12.

30. These conclusions are based on an analysis of conversion accounts in Moser, *Altes und Neues*, from 1733 to 1739.

31. It was titled "Des seel. Herrn Professoris Franckens zu Halle Bekehrungs-Historie," *Altes und Neues* 3 (1733): 56–69. This was not the full autobiography but the narrower version that focused the conversion experience itself. On this edition, see Francke, *Lebensläufe*, 78–79.

32. "Eines Gräflichen Hof-Predigers Nachricht von seiner Bekehrung und Amts-Seegen," *Altes und Neues* 4 (1734): 3–35. At the time of its composition around 1726, Schubert was court preacher in Ebersdorf, but that same year he moved to Potsdam as preacher of the Heiligengeistkirche. A partial manuscript copy of the conversion story is also in AFSt, H A114, 197–205. On Schubert and especially his relationship to King Friedrich Wilhelm, see Marschke, "Wir Halenser," 87–93.

33. See, for instance, "Eines Handwercks-Mannes Beschreibung seiner Führung in dem Werck der Bekehrung," *Altes und Neues* 2 (1733): 56–70.

34. For an example of how first-person accounts could be rewritten in New England, see Seeman, "Lay Conversion Narratives."
35. On the two narratives of Schade's conversion, see above, chapter 3.
36. See the third-person narrative of Martha Margaretha von Schönberg's account in AFSt, W X/1/1.
37. *SAMR* 6 (1732): 659–64.
38. *SAMR* 18 (1734): 202.
39. *SAMR* 11 (1733): 369.
40. Ibid., 369–70.
41. *Altes und Neues* 4 (1734): 44–46.
42. "Das unselige Ende Joh. Ph. P. gewesenen Schuldieners in Ob. verzeichnet von seinem damaligen Pastore, Hn. M.P.," *FSAM* 29 (1735): 620, 622, 630–31.
43. See, for example, the story of Engel Utstiems's conversion as a young woman and her edifying death later in life. *FSAM* 35 (1736): 343–51. The narrator expressly praised her early conversion (343).
44. *SAMR* 6 (1732): 659.
45. *SAMR* 19 (1734): 342–44.
46. For instance, in the *Sammlung* and *Fortgesetzte Sammlung*, five of sixteen third-person accounts of male conversion are clergy or those with university theological training. In the *Verbesserte Sammlung* and *Closter-Bergische Sammlung*, three out of twenty third-person male narratives were clergy or those who had university theological training. The latter is a lower number, but given that many of the other male narratives were of children (four) or executed criminals (six), this is still a relatively high proportion of exemplary, adult male narratives. In Moser's *Altes und Neues*, only one of the nine third-person accounts was by a theological student or clergyman.
47. On the advantage of converted preachers for Pietists like Francke and Lange, see Strom, "Pietism and Revival," 192–93.
48. *Altes und Neues* 4 (1734): 3–35. The manuscript copy in the archives of the Franckesche Stiftungen ends with his conversion at Halle. Cf. AFSt, H A114, 197–205.
49. *CSNM* 5 (1746): 591. This would have been around September 21, 1717, when Francke preached in Idstein. See Francke, *Predigten*, 1:91.
50. The biography lists many of the prominent Pietists in Jena and Halle as important influences, including Buddeus, Walch, G. A. Francke, Rambach, Lange, and Freylinghausen among others. *CSNM* 5 (1746): 592–93.
51. Ibid., 596. Lehr's hymn was popular among Pietists and others who noted its role in conversion. See, for instance, the letter of Jacob Rudolph to G. A. Francke, Dargun, January 25, 1744, StBPK, Francke Nachlass, 18, 2/12, 5.
52. *CSNM* 5 (1746): 603.
53. One conversion account described the non-Pietist clergy's bitter opposition to the conversions in conventicles and other Pietist practices. See *SAMR* 3 (1732): 345–46.
54. Schubert and Dennstädt mention A. H. Francke as a decisive influence on their conversions, while the anonymous noble, Porst, and others, including Jacob Schneider from Mehro, mention Johann Caspar Schade.
55. *SAMR* 10 (1733): 222. Over his career, Francke alone published nearly five hundred editions of pamphlet sermons, with estimated print runs of five thousand copies each. See Raabe and Pfeiffer, *August Hermann Francke*, xv. This would have put into circulation nearly 2.5 million copies of his sermons. For the six years from 1717 to 1723 alone, Obst estimates that the publishing house of the Halle orphanage produced around 350,000 copies of Francke's sermons. See Obst, *August Hermann Francke*, 43.
56. See, for instance, the 1720 letter of Samuel Urlsperger to A. H. Francke, StBPK, Francke Nachlass, 21, 2, 1/7, 69; or the description in von Wreech on the effect of Francke's

sermons among the prisoners of war in Siberia, *Wahrhaffte und umständliche Historie*, 43, 125, 170, 172.

57. *SAMR* 6 (1732): 655.

58. *Altes und Neues* 4 (1734): 56.

59. See, for instance, the accounts of Schwerdtfeger's conversion that appeared almost simultaneously—in *SAMR* 18 (1734): 203–11; and *Altes und Neues* 8 (1734): 57–65—and are, apart from minor orthographic variations and different titles, nearly identical. Similarly, the manuscript of Schubert's conversion account and the first part of the printed account in *Altes und Neues* are very close but not dependent on each other, which suggests common fidelity to a third source. See AFSt, H A114, 197–205; and *Altes und Neues* 4 (1734): 3–35.

60. Lächele points to elisions in reprinted texts in the early editions of the *SAMR* as evidence that Jerichovius deliberately avoided putting Halle and Francke in a favorable light. See, for instance, Lächele, *Erbauungszeitschriften als Kommunikationsmedium*, 206–9. Given the very favorable view of Halle and Francke in other narratives—especially Dennstädt's—it is questionable whether such editing reveals a bias against Francke or Hallensian Pietism.

61. *FSAM* 35 (1736): 345–46.

62. Ibid., 348.

63. *FSAM* 36 (1736): 466.

64. An example of the conversion of a supposed "atheist" is the narrative of Johann Gerhard Neidhardt in *VSAM* 19 (1740): 354–74. See also Maria Elisabeth Bick, who described participation in worship but little connection to God prior to her conversion. *VSAM* 26 (1742): 184–212.

65. *VSAM* 12 (1739), 424–47. For the references to the separatists, perhaps followers of Dippel, and her connection to them, see 428.

66. For explicit reference to the church community and confessional adherence, see ibid., 434, 441.

67. *FSAM* 36 (1736): 472–74.

68. See the biographies of George Weißmann and Andreas Schilder in *SAMR* 6 (1732): 631–49, 650–55, both cases from Silesia; and Valentin and Johann Weißmann in *SAMR* 11 (1733): 370–77, from Austria.

69. Immediately following Schilder's biography, Jerichovius printed the conversion narrative of a servant girl that especially emphasized Lutheran doctrine. *SAMR* 6 (1732): 655–59.

70. "Der große und wunderbare Reichthum der gnade Gottes, wie sich solcher an einer Ao. 1735 in S. verstorbenen Römisch-Catholischen Manns-Person offenbahret hat," *FSAM* 41 (1737): 218–39.

71. See, for instance, the portrayal of a chaplain in *FSAM* 41 (1737): 223. Jesuits, however, fare much less well. The author of the account made one Jesuit responsible for the wife's despair, which nearly led to her suicide (224–25).

72. For instance, "Eines erweckten Sünders Beschreibung seines vorigen Lebens und Bekehrung," *Altes und Neues* 11 (1735): 30–68; or "Heilsame Reflexiones über einen oft kräftig gerührten aber stets unbekehrt gebliebenen Hirten," *SAMR* 7 (1732): 839–67.

73. "Erzehlung der merckwürdigen Bekehrung und darauf erlangten Erfahrung Marien Hurl, wie solche aus ihrem eigenen Munde aufgezeichnet wordenn, die dritte Auflage," *VSAM* 4 (1737): 420–53.

74. *Altes und Neues* 4 (1743): 7–11.

75. For a casual use of *Bußkampf* in this sense of someone already converted, see *Altes und Neues* 1 (1733): 57–59.

76. *VSAM* 14 (1739): 659–79. The account appeared anonymously and, unlike most such published accounts, while the subject was presumably still living.

77. *Altes und Neues* 11 (1735): 3.

CHAPTER 6

1. On early Pietism in Mecklenburg and the turn toward orthodoxy, the best account remains Schmaltz, *Kirchengeschichte Mecklenburgs*, vol. 3. See also Strom, "Conversion, Confessionalization, and Pietism in Dargun." For pre-Pietist reform movements in Mecklenburg, see Strom, *Orthodoxy and Reform*.

2. *Erläuterung der Fürstl. Mecklenburgschen Kirchen-Ordnung*, fol. A3v. See also Schmaltz, *Kirchengeschichte Mecklenburgs*, 3:121.

3. For examples, see Ritter, "Die Inspirierten"; Bernet, "Der Lange Weg"; Wotschke, "Sturm"; and Schmaltz, *Kirchengeschichte Mecklenburgs*, 3:148–51.

4. In the Hamburger Vergleich of 1701, the majority of the territory from the former duchies of Mecklenburg-Güstrow and Mecklenburg-Schwerin were united into the larger duchy of Mecklenburg-Schwerin, which contained the dominant economic and cultural centers of the two predecessor duchies. A smaller territory of Mecklenburg-Strelitz was created, but its importance remained politically and religiously marginal.

5. On Christine's interest in Pietism and her wide-ranging influence on religious affairs in Wernigerode, see the entry by Eduard Jacobs in *Allgemeine Deutsche Biographie*, 4:219–21. On Louise's efforts to instill Pietism at court in Denmark and her effect on the future King Christian VI, see Lausten, *Church History*, 166.

6. On Augusta's youth and religious development, see the long, nearly book-length article by Wilhemi, "Augusta," here 110–27. This article remains the most complete account of Augusta and the movement in Dargun. It remains particularly valuable since some of the archival sources used by Wilhelmi in Mecklenburg and Wernigerode are no longer extant. Also valuable is the overview by Peschke, "Pietismus in Dargun." Peschke is overly broad in his categorizations. A fragment of Augusta's and Christina's correspondence with Petersen is preserved in LASA Wernigerode, Rep. H. Stolberg-Wernigerode, K, Nr. 687, 10.

7. It was originally a Cistercian monastery; after the Reformation the dukes of Mecklenburg-Güstrow refashioned the complex into a second residence. See Kratzke, *Kloster und Schloß*.

8. Though removed from most governmental functions by imperial order, Carl Leopold still retained some ducal authority in ecclesiastical affairs, which led to a series of conflicts within the Mecklenburg Landeskirche of the 1730s and 1740s. See Schmaltz, *Kirchengeschichte Mecklenburgs*, 3:129–42. There is little good literature on the mercurial figure of Carl Leopold. Most recently, see Heitz, "Carl Leopold von Mecklenburg-Schwerin," 303–10, which is sketchy throughout and hardly deals with Carl Leopold after 1720.

9. See the notes to the distribution of Bibles during the years 1723–25 in Landeshauptarchiv Schwerin (hereafter LHA Schwerin), eccl. spec. 1846; Schmaltz, *Kirchengeschichte Mecklenburgs*, 3:152.

10. Wilhelmi, "Augusta," 116–17. Her letter to a niece in 1725 reveals her interest in typically Pietist scriptural reading and devotional literature. LHA Schwerin, Korresp. ducal. 2.12–1/22, 232, letter of June 13, 1725.

11. See the correspondence of Simon Ambrosius Hennings to A. H. Francke in 1722, StBPK, Francke Nachlass, 10, 1/5, 12, 17; as well as the reports of the *Pagenmeister* von Horn to A. H. Francke in establishing prayer sessions and other Pietist practices in Halle from 1722, AFSt, H C139, 9–12. Stieber helped von Horn establish a *collegium biblicum*, and Hellwig and his wife participated in von Horn's prayer meetings. Recknitz—not to be confused with Röckenitz, adjacent to Dargun—was some distance from Dargun but much closer to Güstrow, where Augusta likely made Hennings's acquaintance. Hennings was pastor in Recknitz for his entire career, from 1710 until 1743. Willgeroth, *Pfarren*, 1:400.

12. Shortly after taking up his duties as Hofprediger in Güstrow at the invitation of Augusta and her mother in 1711–12, Stieber wrote several letters to A. H. Francke recalling his time in Halle and describing his work in Güstrow. See AFSt, H C817, Brief Nr. 7; C569, 1–2.

13. Hennings remarked on Augusta's visit to Halle in a 1722 letter, StBPK, Francke Nachlass, 10, 1/5, 12. The letter of von Horn to A. H. Francke of January 1, 1723 (AFSt, H C139, 12), reveals Augusta's ambivalence about Halle.

14. See also the letters of her secretary, Johann Christian Hellwig, to A. H. Francke from 1724 through 1727 praising the reports of the mission to India and sending contributions. AFSt, H C609.

15. Some accounts date the radical turn already to the early 1720s, though the letters of von Horn to Francke from 1722 do not support this. In a 1735 remark, Stieber suggests that he had been fighting against heterodox ideas at court for ten years, which would put the turn toward more radical ideas in the mid-1720s. Letter from Stieber to Augusta, January 22, 1735, LHA Schwerin, eccl. spec. 1853.

16. The extant correspondence is fragmentary, but the exchange between Augusta and her sister Christina in the mid-1720s reveals their engagement and correspondence with J. W. Petersen. See LASA Wernigerode, Rep. H. Stolberg-Wernigerode, K, Nr. 687. Other members of Augusta's circle also mention Petersen's works around this time, including Hennings. See Hennings's letter to A. H. Francke, February 12, 1726, StBPK, Francke Nachlass, 10, 1/5, 13. The polemical and apologetical intent of later reports makes their objectivity on the question suspect, but as Wilhelmi notes, divergent sources (including both supporters and opponents of the later revival in Dargun) agreed on the radical influences at court, especially the doctrine of the *apokatastasis* during the 1720s and early 1730s. See Wilhelmi, "Augusta," 122. On the need to combat the doctrine of the *apokatastasis* among some members at court, especially Hellwig, see the 1736 letter of Carl Heinrich Zachariae to Count Christian Ernst in Wernigerode, LASA Wernigerode, Rep. H. Stolberg-Wernigerode, Nachlass Henrich Ernst II A, Nr. 200.

17. On Hellwig, see Wilhelmi, "Augusta," 120–22. Hellwig was considered one of the instigators of radical ideas at court. In an anonymous account—likely written by the later court preacher Zachariae—the author held Hellwig responsible for introducing heterodox ideas in Dargun. See *Anmerckungen*, 52–53. From a very different position, Stieber also criticized Hellwig. See Wilhelmi, "Augusta," 122. On the Berleburg Bible, see Sheehan, *Enlightenment Bible*, 73–84, Shantz, *German Pietism*, 219–29.

18. Letter from Hennings to A. H. Francke on February 2, 1725, StBPK, Francke Nachlass, 10, 1/5, 13.

19. There is no direct correspondence extant in Schwerin to confirm this. However, both supporters and opponents of Augusta mentioned Tuchtfeld as a possible candidate. See *Walchius Illustratus*, 28. See also Wilhelmi, "Augusta," 129, who sees these reports as credible. On Tuchtfeld, see Lehmann, "Victor Christoph Tuchtfeld," 277–92; Hinrichs, *Preußentum und Pietismus*, 137–45.

20. There is no extant correspondence of Augusta with Zinzendorf or others in Herrnhut, but there is evidence from February 1732 that Augusta and others in Dargun were particularly interested in the project at Herrnhut. See LHA Schwerin, eccl. spec. 1472. In 1735, after being dismissed, the former court preacher Stieber accused those in Dargun of having introduced the sectarian ways of Zinzendorf, but this is more likely a polemical accusation than a clearheaded observation.

21. There is some evidence for this. Augusta had apparently written to Johann Wilhelm Petersen about her spiritual struggles in the mid-1720s, to which Petersen replied, consoling her. Letter from J. W. Petersen to Augusta, June 20, 1725 (copied by Augusta), LASA Wernigerode, Rep. K, Nr. 687, fols. 24v, 25r. Wilhelmi sees Augusta as spiritually unsettled in this period. Wilhelmi, "Augusta," 118–19.

22. The best account of the revival in Wernigerode is still Jacobs, "Johann Liborius Zimmermann."

23. See, for instance, the letters of Simon Ambrosius Hennings and Jacob Christian Hellwig on the conversion of the Jews to Grischow and Callenberg, AFSt, H, K3, 328 (1729) and K6,

7 (1730); as well as the letters of Hellwig to August Hermann Francke on the Malabar mission, AFSt, H C609, 1–3 (1724–27).

24. Schmidt had been a catechist in Wernigerode, but because of his studies in Wittenberg he was not eligible for a clerical position in the county. Ehrenpfort, who was unusually tall, was reportedly sent to Mecklenburg to avoid the recruiters for the Brandenburg-Prussian army. See Wilhelmi, "Augusta," 130–31. See Willgeroth, *Pfarren*, 1:547, 569, 572. Ehrenpfort studied in Halle, matriculating in 1725. See Juntke, *Matrikel*, 131.

25. Letter of Jakob Schmidt to Lady Sophie Charlotte, July 3, 1733, LASA Wernigerode, Rep. H. Stolberg-Wernigerode, Nachlass Sophie Charlotte I, Briefe 75, Nr. 1.

26. Unlike the others, Hövet was from Mecklenburg, but he fully shared the convictions of the new preachers. See Willgeroth, *Pfarren*, 1:572.

27. Letter from Jakob Schmidt to Lady Sophie Charlotte, May 7, 1734, LASA Wernigerode, Rep. H. Stolberg-Wernigerode, Nachlass Sophie Charlotte I, Briefe 75, Nr. 2. Schmidt also reported on the conversions in his own parish, though he lamented the distances between villages within the parochial boundaries.

28. On the initial good relations between the Mecklenburg Pietists and the newcomers, see, for instance, Hellwig's September 1735 letter to Callenberg, AFSt, H K23, fol. 222r; and the anonymous *Anmerckungen*, 61.

29. Wilhelmi, "Augusta," 132–33. Some critics reported that Ehrenpfort preached millenarian ideas prior to 1735, but the credibility of these accounts is not especially strong. See "Specification," composed by Albertus Heinrich Fabricius, April 19, 1735, LHA Schwerin, eccl. gen. 1572.

30. Already in December 1733, Schmidt reported that Hofprediger Stieber had criticized "the truth," presumably the views of the new preachers. AFSt, H C717, 1, letter from Schmidt to G. A. Francke.

31. Though not as impartial as its title suggests, the anonymous report written by the former court physician, Joachim Jasper Johann Hempel, describing the religious practices and ensuing revival at court is telling. See Joachim Jasper Johann Hempel, "Unpartheiische und aufrichtige Historie des Kirchen-Zustandes bey der Gemeine zu Dargun im Mecklenburgischen, von Anno 1733 bis zu Ausgang de Jahrs 1735." On Hempel and his position at court, see Wilhelmi, "Augusta," 134–35.

32. Letter from Stieber to Augusta, January 22, 1735, LHA Schwerin, eccl. spec. 1853. Later reports alleged, for instance, that Stieber refused to hear confession from a lady at court who had gone to hear Ehrenpfort's sermons in Röckenitz rather than his. *Anmerckungen*, 83.

33. Lau's tract on conversion initiated the public debate on the topic of the *Bußkampf* in the 1730s. See Lau, *Schriftmäßige Beantwortung*.

34. On Zachariae's background, see Willgeroth, *Pfarren*, 2:751. Zachariae had also not studied in Halle and had little connection to G. A. Francke or others at Halle.

35. In a 1734 letter to Lady Sophie Charlotte, Schmidt noted that some of his prayer practices were seen as Catholic. LASA Wernigerode, Rep. H. Stolberg-Wernigerode Nachlass Sophie Charlotte I, Briefe 75, Nr. 2. Hempel reports that because of these rumors, a Catholic distiller came to Dargun seeking to take the Eucharist because "he had heard that they had adopted his faith there." Hempel, "Unpartheiische und aufrichtige Historie," fol. [*7v].

36. AFSt, H C717, 2.

37. LASA Wernigerode, Rep. H. Stolberg-Wernigerode, Nachlass Sophie Charlotte, VII, Nr. 9, "Etwas von den darguhnschen Reise," fol. 1r–v. The narrator of this account—almost assuredly a member of the court at Wernigerode—collected this and many other conversion narratives after a visit to Dargun in 1741, recording "what these souls have said." In this account, the author employs an odd diction, perhaps because of Augusta's high station, and occasionally intersperses the "majestic plural" with typical third-person narration. The informal and unpolished nature of these accounts signal that the author only intended for this to circulate privately

within Pietist networks. A brief reference to the duchess's conversion also appears in Hempel's "Historie," fol. *6r.

38. Draft letter to Suckow dated March 16, 1735, LHA Schwerin, eccl. gen. 1572.

39. Ehrenpfort reportedly said that these would "all eat their own way into death." "Specification," LHA Schwerin, eccl. gen. 1572, Nr. 4. See also ibid., Nr. 28, and the "Schorrentin" report of April 13, 1735.

40. "Einige Nachrichten," LHA Schwerin, eccl. gen. 1572. The Pietist Hövet, who was trained in Mecklenburg, reportedly called his own teachers and preachers "false lights, wolves, and blind leaders," who themselves had no experience with the proper path. Ibid., Schorrentin report.

41. "Einige Nachrichten," LHA eccl. gen. 1572.

42. According the "Specification," Schmidt damned fundamentally not only "his current audience but also their descendants as well as his predecessors in office." LHA Schwerin, eccl. gen. 1572, Nr. 3.

43. "Specification," LHA Schwerin, eccl. gen. 1572, Nr. 11.

44. "Specification" LHA Schwerin, eccl. gen. 1572, Nrs. 15, 17. Given that Augusta paid her Pietist clergy extraordinarily well and lavished gifts on them, these allegations cannot be dismissed out of hand. See Wilhelmi, "Augusta," 134.

45. "Einige Nachrichten," Nr. 6, LHA Schwerin, eccl. gen. 1572.

46. "Specification," Nr. 14, ibid.

47. "Specification," Nr. 12, ibid.

48. "Schorrentin" and "Specification," Nr. 24, ibid.

49. Nearly all the accounts from 1735 mention this in one form or another. See "Einige Nachrichten," Nr. 2, ibid.; "Schorrentien" and "Gorrendorf," Nr. 4, ibid.; "Protocollum," ibid.

50. "Gorrendorf," Nr. 4, ibid.

51. "Schorrentin," ibid.

52. "Protocolum," ibid.

53. See Colberg, *Christenthum*, 295; Morgenbesser, *Prüfung*; and Feustking, *Gynaeceum*, 38, 506, 665. Walch mentions it somewhat skeptically with regard to the early Quakers. See Walch, *Einleitung*, 4:763. Similar arguments were also made against the Moravians. See *Büdingische Sammlung*, 1:145.

54. Zorn, *Dissertatio*. Reprints followed in Rostock (1717) and Wittenberg (1745). While less crude than Morgenbesser and acknowledging the pharmacological effects of powders, Zorn still emphasized the possibility of supernatural effects and satanic influences. Ibid., 32–33.

55. The anti-Pietist pastor Morgenbesser was convinced that magic and Satan were at work. Morgenbesser, Samuel. *Prüfung*, fol. B1v. In contrast to Morgenbesser, Kettner proposed that the *Quäcker-Pulver* was made from jimsonweed (*Datura stramonium*), which could have hallucinogenic effects. See Kettner, "Beylage," 59–60. There is no indication that jimsonweed, however, was part of the Halle armamentarium or otherwise present in Dargun. See Wilson, "Traffic," 10–13.

56. Documents in LHA Schwerin, Unterhalt und Leibgedinge, 388–90; and AFSt, Repertorium 2, Schrank VIIa, 297, Nr. 23, both show large amounts of medicines, especially *essential dulcis*, going from Halle to Dargun during the 1730s, both directly to the court and to agents such as Pastor Hennings in Recknitz. Wilhelmi estimated the total from 1733–38 at 350 Reichsthaler. Wilhelmi, "Augusta," 255. The dominance of the elixir *essentia dulcis* among these medicines may be one reason that in Mecklenburg opponents referred to a conversion *Tranck* alongside the more common *Pulver*.

57. "Protocollum" of April 26, 1735, LHA Schwerin, eccl. gen 1572.

58. Ibid. The oven mentioned here was likely the large baker's oven on the grounds of the Dargun palace. Another account mentions that "a number of the converted have found their peace in the cabbage garden behind the oven and in the pig stall." "Specification," Nr. 13, ibid.

59. See the case of Carl Leopold and the Cantor Beatus below.

60. Augusta recruited Johann Andreas Liekefett from Klein-Ilsede near Hildesheim, who had previously been catechist at the court of Christian-Ernst in Wernigerode, and presented him along with Ehrenpfort as candidates. On Liekefett's revivalist orientation and connection to Wernigerode, see Ruprecht, *Pietismus*, 117–20. Augusta reckoned that the parish would not elect Ehrenpfort and therefore choose Liekefett instead.

61. Documents regarding the Jördenstorf election are in LHA Schwerin, eccl. spec. 4899 and 4900. A thorough summary of the election is found in Wilhelmi, "Augusta," 186–93.

62. Letter of Johann Heidemann to Augusta, August 1, 1736 (copy), LASA Wernigerode, Rep. H. Stolberg-Wernigerode, HA A67, Fach. 1–3, Nr. 8.

63. LHA Schwerin, eccl. spec. 4899, fol. 60r.

64. Ibid., fol. 57r.

65. Willgeroth, *Pfarren*, 1:561. The local nobles recruited a substitute preacher for part of this time, so that the parish was not completely without pastoral leadership. However, Augusta prevented the permanent appointment until 1748, when the congregation, despite the Superintendent's opposition, was willing to accept a slate of candidates, all of Augusta's choosing. See Wilhelmi, "Augusta," 196–97.

66. Letter from Zachariae to Count Christian Ernst, January 23, 1736, LASA Wernigerode, Rep. H. Stolberg-Wernigerode, Nachlass Henrich Ernst II, A, Nr. 200, fols. 1r–3r.

67. In 1734, they referred to themselves as the "three-leafed clover." *Walchius Illustratus*, 52–53.

68. LASA Wernigerode, Rep. H. Stolberg-Wernigerode, Nachlass Henrich Ernst I, B, Nr. 20, fol. 3r.

69. Letter to Countess Sophie Charlotte, January 31, 1736, LASA Wernigerode, Stolberg-Wernigerode, Rep. K, Nr. 920.

70. The disputation appeared as Burgmann, *Lucta*.

71. "Neue Nachrichten," *FSAM* 31 (1735): 928.

72. Hövet, *Gewißheit Bey denen Wiedergebohrnen*; Schmidt, *Eine Predigt vom Gebet*; Ehrenpfort, *Eine Predigt von der Heil. Tauffe*. All three bear dedications to Augusta. Suckow apparently prepared a rejoinder early on that was never published. See "Erzählung der meklenburgischen Controvers vom Buskampf," 669–70.

73. *Hamburgische Berichte von neuen gelehrten Sachen*, Nr. 58, July 20, 1736, 526–27.

74. "Vom Anfang der meklenburgischen Streitigkeit," 320–21.

75. Ehrenpfort, *Geheimniß*, preface.

76. Zachariae, *Buß-Kampf*.

77. Albertus Hinrich Fabricius reported on one lay commenter who puzzled over what was meant: "They talk all the time about the narrow gate, but they never want to explain what it is." "Specification," Nr. 26, LHA Schwerin, eccl. gen. 1572. Henning also spoke critically of their emphasis on the "narrow gate" according to Zachariae. Letter from 1736, LASA Wernigerode, Rep. H. Stolberg-Wernigerode, Nachlass Henrich Ernst II, A, Nr. 200, fol. 2v.

78. Zachariae, *Buß-Kampf*, 72. The reference is Chemnitz, *Loci Theologici*, 1:199.

79. Burgmann connected the teaching on the *Bußkampf* here to ideas of repentance in Stenger and Christianus Melodius (pseudonym of Adam Bernd), and "fanatics" such as Gichtel and his followers. See Burgmann, *Lucta*, 19–20. In general, the *Bußkampf* is described as a "cesspool of errors" and "snake in the grass" (ibid., 1, 38). The German translation is somewhat more moderate, calling it "a cover for many dangerous errors." See Burgmann, *Theologische Abhandlung*, 96–97.

80. Burgmann, *De Lucta, poenitentium*, 16–17.

81. Zachariae, *Buß-Kampf*, 77–81. The Dargun Pietists frequently found themselves accused of perfectionism, a position they did not hold.

82. *Theologische Beantwortung Zwoer Fragen*.

83. For Peschke, Zachariae represented the "spirit of Halle theology," whereas Russmeyer represented the Lutheran orthodox position. See Peschke, "Pietismus in Dargun," 94. Neither is quite accurate, and the portrayal of Russmeyer is especially misleading.

84. Diederich von Dobbeler recommended Russmeyer to A. H. Francke as a missionary in 1716. See the letter of von Dobbeler to Francke, StBPK, Francke Nachlass, 4a/7, 15.

85. See the letter of A. H. Francke advising Russmeyer, dated December 31, 1723, StBPK, Francke Nachlass, 1a/1A, 32. On the controversies in Greifswald during which Russmeyer was one of the leading representatives of the Pietist party—and accordingly the target of orthodox opponents—see Lother, *Pietistische Streitigkeiten*, 132–54. In fact, Russmeyer considered a position in Halle, but according to Lother he chose not to accept it because of the inadequate pay. Lother places him squarely in the Pietist tradition. Ibid., 147, 248, 249.

86. Lother, *Pietistsche Streitigkeiten*, 146–54.

87. As early as 1736, the Dargun party apparently suspected Russmeyer of criticizing their approach to conversion in a sermon. See "Erzählung der meklenburgischen Controvers vom Buskampf," 331.

88. Russmeyer here contrasted the diverse ways that Christ dealt with his followers in the process of repentance with a single-minded pursuit of conversion that he identified as an unspiritual *Bekehrsucht* or untoward desire for conversion. See Russmeyer, *Umgang Christi*, 29. Russmeyer saw this sermon as a corrective to the *Bußkampf*. See Russmeyer, *Sonderbare Krafft*, 190. Ardent supporters of zealous conversion practices saw this sermon as a rebuke. See the letter of Wilhelm Christian Hasselbach to Gotthilf August Francke, January 18, 1738, AFSt, H C715, 43.

89. Russmeyer, *Sonderbare Krafft*, 191.

90. Ibid., 128, 185.

91. Ibid., 215, 185.

92. On his criticism of the *Bußkampf* method of conversion as lacking scriptural basis, see ibid., 190, 193. On Francke and the diversity of repentance in conversion, see ibid., 199.

93. Ibid., 204.

94. Ibid., 204–14.

95. Ibid., 215–18.

96. A clear response came in the form of the anonymous *Anmerckungen über des Herrn D. Michael Christian Rußmeyers Schrift*, whose author was likely Zachariae.

97. Universitäts- und Landesbibliothek Halle, MS A 96 (3), "Responsum der Theol. Facultaet zu Halle an H. Diac. Glave in Pasewalck die Lehre vom Buß-Kampff betreff.," fol. 43v. Written by Christian Benedict Michaelis on behalf of his colleagues, the document appears to address a conflict among Pietists, presumably adherents of Russmeyer and supporters of the Dargun party in Pomerania, about the precise definition of the *Bußkampf*.

98. Bertram, *Bedencken*. The treatise vigorously defends the possibility of a true *Bußkampf*, but later chapters implicitly question practices at Dargun by strongly criticizing rigid application of the *Bußkampf* as well as the expectation that one would be able to narrate the details of the "history of his conversion" (102).

99. In a 1737 letter to Christian Berlin in Wollin, Francke expressed his "heartfelt regret" at the public disagreement between Russmeyer and those in Dargun, assigning some blame to both parties. AFSt, H C397, 1. But two years later, after a further escalation of the conflict in print, Francke appeared increasingly frustrated with the Dargun party. Ibid., 5.

100. Letter of Cellarius to Christian Ernst, August 31, 1737, LASA Wernigerode, Rep. H. Stolberg-Wernigerode, Nachlass Henrich Ernst I, B, Nr. 20, fol. 34r.

101. Hellwig, *Des Sehligen Mannes Gottes*, 9–10.

102. *Geprüfete Prüfung*.

103. Stieber likely composed the 1742 tract critical of Dargun and Walch's favorable treatment of the movement, *Walchius Illustratus*.

104. Neumeister provided a preface to Adamsen, *Antwortschreiben*, where Hempel's report appeared. Adamsen, who is otherwise unknown, may have been a pseudonym for Neumeister.

105. Wilhelmi, "Augusta," 135.

106. Wilhelmi characterizes many of the attacks of orthodox Lutherans in Mecklenburg against the Dargun Pietists as "helpless polemics" that the Darguner, despite their own exaggerations and foibles, had little problem countering. See Wilhelmi, "Augusta," 206–7. He singled out Franz Albert Aepinus, professor of theology in Rostock, and Christopherus Nicholas Rampe as especially weak.

107. Wilhelmi follows the intricate battles over consistorial authority in detail. See Wilhelmi, "Augusta," 208–16.

108. See, for instance, the letter of Friedrich Wilhelm to Christian Ludwig dated November 8, 1738, LASA Wernigerode, Rep. H. Stolberg-Wernigerode, HA A67, Fach. 1–3, Nr. 8, fol. 43r. See also Wilhelmi, "Augusta," 216.

109. Wilhelmi, "Augusta," 216.

110. These included schoolmasters and sextons in nearby parishes. A remark in one report from circa 1739 noted, "Among the twelve positions for schoolmasters, Her Most Serene Highness has already filled six with truly believing and well-grounded individuals, to whom she gives free room and board." LASA Wernigerode, Rep. H. Stolberg-Wernigerode, Nachlass Henrich Ernst I, B Nr. 20, "Ausbreitung und Hindernisse der Reiches Gottes im Hertzogthum Mecklenburg," fols. 4v–5r.

111. See the letter to Christian Ernst on June 5, 1736, requesting a *Hofkantor*, LASA Wernigerode, Stolberg-Wenigerode K, Nr. 920, fols. 12r–13r. It is indicative that though the candidate eventually came from Halle, Zachariae's connection went through Wernigerode. After Rudolph arrived, Zachariae wrote thanking Christian Ernst. See the letter of September 4, 1736, ibid., fol. 18r.

112. "Extract eines Briefes aus Suerin vom 6ten Dec. 1736," LASA Wernigerode, Rep. H. Stolberg-Wernigerode, Nachlass Henrich Ernst I, B, Nr. 20, fol. 33r. The author of the letter is not known.

113. See the account from 1741 that Berner related to a visitor from Wernigerode, LASA Wernigerode, Nachlass Sophie Charlotte VII, Nr. 9, fols. 9v–10r.

114. Schmaltz, *Kirchengeschichte Mecklenburgs*. Berner successfully appealed to Duke Carl Leopold for protection. See the letter of April 24, 1739, LHA Schwerin, eccl. spec. 1576.

115. Pastor Vorast in Bützow reported that despite his resolution as a young pastor to form a covenant with God, the "temptations of the world" and "the flattery of important figures" drew him away. Allies of Dargun, he reported, brought him to true conversion, with his breakthrough occurring at a prayer meeting as he heard one of the revivalist hymns of Johann Liborius Zimmermann, "Auf, verzagter Geist und Kämpfe." LASA Wernigerode, Nachlass Sophie Charlotte VII, Nr. 9, fol. 10r. On Zimmermann's hymn, see Jacobs, "Johann Liborius Zimmermann," 214. Wilhelmi describes the growing affiliation of many clergy in Mecklenburg with the Dargun movement. See Wilhelmi, "Augusta," 225, 263–65.

116. LASA Wernigerode, Rep. H. Stolberg-Wernigerode, Nachlass Henrich Ernst I, B, Nr. 20, fol. 8r.

117. The author estimated "twenty-something" in each of the village parishes. Ibid., fol. 4r–v.

118. Ibid., fol. 5v.

119. The accounts are found in "Etwas von der darguhnschen Reise," LASA Wernigerode, Rep. H. Stolberg-Wernigerode, Nachlass Sophie Charlotte VII, Nr. 9. The author of the collection is unknown, but internal evidence and style points to a noble woman from the court of Wernigerode.

120. The author began the collection with the observation that the following included "that which was said of souls in their conduct [i.e., in conversion] appearing noteworthy to me." Later, she referred several times to things being recounted "to me" or that were "told" (*erzählt*),

reinforcing the stories' conversational character. However, the careful numbering of accounts, the clean handwriting, and the nature of the prose itself points to a process of considered revision. Ibid.

121. Ibid., fol. 7r.

122. On a visit to Dargun in 1740, Walbaum wrote in his *Tagebuch* of two women, one the wife of a cook and the other the wife of a carpenter, who prayed with him, "after telling me of their conversions." Quoted in Wilhelmi, "Augusta," 279.

123. For a brief discussion of the function death in these narratives, see Strom, "Constructing Religious Experience."

124. LASA Wernigerode, Rep. H. Stolberg-Wernigerode, Nachlass Sophie Charlotte VII, Nr. 9, fol. 6r.

125. Ibid., fol. 4v. Moltzahn's account is the longest in the collection. The hymn is one by Christian Friedrich Richter and appeared in Freylinghausen's *Geistreiches Gesangbuch*, Nr. 737.

126. This hymn cannot be identified. It has certain similarities to a verse from Luther's "Ein' feste Burg": "Und wenn die Welt voll Teufel wär' / Und wollt' uns gar verschlingen."

127. LASA Wernigerode, Rep. H. Stolberg-Wernigerode, Nachlass Sophie Charlotte VII, Nr. 9, fol. 5r.

128. Ibid., fols. 2v–3r, 5v, 6v, 2r. The most famous Pietist *Spruchkästchen* was that by Bogatzky, *Güldnes Schatz-Kästlein der Kinder Gottes, deren Schatz im Himmel ist*, first published in Breslau in 1718 but reprinted dozens of times in the following decades. One could read Bogatzky's collection in book form or have the specially sized pages cut individually and used in a box or *Kästchen*, as they were here. For other uses of the *Spruchkästchen* in Dargun, see Wilhelmi, "Augusta," 147, 232, 245, 255, 266. Opponents also criticized the use of such *Spruchkästchen* (also *Spruchkapseln*), implying that people used them as a way of divining true conversion. See Wilhelmi, "Augusta," 158. See also Brückner, "Providenz in Zettelkasten."

129. The theologically trained *Pagenhofmeister* Leonhardt compiled fifteen conversion narratives during a period of revival in 1745 titled "Einen (hand)schriftlichen Aufsatz von der Bekehrung verschiedener Seelen, welche Gott am Ende des 1745. Jahres bald nacheinander in der Ordnung wahrer Buße in der Dargunschen Hofgemeinde zum Frieden gebracht." Though available to Wilhelmi in the nineteenth century, it is no longer extant. See Wilhelmi, "Augusta," 232.

130. "Bekehrung eines Kuhhirten in Mecklenb. wie solche im Febr. 1740 aus Dargun berichtet worden," LASA Wernigerode, Rep. H. Stolberg-Wernigerode, Nachlass Henrich Ernst II, B, Nr. 62.

131. Ibid., fol. 1r–v.

132. Ibid., fol. 2r–v.

133. Ibid., fols. 3r–4r.

134. Ibid., fols. 7v–8r.

135. Walbaum named him as Johann Erdmann Kücken from "Grantz" in Mecklenburg-Strelitz. See Wilhelmi, "Augusta," 277.

136. A good example of the circulation of the latter is a bound manuscript conversion narrative of a young woman from Lomersheim in Württemberg found in the Universitätsbibliothek Rostock, Mss. Theol. 133 (5). Though its provenance is unclear, the style of its binding and context within the collection suggest a connection to the court of Dargun.

137. On Friedrich's early life, see Wigger, "Leben Herzog Friedrichs."

138. LASA Wernigerode, Rep. H. Stolberg-Wernigerode, Nachlass Henrich Ernst I, B, Nr. 20, fol. 33r.

139. Letter to G. A. Francke, January 25, 1744, StBPK, Francke Nachlass, 18, 2/12, 4, fol. 1r.

140. Ibid., fol. 1v.

141. *Bekehrung und herrliches Ende*. A more detailed analysis of Ritter's conversion appears in the next chapter.

142. In addition to the first edition published in Magdeburg, Ritter's account was anthologized in Moser, *Seelige Letzte Stunden*, which appeared in four additional editions between 1740 and 1767. Another anthology included Ritter's account as well, Woltersdorff, *Der Schächer am Kreuz* (1753), 543–88, with later editions in 1760/66. It appeared in several other editions and collections. A modern, annotated edition is now available, Jakubowski-Tiessen, *Bekehrung unterm Galgen*.

143. Leonhardt, *Bekehrung und seliges Ende eines eilfjährigen Kindes*, 8, 11, 15.

144. Ibid., 16–29. Zachariae's older brother, Gotthilf Traugott, contributed the second account of his last hours and death.

145. Wilhelmi, "Augusta," 236.

146. Letter from Rudolph to G. A. Francke, January 25, 1744, StBPK, Francke Nachlass, 18, 2/12, 5. The woman's name or the nature of her crime is unclear. Charges of infanticide were often responsible for capital offenses involving women in the early modern period, which is likely the case here.

147. Ibid. The hymn was composed by Leopold Lehr in 1731 and often appeared in Pietist stories of conversion. On Lehr's own conversion, see above, chapter 5.

148. The best account is found in the letters of Jacob Rudolph to Gotthilf August Francke, StBPK, Francke Nachlass, 18, 2/12, 2–5. As a leading figure in the Dargun movement, Rudolph was hardly a disinterested party, but most of his observations are confirmed in documents from the chancery of Carl Leopold, especially LHA Schwerin, eccl. spec. 6226. Jacob Schmidt reported to Francke on the early investigation of the case as well in a letter on October 12, 1743, AFSt, H C717, 6 The clergy in Malchin were split on Beatus. The junior pastor Gottfried Samuel Sigismundi supported him, as did some other members of the community in Malchin who wrote letters to him while he was imprisoned. LHA Schwerin, eccl. spec. 6215, Malchin. 3ff; and eccl. spec. 6226, Malchin Kantorat, 44ff. Augusta also wrote to Duke Carl Leopold on Beatus's behalf. See LHA Schwerin, eccl. spec. 6215, fol. 20r.

149. Letter of Rudolph to G. A. Francke, August 6, 1744. StBPK, Francke Nachlass, 18, 2/12, 2. The legal reasons for the interrogation of Beatus and the justification for torture are found in an opinion by Gottfried Rudolf Ditmar, *Geheimer Sekretär*, to Carl Leopold, LHA Schwerin, eccl. spec. 6226, 54ff. Wilhelmi incorrectly implies that Beatus was spared torture. See Wilhelmi, "Augusta," 262. Ditmar's justification was instrumental for the application of torture. The stories of magical words on slips of paper probably had their origins in the Pietist employment of the *Spruchkästlein*, which were used in Dargun at the time. See LHA Schwerin, Unterhalt und Leibgedinge 389, Ausgaben Osterquartal 1735; and Jacob Rudolph's letter to G. A. Francke, January 25, 1744, StBPK, Francke Nachlass, 18, 2/12, 4–5.

150. Rudolph's letter to G. A. Francke dated August 6, 1744, StBPK, Francke Nachlass, 18, 2/12, 2.

151. Rudolph reported that Beatus was said to have withstood the "third degree of torture" and that his "hands and feet were completely ruined." StBPK, Francke Nachlass, 18, 2/12, 2. On degrees of torture, see Van Dülmen, *Theater des Schreckens*, 32–33.

152. Ibid. See also Beatus's letter thanking Carl Leopold for the appointing him. LHA Schwerin, eccl. spec. 2364, Dömitz Rector, fol. 264r–v.

153. Rudolph noted that all "the world" spoke freely, if inaccurately, about the case. StBPK, Francke Nachlass, 18, 2/12, 2.

154. LHA Schwerin, eccl. spec. 6226, fols. 122r–124v. Carl Leopold's detractors impudently sent the poem directly to the duke.

155. *Mecklenburg's Volkssagen*, 2:193–94.

156. Rudolph provides a detailed description of their use in Dargun. StBPK, Francke Nachlass, 18, 2/12, 5. See also the conversion narratives discussed above as well as LHA Schwerin, Unterhalt und Leibgedinge 389, Ausgaben Osterquartal 1735.

157. This alleged action particularly animated Carl Leopold and his interrogators in the case of Beatus. See the repeated interrogatories in LHA Schwerin, eccl. spec. 6226, fol. 54v. Others interrogated in Dargun later expressed surprise that the authorities questioned them so much about "Zettelfressen" and so little about their Pietist views. Rudolph letter, August 6, 1735, StBPK, Francke Nachlass, 18, 2/12, 5.

158. Johann Georg Rosenbach's attempts to disabuse would-be adherents that he distributed pieces of paper meant to be eaten are almost comical, but opponents seriously accused him of being a *Zettel-Fresser*. See Rosenbach, *Wunder- und Gnaden-volle Führung*, 353–58. The radical Pietist printer Christoph Saur talked about the *Schatzkästlein* and the "lie of the *Zettelfressen*" that it occasioned (qtd. in Sachse, *German Pietists*, 101). Sachse also claimed that Kelpius used a similar *Schatzkästlein* among his followers in the early 1700s, but he gives no source for this claim (100–101).

159. Nineteenth-century folklorists cite instances from southern Germany and Bohemia in which peasants fed farm animals pieces of paper marked with Bible verses, phrases, and crosses to prevent their being bewitched or becoming ill. Treichel, *Rundmarken und Rillen*, 46. See also *Beiträge zur Geschichte Böhmens* 2, no. 2 (1864): 128. For other examples of such *Eßzettel* see Hoffmann-Kreyer and Bächtold-Stäubli, *Handwörterbuch*, 1:383, 9:321–22.

160. Rudolph recounts this "ridiculous" story in a letter to G. A. Francke in order to illustrate the depth of such superstitious convictions in Mecklenburg. StBPK, Francke Nachlass, 18, 2/12, 5.

161. LHA Schwerin, eccl. spec. 1577.

162. Wilhelmi notes that the revival in Sternberg was largely independent from Dargun's direct influence. See Wilhelmi, "Augusta," 265, 281–83.

163. Letter of Jacob Schmidt to G. A. Francke, AFSt, H C 717, 10 (1747). See also AFSt, H C 717, 9 (1746).

164. Letter of Jacob Schmidt to G. A. Francke, AFSt, M3 H32, 148 (1748).

165. Schmaltz, *Kirchengeschichte Mecklenburgs*, 3:163.

166. Universitäts- und Landesbibliothek Halle, Stolberg-Wernigerode Zh-59 (1), fol. 252r. See Willgeroth, *Pfarren*, 1:78, 565. On Sarcander, see ibid., 1:565; Wilhelmi, "Augusta," 144, 156–60.

167. Universitäts- und Landesbibliothek Halle, Stolberg-Wernigerode Zh-59 (1), fol. 252v; Willgeroth, *Pfarren*, 1:243.

168. Originally from Ansbach, Döderlein studied in Halle and took an early interest in the Dargun movement, participating in the revivals on the von Mohlzahn estate in Teschow and elsewhere during the 1740s. See Wilhelmi, "Augusta," 262–63. See also AFSt, H C717, 7. On the founding of the new university, see Asche, *Bürgeruniversität*, 71–79.

169. LASA Wernigerode, Rep. H. Stolberg-Wernigerode, Nachlass Henrich Ernst I, B, Nr. 20, fols. 4v–5r.

170. On Augusta's efforts in the schools in and around Dargun, see Wilhelmi, "Augusta," 251–55.

171. Wilhelmi, "Augusta," 133–34.

172. AFSt, H C71, 4, letter of December 22, 1741.

CHAPTER 7

1. For an introduction to these conversion narratives and further bibliography, see Jakubowski-Tiessen, *Bekehrung unterm Galgen*. See also Strom, "Pietist Conversion Narratives."

2. Stuart coined the term in her article "Suicide by Proxy." See also Krogh, *A Lutheran Plague*, who refers to the phenomenon as "suicide murders."

3. Kittsteiner, *Entstehung*, 347–56.

4. On the role of the clergy in executions, see Evans, *Rituals of Retribution*, 78–86; Lächele, "Maleficanten und Pietisten," 182–84.

5. One of the popular Lutheran manuals had an entire section on pastoral care with the "malefactors" (*Maleficanten*). See Hartmann, *Hand-Buch*, 579–627. Hartmann gives precise directions of how clergy should attend to the condemned, even to the place of execution. Hartmann first published his manual in 1680, and it appeared in numerous editions until 1715.

6. A good example is the Berlin pastor Andreas Schmid, who described how he remained with the convicted murderer, Daniel Stieff, as he slowly died under the crushing blows of the executioner's wheel. See Schmid, *Göttliche Zorn-Macht*, 145–47.

7. On publishing practices surrounding executions, see Evans, *Rituals of Retribution*, 150–59.

8. Typical, perhaps, was the 1730 case of Andreas Lepsch, who after the trial remained in jail for about three weeks before his execution. Moser, *Letzte Stunden 31 Personen*, 766. The period could be considerably longer; Christian Friedrich Ritter was arrested in late January 1738 and the sentence was carried out many months later in September, in part because of the time involved in soliciting outside legal opinions. See Jakubowski-Tiessen, *Bekehrung unterm Galgen*, 17. On Lepsch and Ritter, see below.

9. See, for instance, Schmid, *Historische Lebens-Beschreibung*; and Schmid, *Göttliche Zorn-Macht*. A similar narrative that closely correlates the confession of the crime with repentance and conversion is *Nachricht von denen Prediger-Mördern*. The author of the latter did not identify himself, but he was a Protestant clergyman.

10. A good example is the short pamphlet describing the confession and regret of two members of a criminal band, one of whom supposedly composed a *Buß-Lied*, which he asked to be printed after his execution. See *Die zum Exempel*. See also *Buß-Lied*.

11. The pamphlet detailing the execution of rebels from a revolt in Mühlhausen in 1733 described how the schoolboys from the orphanage intoned a hymn as each individual was executed. See *Kurtzgefaßte Historische Nachricht*, 19.

12. Hartmann recommends that the minister should say to the condemned "Although you must expect temporal death, which moves each person, however, to pity, you also indeed know that you could live eternally in heaven, if, through true repentance, you convert to God. [This comes] from God, who has testified with a faithful oath that he does not desire the death of the sinner (that is his eternal death and damnation), but rather that he [the sinner] convert himself from his nature and live." Hartmann, *Hand-Buch*, 580.

13. Hartmann contrasted *Galgen-Reu* with true repentance. See Hartmann, *Hand-Buch*, 573. Likewise, *Schächers-Buße* colloquially referred to an insincere form of repentance by a criminal. See Moser, *Letzte Stunden 31 Personen*, 240; Jakubowski-Tiessen, *Bekehrung unterm Galgen*, 105. Luther did not use this word in his New Testament translation, but *Schächer*, an older word for robbers and criminals, often evoked the thieves crucified with Jesus (Luke 23). See Grimm and Grimm, *Deutsches Wörterbuch*, s.v. "Schächer."

14. Moser, *Seelige Letzte Stunden 31 Personen*, 4.

15. Ibid., 11–12. The case cited by Moser concerned General Johann Reinhold Patkul (1662–1707), a Baltic German caught up in the intrigues of the Great Northern War and convicted of treason by Charles XII of Sweden. Patkul's last hours circulated widely, including in English translation. Gerber included the account in his collection *Historie der Wiedergebohrnen Sachsen*, for which Moser dismissed him as "honest but otherwise often all too gullible." See Moser, *Letzte Stunden 31 Personen*, 11; Gerber, *Zweyter Anhang*, 316–37.

16. Schubert appears to have published this account in 1730 in pamphlet form, but no extant copy can be located. It also appeared in an appendix to a collection of sermons, Schubert, *Zeugniß von der Gnade*. It later appeared in Moser's 1740 *Letzte Stunden*, as well as the reprint edition of 1753 cited here. It became an explicit model for later conversions of condemned prisoners.

See, for instance, the case of Christian Friedrich Ritter in Jakubowski-Tiessen, *Bekehrung unterm Galgen*, 29.

17. Moser, *Seelige Letzte Stunden 31 Personen*, 767–68.
18. Ibid., 769.
19. Ibid., 25.
20. Ibid., 772–73.
21. Ibid., 774–75.
22. Ibid., 781–82.
23. Henckel, *Die letzten Stunden*. See chapter 3 for an extended discussion of Henckel.
24. The account was first published as *Bekehrung und herrliches Ende Christian Friederich Ritters, Eines ehemaligen zweyfachen Mörders, der den 18ten Sept. 1738. zu Dargun in Mecklenburg von untenauf gerädert worden . . . dem Druck überlassen von denen, so alles selbst mit angesehen und gehöret* (Magdeburg, 1739). It was frequently reprinted, including an edition in the nineteenth century, *Bekehrung und herrliches Ende Christian Friederich Ritters* (Dargun, 1872). Citations here are to the edition in Jakubowski-Tiessen, *Bekehrung unterm Galgen*, 9–60.
25. Universitätsarchiv Rostock, 2.02.2 S2471, 150–61; and 2.02.2 SA2471, 193–209.
26. Jakubowski-Tiessen, *Bekehrung unterm Galgen*, 18, 30.
27. Ibid., 25–29, 38.
28. Ibid., 44, 52, 59.
29. Ibid., 29.
30. There is no extant copy of the pamphlet editions, but Woltersdorff later refers to it as the third edition and identifies the printer. See Woltersdorff, *Der Schächer*, 2:831. Schubert's narrative also appeared appended to his first collection of sermons, Schubert, *Zeugniß von der Gnade*, 716–33. Moser reprinted Lepsch in his first collection of 1740 and in subsequent editions, and it was picked up by others as well. In the nineteenth century, an edited account of Lepsch's conversion appeared in a series of short tracts, *Andreas Lepsch*, as well as in the excerpted version of the nineteenth century, Moser, *Selige letzte Stunden hingerichteter Personen*, 182–85. Embarrassed by the nature of Lepsch's crime, the nineteenth-century accounts sought to be much more decorous in their descriptions.
31. *Bekehrung und herrliches Ende*. Ritter's account appeared next in Steinmetz's periodical, *VSAM* 20 (1740): 458–502; and Moser published the account anonymously in the first edition of *Seelige letzte Stunden*. Ritter's account was reprinted four more times in editions of Moser's *Letzte Stunden* between 1742 and 1767. Woltersdorff reprinted Ritter twice, for a total of nine editions between 1739 and 1767. Lepsch's account appeared twice in Schubert's sermons (see above); five times in Moser; in both editions of Woltersdorff, *Der Schächer am Kreuz*; as well as twice in Cleß, *Wegweiser*, for a total of eleven editions between 1730 and 1767 (if one includes the no-longer-extant pamphlets, then fourteen).
32. In his afterword to a modern edition of two execution narratives, Jakubowski-Tiessen gives more attention to Woltersdorff, but Moser was the innovator after whom Woltersdorff modeled his collection, justifying his new collection in 1753 because Moser hadn't published one since 1745. See Woltersdorff, *Der Schächer am Kreuz*, fol. A2v.
33. Moser, *Seelige Letzte Stunden 31 Personen*, 4–5, 11.
34. Ibid., 24–25.
35. The first editions appeared anonymously: [Moser], *Seelige letzte Stunden* (1740); *Selige letzte Stunden einiger dem zeitlichen Tode übergebener Missethäter, Mit einer Vorrede . . .* (Jena, 1742); *Selige letzte Stunden einiger dem zeitlichen Tode übergebener Missethäter* (Leipzig, 1742); *Selige letzte Stunden einiger dem zeitlichen Tode übergebener Missethäter, Erste Fortsetzung . . .* (Leipzig, 1745). Beginning in 1753, Moser attached his name: *Seelige Letzte Stunden 31 Personen*. A virtually identical edition in terms of page numbers appeared in 1767 with a slightly different title, *Lezte Stunden*. See also the 1861 excerpted version, Moser, *Selige letzte Stunden hingerichteter Personen*, ed. F. M. Kapff.

36. Cleß, *Wegweiser*; Woltersdorff, *Der Schächer am Kreuz*.

37. See note 39 above for the editions of the Ritter and Lepsch accounts, as well as chapter 1 for editions of Francke's conversion narrative.

38. Rosamaria Loretelli emphasizes, in contrast, the function of gallows literature in Britain to validate the process of justice. See Loretelli, "Scaffold," 281. Daniel Cohen primarily emphasizes the cautionary and warning function of gallows literature in early New England, though he notes the possibility of their serving as examples of repentance and contrition, especially with the rise of the Great Awakening. See Cohen, *Pillars of Salt*.

39. At the place of execution, Ritter spoke to the assembled crowd: "Now it is my wedding day. . . . Now it will not last much longer. The angels are already coming and want to take me. The bridal carriage is there, upon which I shall be transported to my bridegroom," 58.

40. Moser, *Seelige Letzte Stunden 31 Personen*, 748.

41. Ibid., 764.

42. Ibid., 240.

43. One possible exception in Moser is Johannes Saßovie, a forger, whose initial *Bußkampf* the clergy questioned as a "vain and deceptive fantasy." Though he makes progress, the account leaves the question of his true conversion somewhat ambivalent, while the author depicts his wife, raised Catholic, as a far better example of true conversion. Ibid., 783–96, here 783.

44. See the comments on Lieutenant von Phul in ibid., 869, 873.

45. Ibid., 101, 236.

46. Evans described the ravenstone (*Rabenstein*) as a permanent scaffold made of stone with a raised wooden platform where executions took place. The name derives from the carrion birds that supposedly gathered around it. See Evans, *Rituals of Retribution*, 77.

47. Tucholsky, *Vorwärts*, Nr. 47.

48. Moser, *Seelige Letzte Stunden 31 Personen*, 268, 326, 160, 161.

49. Ibid., 720.

50. Moser recounts one case of a Danish soldier convicted of murder who survived seventeen agonizing hours after being broken by the wheel, yet never lost his faith. The narrator attributed this as being a feat only "the savior could do." According to the account, he continued to testify to his faith. Ibid., 600.

51. Ibid., 833.

52. Ritter's narrative describes four ministers and two theological students involved in his spiritual care. See Jakubowski-Tiessen, *Bekehrung unterm Galgen*, 18. Schubert mentions four ministers and two students or candidates ensuring nearly daily contact. See Moser, *Seelige Letzte Stunden 31 Personen*, 768, 774.

53. Moser, *Seelige Letzte Stunden 31 Personen*, 19.

54. On Reitz, see above. For Steinmetz and his publication of the *Closter-Bergische Sammlung* and the increasing amount of international material, particularly from England, see Lächele, *Erbauungszeitschriften als Kommunikationsmedium*, 90–94.

55. On Lau and Zachariae, see above.

56. The reference to the penitent thief on the cross (Luke 23:32–43) is prominent in Woltersdorff's title and his introduction. Troubled perhaps by the thief's apparent rapid conversion, Woltersdorff speculated that he converted in jail prior to his crucifixion or had previously encountered Jesus. See Woltersdorff, *Der Schächer am Kreutz*, 1:25–26. Moser refers to the biblical story but does not otherwise emphasize it in his account.

57. Moser, *Seelige Letzte Stunden 31 Personen*, 711, 522, 516.

58. One example of Baroque Lutheran hymnody that appears many times in the narratives is Philipp Nicolai's 1597 hymn "Wie schön leuchtet der Morgenstern." See ibid. 641, 669, 676. On the more extravagant bridal imagery among Moravian men, see Faull, "Temporal Men."

59. Jakubowski-Tiessen, *Bekehrung unterm Galgen*, 39, 52, 53, 58.

60. Moser, *Seelige Letzte Stunden 31 Personen*, 532–33, 541, 548.

61. Ibid., 250.
62. Ibid., 428–29; Sehling, *Kirchenordnungen*, 82.
63. On executions in Germany as ritual rather than carnivalesque, see Evans, *Rituals of Retribution*, 103.
64. *VSAM* 12 (1739): 446–47; *Erbauliches Vorbild*, 72.
65. On the religious significance of tears, see Ebersole, "Tears," 9024.
66. Moser, *Seelige Letzte Stunden 31 Personen*, 693, 781, 757.
67. Zedler, *Universal-Lexikon*, vol. 43, col. 1743.
68. Kord, *Murderesses in German Writing*, 197.
69. Morrison, *Understanding Conversion*, xii–xiii, 186–87. See also Morrison, *Conversion and Text*, 144–45.
70. Woltersdorff, *Der Schächer am Kreuz*, 1:28.
71. Moser, *Seelige Letzte Stunden 31 Personen*, 700.
72. See, for instance, the accounts of Bremmel, in Woltersdorff, *Der Schächer am Kreuz*, 1:408–500; and Moser, *Seelige Letzte Stunden 31 Personen*, 269–326; and of Lepsch, in Woltersdorff, *Der Schächer am Kreuz*, 1:831–67; and Moser, *Seelige Letzte Stunden 31 Personen*, 766–82.
73. Suspicion attended many of these conversions and made them controversial within the community. See, for instance, the case of Beatus in Malchin above, in which angry townspeople questioned the sincerity of the conversion. See also Schmid's comments about skepticism with regard to these conversions, in *Göttliche Zorn-Macht*, 155.
74. Steinbart, *Missethäter*, 15–16.
75. In part, Kord's analysis of Moser is distorted by the inadequate edition she used. The editor of the 1861 edition, F. A. Kapff, greatly condensed most of Moser's narratives and added additional cases from the nineteenth century. Kord complains that Moser omitted most biographical information, but Kapff heavily edited and elided much of this. In Moser's original, for instance, Else Klicken's narrative ran to over a hundred pages, but it was reduced to just twelve in the 1861 version. Moser, *Selige letzte Stunden hingerichteter Personen*, ed. F. M. Kapff, 15–27; Moser, *Seelige Letzte Stunden 31 Personen*, 57–161. Cf. Kord, *Murderesses in German Writing*, 197.
76. Moser, *Seelige Letzte Stunden 31 Personen*, 268; Jakubowski-Tiessen, *Bekehrung unterm Galgen*, 138.
77. The connection is made explicitly to St. Stephen in several accounts in Moser, *Seelige Letzte Stunden 31 Personen*: Hausmann (50), Hungerland (236, 250, 268), Serpes (547), Schmalfuss (687), and Töpler (764).
78. Moser, *Seelige Letzte Stunden 31 Personen*, 163–65.
79. See, for instance, the published account of a woman convicted of infanticide that Moser likely knew but did not choose for his collection, Friccius, *Das nachdrückliche Merckmal*. Here the condemned had neither the depraved background nor the dramatic conversion that Moser prized, and even prior to the death of her child she had already experienced divine mercy, showing that her heart was not entirely obdurate when her conversion began.
80. Stuart explores the legal, cultural, and religious context of this phenomenon in her article "Suicide by Proxy." "Suicide by proxy" is Stuart's term; other historians refer to it as "capital punishment suicide," "concealed suicide," and "suicidal murders." For an overview, see Stuart, 419–20. In the eighteenth century, the jurist Carl Ferdinand Hommel referred to it as *mittelbarer Selbstmord* and considered it far more dangerous than typical suicide. See Hommel, *Rhapsodia*, 1454–55.
81. "Bekehrung und Glaubens-volles Ende Gertrude Magdalene Bremmelin, welche wegen an einem fremden Kinde verübten Mordes A. 1744 in Wernigerode enthauptet worden ist." Moser, *Seelige Letzte Stunden 31 Personen*, 269–326. The first few pages provide a brief description of the crime, investigation, and execution, but the bulk of the narrative focuses on the process of conversion that began with her detention.
82. Ibid., 270, 276.

83. Stuart sees Bremmel's language of doing "good penance" and paying with her blood as clashing with the views of the clergy and an indication of the long-term difficulty of inculcating Lutheran ideas of justification after the Reformation. See Stuart, "Suicide by Proxy," 443–44. Woltersdorff, who does not emphasize extended forms of repentance, adds a commentary on this passage that is missing in the original and in Moser, thereby shifting its meaning in a more Lutheran orthodox direction. Woltersdorff, *Der Schächer am Kreutz*, 1:414. Cf. Moser, *Seelige Letzte Stunden 31 Personen*, 275–76. Given the strongly Pietist orientation of the clergy in Wernigerode at this time, another interpretation of Bremmel's convictions may lie in the context of strict Pietist demands for an extended struggle in repentance (*Bußkampf*). Certainly, from the point of view of the clergy, Bremmel's view was distorted, but it may very well reflect the Pietist celebration of conversion prior to execution and the demands for a profound personal repentance, which—despite the qualifications of the clergy—would not have appeared entirely passive.

84. Samuel Lau, court preacher in Wernigerode, authored one of the earliest literary defenses of the *Bußkampf*; see above and Lau, *Schriftmäßige Beantwortung*. In general, see Brecht et al., *Pietismus*, 2:346–48.

85. Moser, *Seelige Letzte Stunden 31 Personen*, 275, 277.

86. Bremmel's views as recorded by the narrator are obliquely stated, but given that she emphasized "daß wer also stürbe, nicht anders als selig werden müsse" (that whoever dies in this way must necessarily become saved) suggests that the condemned's behavior was particularly pious and likely expressed some sort of conversion-type experience. Ibid., 276.

87. The narrator seeks to leave little doubt in the mind of the reader of the genuine nature of Bremmel's subsequent conversion and her steadfast faith, even as her death at the hand of the executioner is imminent. Ibid., 323–26.

88. AFSt, M 1 K7, 20, letter from Christian Ernst v. Stolberg-Wernigerode to G. A. Francke, January 19, 1745. Ernst sent three copies to Halle.

89. *Die Hirten-Treue*; Moser, *Seelige Letzte Stunden 31 Personen*, 269–326; Woltersdorff, *Der Schächer am Kreutz*, 1:407–500. The narrator describes how at the place of execution, Bremmel walked to the carriage where the "gracious sovereigns" watched the spectacle, thanked them for their generosity, and asked the Lord to bless them (Moser, *Seelige Letzte Stunden 31 Personen*, 322–23).

90. Moser, *Seelige Letzte Stunden 31 Personen*, 27–28.

91. Rambach, *Moral-Theologie*, 122. This compilation of lectures appeared after Rambach's death in 1735.

92. Woltersdorff, *Der Schächer am Kreutz*, fol. [*3r].

93. Krogh, *Lutheran Plague*.

94. Steinbart, *Missethäter*, 25–26. On Steinbart, including his early education in Pietist institutions, see Hildebrand, *Gotthilf Samuel Steinbart*.

95. Steinbart, *Missethäter*, 15–16.

96. Ibid., 8.

97. Ibid., 9–12.

98. Ibid., 14, 25–26.

99. On Steinbart's Pietist background and later development, see Hildebrand, *Gotthilf Samuel Steinbart*, 13–16.

100. See, for instance, the 1782 sermon by Spalding, "Von falschen Bekehrungen," in Spalding, *Neue Predigten*, 73–96.

101. Kittsteiner, *Entstehung*, 347–56.

102. This sparked widespread discussion in the 1770s. For an overview of the literature, see *Allgemeine deutsche Bibliothek* 27 (1775): 436–38.

103. On the Danish and German responses, see Krogh, *Lutheran Plague*, 137ff.

CONCLUSION

1. Francke, *Kurtze, iedoch gründliche Nachricht*. On these and other accounts, see chapter 1, above.
2. Niemeyer, "Uebersicht," 1:34.
3. Knapp, "Beyträge," 2:429ff.
4. Kanne, *Leben*, 175–83; Guericke, *August Hermann Francke*.
5. Brown, *Memoirs of Augustus Hermann Francke*.
6. As examples see "Conversion of Professor Francke in Halle" and "Conversion of Professor Francke."
7. Krämer, *Lebensbild*; Schmid, *Geschichte des Pietismus*, 156–59; Ritschl, *Geschichte des Pietismus*, 1:250–53.
8. Mahrholz, *Deutsche Selbstbekenntnisse*. Mahrholz writes, "What he has experienced and depicted [in his conversion account] is something that hundreds and thousands of German individuals have undergone with him and following him. The entire practice of Pietism turned on the central experience of grace, which in the *Durchbruch* is simultaneously experienced sensually. Thus what Francke has shaped here in a typical fashion was something that was vibrant among the religious feeling of the petty bourgeoisie" (154). See also Wendland, "Die pietistische Bekehrung."
9. Aland, "Bemerkungen," 563. More recently, see Mettele, "Constructions," 15; Wallmann, *Der Pietismus*, 109; Hindmarsh, *Evangelical Conversion Narrative*, 58–59; Wustmann, *Die "begeisterten Mägde*," 67.
10. De Boor, "Erfahrung gegen Vernunft," 135. In a reflection at the end of his life, Francke did refer to his experience in Lüneburg as a *Buß-Kampf* as well as an *Anfechtung*, but this further underscores the variability of meaning surrounding the term. See Krämer, *Beiträge*, 61.
11. In a response to the question of the *Bußkampf* on behalf of the Halle theology faculty, Christian Benedict Michaelis, professor of theology, objected strongly to the way that others scurrilously misrepresented the supposed "Hallensean *Bußkampf*." See Universitäts- und Landesbibliothek Halle, MS A 96 (3), "Responsum." Michaelis's annoyance was targeted at a publication that caricatured practices of conversion at Halle. See Michaelis, *Vollständige So wohl Historisch- als Theologische Nachricht*, 148–52.
12. On the later manuscript account as the definitive interpretation of Schade, see chapter 2, above. Wendland and, following him, Obst read the third-person account as giving more insight into Schade's conversion. See Wendland, "Die pietistische Bekehrung," 221–22; Obst, "Elemente atheistischer Anfechtung," 38–41.
13. Spener published the autobiographical account as part of his *Leichenpredigt* for Schade; see Spener, *Christliches Ehren-Gedächtnüß*. Francke added the autobiography to a collection of spiritual biographies he edited; see Weller, *Marter-Buch*. Similarly, Arnold reproduced the autobiography in *Leben der Gläubigen*. Obst claims that the third-person account was published two years after Schade's death, but the earliest printing I have found is 1710.
14. Francke, *Collegivm Pastorale*, 2:233–34.
15. Reitz, *Historie der Wiedergebohrnen*. Dorothea von Mücke emphasized that Reitz sought to present the diverse ways individuals came to God and avoided identifying this with a "template of conversion." See Mücke, "Experience," 21.
16. *Sammlung auserlesener Materien zum Bau des Reichs Gottes* (1731–34); *Fortgesetzte Sammlung auserlesener Materien zum Bau des Reichs Gottes* (1735–37); *Verbesserte Sammlung auserlesener Materien zum Bau des Reichs Gottes* (1737–43); *Closter-Bergische Sammlung nützlicher Materien zur Erbauung im wahren Christenthume* (1745–61); and *Altes und Neues aus dem Reich Gottes* (1733–39). On the patterns of conversion in these periodicals, see chapter 5 above.

17. For a brief overview of Kanapati Vattiyar's conversion and "apostasy," see Strom, "Constructing Religious Experience." Young and Jeyaraj analyze this conversion in greater depth in "Singer of the 'Sovereign Lord.'"

18. One of Reitz's later narratives, that of Peter Leideneck, illustrates a problem that plagued those who published conversion narratives of living individuals, when the converted soldier fell back into his former ways, forcing Reitz to remove his biography from future editions. See Schrader, "Nachwort," 181–82. See also Schrader, *Literaturproduktion und Büchermarkt*, 85–86.

19. Arnds, *Christlieb Leberecht von Exter*. On Exter's biography, see Whitmer, "Model Children."

20. Ziegenbalg composed his first-person account while in prison in Tranquebar in 1709. See AFSt, H B75–76. After Ziegenbalg's death in 1719, it was recast into the third person and printed with additional material in *Der Königl: Dänischen Missionarien aus Ost-Indien eingesandter Ausführlichen Berichten*, Part 2, Continuation 18 (1720, 2nd ed. 1724), 225–44.

21. De Boor, "Erfahrung gegen Vernunft."

22. See chapter 6, above.

23. Francke, *Kurtze und einfältig iedoch gründliche Anleitung*, 4.

24. For a detailed example of this, see the 1722 sermon, Francke, "Die scharfe Augen Christi in Beurtheilung einer wahren und falschen Herzensbekehrung," AFS, H M15b, 261. In a foreword to one of Wiegleb's devotional tracts, Francke warned of many different possibilities of deceiving oneself on conversion and regeneration. See the foreword (unpaginated) to Wiegleb, *Erbaulicher Unterricht*. Others echoed similar concerns; see, for example, Russmeyer, *Sonderbare Krafft*, 128.

25. Porst in *SAMR* 9 (1733): 81. Though likely composed in the late 1690s, it was first published in 1733. See above.

26. See, for instance, Porst, *Compendium*, 739–43.

27. Francke, *Idea studiosi Theologiae*, 470.

28. Lange, *Mittel-Straße*, 4:373.

29. Rürup, *Johann Jacob Moser*, 36.

30. Spalding, *Neue Predigten*, 193. See also his sermon "Von falschen Bekehrungen," in ibid., 73–96. Rather than telling about one's conversion, Spalding urges his parishioners to show its effect through their behavior.

31. Wiegleb authored one of the most common tracts on conversion in Pietism, *Hindernisse der Bekehrung*, first published in 1698 in Halle and reprinted again in 1701, 1709, 1710, and 1727. See chapter 2, above. On Wiegleb and conversion in Gotha, see also Strom, "Wiegleb."

32. Cf. Mettele, "Constructions," 22.

33. In his masterful if nonetheless problematic narrative on the *Protestant Evangelical Awakening*, Ward declared that "Francke was basically a preacher of reform rather than revival" and that Halle Pietism was "not itself revivalist" (72).

34. Widén, *Bekehrung und Erziehung*, 5.

35. Quoted in Wreech, *Wahrhaffte und umständliche Historie*, 99–100. Wreech was a German officer in Swedish service during the Great Northern War who was captured after the defeat of Charles XII and Swedish forces at the battle of Poltava in 1709. Von Wreech was interned with thousands of others in Siberia and only returned to Germany in 1722. On the prisoners, see Montgomery, "Der Pietismus in Schweden," 495–96.

36. In the extant correspondence with Francke and others in Halle, the focus also shifted distinctly to the running of the school, which von Wreech had tried to organize as closely as possible according to the model of the *Waisenhaus* at Halle. See the correspondence in Halle that increasingly focuses on the school and its functioning, AFSt, H C491.

37. Spener, *Theologische Bedencken*, 197–98.

38. These included Powell's *Spirituall Experiences*, excerpted in Undereyck's *Christi Braut*, and featured much more prominently in the first volume of Reitz, *Historie der Wiedergebohrnen*, in which almost all the conversion narratives were English in origin. Other English examples include the maudlin child conversions of Janeway, *Token for Children*; and Bunyan's autobiographical *Grace Abounding*.

39. Bunyan, *Grace Abounding*. On the later editions, see W. R. Owens's introduction to Bunyan's *Grace Abounding*.

40. Petersen's *Eine kurze Erzehlung, Wie mich die leitende Hand Gottes, bißher geführet* appeared as an appendix to Petersen's *Gespräche des Hertzens mit Gott* (1689). On the lack of a conversion in her autobiography, see Guglielmetti, "Nachwort," 98. For a modern translation, see Petersen, *Life*.

41. The place of Aldersgate as Wesley's definitive conversion is debated in the literature. Outler argues it is an anomaly and notes that "'Aldersgate' simply drops out of sight in the whole of Wesley's subsequent writings." See Outler, ed., *John Wesley*, 51–53. See also Maddox, ed., *Aldersgate Reconsidered*.

42. One possible exception of published conversion narratives might appear to be Christoph Eberhard's *Der Innere und äussere Zustand*, regarding the spiritual condition of the soldiers in Russian exile after the Battle of Poltava in 1709. But where the first issue seemed to promise accounts of conversion, the letters reprinted were more devotional and reflective than narratives of specific conversion experiences. After the first issue in 1718, whose subtitle continued, *Durch Ihre eigene Brieffe, Darinnen Sie Die auf ihre vormahliche fleischliche Sicherheit erfolgte Bekehrung und wunderbahre Erhaltung . . . melden*, conversion (*Bekehrung*) was dropped from the subtitle.

43. On the difference between manuscript and print diffusion of conversion narratives in Germany, see Strom, "Constructing Religious Experience."

44. Reichel, *Senfkordorden*, 30.

45. See his comments quoted in Uttendörfer, *Zinzendorf und die Mystik*, 110. Zinzendorf's comment underscores the lack of a compulsory pattern of conversion at Halle during the height of August Hermann Francke's influence.

46. See Uttendörfer, *Zinzendorf's Religiöse Grundgedanken*, 37; Schmidt, "Kinderweckung in Herrnhut," 116–18. Frederick A. Dreyer, in *Genesis of Methodism*, 38–48, asserts that this was still present in the later 1730s when Moravians encountered John Wesley.

47. For an overview, see Geiger, "Zinzendorfs Stellung." See also chapter 4, above.

48. Schmidt, *Wiedergeburt*, 205.

49. Hindmarsh, *Evangelical Conversion Narrative*, 184.

50. Mettele, "Constructions," 35.

51. See, for instance, the case of Anna Hasse, who despite a "complete awakening" was later excluded from the community. Faull, *Moravian Women's Memoirs*, 44–48.

52. Hindmarsh, *Evangelical Conversion Narrative*, 177. Hindmarsh illustrates the different nature of early Methodist and Moravian spiritual autobiography with the case of Martha Claggett, who was a "typical" Methodist convert under Charles Wesley's influence and after turning to the Moravians portrayed her spiritual biography in very different terms. Ibid., 186–92.

53. Faull, *Moravian Women's Memoirs*, 13, 20, 41, 71; Hindmarsh, *Evangelical Conversion Narrative*, 184.

54. Hindmarsh, *Evangelical Conversion Narrative*, 186.

55. On the structure of these, see Faull, ed., *Moravian Women's Memoirs*, xxxi–xxxvii.

56. See chapter 2, above; and Mücke, "Experience."

57. Rosenbach, *Wunder- und Gnaden-volle Bekehrung*. This autobiographical account also contains a telling of the conversion of Johann Adam Raab, who was instrumental in the process of converting Rosenbach. On Rosenbach and Halle Pietists, see Schneider, "Der radikale Pietismus," 141. See also Weigelt, *Geschichte des Pietismus*, 135–37.

58. See its critical review in *Unschuldige Nachrichten von Alten und Neuen Theologischen Sachen* 4 (1704): 855–64. This formed the basis of many later judgments of Rosenbach, including in *Theologische Beantwortung Zwoer Fragen*, 17.

59. See "Lebens-Lauff" in Tennhardt, *Gott allein*, 69–77. On Tennhardt, see Weigelt, *Geschichte des Pietismus*, 137–41; Engelbrecht, *Warhafftige Geschicht*.

60. In an account published in 1715, the Johann Friedrich Rock described "blessed movements" that preceded his prophecies among the *Inspirierten* but no explicit conversion. See "Kurtze Erzehlung" in Rock, *Wie ihn Gott geführet*, 8–9. However, in two unpublished accounts from around the same time (1707, 1717), Rock did refer to multiple *Erweckungen* that have some similarities with a conversion experience. See Rock, *Wie ihn Gott geführt*, 11–12, 14, 19, 21, 24, 26.

61. For instance, the report of the conversion and execution of a woman convicted of infanticide in *Geistliche Fama* 1 (1733): 68–74 appeared verbatim in Moser, *Seelige Letzte Stunden 31 Personen*, 50–57.

62. *Geistliche Fama*, preface to the second edition of vol. 1 (1733).

63. *Geistliche Fama* 2 (1733): 3–120.

64. Ibid., 40–66.

65. For instance, see chapter 5, above.

66. See, for instance, *Geistliche Fama* 2 (1733): 115; and 2 (1735): 78. In the critical depiction of the attempted conversion of the shepherd (mentioned above) to the "mother church," as the editors referred to the Lutheran church, the shepherd refused to "convert" and attend communion, claiming instead he was illumined directly by God. See *Geistliche Fama* 2 (1733): 44.

67. Meier, *Origin of the Schwarzenau Brethren*, 32, 35.

68. Bach, *Voices of Turtledoves*, 40.

69. The sermon appears in Spalding, *Neue Predigten*, 73–96.

70. Ibid., 76, 77–78, 82.

71. Ibid., 94–95. For a new interpretation of conversion in the German Enlightenment, see Gillo, "Redemption Through Conversion."

72. A good example of this point is Siegmund Jacob Baumgarten, who was an important figure in the early Enlightenment in Halle. See Sorkin, *Religious Enlightenment*, 128–29.

73. Kant, "Über Pädagogik" (1803), quoted in Kittsteiner, *Entstehung*, 354.

74. A good example of this is Wellenreuther's recent biography *Heinrich Melchior Mühlenberg*, 30, 31, 43. Wellenreuther appears to assume a standard *Bußkampf* model of conversion for Mühlenberg and his career, even though Mühlenberg's own description of a signal change in his spiritual life betrays little of this, nor does his subsequent career evince the kind of conversionist attitude one would expect on that basis. Cf. Mühlenberg, *Selbstbiographie*. Missing from his extensive journals are, for instance, any detailed descriptions of the conversion experiences of his parishioners. Mühlenberg viewed conversion less in any schematic sense than as a long, extended, and diverse process. See, for instance, *Korrespondenz*, 1:365.

75. Niggl, *Geschichte*, 11, 12.

76. See, for instance, Becker, *Conversio im Wandel*. On the reprinting of Francke's conversion narrative in the *Erweckungsbewegung*, see Schnurr, *Weltreiche und Wahrheitszeugen*, 80.

77. Hindmarsh, *Evangelical Conversion Narrative*, 340.

78. See above; and Strom, "Pietist Conversion Narratives."

79. On case of Kanapati Vattiyar see Strom, "Constructing Religious Experience"; and Young and Jeyaraj, "Singer of the 'Sovereign Lord.'" In his study of the Institutum Judaicum, Christoph Rymatzki discusses the struggles to maintain an expectation of a pietistic form of conversion among Jewish proselytes. See Rymatzki, *Hallischer Pietismus und Judenmission*, 157, 456.

80. Sorkin, *Religious Enlightenment*, 194. For detailed analysis, including the millenarian context, see Gillo, "Redemption Through Conversion," 65–76.

81. Especially around the time of the hundredth anniversary of Francke's death, a flurry of publications appeared. As an example of the narrative's reach beyond Germany, Princeton's *Biblical Repertory and Theological Review* (1830) recapitulated Francke's conversion story in detail in its review of Guericke's centennial biography, 412–14.

82. This new attitude toward conversion narratives deserves its own study. See, for instance, Becker, *Conversio im Wandel*.

BIBLIOGRAPHY

ARCHIVAL AND MANUSCRIPT MATERIALS

Berlin

   Staatsbibliothek zu Berlin–Preußischer Kulturbesitz, Francke Nachlass, 1a/1A, 32; 2, 15/3; 4a/7, 15; 9/1; 10, 1/5, 12, 17; 10, 1/5, 13; 17, 1/9, 44; 18, 2/12, 2–5; 21, 1/2, 63; 21, 2, 1/7, 69.

Gotha
   Forschungsbibliothek Gotha, Chart A 306.
   Landesarchiv Thüringen–Staatsarchiv Gotha: Oberkonsistorium Loc. 17, Nr. 20.

Halle
   Archiv der Franckeschen Stiftungen, H A114; H B75–76; H C139; H C139; H C241; H C243; H C397; H C433; H C491; H C609; H C71; H C715; H C717; H C817; H D84; H D89; H K23; H K3; H M15b; H M6; H N13; M 1 C 11, 54; M 1 K7; M 3 H32; Rep. 2, Schrank VIIa, 297, Nr. 23; W X/1/1.
   Universitäts- und Landesbibliothek Halle, MS A 96 (3); Stolberg-Wernigerode Zh-59 (1).

Kassel
   Universitätsbibiliothek, 4 Ms. hist. litt. 15[408,2.

Rostock
   Universitätsarchiv Rostock, 2.02.2 S2471, SA2471.
   Universitätsbibliothek Rostock, Mss. Theol. 133 (5).

Schwerin
   Landeshauptarchiv Schwerin: eccl. spec. 1472, 1576, 1577, 1846, 1853, 2364, 4899, 4900, 6215, 6226; eccl. gen. 1572; Korresp. ducal. 2.12–1/22; Unterhalt und Leibgedinge 389.

Wernigerode
   Landesarchiv Sachsen-Anhalt, Abteilung Magdeburg, Standort Wernigerode: Rep. H. Stolberg-Wernigerode, HA A67, Fach. 1–3, Nr. 8; K, Nr. 687; K, Nr. 920; Nachlass Heinrich Ernst I, B, Nr. 20; Nachlass Heinrich Ernst II, A, Nr. 200; Nachlass Sophie Charlotte I, Briefe 75, Nr. 1, 2; Nachlass Sophie Charlotte VII, Nr. 9.

PRINTED MATERIALS

Aalen, Liev. *Die Theologie des jungen Zinzendorfs*. Bielefeld: Lutherisches Verlagshaus, 1966.
Adamsen, Georg Theophil. *Ausführliches Antwortschreiben an seinen guten Freund und Gönner, Herrn Christianum Rodophilum, Betreffend Die nagelneuen Heiligen und sich so nennende Bekehrten zu Dargun*. Hamburg, 1737.

Aland, Kurt. "Bemerkungen zu August Hermann Francke und seinem Bekehrungserlebnis." In *Kirchengeschichtliche Entwürfe*, edited by Kurt Aland, 543–67. Gütersloh: Gerd Mohn, 1960.

Alberti, Michael. *Wohlverdientes Ehrengedächtniß / Welches . . . August Hermann Francken . . . Nachdem derselbe im 65sten Jahr seines Alters den 8. Juni 1727 . . . selig entschlaffen war*. Halle, 1727.

Albrecht, Ruth. *Johanna Eleonora Petersen: Theologische Schriftstellerin des frühen Pietismus*. Arbeiten zur Geschichte des Pietismus 45. Göttingen: Vandenhoeck & Ruprecht, 2005.

Albrecht-Birkner, Veronica. *Francke in Glaucha: Kehrseiten eines Klischees (1692–1704)*. Hallesche Forschungen 15. Halle: Verlag der Franckeschen Stiftungen, 2004.

———. "Franckes Krisen." In *Die Welt verändern: August Hermann Francke—Ein Lebenswerk um 1700*, edited by Holger Zaunstöck, Thomas Müller-Bahlke, and Claus Veltmann, 81–99. Kataloge der Franckeschen Stiftungen 29. Halle: Verlag der Franckeschen Stiftungen, 2013.

Allgemeine deutsche Bibliothek. 1765–94.

Altes und Neues aus dem Reich Gottes und der übrigen guten und bösen Geister. 1733–39. (Periodical.)

Althaus, Paul. "Die Bekehrung in reformatorischer und pietistischer Sicht." *Neue Zeitschrift für systematische Theologie* 1 (1959): 3–25.

Andreas Lepsch, der am 17. Oktober 1730 vor Potsdam lebendig verbrannt wurde. Barmen, 1839.

Anmerckungen über des Herrn D. Michael Christian Rußmeyers Schrift, so den Titul führet: Die sonderbahre Kraft Christi, Die Heucheley zu entdecken. Wernigerode, 1738.

Anton, Paul. *Ein recht-exemplarischer Knecht des Herrn: An dem Exempel Des Hoch-Ehrwürdigen und Hochgelahrten Herrn Herrn August Hermann Francken*. Halle, 1727.

Appold, Kenneth G. *Abraham Calov's Doctrine of "Vocatio" in Its Systematic Context*. Tübingen: Mohr Siebeck, 1998.

Arnds, Wilhelm Erasmus. *Eines zehen-jährigen Knabens Christlieb Leberecht von Exter, aus Zerbst, Christlich geführter Lebens-Lauff*. Edited by August Hermann Francke. Halle, 1708. Translated as *Early Piety Recommended in the Life and Death of Christlieb Leberecht Von-Exter*. London, n.d.

Arndt, Johann. *Vier Bücher von wahrem Christenthumb heilsamer Busse, hertzlicher Rewe und Leid uber die Sünde und wahrem Glauben*. Magdeburg, 1610.

———. *Von wahrem Christenthumb, heilsamer Busse, wahrem Glauben, heyligem Leben und Wandel der rechten wahren Christen*. Frankfurt, 1605.

———. *Von wahrem Christenthumb: Die Urausgabe des ersten Buches (1605)*. Edited by Johann Anselm Steiger. Hildesheim: Olms, 2005.

Arnold, Gottfried. *Die Leben der Gläubigen Oder Beschreibung solcher Gottseligen Personen, welche in denen letzten 200. Jahren sonderlich bekandt worden*. Halle, 1701.

———. *Unpartheyische Kirchen- und Ketzerhistorie*. 2 vols. Frankfurt, 1729. Originally published 1699–1700.

———. *Vitae Patrum, Oder Das Leben Der Altväter und anderer gottseeligen Personen*. 2 vols. Halle, 1700.

Asche, Matthias. *Von der reichen hansischen Bürgeruniversität zur armen mecklenburgischen Landeshochschule: Das regionale und soziale Besucherprofil der Universitäten Rostock und Bützow in der Frühen Neuzeit*. Stuttgart: Franz Steiner, 2000.

Atwood, Craig D. *Community of the Cross: Moravian Piety in Colonial Bethlehem*. University Park: Penn State University Press, 2004.

"Ausführlicher Bericht, von Christlicher Ankunft gottseelig geführtem Leben, treuverwaltetem Amte und seel. Abschiede Herrn Joh. Caspar Schadens." In *Geistreicher und erbaulicher Schrifften*, by Schade, vol. 1. Frankfurt, 1720–21.

Bach, Jeff. *Voices of Turtledoves: The Sacred World of Ephrata*. University Park: Penn State University Press, 2003.

Bach, Thomas. "The Halle Testimonial System: Conflicts and Controversies." *Covenant Quarterly* 65 (2006): 39–55.
Bachmann, J. F. *Zur Geschichte der Berliner Gesangbücher: Ein hymnologischer Beitrag.* Berlin, 1856.
Baird, Robert P. "Miguel de Molinos: Life and Controversy." In *The Spiritual Guide*, by Miguel de Molinos, edited by Robert P. Baird, 1–20. Classics of Western Spirituality. Mahwah, NJ: Paulist Press, 2010.
Bauer, Friedrich. *Erläuterter Grundtext vom Prediger Salomo.* Leipzig, 1732.
Becker, Judith. *Conversio im Wandel: Basler Missionare zwischen Europa und Südindien und die Ausbildung einer Kontaktreligiosität, 1834–1860.* Göttingen: Vandenhoeck & Ruprecht, 2015.
Becker-Cantarino, Barbara. "Pietismus und Autobiographie: Das Leben der Johanna Eleonora Petersen (1644–1724)." In *"Der Buchstab tödt—der Geist macht lebendig": Festschrift zum 60. Geburtstag von H.-G. Roloff*, edited by J. Harding and J. Jungmayr, vol. 2, 917–36. Bern: Peter Lang, 1992.
Bekehrung und herrliches Ende Christian Friedrich Ritters, Eines ehemaligen zweyfachen Mörders, der den 18ten Sept. 1738. zu Dargun in Mecklenburg von untenauf gerädert worden. Magdeburg, 1739. Reprint, Dargun, 1874.
Bernet, Claus. "Der lange Weg aus der Konfession in den radikalen Pietismus. Von Babel in das himmlische Jerusalem—Am Beispiel von Leonhard C. Sturm, Elias Eller und 'Chimonius.'" In *Confessionalism and Pietism: Religious Reform in Early Modern Europe*, edited by Fred van Lieburg, 255–82. Mainz: Philipp von Zabern, 2006.
Bertram, Johann Friedrich. *Schriftmäßiges und unpartheyisches Bedencken, über zwo kürtzlich aufgeworffenen theologische Fragen I. vom Bußkampf II. von Bestimmug der eigentlichen Zeit, wenn einer bekehret worden.* Bremen, 1738.
Bescheidentliche Beantwortung Der Neulicher Zeit an Tag gekommenen Schrifft, Welche Ein Liechtscheuender unter den Nahmen Confessio Oder Glaubens-Bekäntnüß derer Pietisten in Gotha, Samt einem darüber gestellten kurtzen Bedencken, herausgegeben. N.p.: 1693.
Beyreuther, Erich. *Selbstzeugnisse August Hermann Franckes.* Marburg: Francke Buchhandlung, 1963.
Bogatzky, Carl Heinrich von. *Carl Heinrich von Bogatzky's Lebenslauf, von ihm selbst beschrieben: Für die Liebhaber seiner Schriften und als ein Beytrag zur Geschichte der Spenerschen theologischen Schule herausgegeben.* Halle, 1801.
———. *Güldnes Schatz-Kästlein der Kinder Gottes, deren Schatz im Himmel ist.* Breslau, 1718.
Böhme, Jacob. *Sämtliche Schriften.* 11 vols. Stuttgart: Frommann, 1956–61.
Bornkamm, Heinrich, Friedrich Heyer, and Alfred Schindler, eds. *Der Pietismus in Gestalten und Wirkungen: Martin Schmidt zum 65. Geburtstag.* Arbeiten zur Geschichte des Pietismus 14. Bielefeld, 1975.
Brecht, Martin, and Paul Peucker, eds. *Neue Aspekte der Zinzendorf-Forschung.* Göttingen: Vandenhoeck & Ruprecht, 2006.
Brecht, Martin, et al., eds. *Geschichte des Pietismus.* 4 vols. Göttingen: Vandenhoeck & Ruprecht, 1993–2004.
Breithaupt, Joachim Justus. "Breithaupts eigenhändig aufgesetzter Lebens=Lauf." In *Joachim Justus Breithaupt (1658–1732): Aspekte von Leben, Wirken und Werk im Kontext*, edited by Reimar Lindauer-Huber and Andreas Lindner, 23–53. Stuttgart: Steiner, 2011.
———. *Der Ordinanden Examen, Darinnen die Summa Christlicher Lehre begriffen, allen Gottfürchtigen nützlich und nothwendig zu wissen, Geschrieben durch Hn. Philipp. Melanchthon.* Halle, 1701.
Bremmer, Jan N., Wouter J. van Bekkum, and Arie L. Molendijk, eds. *Paradigms, Poetics and Politics of Conversion.* Groningen: Peeters, 2006.
Breuer, Dieter. "Konversionen im konfessionellen Zeitalter." In *Konversion im Mittelalter und in der Frühneuzeit*, edited by Friedrich Niewöhner and Fidel Rädle, 59–66. Hildesheim: Olms Verlag, 1999.

Breul, Wolfgang, and Jan Carsten Schnurr, eds. *Geschichtsbewusstsein und Zukunftserwartung in Pietismus und Erweckungsbewegung*. AGP 59. Göttingen: Vandenhoeck & Ruprecht, 2013.
Brown, Abraham Rezeau. *Memoirs of Augustus Hermann Francke*. Philadelphia, 1830.
Brückner, Shirley. "Die Providenz in Zettelkasten: Divinatorische Lospraktiken in der pietistischen Frömmigkeit." In *Geschichtsbewusstsein und Zukunftserwartung in Pietismus und Erweckungsbewegung*, edited by Wolfgang Breul and Jan Carsten Schnurr, 351–66. AGP 59. Göttingen: Vandenhoeck & Ruprecht, 2013.
Büdingische Sammlung einiger in die Kirchenhistorie einschlagender sonderlich neuerer Schriften. Büdingen, 1742.
Bullen, Christian. *Vox Clamantis in deserto oder Stimme Johannis des Teuffers*. Amsterdam, 1668.
Bunyan, John. *Grace Abounding to the Chief of Sinners*. London, 1666.
Burgmann, Johann Christian. *De Lucta poenitentium, vulgo Vom Buß-Kampf*. Rostock, 1736.
———. *Theologische Abhandlung vom Buß-Kampff*. Translated by Johann Henrich Burgmann. Rostock, 1737.
Buß-Lied des bekannten und so genannten schönen Böttgers, so sonst zu Leipzig im Goldhahn Gäßlein soll gewohnet haben, Welches, Als er Nebst andern Malificanten den 8. Martii, 1715. in Dreßden zur Execution gebracht wurde, in seinen Arrest selber auffgesetzt. N.p.: 1715.
Caldwell, Patricia. *The Puritan Conversion Narrative: The Beginnings of American Expression*. Cambridge: Cambridge University Press, 1983.
Carlebach, Elisheva. *Divided Souls: Converts from Judaism in Germany, 1500–1750*. New Haven: Yale University Press, 2001.
[Carpzov, Johann Benedict]. *Außführliche Beschreibung Des Unfugs, Welchen Die Pietisten zu Halberstadt im Monat Decembri 1692. ümb die heilige Weyhnachts-Zeit gestifftet*. N.p.: 1693.
Chemnitz, Martin. *Loci Theologici*. Wittenberg, 1615.
Cleß, Wilhelm Jeremias Jacob. *Stifts-Archi-Diaconi in Stuttgart sicherer und getreuer Wegweiser für arme Maleficanten in den Gefängnissen: Begreifend 1.) Einen schriftmässigen Unterricht von Busse, Glauben, und seligem Sterben. 2.) Erweckliche Gebete auf allerhand Umstände. 3.) Erbauliche Exempel wolbereiteter Maleficanten*. Stuttgart, 1753; 2nd ed., Leipzig, 1755.
Closter-Bergische Sammlung nützlicher Materien zur Erbauung im wahren Christenthume. 1745–61. (Periodical.)
Cohen, Daniel. *Pillars of Salt and Monuments of Grace: New England Crime Literature and the Origins of Popular Culture*. Amherst: University of Massachusetts Press, 2006.
Colberg, Ehregott Daniel. *Das platonisch-hermetisches [sic] Christenthum: Begreiffend die historische Erzehlung vom Ursprung und vielerley Secten der heutigen fanatischen Theologie*. Erfurt, 1690.
"Conversion of Professor Francke." *Christian Advocate and Journal and Zion's Herald*, October 8, 1830, 21.
"Conversion of Professor Francke in Halle." *Millennial Harbinger*, November 1, 1830, 494–95.
Corpis, Duane J. *Crossing the Boundaries of Belief: Geographies of Religious Conversion in Southern Germany, 1648–1800*. Charlottesville: University of Virginia Press, 2014.
De Boor, Friedrich. "Erfahrung gegen Vernunft: Das Bekehrungserlebnis A. H. Franckes als Grundlage für den Kampff des Hallischen Pietismus gegen die Aufklärung." In *Der Pietismus in Gestalten und Wirkungen: Martin Schmidt zum 65. Geburtstag*, edited by Heinrich Bornkamm, Friedrich Heyer, and Alfred Schindler, 120–38. Arbeiten zur Geschichte des Pietismus 14. Bielefeld: Luther-Verlag, 1975.
Degenhardt, Jane Hwang. *Islamic Conversion and Christian Resistance on the Early Modern Stage*. Edinburgh: Edinburgh University Press, 2010.
Delius, Walter. "Aus dem Briefwechsel des Berliner Propstes Johann Porst mit A. H. Francke in Halle a.S." *Jahrbuch für Berlin-Brandenburgische Kirchengeschichte* 39 (1964): 89–113.
Dellsperger, Rudolf. *Die Anfänge des Pietismus in Bern*. Arbeiten zur Geschichte des Pietismus 22. Göttingen: Vandenhoeck & Ruprecht, 1984.

Deppermann, Andreas. *Johann Jakob Schütz und die Anfänge des Pietismus*. Tübingen: Mohr Siebeck, 2002.
Dreyer, Frederick A. *Genesis of Methodism*. Bethlehem: Lehigh University Press, 1999.
Duggan, Lawrence. "'For Force Is Not of God': Compulsion and Conversion from Yahweh to Charlemagne." In *Varieties of Religious Conversion in the Middle Ages*, edited by James Muldoon, 49–62. Gainesville: University Press of Florida, 1997.
Ebenfeld, Johann [Samuel Walther]. *Entdeckung einiger Unrichtigkeiten, welche Der Herr Leut. von Blanckensee in seinem ao. 1728 gedruckten Lebenslauf einfliessen lassen*. Magdeburg, 1728.
[Eberhard, Christoph]. *Der Innere und äussere Zustand Derer Schwedischen Gefangenen In Rußland*. 8 vols. Frankfurt and Leipzig, 1718–21.
Ebersole, Gary. "Tears." In *Encyclopedia of Religion*, edited by Lindsay Jones, 2nd ed., vol. 13, 9023–27. Detroit: Macmillan, 2005.
Ehrenpfort, Henning Christoph. *Das Geheimnis der Bekehrung eines Menschen zu Gott*. Alt-Stettin, 1736.
———. *Eine Predigt von der Heil. Tauffe*. Alten-Stettin, 1735.
Engelbrecht, Hans. *Eine Warhafftige Geschicht und Gesicht vom Himmel und der Hellen*. N.p.: 1640.
Erb, Peter C., ed. *The Pietists: Selected Writings*. Classics of Western Spirituality. Mahwah, NJ: Paulist Press, 1983.
Erbauliches Vorbild Heinrich Gottlieb Schuberts, gewesenen Alumni der Lateinischen Schule des Wäysenhauses. Halle, 1743.
Erickson, Peter. "Religious Conversion in the Late German Enlightenment: Goethe, Schiller, and Wieland." Ph.D. diss., University of Chicago, 2014.
Erläuterung der Fürstl. Mecklenburgschen Kirchen-Ordnung. Schwerin, 1708.
"Erzählung der meklenburgischen Controvers vom Buskampf." *Acta historico-ecclesiastica* 4 (1740): 315–44.
Evans, Richard J. *Rituals of Retribution: Capital Punishment in Germany, 1600–1987*. Oxford: Oxford University Press, 1996.
Fabricius, Johann Jakob [Justus Kläger]. *Kurtze und warhaffte Beschreibung der geistlosen Geistlichen: Zu fernern Prüfung den rechtschaffenen Dienern des göttlichen Worts; Und ernste Warnung Den Miedlingen und Heuchelern*. N.p.: 1668.
Faull, Katherine M. "Temporal Men and the Eternal Bridegroom: Moravian Masculinity in the Eighteenth Century." In *Masculinity, Senses, Spirit*, edited by Katherine M. Faull, 55–79. Lewisburg: Bucknell University Press, 2011.
Faull, Katherine M., ed. *Moravian Women's Memoirs: Related Lives, 1750–1820*. Syracuse: Syracuse University Press, 1997.
Fergen, Heinrich. *Waarhafftiger Bericht, an statt einer gründlichen Beantwortung, auff die unverdiente Beschuldigungen, damit Er und unterschiedliche andere mehr in Gotha in einer Lästerschrifft, genannt Ausführliche Beschreibung des Unfugs, welchen die Pietisten zu Halberstadt gestifftet*. Jena, 1694.
Feustking, Johann Heinrich. *Gynaeceum haeretico fanaticum oder Historie und Beschreibung der falschen Prophetinnen, Quäkerinnen, Schwärmerinnen und andern sectirischen und begeisterten Weibes-Personen*. Frankfurt, 1704.
Förstemann, Ernst. *Die gräflich Stolbergische Bibliothek zu Wernigerode*. Nordhausen, 1866.
Fortgesetzte Sammlung auserlesener Materien zum Bau des Reichs Gottes. 1735–37. (Periodical.)
Fortgesetzte Sammlung von alten und neuen theologischen Sachen, Büchern, Uhrkunden, Controversien, Anmerckungen und Vorschlägen. 1720–50. (Periodical.)
Francke, August Hermann. *Das Amt u. Werck Johannis des Täufers: Zur nöthigen Erinnerung des Amts und Wercks des durch den Tod vom Herrn hinweggenommenen treuen Knechtes Gottes . . .* Halle, 1728.
———. *Die Bekehrung Durch Leibliche Trübsal: Wie solche Zwar öffters scheinbar, aber selten rechtschaffen sey*. 2nd ed. Berlin, 1723. First published 1719.

———. *Collegivm Pastorale über D. Io. Lvdov. Hartmanni Pastorale Evangelicvm*. Edited by Gotthilf August Francke. 2 vols. Halle, 1741–43.

———. "Erbauliche Briefe, Des sel. Herrn Prof. Franckens in Halle an den nun auch sel. Herrn R. W." *Theologia Pastoralis Practica* 4 (1752): 837–40.

———. Foreword to *Erbaulicher Unterricht vom rechten Grund und Gebrauch des Catechismi Lutheri*, by Johann Hieronymus Wiegleb. Halle: Schütze, 1697.

———. *Gedächtniß- und Leichen-Predigten: Nebst denen Mehrentheils besonders beygefügten erbaulichen Umständen des Lebens und seligen Abschieds mancher Christlichen Personen*. Halle, 1723.

———. *Idea studiosi Theologiae oder Abbildung eines der Theologie beflissenen, wie derselbe sich zum Gebrauch und Dienst des Herrn zu allem guten Werck gehöriger Maassen bereitet*. Halle, 1712. Reprinted in *A. H. Francke's pädagogische Schriften: Nebst der Darstellung seines Lebens und seiner Stiftungen*. Edited by Gustav Krämer. Langensalza, 1876.

———. *Kurtze, iedoch gründliche Nachricht, von dem sehr merckwürdigen und erbaulichen Lebens-Lauffe Des weyland Hoch-Ehrwürdigen, in Gott Andächtigen und Hochgelehrten Herrn, Herrn August Hermann Franckens* ... In *Lebensläufe August Hermann Franckes*, by Francke, edited by Markus Matthias, 33–70. Leipzig: Evangelisches Verlagshaus, 1999.

———. *Kurtze und einfältig iedoch gründliche Anleitung zum Christenthum*. Halle, 1696.

———. *Kurtzer und Einfältiger Unterricht, Wie Die Kinder zur wahren Gottseligkeit, und Christlichen Klugheit anzuführen sind*. Halle, 1702. Reprinted in *A. H. Francke's pädagogische Schriften: Nebst der Darstellung seines Lebens und seiner Stiftungen*. Edited by Gustav Krämer. Langensalza, 1876.

———. *Kurtzer Unterricht von der Möglichkeit der wahren Bekehrung zu Gott und des thätigen Christenthums*. Halle, 1709.

———. *Lebensläufe August Hermann Franckes*. Edited by Markus Matthias. Leipzig: Evangelisches Verlagshaus, 1999.

———. *Lectiones paraeneticae oder öffentliche Ansprachen an die studiosos theologiae auf der Universität zu Halle in dem so genannten collegio paraenetico*. Edited by Gotthilf August Francke. 7 vols. Halle, 1726–36.

———. *Der letzte und schöne Glaubens-Kampff des Israels Gottes*. Halle, [1703/4]. Reprinted in *Gedächtniß- und Leichen-Predigten: Nebst denen Mehrentheils besonders beygefügten erbaulichen Umständen des Lebens und seligen Abschieds mancher Christlichen Personen*, by Francke. Halle, 1723.

———. *Der letzte und schöne Glaubens-Kampff des Israels Gottes: Aus dem Propheten Jesaia am XLIII, v. 1.2: Bey Beerdigung Der weyland Wohlgebornen, Fräulein Marthä Margarethä von Schönberg*. Halle, [1703/4].

———. *Observationes Biblicae oder Anmerckungen über einige Oerter H. Schrifft*. Halle, 1695. Reprinted in *Schriften zur biblischen Hermeneutik*, by August Hermann Francke, edited by Erhard Peschke et al. Berlin: Walter de Gruyter, 2003.

———. *Predigten*. Edited by Erhard Peschke. 2 vols. Berlin: Walter de Gruyter, 1987–89.

———. *Sonn- und Fest-Tags-Predigten, welche Theils in Halle, theils an verschiedenen auswärtigen Oertern von wichtigen und auserlesenen Materien gehalten worden*. Halle, 1724.

———. *Untergang des Reichs des Satans in uns, als ein unbetrügliches Kennzeichen der wahren Bekehrung. Am Sonntag Oculi Anno 1699* ... Halle, 1702.

———. *Vom erbaulichen Predigen, Oder die Frage: Wie ein treuer Lehrer, der gern seine Predigten zur Gewinnung und Erbauung seiner Zuhörer immer weißlicher einrichten*. Halle, 1725.

———. *Zweyfache Schriftliche Ansprache An Einige auswärtige Christliche Freunde, etliche besondere zum Christenthum gehörige Puncte betreffend, Auf Begehren zum Druck gegeben Anno 1701*. 3rd ed. Halle, 1735.

Francke, Johann Georg. *Einen treuen Lehrer der Kirche, welcher in dem Vertrauen zu Gott und seiner Gnade arbeitet, Stelte An dem Exempel Des ... Herrn Aug. Hermann Franckens*. Halle, 1727.

Franckenberg, Abraham von. *Gründlicher und wahrhafter Bericht von den Leben und Abschied des in Gott selig-ruhenden Jacob Böhmens*. 1651. In *Sämtliche Schriften*, by Jacob Böhme, vol. 10. Stuttgart: Frommann, 1956–61.
Freylinghausen, Johann Anastasius. *Das Amt u. Werck Johannis des Täufers: Zur nöthigen Erinnerung des Amts und Wercks des durch den Tod vom Herrn hinweggenommenen treuen Knechtes Gottes (Weyland Hernn August Hermann Franckens . . .)*. Halle, 1728.
———. *Geistreiches Gesangbuch*. Halle, 1704.
———. *Grundlegung der Theologie darinnin die Glaubens-Lehren aus Göttlichen Wort deutlich fürgetragen*. Halle, 1703. Reprint, Hildesheim: Olms, 2005.
———. *Ordnung des Heyls, Nebst einem Verzeichnis Der wichtigsten Kern-Sprüche H. Schrifft, darinn die führnehmsten Glaubens-Articul gegründet sind, Wie auch einem so genannten güldenen A, B, C und Gebetlein*. Halle, 1713.
———. *Wohlverdientes Ehren-Gedächtniß Des Um die Kirche Christi treuverdienten Theologi, Deß weyland Hoch-Ehrwürdigen, in Gott Andächtigen und Hochgelahrten Herrn, Herrn Johann Anastasii Freylinghausens*. Halle, 1740.
Friccius, Caspar Georg. *Das nachdrückliche Merckmal der Göttlichen Gerechtigkeit und Barmhertzigkeit, So bey der Execution Elisabeth Ahls, Einer Kinder-Mörderinn*. Salzwedel, 1726.
Gaventa, Beverly Roberts. *From Darkness to Light: Aspects of Conversion in the New Testament*. Philadelphia: Fortress Press, 1986.
Gawthrop, Richard. *Pietism and the Making of Eighteenth-Century Prussia*. Cambridge: Cambridge University Press, 1993.
Geiger, Erica. "Zinzendorfs Stellung zum Halleschen Bußkampf und Bekehrungserlebnis." *Unitas Fratrum* 49–50 (2002): 13–22.
Geistliche Fama: Mittheilend einige neuere Nachrichten von göttlichen Erweckungen, Wegen, Führungen u. Gerichten. 1730–44. (Periodical.)
Geprüfete Prüfung oder Untersuchung der sogenannten Aufrichtigen Prüfung so Dr. M. Bernh. Henr. Rönnberg, . . . Nebst einem Anhange, darinn der sich so nennende Dargunische Emigrante wie auch der Herr Mag. Burgmann kürtzlich abgefertigt wird. Berlin, 1742.
Gerber, Christian. *Historia derer Wiedergebohrnen in Sachsen, Oder Exempel solcher Personen, mit denen sich im Leben, oder im Tode viel merckwürdiges zugetragen*. Dresden, 1725–29.
———. *Zweyter Anhang zu der Historie der Wiedergebohrnen in Sachsen: Nebst einer nöthigen Vertheidigung dieser Historie, Wider die unfreundliche Censur derer Herren Sammler Altes und Neues*. Leipzig and Dresden, 1729.
Gierl, Martin. *Pietismus und Aufklärung: Theologische Polemik und die Kommunikationsreform der Wissenschaft am Ende des 17. Jahrhunderts*. Göttingen: Vandenhoeck & Ruprecht, 1997.
Gillo, Idan. "Redemption Through Conversion: The Conversion and Rebirth Discourse in Eighteenth Century Germany." Ph.D. diss., Stanford University, 2016.
Die Glaubens-Kraft Eines Evangelischen Lehrers, Wurde An dem Exempel Des Weyland Hochehrwürdigen in Gott andächtigen und Hochgelahrten Herrn, Herrn August Hermann Franckens. Halle, 1727.
Greschat, Martin. *Zwischen Tradition und neuem Anfang: Valentin Ernst Löscher und der Ausgang der lutherischen Orthodoxie. Untersuchungen zur Kirchengeschichte 5*. Witten: Luther Verlag, 1971.
Greyerz, Kaspar von. *Selbstzeugnisse der Frühen Neuzeit*. Munich: Oldenbourg, 2007.
———. "Was It Enjoyable? Attitudes Towards Pleasure of English and German Early Modern Autobiographers." In *Von der dargestellten Person zum erinnerten Ich: Europäische Selbstzeugnisse als historische Quellen (1550–1850)*, edited by Kaspar von Greyerz, Hans Medick, and Patrice Veit, 183–98. Cologne: Böhlau, 2001.
Greyerz, Kaspar von, Hans Medick, and Patrice Veit, eds. *Von der dargestellten Person zum erinnerten Ich: Europäische Selbstzeugnisse als historische Quellen (1550–1850)*. Cologne: Böhlau, 2001.

Gross, Andreas Y., Vincent Kumaradoss, and Heike Liebau, eds. *Halle and the Beginning of Protestant Christianity in India.* 3 vols. Halle: Verlag der Franckeschen Stiftungen, 2006.

Großgebauer, Theophil. "Treuer Unterricht von der Wiedergeburt." Appendix to *Wächterstimme aus dem verwüsteten Zion.* Frankfurt am Main, 1661.

———. *Wächterstimme aus dem verwüsteten Zion: Das ist, Treuhertzige und nothwendige Entdeckung, aus was Ursache die vielfältige Predigt des Worts Gottes bey Evangelischen Gemeinen wenig zur Bekehrung und Gottseligkeit fruchte und warumb Evangelische Gemeinen bey den häutigen Predigten des H. Worts Gottes ungeistlicher und ungöttlicher werden. Sambt einem treuen Unterricht von der Wiedergeburt.* Frankfurt am Main, 1661.

Guericke, Heinrich Ernst Ferdinand. *August Hermann Francke: Eine Denkschrift zur Säcularfeier seines Todes.* Halle, 1827.

Guglielmetti, Prisca. "Nachwort." In *Leben, von ihr selbst mit eigener Hand aufgesetzet: Autobiographie,* by Johanna Eleonora Petersen, edited by Prisca Guglielmetti, 89–109. Leipzig: Evangelische Verlagsanstalt, 2003.

Harran, Marilyn J. *Luther on Conversion: The Early Years.* Ithaca: Cornell University Press, 1983.

Hartmann, Johann Ludewig. *Hand-Buch für Seelsorger: In Sechs Theilen vorstellend Monita, Alloquia, Suspiria, Colloquia, Dicta, Exempla, Cantica, Superpondia &c. . . .* Nuremberg, 1689.

Heitz, Gerhard. "Carl Leopold von Mecklenburg-Schwerin (1679–1747)." In *Kaiser, König, Kardinal: Deutsche Fürsten, 1500–1800,* edited by Rolf Straubel and Ulman Weiss, 303–10. Leipzig: Urania Verlag, 1991.

Hellwig, Johann Christian. *Des Sehligen Mannes Gottes Lutheri Zeugniß, gegen das sogenandte Geheimniß der Bekehrung: In neun Sätzen: Sammt einer kurtzen Beschreibung der neuen Propheten, in gebundner Rede, aus eigener gnughaffter Erfahrung verfasset, von einem Dargunschen Emigranten.* Rostock, 1739.

Hempel, Joachim Jasper Johann. "Unpartheiische und aufrichtige Historie des Kirchen-Zustandes bey der Gemeine zu Dargun im Mecklenburgischen, von Anno 1733. bis zu Ausgang de Jahrs 1735." In *Ausführliches Antwortschreiben an seinen guten Freund und Gönner, Herrn Christianum Rodophilum, Betreffend Die nagelneuen Heiligen und sich so nennende Bekehrten zu Dargun,* by Georg Theophil Adamsen. Hamburg, 1737.

Henckel von Donnersmarck, Erdmann Heinrich. *Die letzten Stunden einiger Der Evangelischen Lehre zugethanen und in diesem und nechst verflossenen Jahren selig in dem Herrn Verstorbenen Persohnen.* 4 vols. Halle, 1720–34.

Henningsen, Jürgen. "Leben entsteht aus Geschichten: Eine Studie zu August Hermann Francke." *Neue Zeitschrift für Systematische Theologie und Religionsphilosophie* 19 (1977): 261–83.

Herbst, Michael. *Wie finden Erwachsene zum Glauben?* Frankfurt am Main: Gemeinschaftswerk der Evangelischen Publizistik, 2009.

Hertz, Deborah. *How Jews Became Germans: The History of Conversion and Assimilation in Berlin.* New Haven: Yale University Press, 2007.

———. *Wie Juden Deutsche wurden: Die Welt jüdischer Konvertiten vom 17. bis zum 19. Jahrhundert.* Translated by Thomas Bertram. Frankfurt am Main: Campus Verlag, 2010.

Herzog, Frederick. *European Pietism Revisited.* San Jose: Pickwick, 2003.

Heshus, Tilemann. *Vier Predigten von der Busse und Bekehrung zu Gott.* Königsberg, 1575.

Hildebrand, Richard. *Gotthilf Samuel Steinbart: Ein Beitrag zur Geschichte der Popularphilosophie im achtzehnten Jahrhundert.* Herne: C. T. Kartenberg, 1906.

Hindmarsh, D. Bruce. *The Evangelical Conversion Narrative: Spiritual Autobiography in Early Modern England.* Oxford: Oxford University Press, 2005.

Hinrichs, Carl. *Preußentum und Pietismus: Der Pietismus in Brandenburg-Preußen als religiössoziale Reformbewegung.* Göttingen: Vandenhoeck & Ruprecht, 1971.

Die Hirten-Treue Christi, welche er an einem seiner verlornen Schafe, nemlich an Gertrude Magdalene Bremmelin, einer vorsetzlichen Kindermörderin, erwiesen: zum Preise desselben unendli-

cher Menschenliebe, wie auch zur Warnung und Besserung beschrieben; nebst einer auf dem Rabenstein gehaltenen Rede. Wernigerode, 1744. 2nd ed., 1745.

Hoffmann-Krayer, Eduard, and Hanns Bächtold-Stäubli, eds. *Handwörterbuch des deutschen Aberglaubens*. 10 vols. Berlin: de Gruyter, 1927–42.

Holl, Karl. "Die Bedeutung der großen Kriege für das religiöse und kirchliche Leben innerhalb des deutschen Protestantismus." In *Der Westen*, vol. 3 of *Gesammelte Aufsätze zur Kirchengeschichte*, 302–84. Tübingen: Mohr-Siebeck, 1928.

Holterhoff, Engelbert. *Memoria Johannis Jacobi Fabricii, Westphali; Oder Warhaftige Beschreibung des nun in Gott ruhenden Mannes Joh. Jacobi Fabricii*. Frankfurt am Main, 1692.

Hommel, Carl Ferdinand. *Rhapsodia qvaestionvm in foro qvotidie obventivm neqve tamen legibvs decisarvm*. Vol. 5. Bayreuth, 1769.

Hövet, August. *Gewißheit Bey denen Wiedergebohrnen, daß sie Gottes Kinder seynd*. Alten-Stettin, 1735.

Der Innere und äussere Zustand Derer Schwedischen Gefangenen In Rußland, Durch Ihre eigene Brieffe . . . 8 vols. Frankfurt and Leipzig, 1718–21.

Jacobs, Eduard. "Johann Liborius Zimmermann und die pietistische Bewegung in Wernigerode." *Zeitschrift des Harz-Vereins für Geschichte und Altertumskunde* 31 (1898): 121–226.

Jakubowski-Tiessen, Manfred. *Bekehrung unterm Galgen: Malefikantenberichte*. Leipzig: Evangelische Verlagsanstalt, 2011.

James, William. *The Varieties of Religious Experience: A Study in Human Nature*. London: Routledge, 2002.

Janeway, James. *A Token for Children: Being an Exact Account of the Conversion, Holy and Exemplary Lives, and Joyful Deaths of Several Young Children*. London, 1672.

Juntke, Fritz, ed. *Matrikel der Martin-Luther-Universität Halle-Wittenberg (1690–1730)*. Vol. 1. Halle: Universitäts- und Landesbibliothek, 1960.

Kaiser, Michael, and Stefan Kroll, eds. *Militär und Religiosität in der frühen Neuzeit*. Münster: LIT Verlag, 2004.

Kanne, J. A. *Leben und aus dem Leben merkwürdiger und erweckter Christen aus der protestantischen Kirche*. Bamberg and Leipzig: Kunz, 1817.

Kettner, Friedrich Ernst. "Beylage." In *Kirchen- und Reformations-Historie, Des Käyserl. Freyen Weltlichen Stiffts Quedlinburg*. Quedlinburg, 1710.

Kieckhefer, Richard. "Convention and Conversion: Patterns in Late Medieval Piety." *Church History* 67 (1998): 32–51.

Kirn, Hans-Martin. "The Penitential Struggle ('Busskampf') of August Hermann Francke (1633–1727): A Model of Pietistic Conversion?" In *Paradigms, Poetics and Politics of Conversion*, edited by Jan N., Wouter J. van Bekkum, and Arie L. Molendijk, 123–32. Groningen: Peeters, 2006.

Kittsteiner, Heinz-Dieter. *Die Entstehung des modernen Gewissens*. Frankfurt: Insel, 1991.

Klueting, Harm. *Reformatio vitae: Johann Jakob Fabricius (1618/20–1673): Ein Beitrag zu Konfessionalisierung und Sozialdisziplinierung im Luthertum des 17. Jahrhunderts*, 75–96. Münster: LIT Verlag, 2003.

Knapp, Georg Christian. "Beyträge zur Lebensgeschichte Aug. Herm. Frankens aus ungedruckten Nachrichten." *Frankens Stiftungen* 2 (1794) 416–50.

Kolb, Robert. *For All the Saints: Changing Perceptions of Martyrdom and Sainthood in the Lutheran Reformation*. Macon, GA: Mercer, 1987.

Der Königl: Dänischen Missionarien aus Ost-Indien eingesandter Ausführlichen Berichten. 1718–72. (Periodical.)

Kord, Susanne. *Murderesses in German Writing, 1720–1860: Heroines of Horror*. New York: Cambridge University Press, 2009.

Kormann, Eva. *Ich, Welt und Gott: Autobiographik im 17. Jahrhundert*. Cologne: Böhlau, 2004.

Krämer, Gustav. *August Hermann Francke: Ein Lebensbild*. Halle, 1882.

Krämer, Gustav, ed. *A. H. Francke's pädagogische Schriften: Nebst der Darstellung seines Lebens und seiner Stiftungen*. Langensalza, 1876.

———. *Beiträge zur Geschichte August Hermann Francke's enthaltend den Briefwechsel Francke's und Spener's*. Halle, 1861.

Kratzke, Christine. *Kloster und Schloß zu Dargun in Mecklenburg-Vorpommern: Baugeschichte der Kloster-Schloßanlage unter besonderer Berücksichtigung der mittelalterlichen Bauteile*. Dargun: Förderverein Kloster-Schlosskomplex Dargun, 1995.

Krogh, Tyge. *A Lutheran Plague: Murdering to Die in the Eighteenth Century*. Leiden: Brill, 2012.

Krusenstjern, Benigna von. "Was sind Selbstzeugnisse? Begriffskritische und quellenkundliche Überlegungen anhand von Beispielen aus dem 17. Jahrhundert." *Historische Anthropologie* 2 (1994): 462–71.

Kümmel, Werner Friedrich. "Der sanfte und selige Tod: Verklärung und Wirklichkeit des Sterbens im Spiegel lutherischer Leichenpredigten des 16. bis 18. Jahrhunderts." In *Leichenpredigten als Quelle historischer Wissenschaften*, vol. 3, edited by Rudolf Lenz, 199–226. Marburg: Johannes Gutenberg-Universität, 1997.

Kurten, Petra. *Umkehr zum lebendigen Gott: Die Bekehrungstheologie August Hermann Franckes als Beitrag zur Erneuerung des Glaubens*. Paderborn: Schöningh, 1985.

Kurtzgefaßte Historische Nachricht von der Mühlhäusischen Unruhe, und der darauf am 30. Decembr. 1734. erfolgten Execution und durch Urtheil und Recht erkannten Bestraffung einiger Rädelsführer. N.p.: 1735.

Lächele, Rainer. "Einführung." In *Erlebnisse eines frommen Handwerkers im späten 17. Jahrhundert*, by Hans Ludwig Nehrlich, edited by Rainer Lächele, 1–19. Tübingen: Max Niemeyer, 1997.

———. "'Maleficanten' und Pietisten auf dem Schafott." *Zeitschrift für Kirchengeschichte* 107 (1996): 179–200.

———. *Pietistische Öffentlichkeit und religiöse Kommunikation: Die "Sammlung Auserlesener Materien zum Bau des Reichs Gottes" (1730–1761); Ein Repertorium*. Epfendorf: Bibliotheca-Academica-Verlag, 2004.

———. *Die "Sammlung auserlesener Materien zum Bau des Reichs Gottes" zwischen 1730 und 1760: Erbauungszeitschriften als Kommunikationsmedium des Pietismus*. Hallesche Forschungen 11. Tübingen: Verlag der Franckeschen Stiftungen Halle im Max Niemeyer Verlag, 2006.

Lagny, Anne. "Breithaupts Lebensbeschreibung: Als Zeugnis über die Etablierung des Pietismus." In *Joachim Justus Breithaupt (1658–1732): Aspekte von Leben, Wirken und Werk im Kontext*, edited by Reimar Lindauer-Huber and Andreas Lindner, 55–63. Stuttgart: Steiner, 2011.

———. "Lebenslauff et Bekehrung: De la relation autobiographique à la méthode de conversion religieuse." In *Les piétismes à l'âge classique: Crise, conversion, institutions*, edited by Anne Lagny, 89–110. Villeneuve-d'Ascq: Presses Universitaires du Septentrion, 2001.

Lange, Joachim. *Lebenslauf, Zur Erweckung seiner in der Evangelischen Kirche stehenden, und ehemal gehabten vielen und wehrtesten Zuhörer, Von ihm selbst verfaßet, und mit einigen Erläuterungen, auch eingeschalteten Materien, ausgefertiget*. Halle and Leipzig, 1744.

———. *Die richtige Mittel-Straße*. 4 vols. Halle, 1712–14.

Lau, Samuel. *Schriftmäßige Beantwortung der Frage: Ob es nothwendig, die Zeit seiner Bekehrung zu wissen, oder sonst ein Kenzeichen eines unbekehrten Zustandes daraus zu nehmen?* Jena, 1732. 2nd ed., Jena, 1734. 3rd ed., Jena, 1738.

Lausten, Martin Schwarz. *A Church History of Denmark*. Translated by Frederick H. Cryer. Aldershot, UK: Ashgate, 2002.

La Vopa, Anthony J. *Grace, Talent, and Merit: Poor Students, Clerical Careers, and Professional Ideology in Eighteenth-Century Germany*. Cambridge: Cambridge University Press, 1988.

Lehmann, Andrea. "Breithaupts Berufung an die Universität Halle." In *Joachim Justus Breithaupt (1658–1732): Aspekte von Leben, Wirken und Werk im Kontext*, edited by Reimar Lindauer-Huber and Andreas Lindner, 129–39. Stuttgart: Steiner, 2011.

Lehmann, Hannelore. "Victor Christoph Tuchtfeld und das Tuchtfeldische Soldatenkonventikel in Potsdam 1726/27: Erziehung zum frommen Soldaten oder 'Verleidung' des Soldatenstandes." In *Militär und Religiosität in der frühen Neuzeit*, edited by Michael Kaiser and Stefan Kroll, 277–92. Münster: LIT Verlag, 2004.

Lehmann, Hartmut. "Perspektiven für die Pietismusforschung." *Theologische Rundschau* 77 (2012): 226–40.

Lehmann, Hartmut, et al., eds. *Glaubenswelt und Lebenswelten: Geschichte des Pietismus.* Vol. 4. Göttingen: Vandenhoeck & Ruprecht, 2004.

Lenz, Rudolf. *Leichenpredigten als Quelle historischer Wissenschaften.* Vol. 3. Marburg: Johannes Gutenberg-Universität, 1997.

Leonhardt, Ludolph Balthasar. *Bekehrung und seliges Ende eines eilfjährigen Kindes, August Ernst Friederich Zachariä.* Stettin, 1747.

Leube, Hans. *Die Reformideen in der deutschen lutherischen Kirche zur Zeit der Orthodoxie.* Leipzig: Dörffling & Franke, 1924.

Lindberg, Carter, ed. *Pietist Theologians.* Malden, MA: Blackwell, 2005.

Loretelli, Rosamaria. "The Scaffold and Its Literature: The Interweaving of Justice and Narrative in Eighteenth-Century England." *Études Thanatologiques / Studi Tanatologici / Thanatological Studies* 3 (2008): 271–98.

Lother, Helmut. *Pietistische Streitigkeiten in Greifswald: Ein Beitrag zur Geschichte des Pietismus in der Provinz Pommern.* Gütersloh: C. Bertelsmann, 1925.

Lotz-Heumann, Ute, Jan-Friedrich Mißfelder, and Matthias Pohlig. "Konversion und Konfession in der Frühen Neuzeit." In *Konversion und Konfession in der Frühen Neuzeit*, edited by Ute Lotz-Heumann, Jan-Friedrich Mißfelder, and Matthias Pohlig, 11–32. Schriften des Vereins für Reformationsgeschichte 205. Gütersloh: Bertelsmann, 2007.

―――, eds. *Konversion und Konfession in der Frühen Neuzeit.* Schriften des Vereins für Reformationsgeschichte 205. Gütersloh: Bertelsmann, 2007.

Luebke, David M., Jared Poley, Daniel Ryan, and David Warren Sabean, eds. *Conversion and the Politics of Religion in Early Modern Germany.* New York: Berghahn, 2012.

Luria, Keith. "The Politics of Protestant Conversion to Catholicism in Seventeenth-Century Germany." In *Conversion to Modernities: The Globalization of Christianity*, edited by Peter van der Meer, 23–46. New York: Routledge, 1996.

Maddox, Randy L., ed. *Aldersgate Reconsidered.* Nashville: Kingswood Books, 1990.

Mahrholz, Werner. "Der Wert der Selbstbiographie als geschichtliche Quelle." In *Die Autobiographie: Zu Form und Geschichte einer literarischen Gattung*, edited by Günter Niggl, 72–74. Darmstadt: Wissenschaftliche Buchgesellschaft, 1998.

―――. *Deutsche Selbstbekenntnisse, ein Beitrag zur Geschichte der Selbstbiographie von der Mystik bis zum Pietismus.* Berlin: Furche, 1919.

Marschke, Benjamin. "'Wir Halenser': The Understanding of Insiders and Outsiders Among Halle Pietists in Prussia Under Frederick William I (1713–1740)." In *Pietism and Community in Europe and North America: 1650–1850*, edited by Jonathan Strom, 81–93. Leiden: Brill, 2010.

Mather, Samuel, ed. *Vita B. Augusti Hermanni Franckii S.S. theologiae in Academia Fridericiana nuper professoris eximii; nec non V.D.M apud Glaucham, &c. prope Hallam Magdeburgicam: Cui adjecta est, Narratio rerum memorabilium in ecclesiis evangelicis per Germaniam &c.* Boston, 1733.

Matthias, Markus. "Bekehrung und Wiedergeburt." In *Geschichte des Pietismus*, vol. 4, edited by Martin Brecht et al., 49–79. Göttingen: Vandenhoeck & Ruprecht, 1993–2004.

———. "Franckes Erweckungserlebnis und seine Erzählung." In *Die Welt verändern: August Hermann Francke; Ein Lebenswerk um 1700*, edited by Holger Zaunstöck, Thomas Müller-Bahlke, and Claus Veltmann, 69–79. Halle: Verlag der Franckeschen Stiftungen, 2013.

———. "Gewissheit und Bekehrung: Die Bedeutung der Theologie des Johannes Musaeus für August Hermann Francke." *Pietismus und Neuzeit* 41 (2015): 11–31.

McGinn, Bernard. "Miguel de Molinos and the *Spiritual Guide*: A Theological Reappraisal." In *The Spiritual Guide*, by Miguel de Molinos, edited by Robert P. Baird, 21–39. Classics of Western Spirituality. Mahwah, NJ: Paulist Press, 2010.

Mecklenburg's Volkssagen. Leipzig, 1859.

Meier, Marcus. *The Origin of the Schwarzenau Brethren*. Translated by Dennis L. Slabaugh. Philadelphia: Brethren Encyclopedia, 2008.

Mettele, Gisela. "Constructions of the Religious Self: Moravian Conversion and Transatlantic Communication." *Journal of Moravian History* 2 (2007): 7–36.

Michaelis, Christian Benedict. *Vollständige So wohl Historisch- als Theologische Nachricht von der Herrnhuthischen Brüderschafft: Durch eine nach Herrnhut angestellte Reise persönlich eingeholet*. Frankfurt and Leipzig, 1735.

Misch, Georg. *Geschichte der Autobiographie*. 3rd ed. 4 vols. Frankfurt am Main: Schulte-Bulmke, 1949–69.

Mohr, Rudolf, "Über die 'Historie der Wiedergebohrnen' von Johann Reitz." *Monatshefte für evangelische Kirchengeschichte des Rheinlandes* 23 (1974): 80–91.

Molinos, Miguel de. *The Spiritual Guide*. Edited by Robert P. Baird. Classics of Western Spirituality. Mahwah, NJ: Paulist Press, 2010.

Montgomery, Ingun. "Der Pietismus in Schweden im 18. Jahrhundert." In *Geschichte des Pietismus*, vol. 2, edited by Martin Brecht et al., 489–522. Göttingen: Vandenhoeck & Ruprecht, 1993–2004.

Morgan, Edmund. *Visible Saints*. Ithaca: Cornell University Press, 1965.

Morgenbesser, Samuel. *Prüfung des Holländischen Qvaker-Pulvers*. Sorau, 1697.

Mori, Ryoko. *Begeisterung und Ernüchterung in christlicher Vollkommenheit: Pietistische Selbst- und Weltwahrnehmungen im ausgehenden 17. Jahrhundert*. Tübingen: Niemeyer, 2004.

Morrison, Karl F. *Conversion and Text: The Cases of Augustine of Hippo, Herman-Judah, and Constantine Tsatsos*. Charlottesville: University Press of Virginia, 1992.

———. *Understanding Conversion*. Charlottesville: University of Virginia Press, 1992.

Moser, Johann Jacob. *Beytrag zu einem Lexico der jetztlebenden Lutherisch- und Reformirten Theologen in und um Teutschand*. Züllichau, 1740.

———. *Lezte Stunden ein und dreyßig durch die Hand des Scharfrichters unterschiedener Verbrechen wegen hingerichteter Personen*. Stuttgart, 1767.

———. *Seelige letzte Stunden einiger dem zeitlichen Tode übergebener Missethäter*. Leipzig, 1740.

———. *Seelige Letzte Stunden, 31 Personen, so unter des Scharfrichters Hand gestorben: Vor der Welt, als Kindes- und andere Mörder, Duellanten, Räuber, Jauner vor Gott aber, gerechtfertigte Seelen, gesammelt, mit einer Vorrede von Johann Jacob Moser*. Stuttgart: G. F. Jenisch, 1753.

———. *Selige letzte Stunden einiger dem zeitlichen Tode übergebener Missethäter*. Leipzig, 1742.

———. *Selige letzte Stunden einiger dem zeitlichen Tode übergebener Missethäter, Erste Fortsetzung*. Leipzig, 1745.

———. *Selige letzte Stunden einiger dem zeitlichen Tode übergebener Missethäter, Mit einer Vorrede*. Jena, 1742.

———. *Selige letzte Stunden hingerichteter Personen*. Edited by F. M. Kapff. Stuttgart, 1861.

Mücke, Dorothea von. "Experience, Impartiality, and Authenticity in Confessional Discourse." *New German Critique* 79 (2000): 5–35.

Mühlenberg, Heinrich Melchior. *Die Korrespondenz Heinrich Melchior Mühlenbergs aus der Anfangszeit des deutschen Luthertums in Nordamerika*. 3 vols. Berlin: Walter de Gruyter, 1986–.

———. *Selbstbiographie*. Allentown, 1881.
Muldoon, James, ed. *Varieties of Religious Conversion in the Middle Ages*. Gainesville: University Press of Florida, 1997.
Mulsow, Martin, and Richard Henry Popkin, eds. *Secret Conversions to Judaism in Early Modern Europe*. Leiden: Brill, 2004.
Murakami-Mori, Ryoko. "Der Berliner Beichtstuhlstreit: Frömmigkeit und Zeitwende im späten 17. Jahrhundert." *Pietismus und Neuzeit* 17 (1991): 62–94.
Nachricht von denen Prediger-Mördern, Raubern und Spitzbuben, Welche den 28. Januar. 1713. Nachts zwischen 12. und 1. Uhr Ihren allerseits Beicht-Vater und 22. jährigen Prediger, Herrn Johann Heinrich Meiern, Zu Rehburg (im Ambte Stoltzenau) jämmerlich ermordet . . . N.p.: 1715.
Nehrlich, Hans Ludwig. *Erlebnisse eines frommen Handwerkers im späten 17. Jahrhundert*. Edited by Rainer Lächele. Tübingen: Max Niemeyer, 1997.
Neumeister, Erdmann. Preface to *Ausführliches Antwortschreiben an seinen guten Freund und Gönner, Herrn Christianum Rodophilum, Betreffend Die nagelneuen Heiligen und sich so nennende Bekehrten zu Dargun*, by Georg Theophil Adamsen. Hamburg, 1737.
Niceron, Jean Pierre. *Nachrichten von Begebenheiten und Schriften berühmten Gelehrten*. Edited by Siegmund Jakob Baumgarten and Friedrich Eberhard Rambach. 24 vols., Halle, 1749–77.
Niemeyer, August Hermann. "Allgemeine chronologische Uebersicht des Lebens und der Stiftungen August Hermann Franckes." *Frankens Stiftungen, Eine Zeitschrift zum Besten vaterlosen Kinder* 1 (1792): 19–52; 2 (1794) 273–304.
Niewöhner, Friedrich, and Fidel Rädle, eds. *Konversion im Mittelalter und in der Frühneuzeit*. Hildesheim: Olms Verlag, 1999.
Niggl, Günther, ed. *Die Autobiographie: Zu Form und Geschichte einer literarischen Gattung*. Darmstadt: Wissenschaftliche Buchgesellschaft, 1989.
———. *Geschichte der deutschen Autobiographie im 18. Jahrhundert: Theoretische Grundlegung und literarische Entfaltung*. Stuttgart: Metzlersche J. B. Verlagsbuchhandlung, 1988.
———. "Zur Säkularisation der pietistischen Autobiographie." In *Die Autobiographie: Zu Form und Geschichte einer literarischen Gattung*, edited by Günter Niggl, 367–91. Darmstadt: Wissenschaftliche Buchgesellschaft, 1989.
Nischan, Bodo. *Prince, People, and Confession: The Second Reformation in Brandenburg*. Philadelphia: University of Pennsylvania Press, 1994.
Nüssel, Frederike. *Bund und Versöhnung: Zur Begründung der Dogmatik bei Johann Franz Buddeus*. Göttingen: Vandenhoeck & Ruprecht, 1996.
Obst, Helmut. *August Hermann Francke und die Franckeschen Stiftungen in Halle*. Göttingen: Vandenhoeck & Ruprecht, 2002.
———. *Der Berliner Beichtstuhlstreit: Die Kritik des Pietismus an der Beichtpraxis der lutherischen Orthodoxie*. Arbeiten zur Geschichte des Pietismus 11. Witten: Luther-Verlag, 1972.
———. "Elemente atheistischer Anfechtung im pietistischen Bekehrungsprozeß." *Pietismus und Neuzeit* 2 (1975): 33–42.
Olearius, Johann. *Geistliches Hand-Buch Der Kinder Gottes*. Halle and Leipzig, 1668.
Outler, Albert C., ed. *John Wesley*. New York: Oxford University Press, 1964.
Owens, W. R. Introduction to *Grace Abounding to the Chief of Sinners*, by John Bunyan. London: Penguin Classics, 1987.
Patzelt, Herbert. *Der Pietismus im Teschener Schlesien, 1709–1730*. Göttingen: Vandenhoeck & Ruprecht, 1969.
Paul, Matthias. *Johannes Anastasius Freylinghausen als Theologe des hallischen Pietismus*. Hallesche Forschungen 36. Halle: Verlag der Franckeschen Stiftungen, 2014.
Peschke, Erhard. *Bekehrung und Reform: Ansatz und Wurzeln der Theologie August Hermann Franckes*. Arbeiten zur Geschichte des Pietismus 15. Bielefeld: Luther-Verlag, 1977.

———. *Die frühen Katechismuspredigten August Hermann Franckes, 1693–1695*. Arbeiten zur Geschichte des Pietismus 28. Göttingen: Vandenhoeck & Ruprecht, 1992.

———. "Der Pietismus in Dargun." *Pietismus und Neuzeit* 1 (1974): 82–99.

———. *Studien zur Theologie August Hermann Franckes*. 2 vols. Berlin: Evangelische Verlagsanstalt, 1963.

Peschke, Erhard, ed. *Katalog der in der Universitäts- und Landesbibliothek Sachsen-Anhalt zu Halle (Saale) vorhandenen handschriftlichen und gedruckten Predigten August Hermann Franckes*, Halle: Univ.- und Landesbibliothek Sachsen-Anhalt, 1972.

Petersen, Johanna Eleonora. *Eine kurtze Erzehlung, Wie mich die leitende Hand Gottes, bißher geführet*. Appendix to *Gespräche des Hertzens mit Gott*, by Petersen, 235–95. Plön, 1689.

———. *Leben, von ihr selbst mit eigener Hand aufgesetzet: Autobiographie*. Edited by Prisca Guglielmetti. Leipzig: Evangelische Verlagsanstalt, 2003. Original ed., 1718.

———. *The Life of Lady Johanna Eleonora Petersen, Written by Herself*. Edited and translated by Barbara Becker-Cantarino. Chicago: University of Chicago Press, 2005.

Pettit, Norman. *The Heart Prepared: Grace and Conversion in Puritan Spiritual Life*. 2nd ed. Middletown: Wesleyan University Press, 1989.

Podczeck, Otto. *August Hermann Franckes Schrift über eine Reform des Erziehungs- und Bildungswesens als Ausgangspunkt einer geistlichen und sozialen Neuordnung der Evangelischen Kirche des 18. Jahrhunderts: Der große Aufsatz*. Berlin: Akademie-Verlag, 1962.

Pollack, Detlef. "Überlegungen zum Begriff und Phänomen der Konversion aus religionssoziologischer Perspektive." In *Konversion und Konfession in der Frühen Neuzeit*, edited by Ute Lotz-Heumann, Jan-Friedrich Mißfelder, and Matthias Pohlig, 33–55. Gütersloh: Bertelsmann, 2007.

Porst, Johann. *Compendium theologiae viatorum et regenitorum practicae: Oder die göttliche Führung der Seelen, und Wachsthum der Gläubigen, in einem kurtzen Auszug vorgestellet*. Halle: Waysenhaus, 1723.

Powell, Vavasor. *Spirituall Experiences, of Sundry Beleevers*. Ibbiston, 1651. 2nd ed., 1653.

Raabe, Paul, and Almut Pfeiffer, eds. *August Hermann Francke, 1663–1727: Bibliographie seiner Schriften*. Hallesche Quellenpublikationen und Repertorien 5. Halle: Verlag der Franckeschen Stiftungen in Max Niemeyer Verlag, 2001.

Rambach, Johann Jacob. *Moral-Theologie oder christliche Sitten-Lehre*. Frankfurt, 1738.

Rambo, Lewis. *Understanding Religious Conversion*. New Haven: Yale University Press, 1993.

Rambo, Lewis, and Charles E. Farhadian, eds. *The Oxford Handbook of Religious Conversion*. Oxford: Oxford University Press, 2014.

Rau, Johann. *Daß Ausnehmende Göttliche Wohlthaten. . . .* Berlin: Möller, 1728.

Reichel, Gerhard. *Der "Senfkornorden" Zinzendorfs: Ein Beitrag zur Kenntnis seiner Jugendentwicklung und seines Charakters*. Berichte des theologischen Seminars der Brüdergemeinde in Gnadenfeld. Leipzig: Friedrich Jansa, 1914.

Reitz, Johann Heinrich. *Historie der Wiedergebohrnen, Oder Exempel gottseliger, so bekandt- und benant- als unbekandt- und unbenanter Christen, Männlichen und Weiblichen Geschlechts, In Allerley Ständen: Wie dieselbe erst von Gott gezogen und bekehret, und nach vielem Kämpfen und Aengsten, durch Gottes Geist und Wort, zum Glauben und Ruh ihrer Gewissens gebracht seynd*. 7 vols. Offenbach, 1698–1745. Reprinted as *Historie der Wiedergebohrnen: Vollständige Ausgabe der Erstdrucke aller sieben Teile der pietistischen Sammelbiographie (1698–1745): Mit einem werkgeschichtlichen Anhang der Varianten und Ergänzungen aus den späteren Auflagen*. Edited by Hans-Jürgen Schrader. 7 vols. Tübingen: Niemeyer, 1982.

Rieger, Miriam. "Besessenheit und Pietismus: Zur Deutung einer Teufelsgeschichte in Breithaupts Lebensbeschreibung." In *Joachim Justus Breithaupt (1658–1732): Aspekte von Leben, Wirken und Werk im Kontext*, edited by Reimar Lindauer-Huber and Andreas Lindner, 65–77. Stuttgart: Steiner, 2011.

———. "Eine pietistische Ausbildungsstätte? Der Streit um das Gymnasium Illustre um 1700." In *Gotha macht Schule: Bildung von Luther bis Francke*, edited by Sascha Solatowksy, 89–95. Gotha: University of Erfurt, 2013.
Ritschl, Albrecht. *Geschichte des Pietismus: Der Pietismus in der lutherischen Kirche des 17. und 18. Jahrhunderts*. 3 vols. Bonn: Adolph Marcus, 1880–86.
Ritter, D. "Die Inspirierten in Rostock." *Jahrbücher des Vereins für Mecklenburgische Geschichte und Altertumskunde* 66 (1901): 141–54.
Rock, Johann Friedrich. *Wie ihn Gott geführet und auf die Wege der Inspiration gebracht habe. Autobiographische Schriften*. Edited by Ulf-Michael Schneider. Leipzig: Evangelische Verlagsanstalt, 1999.
Rogall, Georg Friedrich. "Paranesis publica, oder Oeffentliche Erweckungs-Rede an die Studiosos Theol. Auf der Königsbergischen Universität." In *Epicedia, Oder Klag- und Trost-Carmina und andere dazu gehörige Schriften, Bey dem seeligen Ableben Weyland August Hermann Francken . . .*, 187–94. Halle, 1727.
Rosenbach, Johann Georg. *Wunder- und Gnaden-volle Bekehrung, Zweyer in der Irre gegangenen verlohrn gewesenen Schaafe*. N.p.: 1703.
———. *Wunder- und Gnaden-volle Führung Gottes Eines auff dem Wege der Bekehrung Christo nachfolgenden Schaafs Oder Historische Erzehlung Was sich mit mir . . . von 1701 biß 1704 zugetragen*. N.p.: 1704.
Rotermund, Hans-Martin. *Orthodoxie und Pietismus: Valentin Ernst Löschers "Timotheus verinus" in der Auseinandersetzung mit der Schule August Hermann Franckes*. Berlin: Evangelische Verlagsanstalt, 1959.
Ruprecht, Rudolf. *Der Pietismus des 18. Jahrhunderts in den Hannoverschen Stammländern*. Göttingen: Vandenhoeck & Ruprecht, 1919.
Rürup, Reinhard. *Johann Jacob Moser: Pietismus und Reform*. Wiesbaden: Franz Steiner Verlag, 1965.
Russmeyer, Michael Christian. *Die Sonderbare Krafft Christi, die Heucheley zu entdecken*. Greifswald, 1737.
———. *Der Umgang Christi, Welchen er in den Tagen seines Fleisches mit den verschiedenen Arten von Menschen, Mit seinen Jüngern, mit den Mühseligen und Beladenen, mit denen Sündern, und mit denen Heuchlern, gepflogen hat*. Greifswald, 1736.
Rymatzki, Christoph. *Hallischer Pietismus und Judenmission: Johann Heinrich Callenbergs Institutum Judaicum und dessen Freundeskreis (1728–1736)*. Hallesche Forschungen 11. Halle: Verlag der Franckeschen Stiftungen, 2004.
Sachse, Julius Friedrich. *The German Pietists of Provincial Pennsylvania, 1694–1708*. Philadelphia, 1895.
Sammlung auserlesener Materien zum Bau des Reichs Gottes. 1731–34. (Periodical.)
Schade, Johann Caspar. *Geistreicher und erbaulicher Schrifften*. 5 vols. Frankfurt, 1720–21.
———. *Lebenslauff*. In *Geistreicher und erbaulicher Schrifften*, by Schade, vol. 1. Frankfurt, 1720–21.
———. "Merckwürdige und erbauliche Erzehlung von Einem Menschen Der in schweren Unglauben und Atheismus geführet, Aber Von Gott herrlich heraus gerissen worden." In *Geistreicher und erbaulicher Schrifften*, by Schade, vol. 5. Frankfurt, 1720–21.
Schäfer, Peter, and Mark Cohen, eds. *Toward the Millennium: Messianic Expectations from the Bible to Waco*. Leiden: Brill, 1996.
Schian, Martin. *Orthodoxie und Pietismus im Kampfe um die Predigt: Ein Beitrag zur Geschichte des endenden 17. und des beginnenden 18. Jahrhunderts*. Gießen: Töpelmann, 1912.
Schlette, Magnus. *Die Selbst(er)findung des Neuen Menschen: Zur Entstehung narrativer Identitätsmuster im Pietismus*. Göttingen: Vandenhoeck & Ruprecht, 2005.
Schmaltz, Karl. *Kirchengeschichte Mecklenburgs*. Vols. 1–2, Bahn: Schwerin, 1935–36; Vol. 3, Berlin: Evangelische Verlagsanstalt, 1952.

Schmid, Andreas. *Die erwiesene Göttliche Zorn-Macht, in Offenbahrung und Heimsuchung heimlicher Sünden.* Berlin: J. A. Rüdigern, 1720.

———. *Historische Lebens-Beschreibung des gewesenen Kürschner-Gesellens, Erdmann Briesemannes.* Berlin, 1717.

Schmid, Heinrich. *Geschichte des Pietismus.* Nördlingen: Beck, 1863.

Schmidt, Jacob. *Eine Predigt vom Gebet.* Alten-Stettin, 1735.

Schmidt, Martin. *Wiedergeburt und neuer Mensch: Gesammelte Studien zur Geschichte des Pietismus*, Arbeiten zur Geschichte des Pietismus 2. Witten: Luther Verlag, 1969.

Schmidt, Pia. "Die Kindererweckung in Herrnhut am 17. August 1727." In *Neue Aspekte der Zinzendorf-Forschung*, edited by Martin Brecht and Paul Peucker, 115–33. Göttingen: Vandenhoeck & Ruprecht, 2006.

Schmidt-Biggemann, Wilhelm. "Salvation Through Philology: The Poetical Messianism of Quirinius Kühlmann (1651–1689)." In *Toward the Millennium: Messianic Expectations from the Bible to Waco*, edited by Peter Schäfer and Mark Cohen, 259–98. Leiden: Brill, 1996.

Schneider, Hans. *Der fremde Arndt: Studien zu Leben, Werk und Wirkung Johann Arndts (1555–1621).* Göttingen: Vandenhoeck & Ruprecht, 2006.

———. *German Radical Pietism.* Translated by Gerald T. MacDonald. Lanham, MD: Scarecrow Press, 2007.

———. "Der radikale Pietismus im 18. Jahrhundert." In *Geschichte des Pietismus*, vol. 2, edited by Martin Brecht et al., 107–97. Göttingen: Vandenhoeck & Ruprecht, 1993–2004.

Schnurr, Jan Carsten. *Weltreiche und Wahrheitszeugen: Geschichtsbilder der protestantischen Erweckungsbewegung in Deutschland, 1815–1848.* Göttingen: Vandenhoeck & Ruprecht, 2011.

Schrader, Hans-Jürgen. *Literaturproduktion und Büchermarkt des radikalen Pietismus: Johann Henrich Reitz' "Historie der Wiedergebohrnen" und ihr geschichtlicher Kontext.* Palaestra 283. Göttingen: Vandenhoeck & Ruprecht, 1989.

———. "Nachwort des Herausgebers." In *Historie der Wiedergebohrnen: Vollständige Ausgabe der Erstdrucke aller sieben Teile der pietistischen Sammelbiographie (1698–1745): Mit einem werkgeschichtlichen Anhang der Varianten und Ergänzungen aus den späteren Auflagen*, by Johann Heinrich Reitz, edited by Hans-Jürgen Schrader, 4:127–203. Tübingen: Niemeyer, 1982.

Schubert, Heinrich. *Zeugniß von der Gnade u. Wahrheit in Christo: In einigen Predigten über verschiedene Texte der heiligen Schrifft abgeleget.* Magdeburg, 1733.

———. *Zeugniß von der Gnade und Wahrheit in Christo: Abgelegt in Predigten, Welche Uber die ordentliche Sonn- und Fest-taegliche Episteln Zu Potsdam in der Heiligen-Geist-Kirche, Unter göttlichem Beystand, gehalten.* Halle, 1741.

Schwentzel, Johann Ulrich. *Einen Salomon unsrer Zeit Zeigte An Dem nunmehro selig-verstorbenen Hoch-Ehrwürdigen, in Gott Andächtigen und Hochgelahrten Herrn Herrn August Hermann Francken.* Halle, 1727.

Scriver, Christian. *Seelen-Schatz: Darinn von der menschlichen Seelen hohen Würde, tieffen und kläglichen Sünden-Fall, Busse und Erneuerung durch Christum . . . gehandelt wird.* 2 vols. Magdeburg, 1701.

Seeman, Erik R. "Lay Conversion Narratives: Investigating Ministerial Intervention." *New England Quarterly* 71 (1998): 629–34.

Sehling, Emil. *Die evangelischen Kirchenordnungen des XVI. Jahrhunderts.* Vol. 3. Leipzig: O. R. Reisland, 1902.

Shantz, Doug. "Conversion and Sarcasm in the Autobiography of Johann Christoph Edelmann." In *Conversion and the Politics of Religion in Early Modern Germany*, edited by David M. Luebke, Jared Poley, Daniel Ryan, and David Warren Sabean, 153–68. New York: Berghahn, 2012.

———. *German Pietism: An Introduction.* Baltimore: Johns Hopkins University Press, 2013.

Sheehan, Jonathan. *The Enlightenment Bible: Translation, Scholarship, Culture*. Princeton: Princeton University Press, 2005.
Siebenhüner, Kim. "Glaubenswechsel in der Frühen Neuzeit: Chancen und Tendenzen einer historischen Konversionsforschung." *Zeitschrift für Historische Forschung* 34 (2007): 243–72.
Sorkin, David. *The Religious Enlightenment: Protestants, Jews, and Catholics from London to Vienna*. Princeton: Princeton University Press, 2008.
Spalding, Johann Joachim. *Neue Predigten Zweyter Band (1784)*. Edited by Malte van Spankeren and Christian Elmo Wolff. Tübingen: Mohr Siebeck, 2009.
Spangenberg, August Gottlieb. *Leben des Herrn Nicolaus Ludwig Grafen und Herrn von Zinzendorf und Pottendorf*. 7 vols. Reprint of Barby edition, 1773–75. Hildesheim: Olms, 1971.
Spener, Philipp Jakob. *Briefwechsel mit August Hermann Francke, 1689–1704*. Edited by Johannes Wallmann Udo Sträter, with Veronika Albrecht-Birkner. Tübingen: Mohr-Siebeck, 2006.
———. *Christliches Ehren-Gedächtnüß Des weyland WohlEhrwürdigen, Großachtbaren und Hochwohlgelahrten, Herrn M. Johann Caspar Schadens*. Berlin, 1698.
———. *Deutsche und lateinische Bedenken. In einer zeitgemäßen Auswahl*. Edited by F. A. G. Hennicke. Halle, 1838.
———. *Letzte theologische Bedencken*. 3 vols. Halle, 1711.
———. *Theologische Bedencken und andere Briefliche Antworten*. Vol. 1, pts. 1–2. Halle, 1700.
———. *Die Werke Philipp Jakob Speners: Studienausgabe*. Edited by Kurt Aland and Beate von Tschischwitz. 2 vols. Gießen: Brunnen Verlag, 1996–.
Stahl, Herbert. *August Hermann Francke, der Einfluss Luthers und Molinos' auf ihn*. Stuttgart: Kohlhammer, 1939.
Steinbart, Gotthilf Samuel. *Ist es rathsam Missethäter durch Geistliche zum Tode vorbereiten und zur Hinrichtung begleiten zulassen?* Berlin, 1769.
Steinmetz, David. "Reformation and Conversion." *Theology Today* 35 (1978): 25–32.
Stievermann, Jan. "Halle Pietism and Its Perception of the American Great Awakening." In *The Transatlantic World of Heinrich Melchior Mühlenberg in the Eighteenth Century*, edited by Hermann Wellenreuther, Thomas Müller-Bahlke, and A. Gregg Roeber, 213–46. Halle: Verlag der Franckeschen Stiftungen, 2013.
Stoeffler, F. Ernest. *German Pietism During the Eighteenth Century*. Leiden: Brill, 1973.
Sträter, Udo. "August Hermann Francke und Martin Luther." *Pietismus und Neuzeit* 34 (2008): 27–28.
Straubel, Rolf, and Ulman Weiss, eds. *Kaiser, König, Kardinal: Deutsche Fürsten, 1500–1800*. Leipzig: Urania Verlag, 1991.
Strom, Jonathan. "Constructing Religious Experience: Conversion Narratives in Hallensian Pietism." In *"Aus Gottes Wort und eigener Erfahrung gezeiget": Erfahrung—Glauben, Erkennen und Gestalten im Pietismus; Beiträge zum III. Internationalen Kongress für Pietismusforschung, 2009*, edited by Christian Soboth et al., 106–29. Hallesche Forschungen 33. Halle: Verlag der Franckeschen Stiftungen, 2012.
———. "Conversion, Confessionalization, and Pietism in Dargun." In *Confessionalism and Pietism: Religious Reform in Early Modern Europe*, edited by Fred van Lieburg, 149–68. Mainz: Philipp von Zabern Verlag, 2006.
———. "Johann Hieronymus Wiegleb and the Experience of Conversion." In *Pietismus in Thüringen*, edited by Veronika Albrecht-Birkner et al. In press, 2018.
———. *Orthodoxy and Reform: The Clergy in Seventeenth Century Rostock*. Tübingen: Mohr Siebeck, 1999.
———. "Pietism and Revival." In *Preaching, Sermon, and Cultural Change in the Long Eighteenth Century*, edited by Joris van Eijnatten, 173–218. Leiden: Brill, 2009.
———. "Pietist Conversion Narratives and Confessional Identity." In *Conversion and the Politics of Religion in Early Modern Germany*, edited by David M. Luebke, Jared Poley, Daniel Ryan, and David Warren Sabean, 135–52. New York: Berghahn, 2012.

———. "Problems and Promises of Pietism Research." *Church History* 71 (2002): 536–54.
Strom, Jonathan, ed. *Pietism and Community in Europe and North America, 1650–1850*. Leiden: Brill, 2010.
Stuart, Kathy. "Suicide by Proxy: The Unintended Consequences of Public Executions in Eighteenth-Century Germany." *Central European History* 41 (2008): 413–45.
Tennhardt, Johann. *Gott allein soll die Ehre seyn*. Nuremberg, 1710.
Teufel, Eberhard. "Die Beziehungen zwischen Herrnhut und Sorau von 1727 bis 1745." *Jahrbuch für brandenburgische Kirchengeschichte* 20 (1925): 172–84.
Theologische Beantwortung Zwoer Fragen Die eigentliche Zeit und Beschaffenheit Der beyden Stücke Bekehrung und Buß-Kampff Betreffend, Betreffend Nemlich . . . Aus Heil. Göttlicher Schrifft Denen Evangelisch-Lutherischen Glaubens-Symbolis und Zeugnissen reiner Lehrer. Frankfurt, 1732.
Tholuck, August. *Geschichte des Rationalismus*. Berlin, 1865.
Treichel, Alexander. *Rundmarken und Rillen an Kirchenwänden*. Berlin, 1880.
Tucholsky, Kurt. "Wie sie starben." *Vorwärts*, March 7, 1914. http://www.textlog.de/tucholsky-wie-sie-starben.html.
Undereyck, Theodor. *Christi Braut unter den Töchtern zu Laodicaea*. Hanau, 1670.
Unschuldige Nachrichten von Alten und Neuen Theologischen Sachen. 1701–19. (Periodical.)
Uttendörfer, Otto. *Zinzendorfs religiöse Grundgedanken*. Herrnhut: Missionsbuchhandlung, 1935.
———. *Zinzendorf und die Mystik*. Berlin: Christlicher Zeitschriften-Verlag, 1952.
Van de Meer, Peter. *Conversion to Modernities: The Globalization of Christianity*. New York: Routledge, 1996.
Van Dülmen, Richard. *Theater des Schreckens: Gerichtspraxis und Strafrituale in der frühen Neuzeit*. Munich: C. H. Beck, 1995.
Van Eijnatten, Joris. *Preaching, Sermon, and Cultural Change in the Long Eighteenth Century*. Leiden: Brill, 2008.
Verbesserte Sammlung auserlesener Materien zum Bau des Reichs Gottes. 1737–43. (Periodical.)
Vogt, Peter. "Nicholas Ludwig von Zinzendorf (1700–1760)." In *Pietist Theologians*, edited by Carter Lindberg, 207–23. Malden, MA: Blackwell, 2005.
"Vom Anfang der meklenburgischen Streitigkeit, aus einem Schreiben vom 28 Aug. 1739." *Acta historica-ecclesiastica* 4 (1740): 315–25.
Walch, Johann Georg. *Historische und Theologische Einleitung in die Religions-Streitigkeiten, welche sonderlich ausser der Evangelisch-Lutherischen Kirchen entstanden*. 5 vols. Jena, 1730–39.
Walchius Illustratus D. i. Abgenöthigte und nach der Wahrheit angestellte Beleuchtung . . . von denen Dargunischen Streitigkeiten. [Jena], 1742.
Wallmann, Johannes. "Erfurt und der Pietismus." In *Erfurt, 742–1992: Stadtgeschichte, Universitätsgeschichte*, edited by Ulman Weiß, 403–22. Weimar: Verlag Hermann Böhlaus Nachfolger, 1992.
———. *Philipp Jakob Spener und die Anfänge des Pietismus*. 2nd ed. Tübingen: Mohr, 1986.
———. *Der Pietismus*. Göttingen: Vandenhoeck & Ruprecht, 2005.
Walker, Mack. *Johann Jakob Moser and the Holy Roman Empire of the German Nation*. Chapel Hill: University of North Carolina Press, 1981.
Ward, W. R. *The Protestant Evangelical Awakening*. Cambridge: Cambridge University Press, 1992.
Weigelt, Horst. *Geschichte des Pietismus in Bayern: Anfänge, Entwicklung, Bedeutung*. Göttingen: Vandenhoeck & Ruprecht, 2001.
Wellenreuther, Hermann. *Heinrich Melchior Mühlenberg und die deutschen Lutheraner in Nordamerika, 1742–1787*. Münster: LIT Verlag, 2013.
Weller, Hieronymus. *Creutz-Schule: Oder Etlicher Märterer und andere vornehme Historien*. Edited by August Hermann Francke. Halle, 1697.

———. *Marter-Buch: Darinnen einige vornehme Historien der Märterer mit ihren Lehren und Trostsprüchen*. Edited by August Herman Francke. Halle, 1700.
Wendland, Walter. "Die pietistische Bekehrung." *Zeitschrift für Kirchengeschichte* 38 (1920): 193–238.
Wengert, Timothy, and Robert Kolb, eds. *The Book of Concord: The Confessions of the Evangelical Lutheran Church*. Minneapolis: Fortress Press, 2000.
Whitmer, Kelly J. *The Halle Orphanage as Scientific Community: Observation, Eclecticism, and Pietism in the Early Enlightenment*. Halle: Waisenhaus, 2015.
———. "Model Children and Pious Desire in Early Enlightenment Philanthropy." In *Childhood and Emotion: Across Cultures, 1450–1800*, edited by Claudia Jarzebowski and Thomas Max Safley, 15–27. London: Routledge, 2014.
Widén, Bill. *Bekehrung und Erziehung bei August Hermann Francke*. Åbo: Åbo Akademi, 1967.
Wiegleb, Johann Hieronymus. *Erbaulicher Unterricht von rechten Grund und Gebrauch des Catechisi Lutheri*. Halle: Schütze, 1697.
———. *Haupt-Summa der Christlichen Lehre, Lehre zu einem kurtzen, iedoch deutlichen, gründlichen und ordentlichen Begriff aller Glaubens Artickel in Frage und Antwort verfasset*. Halle, 1697.
———. *Hindernisse der Bekehrung*. Halle, 1698, 1701, 1709, 1710, 1727.
Wiegleb, Johann Hieronymus, et al. *Confessio Oder Glaubens-Bekäntniß derer Pietisten in Gotha: Sampt einen draüber gestellten kurtzen Bedencken*. N.p.: 1693.
Wigger, Friedrich. "Aus dem Leben Herzog Friedrichs des Frommen bis zu seinem Regierungsantritt." *Jahrbücher des Vereins für Mecklenburgische Geschichte und Altertumskunde* 45 (1880): 53–176.
Wilhelmi, Heinrich, "Augusta, Prinzessin von Meklenburg-Güstrow, und die Dargunschen Pietisten." *Jahrbücher des Vereins für Mecklenburgische Geschichte und Altertumskunde* 48 (1883): 89–284.
Willgeroth, Gustav. *Die Mecklenburg-Schwerinschen Pfarren seit dem dreißigjährigen Kriege*. 4 vols. Wismar: Self-published, 1924.
Wilson, Renate. "The Traffic in Halle Orphanage Medications: Medicinals, Philanthropy, and Colonial Mission." *Caduceus* 13 (1997): 6–22.
Winkler, Eberhard. "Christen als Minderheit—bei August Hermann Francke und heute." In *Reformation und Neuzeit: 300 Jahre Theologie in Halle*, edited by Udo Schnelle, 399–418. Berlin: Walter de Gruyter, 1994.
Witt, Ulrike. *Bekehrung, Bildung und Biographie: Frauen im Umkreis des Halleschen Pietismus*. Halle: Franckesche Stiftungen, 1996.
———. "Eine pietistische Biographiensammlung: Erdmann Heinrich Graf Henckels 'Letzte Stunden' (1720–1733)." *Pietismus und Neuzeit* 21 (1997): 184–215.
Woltersdorff, Ernst Gottlieb. *Der Schächer am Kreutz: Das ist, vollständige Nachrichten von der Bekehrung und seligem Ende hingerichteter Missethäter*. 2 vols. Görlitz, 1753–60/66.
Wotschke, Theodor. "Leonhard Christoph Sturms religiöse und kirchliche Stellung." *Mecklenburgische Jahrbücher* 95 (1931): 103–42.
Wreech, Curt Friedrich von. *Wahrhaffte und umständliche Historie von den Schwedischen Gefangenen in Rußland und Siberien*. Sorau, 1728.
Wustmann, Claudia. *Die "begeisterten Mägde": Mitteldeutsche Prophetinnen im Radikalpietismus am Ende des 17. Jahrhunderts*. Leipzig: Edition Kirchhof & Franke, 2008.
Young, Richard Fox, and Daniel Jeyaraj. "Singer of the 'Sovereign Lord': Hindu Pietism and Christian *Bhakti* in the Conversions of Kanapati Vattiyar, a Tamil 'Poet.'" In *Halle and the Beginning of Protestant Christianity in India*, edited by Andreas Gross, Y. Vincent Kumaradoss, and Heike Liebau, vol. 2, 951–72. Halle: Verlag der Franckeschen Stiftungen, 2006.

Zachariae, Carl Heinrich. *Der in Gottes Wort und unsern Symbolischen Büchern wohlgegründete Buß-Kampf wurde aus dringenden Ursachen dargethan, mit Zeugnissen Alter und Neuer Evangelisch-Lutherischer Lehrer bestättiget*. Peina, 1736.

Zaunstöck, Holger, Thomas Müller-Bahlke, and Claus Veltmann, eds. *Die Welt verändern: August Hermann Francke; Ein Lebenswerk um 1700*. Halle: Verlag der Franckeschen Stiftungen, 2013.

Zeller, Winfried. "Geschichtsverständnis und Zeitbewußtsein: Die 'Geistliche Fama' als pietistische Zeitschrift." *Pietismus und Neuzeit* 2 (1975): 89–99.

Zorn, Peter. *Dissertatio historica Theologicade Philtris enthusasticis anglico batavis H. E. von dem Englisch- und Holländischen Qvaker-Pulver*. Rostock, 1707.

Die zum Exempel Aller verruchten und frevelen Sünder, Auf langweiliges Sitzen und Verleugnung ihrer Missethat, Endlich vollzogene Execution Zweyer von vorigen Maleficanten wieder eingezogenen Armen Sünder, Nahmens Martin Knauth, eines Todten-Gräbers Sohn aus Jena, seines Alters 22. Jahr, und Christian Mölle, aus dem Thüringischen gebürtig, seines Alters 30. Jahr. Berlin, 1739.

INDEX

Aland, Kurt, 28, 42, 145
Albrecht-Birkner, Veronica, 22, 42, 163n32
Althaus, Paul, 10
Anfechtung, 40, 43, 51, 78, 108, 145
    Francke, August Hermann, and, 25, 43, 51, 195n10
    Schade, Johann Caspar, and, 35–36, 146
    See also *Bußkampf*
Angela of Foligno, 40
Anklam, 106
Anton, Paul, 23, 156
apokatastasis panton, doctrine of, 92, 94–95, 100, 181n16
Apollonius, 40
Arndt, Johann, 20, 38, 40, 111, 149, 160n39
    conversion, and, 10–11, 45, 161n59
    repentance, and (*see* repentance: Arndt, Johann)
Arnold, Gottfried, 13, 36, 40–42, 46, 146, 195n13
atheism, 4, 13, 37, 78, 87, 162n64, 179n64
    Francke, August Hermann and, 2, 19, 30, 32, 149
Augusta, Duchess of Mecklenburg, 90–100, 105–20, 180n6. *See also* Dargun
autobiography, 6, 8, 19, 109, 156
    Moravian, 153, 197n52
    spiritual, 8–9, 12–14, 40, 161n57, 162n70 (*see also* conversion narratives)

Bauer, Christian Friedrich, 66
Baumgarten, Siegmund Jacob, 66, 175n39, 198n72
Beatus, Wilhelm Wolrath, 115–17, 188n149
Beissel, Johann Conrad, 155
Bekehrsucht, 75–77, 150, 185n88
Bekehrung. *See under* conversion
Bekehrungs-Pulver. *See* powders and elixirs
Berghaus, Hermann Peter, 56
Berleburg Bible, 92
Berlin, 49, 55, 72–76, 79, 123, 146
Berner, Laurentz Henrich, 106, 186n114
biography, spiritual, 40–41, 49, 53, 58–59. *See also* autobiography; conversion narratives
Blankensee, Joachim Friedrich, 174n26

Böhme, Jacob, 13, 29–30, 38, 154
Brandenburg-Prussia, 62, 73, 99, 105, 119, 143
Breckling, Friedrich, 13
Breithaupt, Joachim Justus, 29–32, 45, 63, 156, 163n32, 164n45, 165n12, 169n88
Bremmel, Gertrude Magdalene, 133, 139–40, 194n83
bridal imagery. *See under* execution narratives
Brückner, Georg Heinrich, 29–32, 48, 145–46
Buddeus, Johann Franz, 68–69, 72, 102, 175n53
Buk, Christian, 118
Bullen, Christian, 13
Bunyan, Paul, 40, 151
Burgmann, Johann Christian, 101–4
Buße. *See* repentance
Bußkampf, 8–9, 36, 42–49, 56–57, 61–77, 88–90, 145–46, 172n46, 185n98, 194n83, 194n84, 195n11, 198n74
    Anfechtung, and, 36, 43, 89, 108, 145, 169n88
    criticisms of, 63–64, 66–70, 100–2, 115, 145–46, 182n33, 184n79, 185n92, 185n98
    Dargun, and, 94–105, 108, 111, 114–15, 120 (*see also* Dargun)
    diversity of meaning, 44–45, 145, 168n83, 172n46, 179n75, 185n97
    Durchbruch, and (*see* conversion: schematic triad of)
    execution narratives, and, 120, 125, 127, 129–30
    Francke, August Hermann, and, 23–25, 28–32, 42–45, 61, 88
    Freylinghausen, Johann Anastasius, and, 25, 31, 45, 61, 169n84
    Halle, and, 42–45, 48–49, 56–57, 64–65, 72
    Moravians, and, 152–153, 174n18, 174n25
    Pietists, radical, and, 94, 99, 101, 104, 174n26
    Rührung, and (*see* conversion: schematic triad of)
    Russmeyer, Michael Christian, and, 102–5, 185n88, 185n97
    translation, 168n70
    See also Lau, Samuel: *Bußkampf*; conversion: schematic triad of

222 INDEX

Bußprediger. See repentance preacher
Bützow, 118

Calov, Abraham, 7
Cammin, 106
Canstein, Carl Hildebrand von, 22, 154
Canstein Bible Institute, 91
Carl Leopold, Duke of Mecklenburg-Schwerin. See under Mecklenburg-Schwerin, Duke of
Carpsov, Johann Benedict, 166n23
Catherine of Genoa, 40
Chantal, Jeanne de, 40
Chemnitz, Martin, 101
Christian VI of Denmark (king), 94, 105, 119
Christian Ernst, Count of Stolberg-Wernigerode. See Stolberg-Wernigerode, Count of (Christian Ernst)
Christian Ludwig, Duke of Mecklenburg-Schwerin. See under Mecklenburg-Schwerin, Duke of
Christine, Countess of Stolberg-Wernigerode. See under Stolberg-Wernigerode, Countess of
Cleß, Johannes, 131
Closter-Bergische Sammlung Nützlicher Materien zur Erbauung im Wahren Christenthum, 79, 135, 176n1
collegia pietatis, 13, 103. See also conventicles
Collegium Philobiblicum. See under Francke, August Hermann
conventicles, 29, 32–33, 88, 98, 108, 116
conversion
  Bekehrung as, 3, 5–6, 157–58
  Bußkampf in (see *Bußkampf*)
  certainty of, 51–52, 56–57, 65–69, 73–76, 81, 111, 129, 149
  clergy, and, 47, 62–63, 65–66, 84–86
  coercion, and, 115, 137, 151
  death and dying, and, 50–60, 83–84, 88, 89, 147–50, 153 (see also execution narratives)
  definition of, 2, 6–7
  distinction between accounts and experiences, 6–7
  enthusiasm, and, 68, 97, 104, 154–55
  Erweckung, and, 107, 153
  failed, 81–84, 89, 133
  Halle and, 8–9, 21–27, 42–48, 61–64, 145 (move to Halle)
  Konversion, as, 5–6, 157–58
  moment, as, 29–30, 34, 37–39, 46, 66–72, 127, 152, 155, 160n30, 161n48
  narratives (see conversion narratives)
  schematic triad of, 36, 43, 57, 65, 88–89, 145–46, 171n15 (see also *Bußkampf; Durchbruch; Rührung*)
  typologies of, 3–4
  See also regeneration; repentance
conversion narratives
  ambivalence regarding, 41–42, 57, 149
  clergy, role in, 58, 76–80, 84–86, 89, 122–23, 134–37
  deathbed, 53–55, 58, 80, 85–88, 167n58
  diversity of, 41, 57, 146
  editing of, 85–86, 111–15
  Eucharist in, 86–88
  execution (see execution narratives)
  Halle and, 41–42, 46–49
  instability of, 49, 57, 118
  manuscript dissemination of, 21, 60, 89, 113–14
  publication of, 21, 41–42, 46, 61, 64, 69, 71–89
  Roman Catholics, portrayal in, 58–59, 88
  thanatography and, 50, 130–31
  third-person narration, 59, 79–86, 148
Corpis, Duane, 4–5
Cubehn, Christoph, 83

Dargun, 9, 70, 90–121
De Boor, Friedrich, 149
Demmin, 106
Denmark, 87, 94, 99, 131, 143, 180n5
Dennstädt, Johanna Sophia von, 77–79, 85–89, 177n24, 179n60
Döderlein, Albrecht, 118
Durchbruch (breakthrough). See also conversion: schematic triad of
  assurance, and, 29, 57, 69
  Bußkampf, relation to, 44
  omission, 51, 78, 81, 127, 169n95
  schematic nature of, 36, 43–44, 57, 69, 72, 88, 175n51
  turning point of conversion narrative, 24, 29, 51, 57, 65, 195n8

Ebersdorf, 84, 177n32
Edward VI (king of England), 39
Edwards, Jonathan, 152
Edzard, Esdras, 17
Ego-Dokumente, 161n57. See also autobiography
Ehrenpfort, Henning Christoph, 93–105, 119, 182n29
Elard, Samuel, 55–56
elixirs. See powders and elixirs
Engelbrecht, Hans, 12, 39, 154, 161n55
Ephraem Syrus, 40
Erfurt, 28–33, 40–42, 48–50, 79, 145
Erweckung (awakening), 107, 153, 174n25, 176n6
essentia dulcis, 98, 183n56
examinations, spiritual, 48, 62

execution narratives, 9, 40, 59–60, 115, 122–43
    authenticity of, 122–23
    bridal imagery, 134, 136, 167n39
    circulation, 123, 130–35
    criticisms, 141–43
    gender, and, 135–37
    reliability of, 137–39
Exter, Christlieb Leberecht von, 148
Eyseneck, Juliana Baur von, 38

Fabricius, Johann Jacob, 13, 161n58
Flörke, Leopold, 118
Flüe, Nicolaus von, 40
Fortgesetzte Sammlung auserlesener Materien zum Bau des Reichs Gottes, 79, 82, 88, 100, 176n1
Franck, David, 117
Franck, Johann Georg. *See* Francke, Johann Georg
Franck, Sebastian, 29–30
Francke, Anna Magdalena, 51
Francke, August Hermann
    Anfechtung, and (see *Anfechtung*: Francke, August Hermann)
    Bußkampf, and (see *Bußkampf*: Francke, August Hermann)
    Collegium Philobiblicum, founding of, 17–18
    conversion: importance of, 41–44, 149; moment of conversion, 46
    schematic variety, 42–44, 168n83
    self-deception, and, 46, 48, 147
    conversion experience, 2, 7, 15–27, 144, 165n54, 173n1; normativity of, 42
    conversion narrative (Francke's), 8, 15–23, 25, 164n43
    composition, 16, 20
    Halle, influence in, 42–45
    influences on, 20–21
    paradigm, as, 9, 15, 27, 89, 132, 143
    reception of, 9, 21–27, 32, 144–45
    conversion narratives:
    ambivalence regarding, 15, 41–42, 46, 62, 147, 150
    composition of, 32, 168n62
    featured in, 22, 29–32, 77–79, 84–85, 177n27
    Lebenslauff (see Francke, August Hermann: conversion narrative)
    memorial publications on, 23–26
    Schade, Johann Caspar, and, 35–37, 49, 146
    scriptures, truthfulness of, 19
    Spener, Philipp Jakob, and (see Spener, Philipp Jakob: Francke, August Hermann)

Francke, Gotthilf August, 25, 61, 92, 104–5, 113, 144
Francke, Johann Georg, 24
Francke Foundations, 22, 27, 45, 48, 152, 164n42
Franckenberg, Abraham, 38
Franckesche Stiftungen. See Francke Foundations
Frankfurt am Main, 13–14, 40, 105
Fratzscher, Nikolaus, 30, 48
Freylinghausen, Johann Anastasius, 25–26, 31, 45, 61, 144, 166n14, 173n2. *See also Bußkampf*; repentance
Friedrich, Duke of Mecklenburg-Schwerin. *See under* Mecklenburg-Schwerin, Duke of
Friedrich Wilhelm I, Duke of Mecklenburg-Schwerin. *See under* Mecklenburg-Schwerin, Duke of
Friedrich Wilhelm I, King of Brandenburg-Prussia, 47–48, 62, 105, 119
furnace of affliction, 52

Geistliche Fama, 71, 154–55
Gerber, Christian, 26, 123, 165n54, 170n114, 190n15
Gerhard, Ludwig, 91
Gichtel, Johann Georg, 39, 78, 87
Glaubenskampf, 51, 54, 56. *See also Bußkampf*
Glaucha, 23, 42, 44, 55
Gotha, 29, 41, 79, 166n28
    Wiegleb, Johann Hieronymus, and, 33–34, 150, 196n31
Greifswald, 102–3, 185n85
Greschat, Martin, 47, 169n104
Großgebauer, Theophil
    baptismal regeneration, 12
    conversion, on, 11–12, 20, 65, 161n47
    Francke, August Hermann, influence on, 12, 20–21, 163n25
Groß-Methling, 93, 106
Guericke, Heinrich Ernst, 27, 144, 199n81
Güstrow, 91, 97, 105

Halle, 8, 15, 21–32, 42–53, 144–47, 150–53
    conflict over *Bußkampf*, 63–64, 185n97
    Pietism, and, 8–9, 28, 45, 89–90, 92, 102, 153
    testimonial conflict (*Testimoniumstreit*), 62–63
    theology faculty, 52, 62–63, 104, 185n97
Hamburgische Berichte von neuen gelehrten Sachen, 100–1, 105
Hellwig, Jacob Christian, 92–93, 99–100, 104
Hempel, Joachim Jasper Johann, 103, 105
Henckel von Donnersmarck, Erdmann Heinrich
    letzten Stunden, Die, 52–60, 80, 84, 88–89, 128, 131, 133, 148, 172n53

Hennings, Simon Ambrosius, 92, 99, 180n11, 183n56
Henningsen, Jürgen, 22, 163n31
Herrnhut, 63–64, 92, 152
Heshus, Tilemann, 10
Hindmarsh, Bruce, 153, 156–57, 197n52
Hoburg, Christian, 39
Hof, 73
Holl, Karl, 11
Horn, George von, 92, 180n11
Hövet, August, 93, 100, 105, 182n26
Hungerland, Anne Marthe, 133, 136, 138

James, William, 2, 6
Janeway, James, 40, 197n38
Jena, 21, 31, 56, 66, 69, 72, 84, 102, 131
Jerichovius, Immanuel Traugott, 71–72, 80, 88, 179n60
John of the Cross, Saint, 40
Jördenstorf, 98–99, 106, 118–19

Kanne, J. A., 27, 144
Kiel, 17
Kißner, Elisabeth, 40, 167n58
Kittsteiner, Heinz-Dieter, 142
Kläger, Justus. *See* Fabricius, Johann Jacob
Klicken, Else, 133, 193n75
Knapp, Georg Christian, 27, 144–45
Konversion. *See under* conversion
Kord, Susanne, 137–39, 193n75
Krämer, Gustav, 27, 144–45
Krimmer, Gottlieb Joachim, 72, 86
Krogh, Tyge, 141
Kücken, Johann Erdmann, 187n135
Kühlmann, Quirinius, 13

Lächele, Rainer, 86, 177n23, 179n60
Lange, Joachim, 62–63, 150, 156, 164n45
Lange, Nicholas, 57
Lau, Samuel, 64–71, 88, 90–92, 101–2, 121, 135, 194n84
  Bußkampf, and, 64–66
Läuterung. *See* purification and refinement
Lehr, Leopold Franz Friedrich, 84–85
Leipzig, 17–18, 20, 23, 29, 35, 41, 73–74, 105, 131, 168n62
Lepsch, Andreas, 125–28, 130–32, 136–38, 148, 190n8
Levin, 93, 97, 106
Lomersheim, 187n136
Löscher, Valentin Ernst, 47, 169n104, 176n54
Lotz-Heumann, Ute, 4–5
Louise, Queen of Denmark, 91
Lübeck, 23, 27, 29

Lüneburg, 16, 18–20, 22–27, 61, 144, 165n54, 173n1, 195n10
Luther, Martin, 9–10, 19–20, 30, 59, 164n48, 190n13

Magdeburg, 62, 130
magic and superstitious practices, 97–99, 104, 115–17, 120–21, 149, 156. *See also Zettelfressen*
Malchin, 115–17, 188n148, 193n73
Martini, Christine Sophie, 55, 59
Matthias, Markus, 21, 24, 45, 61–62, 159n18, 162n1, 163n25, 163n27
Mecklenburg, 9, 90–96, 100–3, 105–6, 115–21
  revivals in, 117–18 (*see also* Dargun)
Mecklenburg-Schwerin, Duke of
  Carl Leopold, 91, 96, 99, 105, 116–19, 180n8, 188n149, 189n157
  Christian Ludwig, 105, 113
  Friedrich, 113, 118
  Friedrich Wilhelm I, 91
Meidinger, Johann Wendel, 34
Mendelssohn, Moses, 158
Mettele, Gisela, 152–53
Michaelis, Johann Heinrich, 62
Mischke, Johannes, 63, 174n18
Mohr, Rudolf, 38
Molinos, Miguel de, 17–18, 20, 29–30, 145
Moltzahn, Carl Friedrich von, 107–8, 113
Moore, Elizabeth, 39
Moravians (Renewed Unity of the Brethren), 63–64, 136, 152–53
Morrison, Karl, 5, 49, 137
Moser, Johann Jacob, 123, 125–26, 131–42, 150, 193n75
  Altes und Neues aus dem Reich Gottes, 26, 71, 79, 81–89, 178n46, 179n59
  Seelige letzte Stunden, 60, 130, 154–55, 173n58
Moser, Johann Jakob. *See* Moser, Johann Jacob
Mücke, Dorothea von, 39, 195n15
Musaeus, Johannes, 21

Nadler, Anton, 136
Nehrlich, Hans Ludwig, 30–32, 165n12
Neumeister, Erdmann, 105, 186n104
Neustadt an der Aisch, 74
Niceron, Jean Pierre, 26–27
Niemeyer, August Hermann, 27, 144–45, 164n39
Niggl, Günther, 8, 16, 156, 164n45

Oppenheimer, Joseph Süsskind, 158
Örtzen, Lady von, 108

INDEX

Paphnutius, 40
Pascal, Blaise, 39, 167n51
Peschke, Erhard, 20, 43–44, 102–3, 168n72, 180n6, 185n83
Petersen, Johann Wilhelm, 87–88, 91–92, 181n21
Petersen, Johanna Eleonora, 14, 151
Pietism
   church, 8, 9, 15, 70–71, 85, 88–89, 102, 145, 152–53, 160n29
   definition, 1, 159n1
   radical, 71, 75, 88, 92–94, 104, 153–55, 160n29
Pölzig, 53
Porst, Johann, 73–79, 85–87, 149–50
Potsdam, 80, 89, 125, 130, 177n32
powders and elixirs, 97–98, 117, 120, 149, 183n54
Powell, Vavasor, *Spirituall Experiences*, 38–39
purification and refinement, 52–54, 59

Quaker
   derisive term, 98–99, 101
   powder, 99, 101, 117, 149 (*see also* powders and elixirs)
Quakers, 183n53

Rambach, Johann Jakob, 62–63, 141
Rambo, Lewis, 3–4, 6
ravenstone, 192n46
rebirth. *See* regeneration
Recknitz, 92, 99–100, 180n11
refinement. *See* purification and refinement
regeneration, 1–2, 4, 41, 47, 77, 104, 112, 153
   baptism, and, 11–12, 116, 161n50, 172n53
   moment of, 33, 71
   See also conversion
Reitz, Johann Henrich, 9, 153
   Historie der Wiedergebohrnen, 38–42, 46, 58, 135, 146, 153
Renewed Unity of the Brethren. *See* Moravians (Renewed Unity of the Brethren)
Renner, Anna Margaretha, 136
repentance, 2, 10–12, 30–31, 145, 168n70
   Arndt, Johann, and, 10, 45, 161n59
   Francke, August Hermann, and, 43–44, 48
   Freylinghausen, Johann Anastasius, and, 45
   godly grief, and, 67
   manuals, clerical and, 123
   Moser, Johann Jacob, and, 125–26, 130–32
   Porst, Johann, and, 74–77
   Reformation view of, 160n31
   robber's, 123, 133, 190n13
   Schade, Johann Caspar, and, 35–36, 49, 75
   suicide by proxy, and, 139
   See also Bußkampf; conversion
repentance preacher, 11, 83, 136

Reuß, Count of (Heinrich I), 58
Ritschl, Albrecht, 27, 144
Ritter, Christian Friedrich, 114–15, 120, 128–39
Rock, Johann Friedrich, 154, 198n60
Röckenitz, 93–94, 97, 182n32
Rogall, Georg Friedrich, 24
Roosen, Andreas, 134–35
Rosenbach, Johann Georg, 48–49, 67, 154, 189n158
Rostock, 90–91, 98, 100–2, 105, 118–20, 128
Rotermund, Hans-Martin, 47
Rudolph, Jacob, 106, 113, 116
Rührung (stirring), 36, 43, 50, 57, 65, 77, 88, 107, 125, 171n15. *See also* conversion: schematic triad of
Russmeyer, Michael Christian, 102–5, 121, 185n83, 185n85
   Sonderbare Krafft Christi, die Heucheley zu entdecken, Die, 103

Saggitarius, Kaspar, 21
Sammlung auserlesener Materien zum Bau des Reichs Gottes, 60, 71–72, 79–83, 86, 88–89, 107, 146, 154–55
Sarcander, Joachim Friedrich, 118
Schächers-Buße. See repentance: robber's
Schade, Johann Caspar, 8, 32–37, 177n16
   Anfechtung (*see Anfechtung*: Schade, Johann Caspar)
   conversion narratives, 34–37, 40–41, 80, 146, 195n12
   Francke, August Hermann, and (*see* Francke, August Hermann: Schade, Johann Caspar)
   influence on conversion experiences, 49, 72, 74–76
   Spener, Philipp Jakob, and (*see* Spener, Philipp Jakob: Schade, Johann Caspar)
Scharff, Hermann Wilhelm, 20, 163n25
Schaumberg-Lippe, Countess of (Johanna Sophie), 25, 61
Schlette, Magnus, 8, 159n18
Schmid, Andreas, 123, 184n60
Schmid, Heinrich, 27, 144
Schmidt, Jakob, 93–95, 99–100, 105, 108, 119–20
Schmidt, Martin, 152
Schneider, Jacob, 22, 87–88
Schönberg, Martha Margaretha von, 31, 50–56, 84, 133, 147
Schorrentin, 97
Schrader, Hans-Jürgen, 38
Schubert, Heinrich, 80, 84, 89, 125–30, 138, 148, 179n59
Schultze, Benjamin, 169n95
Schumacher, Samuel, 39, 167n54

Schütz, Johann Jacob, 13–14
Schwaan, 118
Schwenckfeld, Caspar, 39
Schwentzel, Johann Ulrich, 24
Schwerin, 90–91, 105, 106, 113, 118
Scriver, Christian, 12, 161n56
Serpes, Johann Christoph, 136
Silesia, 63–64, 174n22, 179n68
Sophie Charlotte, Countess of Stohlberg-Wernigerode. *See under* Stolberg-Wernigerode, Countess of
Spalding, Johann Joachim, 150, 155, 196n30
Spener, Philipp Jakob, 14, 27, 62–63, 73–74, 76, 85
  collegia pietatis, 13
  conversion account, 72
  conversion narratives, skepticism regarding, 28, 41–42, 49, 68–69, 147, 151
  Francke, August Hermann, and, 18, 21, 32, 49
  Lebenslauf, 14, 72, 156
  regeneration, 12, 161n51
  Schade, Johann Caspar, and, 36–37, 41–42, 146
Stahl, Herbert, 20
Steinbart, Gotthilf Samuel, 141–42
Steinmetz, Johann Adam, 64, 71, 80, 88, 176n1
Stephen Martyr, Saint, 133, 139, 193n77
Sternberg, 117, 189n162
Stieber, Georg Friedrich, 92–94, 104, 181n15, 185n103
Stoeffler, F. Ernest, 45
Stolberg-Wernigerode, Count of (Christian Ernst), 66, 92, 95, 104, 106
Stolberg-Wernigerode, Countess of
  Christine, 91
  Sophie Charlotte, 66, 93
Stuart, Cathy, 189n2, 193n80, 194n83
Sturm, Leonhard Christian, 91
Suckow, Jacob Sigismund, 96–98, 184n72
suicide by proxy, 139–41, 143, 148–49, 189n2, 193n80

Tennhardt, Johann, 154, 174n26
Teresa of Avila, 40
Testimoniumstreit, 62–63
Thais, 40
thanatography, 50, 130–31
Theological Answer to Two Questions, 66–68
Töllner, Justus, 55
Tölper, Anna Regina, 136–37
Trunck. See powders and elixirs

Tucholsky, Kurt, 133
Tuchtfeld, Victor Christoph, 92, 181n19
Turmerlebnis. See Luther, Martin

Uhl, Catharina Elisabeth, 139
Utstiem, Engel, 86–87
Uttendörfer, Otto, 63

Vattiyar, Kanapati, 157–58
Verbesserte Sammlung auserlesener Materien zum Bau des Reichs Gottes, 79, 88–89, 130, 176n1
Vetter, Anna, 12, 161n55

Walbaum, Anton Heinrich, 22, 26, 113, 187n122
Wallmann, Johannes, 20, 163n25
Ward, W. R., 45, 151, 169n92
Weidner, Johann Martin, 163n32
Weller, Hieronymus, 36, 41
Wendland, Walter, 32, 145, 167n43
Wesley, John, 22, 151–52, 197n41
Whitefield, George, 151
Widén, Bill, 47, 151
Wiegleb, Johann Hieronymus, 31, 33–34, 79, 149–50
Wilhelmi, 91–93, 115, 182n29, 183n56, 188n149
Witt, Ulrike, 14, 43, 51, 57–59, 171n15
Wittenberg, 35, 67, 176n54
Woltersdorff, Ernst Gottlieb, 131–38, 140–42, 194n83
Wreech, Curt Friedrich von, 151
Wurm, Anna Magdalena von. *See* Francke, Anna Magdalena
Wurmb, Louise Sophie von, 55
Württemberg, 71, 131, 158

Zachariae, Carl Heinrich, 119–20, 135, 181n17, 182n34
  Bußkampf, defense of, 94–96, 100–7,
  conversion narratives, manuscript, and, 109–13
  conversion narratives, published, and, 114–15
  heterodoxy, opposition to, 95, 99–100, 120
Zettelfressen, 116–17, 189n157
Ziegenbalg, Bartholomäus, 147–48, 158, 196n20
Ziethen, 83
Zimmermann, Johann Liborius, 66, 69, 92
Zinzendorf, Count of (Nicholas Ludwig), 63–64, 92, 152
Züllichau, 136, 142

www.ingramcontent.com/pod-product-compliance
Lightning Source LLC
Chambersburg PA
CBHW021943290426
44108CB00012B/948